HAPPINESS, DEMOCRACY,
and the
COOPERATIVE MOVEMENT

SUNY series in New Political Science
Bradley J. Macdonald, editor

HAPPINESS, DEMOCRACY, *and the* COOPERATIVE MOVEMENT

The Radical Utilitarianism of William Thompson

Mark J. Kaswan

Published by State University of New York Press, Albany

© 2014 State University of New York

All rights reserved

Printed in the United States of America

No part of this book may be used or reproduced in any manner whatsoever without written permission. No part of this book may be stored in a retrieval system or transmitted in any form or by any means including electronic, electrostatic, magnetic tape, mechanical, photocopying, recording, or otherwise without the prior permission in writing of the publisher.

For information, contact State University of New York Press, Albany, NY
www.sunypress.edu

Production by Ryan Morris
Marketing by Michael Campochiaro

Library of Congress Cataloging-in-Publication Data

Kaswan, Mark J., 1962–
 Happiness, Democracy, and the Cooperative Movement: The Radical Utilitarianism of William Thompson / Mark J. Kaswan.
   pages cm. — (Suny series in new political science)
 Includes bibliographical references and index.
  ISBN 978-1-4384-5204-3 (paperback : alk. paper)
  ISBN 978-1-4384-5203-6 (hardcover : alk. paper) 1. Happiness. 2. Democracy. 3. Cooperation. 4. Utilitarianism. 5. Thompson, William, 1775-1833. 6. Bentham, Jeremy, 1748-1832. I. Title.
 BJ1481.K35 2014
 320.01'9--dc23
                                                              2013028902

To Jaques

It is evident, therefore, that a physical change in the condition of man must precede the moral change which every sympathizing mind ardently wishes to see effected; and without some operation, some new and honest mode of traffic, which shall cauterize that plague-spot,—the present commercial system,—we may look in vain for human virtue and social harmony. Precept has ever fallen powerless before the rootedly sordid, mean, selfish, money-changing character which this wicked commercial system has given, with few exceptions, to every human being throughout the civilized world: and more particularly are its debasing effects conspicuous in our own country, where the principle has been pushed to its utmost limits. The system must cease.

—"Death of Mr. Thompson," in John Minter Morgan, *Hampden in the 19th Century,* 1834

A more important and more extensive change in human society was never contemplated by the mind of man.

—William Thompson

Contents

	Preface	ix
	Introduction	1

PART I: WHAT IS HAPPINESS?

1:	The Two Faces of Happiness: A Brief History	19
2:	Between Pleasure and Well-being: Bentham	31
3:	William Thompson's Social Happiness	55

PART II: THE POLITICS OF HAPPINESS

4:	Happiness and Utility	95
5:	The Politics of Happiness and Democratic Principles	133
6:	From Theory to Practice: Cooperatives, Happiness, and Democratic Social Change	163
	Conclusion	197

Appendix 1: Laws and Objects of the Rochdale Society of Equitable Pioneers, adopted 1844 (abridged)	209
Appendix 2: International Co-operative Alliance Statement on the Co-operative Identity, adopted 1995	211
Notes	215
Bibliography	271
Index	289

Preface

This book has two primary topics, or, as I like to think of them, valences: First, it seeks to demonstrate that the concept of happiness is a significant political concept, and that different ways of conceptualizing happiness have very significant political consequences. Second, it seeks to resuscitate a political theory of cooperatives as agents for broadbased social change. I started with the second of these two objects, and admittedly it was not without surprise that I found myself working on the first. However, the more attention that I gave to happiness, the stronger my sense became that it was a matter of vital importance to political theory that had long been overlooked.

I arrived at happiness as a central topic because in my work to develop a political theory of cooperatives I started with the first person to articulate such a theory, William Thompson, who I soon learned had a close association with Jeremy Bentham. But, although Thompson and Bentham share a conceptual framework, they arrive at very different conclusions—Bentham being one of the great theorists of liberal capitalism, and Thompson one of the founders of socialism. One day, in an empty classroom at UCLA, I drew out a conceptual map of their ideas in parallel, to try to trace out the point at which they diverged. That point was happiness; they understand happiness differently, and the rest of their differences flow from there. The rest, as they say, is history.

I have received inspiration, ideas and advice from many sources, but the first to acknowledge here is my father, Jaques, as his contribution extends far beyond the love and support one might hope for from one's parents. His interest and active involvement in the development of cooperatives as a means to build a better society based on principles of justice and equality not only inspired me, but gave me practical experience in the kinds of organizational settings that are the ultimate object of my theoretical work. That my parents gave me the space and ample time to arrive at their conclusions through my own circuitous route speaks volumes for the quality of not only their ideas but also their character. Though my approach leaves my father and me with plenty to talk about, the fact of the matter is that this book reflects a perspective developed through discussions we have had over many years.

As with so many academic "first books," this one started as a doctoral dissertation, and Carole Pateman, my advisor at UCLA, deserves as much credit as can be given for someone in her position. Her influence extends much farther than just shepherding the dissertation, of course, as I first encountered William Thompson in her work; early on she pointed out the importance of subordination; and from her I learned that there was more to utilitarianism than Jeremy Bentham's felicific calculus. And, post-completion, I have benefited in many ways from her ongoing support, mentorship, and, dare I say, friendship. The other members of my dissertation committee, Ray Rocco, Perry Anderson, and Giulia Sissa, also provided much valuable insight and support, both in and out of the classroom, for which I am grateful. One of the great values of graduate school is the opportunity to forge strong supportive relationships with one's peers, and I feel that I have been especially fortunate in this regard. In this light I warmly acknowledge the help of my friends, Helen McManus, Fred Lee, Rebekah Sterling, Paul Osher, Theo Christov, Alex Schulman, Mary McThomas, and Hector Perla.

A number of individuals have provided me with valuable inspiration, encouragement, support and feedback for this project. One of the most important was an anonymous reviewer for SUNY Press (whom I now know to have been Stephen Engelmann) who gave the work both high praise and detailed criticism from a close read that enabled me to strengthen the text considerably. I must also thank Helen McManus for agreeing with the reviewer and helping me think through the revisions. Carlos Figueroa provided lastminute comments along with the solution to a problem that had troubled me almost from the very beginning of the work. And Jim Crimmins's detailed feedback on an earlier version of the manuscript was also of great value. These individuals deserve absolutely no part of the blame for any errors, but much of the praise for the better qualities of this work.

Other individuals who deserve special mention are Dolores Dooley, who generously provided information and material in true cooperative spirit, and Michael Quinn and Stephen Engelmann, whose comments greatly improved chapter 2. Chapter 4 was substantially strengthened thanks to a lengthy discussion and subsequent email exchange with Phillip Schofield. Some of the ideas expressed in this work appeared in early form in 2007 in my article, "Happiness, Politics and the Co-operative Principles" (*Journal of Cooperative Studies* 40, no. 1 (April): 30–40; London: UK Society for Cooperative Studies), and I thank the editor, Paul A. Jones, as well as Molly Scott Cato and two anonymous reviewers for their valuable comments. Terence Ball provided crucial early encouragement, support, and advice about publishing. Others who provided encouragement and feedback include Gar Alperovitz, Mark Bevir, Craig Borowiak, Marc Stears, Bradley MacDonald, Sandy Thatcher, and John Parrish.

Work on the book was greatly aided by my receipt of a J. Robert Beyster Fellowship in 2010 and the Michael W. Huber Fellowship in 2011 through the Rutgers University School of Management and Labor Relations. Although much of the work I am doing through the fellowship pertains to a future project, I must express my gratitude for the generosity of Mary Ann Beyster and the support of Joseph Blasi and Doug Kruse, who direct the Beyster Fellowship program at Rutgers SMLR. The people I have gotten to know through the Beyster Program, particularly Joan Meyers, Erik Olsen, Phil Melizzo, Daphne Berry, Christopher Mackin, David Ellerman, Frank Shipper, and Francesco Bova, have given me much support and encouragement, and have helped me understand that there are many ways of working toward the same goals.

The role of family with respect to happiness is not discussed much in this book, but my own experience has demonstrated to me its importance. No mere acknowledgment can express the depth of gratitude I have for Elizabeth MacDowell. Her critical eye has improved my writing and challenged my thinking in innumerable ways, but more important, she has demonstrated the value of focus and perseverance, of the possibility of change, and of dreaming the impractical. And our daughter, Zoë, I thank for putting up with her father sometimes being a wee bit overstressed, especially in the dissertation stage, and for the remarkable clarity and cogency of youth. I also want to thank my sister, Alice, who provided much crucial support at critical times, and who, as always, went first. Last but not least, these acknowledgments would not be complete without an expression of gratitude for the canine members of my family, Emma, Echo, and Lucy. They taught me a lot about happiness, and it was on our daily walks that many of the ideas of the book got worked out.

Introduction

Happiness is political. We know this, of course: the individual right to the pursuit of happiness is enshrined in one of our greatest political documents, the Declaration of Independence. The way we think about happiness affects what we do, how we relate to other people and the world around us, our moral principles, and even our ideas about how society should be organized. Happiness has been associated with everything from unlimited consumption with wanton abandon on one side to self-denial and the ability to love one's torturer on the other. What it means to pursue one's happiness, then, depends heavily on what one understands by the term.

Indeed, happiness has been expressly recognized as a political concept at various points in history. Happiness was so clearly in the forefront of political thinking at the end of the eighteenth century that it prompted the French Jacobin leader Saint-Just to assert, "Happiness is a new idea in Europe."[1] It was around this same time that Jeremy Bentham was busy formulating the principles of utilitarianism, a political philosophy with happiness at its very center. Bentham's hedonistic model of happiness[2] is one of two that will be examined in this book. The other model, which I will refer to as eudaemonistic,[3] was championed by William Thompson, a contemporary and friend of Bentham. Bentham's hedonistic happiness is generally recognized as one of the major theoretical cornerstones of the liberal capitalist system. Thompson's is much less familiar and less often examined, but his eudaemonistic happiness is a major part of the foundations of democratic socialism as well as the modern cooperative movement.

William Thompson's work has much to offer to contemporary debates. The economic crisis of the past few years has contributed a new intensity to calls for a "new economy" based on alternative economic models.[4] Cooperatives, with over a billion members in more than one hundred countries worldwide, are important to many of these alternative models because they represent the most extensive alternative to the traditional liberal capitalist model. What makes them different is that these autonomous enterprises are founded on a set of principles, articulated expressly as the Co-operative Principles, that includes democracy, equality, and the common ownership of property, and are linked to each other through the International Co-operative Alliance (ICA), one of the world's largest and oldest transnational organizations. But, while the cooperative movement is often seen as largely apolitical today, it had its beginnings in the early nineteenth century as a radical movement for social change, precisely as a reaction to the ravages of the newly developing liberal capitalist system. Out of one of the most thorough early critiques of that system, Thompson worked out a political theory of cooperatives, a theory that came to be called, in fairly short order, socialism.[5] But far from the state socialism that developed in the twentieth century, which left people as alienated from each other and the means of production as did the liberal capitalist alternative,[6] Thompson's ideas have more in common with contemporary anarchist ideas of participatory democracy and local control as the means by which to establish the conditions for the greatest happiness of the greatest number.

Thompson receives little attention from political theorists, but in many ways he prefigures important elements of radical democratic theory today. Indeed, advances often attributed to Marx—for example, where Brown credits Marx with the "discovery of power in the social and specifically economic realm"[7]—could as easily be references to Thompson who, after all, wrote his major work twenty years before Marx wrote the *Economic and Philosophical Manuscripts*. Where Laclau and Mouffe in defining their vision of radical democracy say that they "have proposed that [the] proliferation of antagonisms and calling into question of relations of subordination should be considered as a moment of deepening of the democratic revolution,"[8] they might be interested to find similar ideas expressed in Thompson's critique of subordination and his discussion of the requirements of democracy.

Thompson offers contemporary political theory something it largely lacks, a close attention to the functions of institutions. Lamenting that the "Marxist project of illuminating the place of capitalism in political and social life has pretty much vanished from the orbit of political theory," Brown writes that "to theorize the politics of recognition, the sexual order of things, the nature of citizenship, or the reconfiguration of privacy, without taking the measure of their historically specific production by capitalism, is literally not to know the constitutive conditions of one's object of analysis."[9] Thompson's work is instructive in this regard, as he clearly connects the problems of subordination to the institutional apparatuses that produce it, even as the shape and nature of those institutions have become more firmly entrenched and hardened. But Thompson goes farther: he connects his theory to institutional forms that are meant to address the problems he identifies.

If institutions in general and the cooperative movement more specifically have received little attention from political theorists, it is also the case that the cooperative movement has lost sight of its political nature—especially in the United States.[10] This has not always been the case in the U.S., as cooperatives have been associated with populist movements at various points in its history[11] and, as any reader of the online journal *Grassroots Economic Organizing* knows,[12] within the movement itself there exist elements that clearly understand its political character. Despite this, the vast mainstream of the cooperative movement in the United States—one of the largest in the world, with more than 120 million members, over $3 trillion in assets, and over $500 billion in annual revenue[13]—has little sense of itself as a political movement. While this book may do little to affect the depoliticization of the cooperative movement in the mainstream, it may help to provide a clearer sense of the ideological roots of the movement and strengthen arguments that cooperatives may be an important component of deep-seated social change to build a more just and equitable society.

William Thompson

There exists a vast secondary as well as biographic literature on Bentham (1748–1832), legal and political theorist and acknowledged founder of utilitarianism,[14] to which nothing substantial may be added here. Because Thompson is not nearly so well known,[15] a short introduction is warranted. Although often overlooked and not always acknowledged, Thompson's contributions to socialist theory[16] and feminism[17] have at least been fairly well established. He also receives at least a mention—although rarely much more—in most historical work on the cooperative movement, at least where the pre-Rochdale period prior to 1844 is discussed,[18] but in some his contribution is ignored entirely.[19] What is lacking in all this is a sustained, systematic consideration of Thompson's philosophy and political thought. This book is intended to at least begin to fill that gap by connecting these strains in order to establish both Thompson's importance as a political thinker and the cooperative movement's importance (or potential) as a political movement.

Thompson's Life and Works

Although he would deny it, Thompson (1775–1833) represents perhaps the paradigmatic case of a traitor to his class:[20] born the only son of a wealthy Protestant merchant in Cork, Ireland, Thompson went on to become one of the founding theorists of socialism. As Claeys notes, his *Inquiry into the Principles for the Distribution of Wealth Most Conducive to Human Happiness* (1824) became "the most substantial textbook" of the early British socialist movement.[21] Having become a supporter of the republican cause early on (he was said to carry the French tricolor attached to his walking stick as he walked the Irish countryside),[22] he came into contact with Robert Owen, the Welsh industrialist whom many consider the founder of the cooperative movement, when Owen came to Ireland on a speaking tour in 1822. Although initially dismissive of Owen's plans for cooperative communities as little more than an "improved system of pauper management,"[23] in the *Inquiry* he presents a full-throated endorsement for the Owenite system. In Thompson's hands, however, the Owenite communities become not only a way to address the problems of poverty, as Owen initially considered them, but a vehicle for deeply rooted social change.

Thompson came into contact with Bentham through his interest in education. Along with his father, he was a trustee (or "proprietor") of the Cork Institution (now University College Cork), which was founded with the objective of providing education for poor working men.[24] In 1818, Thompson published a series of letters on the management of the Cork Institution (of which he was highly critical) and the value of education in the *Cork Southern Reporter,* a local paper; these were later compiled into his first publication, a pamphlet titled *Practical Education for the South of Ireland*.[25] In this context, Thompson drew up plans for a school based on principles expounded by Bentham in his *Chrestomathia*, which led him to write to Bentham in October 1818.[26] Their correspondence eventually led to a three-month stay by Thompson in Bentham's house in 1822–23, where he began writing the *Inquiry*.

Thompson's *Inquiry,* his primary work, is a very interesting book. All but dedicated to Bentham, Thompson refers to both utility and happiness throughout, beginning the first chapter with the statement that "*Utility* ... the pursuit of the greatest possible sum of human happiness, is the leading principle constantly kept in view ... in this inquiry."[27] Similarly, the principle of security, which is of utmost importance to Bentham as a principle subsidiary to utility, is central to Thompson's concerns. However, their differences are substantial: Where Bentham argues that security and equality usually conflict (and that equality must give way when they do), Thompson argues for their reconciliation. Where Bentham argues for the benefits of competition and private property, Thompson argues that these undermine the very possibility of happiness for the vast majority of people and argues instead for systems based on cooperation and common property. Where Bentham argues that there should be no limits to the accumulation of wealth and points to the positive aspects of opulence, Thompson argues that with great wealth come great vices, which have a debilitating effect on society. Where Bentham focuses his attention on the requirements of happiness for discrete individuals independently pursuing their self-interest (subject to the constraints, such as laws, imposed by social forces), Thompson is concerned with establishing the social conditions for individuals to achieve happiness such that their self-interest is aligned with the common interest.

At some point—perhaps during his stay in Bentham's house—Thompson met Anna Doyle Wheeler, which led to the publication in 1825 of the *Appeal of One Half of the Human Race, Women, Against the Pretensions of the Other Half, Men, to Retain Them in Political, and Thence in Civil and Domestic, Slavery.* The *Appeal* is a radical work that begins with a condemnation of the exclusion of women from political participation, presents a powerful argument against all systems of subordination, and ends with the claim that the empowerment of women cannot take place until new social institutions are developed that replace systems of exploitation with systems based on equality and cooperation.

Around this time Thompson became heavily involved in efforts by Robert Owen and others to establish a cooperative society in London, while continuing to oversee his lands in Ireland[28] and promote the idea of cooperation. In response to Thomas Hodgskin's *Labour Defended Against the Claims of Capital*,[29] Thompson published a short essay, *Labor Rewarded: The Claims of Labor and Capital Conciliated*, in 1827, in which he argues that the only effective way for workers to combat the exploitation of the capitalists was to gain control of capital themselves, and "UNITE IN LARGE NUMBERS" in cooperative communities.[30] Clearly identified as a leader of the cooperative movement, he was also active during this time lecturing and publishing essays in journals dedicated to promoting cooperative ideas and the establishment of cooperative communities.[31]

In 1830 Thompson published his last work, *Practical Directions for the Speedy and Economical Establishment of Communities on the Principles of Mutual Co-operation, United Possessions and Equality of Exertions and of the means of Enjoyments,* and worked with Owen and others to convene the first Cooperative Congress in England in 1831. The plan he laid out in *Practical Directions* was formally adopted by the Congress and he was given the task, with Owen and others, to convene meetings in London in order to begin the effort to establish a community. As part of this, Thompson offered his own lands for those who would work to establish a community there,[31] although no society was formed.

The Congress met again in 1831 and once more in 1832, before Thompson succumbed to a lifelong respiratory condition and died in 1833, at the relatively young age of fifty-six. His attempt to leave his body to science and his estate to the formation of a cooperative community (with the exception of an annuity for Anna Wheeler) led to his sisters filing a suit to overturn his will. In the nearly twenty years it took to settle the case, the lands were sold to pay for attorneys' fees.[33] When the suit was finally settled, William Pare, Thompson's executor, received "some residue," which he used to publish an abridged edition of the *Inquiry* in 1850, reissued in 1869.[34]

Thompson's Legacy

The existence of Pare's abridged version may have had some effect on Thompson's reception after his death. The abridged version, one reviewer notes, had "a number of the more philosophical sections... deleted" and the book was also "depoliticized in places," including the removal of "an important critique of family inheritance."[35] Karl Marx, who cites Thompson in some of his later work, presents a particularly interesting case. As an Irish historian (who might be accused of some bias in the matter) puts it, Marx was "less than generous in his acknowledgments to Thompson."[36] Nonetheless, Marx does cite Thompson at some important points. Always a critic, what is remarkable about Marx's citations of Thompson is that they come without criticism. For example, Marx includes two very lengthy extracts from the *Inquiry* in his discussion of surplus value in *Capital, volume II*—without comment.[37] Based on his citations to Thompson in *Capital, volume I,* which he saw through to completion, we know that Marx read the original 1824 edition, but Engels, who prepared *Capital, vol. II* for publication, appears to have only been familiar with the abridged edition, based on the citations we may assume he added to Marx's text.[38] But while Engels attributes the "discovery" of surplus value to Marx,[39] Anton Menger, who provides one of the first critical examinations of Thompson's political and economic theory, argues that Marx's "whole theory of surplus value, its conception, its name, and the estimates of its amount are borrowed in all essentials from Thompson's writings."[40] These claims, including Thompson's theory of surplus value, will receive greater attention in chapter 4.

Thompson's relationship with another leading intellectual of the nineteenth century, John Stuart Mill, is more difficult to assess. As a young man, in 1825, Mill was part of a group of Radicals who engaged in a series of debates organized by the London Cooperative Society. The side of the Owenites was championed by Thompson, and it is in the context of a discussion of these debates in his autobiography that Mill's only reference to Thompson, anywhere in his work, appears, as he indicates familiarity with both the *Inquiry* and the *Appeal*, and says that Thompson was "a very estimable man, with whom I was well acquainted."[41] However, Mill ignores Thompson in his political economics, and even in his later writing on socialism. Nonetheless, contemporary scholars have suggested that Mill's feminism was strongly influenced by Thompson,[42] and when reading Mill's *On the Subjection of Women* next to Thompson's *Appeal* one may be struck by the many similarities. It should be noted, of course, that Thompson was not the only feminist writer in the period, nor the only one with whom Mill may have had a personal relationship (Anna

Wheeler, with whom Thompson wrote the *Appeal,* was certainly one of these), but it is difficult to overlook the parallels between the two works.

More contemporary writing on Thompson suffers from various deficiencies. E. K. Hunt's two essays on his political economics reference the original edition in the text but include the abridged version in the citations, and Hunt fails to consider any of Thompson's other work in coming to the conclusion that Thompson is, in effect, insufficiently radical.[43] Gregory Claeys's work, while far more firmly grounded in the literature,[44] shares a curious feature with Hunt's, which is the tendency to misread Thompson's careful working through of counterarguments, specifically around the question of the possibility of a competitive system based on what he refers to as the "natural laws for the distribution of wealth." Like Hunt, Claeys takes this to reflect support for competition under certain conditions. However, as I argue in chapter 4, Thompson's powerful arguments regarding the debilitating social effects of competition under any conditions cannot possibly be read as an endorsement.

Another curious feature of the literature on Thompson is that his relationship with Bentham is generally dismissed as having any significant impact on his work—despite the fact that Thompson references Bentham with reverence. There is no question that they had their differences regarding theory, but as I think the subsequent chapters will make clear, it would be difficult to agree with Lowenthal that "there was no real connection, but in fact the widest divergence between Bentham and Thompson,"[45] with Hunt's statement that "Thompson's claim to being a disciple of Bentham has to be rejected,"[46] or with Claeys that "despite Thompson's immediate acquaintance with Jeremy Bentham, the influence of the latter upon his thought has probably been exaggerated."[47] Theirs was not simply an "acquaintance," as Claeys puts it, and Thompson did not simply "use the greatest-happiness principle merely as a convenient formula for expressing his own benevolent inclinations."[48] While their differences are substantial, the parallels and similarities are, as well. Thompson's conceptual framework is heavily dependent upon Bentham's: happiness is the basis for utility, and a set of subsidiary principles provides the foundations for the theory that follows. As will be discussed in later chapters, Bentham's subsidiary principles are incorporated into Thompson's. Indeed, Thompson could be interpreted as providing a kind of alternate reading of Bentham's ideas, different from that of the political economists of his day, as is suggested by Minter Morgan, someone who knew both men well.⁴⁹

The central concepts of Bentham's and Thompson's theories—happiness, utility, and the subsidiary principles of security, subsistence, abundance, and equality (for Bentham) and security, equality, voluntarism, democracy, and common effort/common property (for Thompson) are explored in detail through much of the book. Before getting to that, another important area of difference, having to do with analytic categories, needs to be discussed, that will help in understanding the contours of what follows.

Conceptual Contrasts between Bentham and Thompson

There is a long-running debate between critical theorists and postmodernists over whether it is helpful or not to identify distinct realms, or spheres, of human activity, one "public" and the other "private."⁵⁰ In some ways it is anachronistic to bring up here, since Bentham and Thompson were long gone by the time Habermas and Foucault, two figures often cited in this debate, came on the scene. Nevertheless, it provides a useful framework by which to understand some of the differences between Bentham and Thompson. To be sure, neither Bentham nor Thompson refer to anything like a "public sphere" or a "private sphere," and, in fact, in what follows I will use a different set of categories. The point here is not to debate whether or not the public and private spheres exist in any meaningful way, but to see how the specific concepts raised here, of politics, society, and democracy, take on different meanings depending on whether one understands them as autonomous but interrelated, or as describing different dimensions of human relationships in all the domains of our lives.

Central Concepts: Politics, Society, and Democracy

Bentham's primary interest in his work was legal reform, and the instrument for this was the legislative institutions. This is, for Bentham, the domain of politics. In order to reform legal institutions, it was necessary to reform the state institutions. So, politics is concerned with matters that pertain to the institutions of government—the actions of the sovereign (be that a monarch or understood as the people in their function as the sovereign), the legislature, the judiciary, and those administrative bodies they establish to carry out their will. This perspective is evident, for example, in an unpublished manuscript, the *Institute of Political Economy*, in which he says in a footnote that, "Politics... is an experimental science.... Each science has its pathology. Laws are the material medica of the political body—[its] therapeutics [is] legislation."[51]

If politics is a domain of activity primarily pertaining to the legislative body and legislating, then society is the object to which those laws are directed. Indeed, even here "society" is probably too broad a term, as it was with *individuals* that Bentham was principally concerned.[52] These were, of course, private individuals, whose actions are guided by their expectations of pleasure and pain or, read a different way, their expectations of reward and punishment, which are shaped in part by political institutions (that is, by law and its enforcement).[53] Society is an important domain, as this is where people either do or do not realize their happiness, but even as it is *shaped* in important ways by political institutions, it is a domain otherwise separate from the political realm. In other words, it is an object on which politics acts, but that does not in itself contain politics.

From this perspective, democracy is understood as a formal mechanism that pertains to politics. It has a specific purpose: to hold legislators accountable. In Bentham's political theory, the people are limited to two political functions: as the sovereign, to constitute the legislative body to which is delegated the sovereign power, and to hold the legislative body accountable through what he calls the Public Opinion Tribunal.[54] This will be discussed at further length in chapter 5, but here let it just be said that democracy is, in Bentham's theory, instrumental: the primary reason Bentham endorsed the representative system for electing legislators was because he believed that this was the best way to align legislators' own interests in maintaining their power with the people's interests. A different way of expressing this is to say that the purpose of the political system is to ensure security to enable individuals to pursue their interests without causing harm to other individuals—essentially, by protecting their property and wealth. Democracy ensures the proper functioning of government in this regard, as a mechanism to enforce the fiduciary responsibility of legislators to serve the public interest rather than their own.

On virtually all of these points, Thompson's perspective is entirely different. Thompson is much more concerned with relations of power, whether these occur in formal institutions or relationships, or within informal institutions or relationships. This is demonstrated most clearly in the *Appeal,* which is ostensibly an argument for suffrage for adult women but that gets much of its rhetorical power from a sweeping argument against all systems of subordination, demonstrating how the *domestic* subordination of women is part and parcel of the *political* subordination of women. In other words, the relations between men and women in the home that place women in a subordinate position to men is a *political* relation. If we understand subordination as a kind of power relationship, then we can recognize that any relationship in which power is instantiated in some way has politics. Politics, in this sense, is a dynamic or a dimension of relationships, whether those relationships are understood as existing within a particular institution (or set of institutions), between institutions, or even between an individual and an institution(s).[55]

Society is also something much broader for Thompson than it is for Bentham. In effect, society is the collection of relations between the individuals of which it is composed. These relations are shaped by a variety of social institutions—of which the institutions of government are one part. This is evident in the way Thompson discusses "social science" in the *Inquiry*.[56] Here he calls "the application" of "*social science* . . . the art of social happiness."[57] Later, he says that the pursuit of this science is necessary, "to assist in wiping out the stain from science, noticed thirty years ago by Condorcet, but still adhering, that though she had done much for the *glory* of mankind, she had done nothing or little for their *happiness.*"[58] His examination of society—the social science—incorporates all of the institutions of society, including state institutions, economic institutions, and what are sometimes termed "social institutions," such as marriage. These are *all* social institutions to Thompson, because they all shape society in various ways; each does so in different ways and may be subject to different forces, but each describes a different means by which the relations of individuals within society are shaped.[59]

With his radical understanding of equality and social institutions, democracy clearly carries a different meaning for Thompson than it does for Bentham. Democracy is integrated into Thompson's political theory not as an instrumental procedure for ensuring that rulers fulfill their fiduciary duties and are accountable to the ruled, but as a principle of social interaction. If security stands as a principal organizing principle for Bentham, equality plays that role for Thompson. Relationships conducted on the basis of equality can be understood as democratic in a deep and radical way that a more formal, restricted conception of democracy cannot encompass. Of course, not every social relationship can be equal in this way—for example, children will always be, in some ways at least, subordinate to adults. But there are many dimensions to our relationships, and we may be equal in some respects—for example, being equal in terms of moral worth—while unequal in others. The question is the extent to which the inequalities that exist justify the exercise of authority of one person over another within a particular domain of action.

While Thompson makes a place in his theory for representative institutions of governance, democracy functions in his theory through public opinion. But where the Public Opinion Tribunal in Bentham's theory operates as an external force on the institutions of government, and the people's self-government is attenuated through representative institutions, in Thompson's theory public opinion serves as a means through which people directly engage in self-government in their daily interactions with those around them. If social institutions are structured in such a way as to promote cooperation, then people will be naturally self-governing in the sense that they will act in ways that benefit the community rather than selfishly seeking their own self-interest at the expense of the community. Thus, through the careful structuring of social institutions, the alignment of self- and social interest—the Holy Grail of moral philosophy at least since Cicero—can be achieved.

Political Economics

The conceptual distinctions between Bentham and Thompson ultimately affect their ideas about political economics. There is not much to be said here about Bentham's views—despite some minor disagreements, he is a devoted disciple of Adam Smith, as he freely admits.[60] Thompson was also influenced by Smith's work, but he diverges from Smith on a number of important points, and I want to highlight some of the major elements of his thought here. A much fuller discussion will be found in the following chapters, especially chapter 4.

Thompson takes much from Smith, including the value of the division of labor and class conflict between what Smith calls the "masters" and the "labourers." The labor theory of value, from Locke to Smith to Ricardo, is crucial to his analysis and his argument that the full produce of labor should, by right, belong to the person who produces it. However, Thompson is not really interested in some of the central concerns of the political economists, for example the determinants of rent versus profit and how the level of wages affects these things, or policies with respect to international trade. Rather, in a manner that broadly anticipates Marx, Thompson critiques the fundamental premises of the earlier political economists.

Just as women's happiness is incompatible with their subordination to men, the greatest happiness is incompatible with labor subordinated to capital. Thompson goes to great lengths in the *Inquiry*—it occupies the first quarter of a very long book—to discover what he calls the "natural laws for the distribution of wealth" under the ideal conditions for the "system of individual competition" (which is as close an analog to "capitalism" as Thompson gets). These laws require that (1) all labor is voluntary, (2) the worker receive the full produce of his or her labor, and (3) all exchange is voluntary.[61] However, even if these conditions were obtained, two facets of the capitalist system would prevent them from leading to the greatest happiness: competition and private property. The problem with the former is that it sets individuals against each other in the race to accumulate property. Thus, other members of society are seen not as one's compatriots but as rivals. Private property presents a further challenge, in the first place because it is the object of competition, and secondly because the winners in the competitive system are then able to subordinate the losers, and use their relative advantage to further advance their position.

Thompson's proposed solution, a version of the Owenite cooperative community model, resolved these problems while still enabling what was, in his terms, "large-scale" industrial production. Members of a community—at least five hundred but not more than two thousand—would produce all that was needed by the community. The communities were to be large enough to take advantage of the benefits of the division of labor while maintaining a high degree of equality. All would share equally in the proceeds of all of the productive activity of all of the members—it was, in effect, a labor exchange, although not formalized as such. No one outside the community would extract its surplus and whatever surplus they produced would be shared equally by all the members.

An important feature of these communities is that all property is to be held in common by the members, with each having an equal share. In this way, the problems of private property and competition are avoided. Where the competitive capitalist system establishes a tension between self-interest and the social interest, a community or enterprise in which all are owners on an equal basis unites individuals and aligns individual interest with social interest. Democratic governance is built into the structure of the institution, because under no other arrangement could property be said to be truly held in common. Such a system must also maintain a high level of equality, including through the equal distribution of the fruits of labor.

No community based on Thompson's plan was ever established, even though he offered his own lands for one. After his death in 1833 the cooperative movement he helped to lead nearly died out. However, new experiments began in the early 1840s that took root and eventually grew into an important part of the global economy. The cooperative movement he helped birth looks very different today from what he had envisioned, as it is based on autonomous enterprises rather than autarkic communities—but it is also far larger than he could have imagined. The cooperative movement—Thompson's role, its later development and its current state—will be discussed in chapter 6. But that comes by way of conclusion. An explication of the theory behind it comes first.

Plan of the Book

While Bentham's work is widely known and has been subjected to a great deal of scrutiny, there exists no thorough, extended examination of Thompson's political thought, a gap in the literature this work is intended, in part, to address. While my primary focus is on Thompson, I do not ignore Bentham. Thompson at least appears to appropriate many of Bentham's ideas, but he follows them to very different conclusions, and the starting point for my research was a desire to understand why that is so. What follows, then, is some back-and-forth through the chapters in examining the work of these two men, who in many respects were closely allied despite substantial and significant differences in their arguments.

What follows is broken up into two parts, explicitly organized so as to follow a path from abstract philosophy to political theory to political practice. Part I is concerned with the concept of happiness. It begins with a very brief chapter on the history of the concept in order to help orient the reader to its development from the ancient Greeks to the present day. Those who would prefer to get to the meat of the matter—the exploration of Bentham's and Thompson's ideas—can skip this chapter. Chapters 2 and 3 are concerned with Bentham's and Thompson's ideas about happiness, and form the philosophical bedrock for what comes after. These are the only two chapters in which Bentham and Thompson are treated separately (except for chapter 6, as Bentham has no part in that particular story). A full chapter on Bentham's ideas on happiness was considered necessary because this is—perhaps surprisingly—a relatively neglected part of Bentham's thought. Despite the vast secondary literature on the notion of "the greatest happiness," it appears that just what Bentham means by "happiness" has received little attention. In the subsequent chapters, Bentham is discussed primarily in order to establish a ground for a more detailed discussion of Thompson. The contrast between the two helps to bring Thompson's ideas into sharper view; on occasion, it sheds some new light on Bentham, as well.

Part II is concerned with the political theory based on happiness—utilitarianism. The first of these chapters, chapter 4, examines the theory of utility itself, with particular attention to political economics. Of course, many books have been written to explore Bentham's utilitarianism, and what is of greatest interest here are only those parts of Bentham's theory that most clearly relate to Thompson's. Thus, most of the chapter is concerned with Thompson's ideas. The next chapter takes the prior chapter's differential development of the concept of utility forward into an exploration of Bentham's and Thompson's democratic theory. Here again, there is plenty of material available on Bentham's ideas,[62] so while enough Bentham is provided to form a clear contrast, most of the chapter is given over to Thompson's ideas. Finally, chapter 6 explores how Thompson's ideas were taken up by the cooperative movement, in order to demonstrate the persistence of Thompson's ideas as well as to suggest that this provides a way to think about the cooperative movement on political terms, as a political movement supported by a coherent political theory.

But it starts with happiness.

PART I
WHAT IS HAPPINESS?

1
The Two Faces of Happiness: A Brief History

Hedonic versus Eudaemonic Happiness

The argument presented in this book—its core argument—is that the differences between Bentham and Thompson rest on the fact that they are working with different conceptions of happiness. For Bentham, happiness is almost an ecstatic experience where the pleasure is substantial and there is no or little corresponding pain;[1] for Thompson, happiness is equivalent to well-being and is best understood as the condition of a person's life. This difference is reflected in the contemporary literature on happiness,[2] which reveals that although there are a variety of ways of thinking about it, for the most part happiness can be understood to wear two faces. One of these, hedonism, looks toward pleasure or a person's level of satisfaction with their current state, while the other, eudaemonism, looks toward well-being and the general conditions of life; one tends to be largely subjective, the other more objective.

These differences have a long history. After all, happiness is, without doubt, one of the oldest philosophical concepts in the Western tradition,[3] and it has remained a subject of active inquiry at least since Socrates began stopping strangers on the streets of Athens to ask them about the purpose of life. Bentham may have popularized the idea that the principal object of government is the "greatest happiness of the greatest number," but this can be seen as a repackaging of Plato, who argued that the task of the Guardians was nothing less than "the greatest possible happiness" for the city.[4]

The concept of happiness has changed substantially since the ancient Greeks, although, in fact, there were significant disagreements among the Greeks themselves. However, the Greeks largely agreed on three points: That happiness cannot be measured in the moment, but has to do with the general conditions of one's life; that virtue is the mode of conduct most conducive to happiness; and that desire undermines happiness and must, therefore, be limited. These are all interrelated, the result of which is that individual happiness is tightly bound to the *polis* (or city-state, around which Greek life was organized). While happiness may be an individual matter in the sense that it requires a kind of mental discipline, the requirements of virtue mean that it must be other-regarding in important ways. And where the temporal frame is the lifespan, the conditions of life, including the conditions of life of the other members of the society within which one lives, are also crucial to happiness.[5]

This "political" character of happiness (political in the sense that it is associated with life in the *polis,* although over time the context changes from *polis* to village) becomes lost—"submerged" might be a better term—in the shift to modernity. Indeed, one of the major signposts of the shift from ancient to modern is in the way happiness becomes individualized, associated with specific sensations or experiences in a way that is largely missing from the ancients. Generally speaking, Greek philosophy did not celebrate the pursuit of pleasure understood as desire-fulfillment; in the modern era, it is taken as a basic premise. As with many other things, the shift can be connected to the rise of commercial society and, ultimately, capitalism, in the way that the fulfillment of desire becomes the primary engine of economic growth. But while the political character of happiness may have become obscured in this development, Jeremy Bentham's work demonstrates its continuing political character as an underlying premise—a point that becomes clear in later chapters when Bentham's political theory is contrasted with William Thompson's counterhegemonic alternative.

The major focus in this section is on three related points, having to do with the relationship of happiness to pleasure and desire; the question of access, or what we might call the right to happiness; and its temporal frame. There is a distinctly historical element to this, as the groundwork for the debate is laid by the ancient Greeks and major shifts develop over time. Of the ancient Greek schools, I concentrate on the thought of Epicurus and the Epicureans here for two reasons: First, because they most clearly laid out the terms of the debate, and because the classical utilitarians (and, perhaps, their descendants in the social sciences) have been seen as following in the Epicurean tradition.[6]

Desire, Pleasure, and Happiness

Epicureanism is generally associated with hedonism, but there is more to it than that. As Rosenbaum puts it, Epicurus articulated "a set of constraints on human behavior, developed . . . for the purpose of creating social conditions in which people are best able to be happy."[7] How people relate to one another and the conditions in which their interactions occur are then seen as crucial for happiness. And while *hedone* (pleasure) is clearly at its center, it is, paradoxically, an ascetic sort of hedonism.[8]

The paradox exists because Epicurus recognized different sorts of pleasure, kinetic and katastematic. Kinetic pleasure is fleeting, unstable, and inherently insecure. Katastematic pleasure is static, stable, and secure. Kinetic pleasure is active and transient, experienced in the course of fulfilling a need or addressing a lack. Static pleasure is passive and constant, of a sort that is experienced in the absence of pain and that realizes its maximum when all pain has been removed. Kinetic pleasures are particular to a specific need or desire, while static pleasure is a general state and an end unto itself. This latter form, according to Annas, Epicurus refers to as "tranquility or *ataraxia,*" and it is this that he "identifies [as] our final end."[9]

A related point has to do with the relationship between pleasure and pain, and the character of pleasure, particularly of the katastematic sort. In effect, pain establishes the limits for pleasure. "Pleasure," as Epicurus puts it, "reaches its maximum limit at the removal of all sources of pain. . . . When pain arising from need has been removed, bodily pleasure cannot increase—it merely varies. But the limit of mental pleasure is reached after we reflect upon these bodily pleasures and the related mental distress prior to fulfillment."[10] The act of fulfilling a pain-causing need gives rise to kinetic pleasure, which is experienced directly and is limited to the action of relieving the pain. This sort of pleasure is limited in two ways: first, it only lasts as long as the action itself, and, second, certain ways of fulfilling the need may give rise to new pains (for example, the pain associated with overeating). Further, kinetic pleasure is particularized: it is associated not with the general condition of hunger but with the specific condition of being hungry, so the pleasure of eating is restricted to that particular instance of being hungry, involving elements not directly associated with the pain of hunger, such as the taste of the food or the conditions in which it is consumed. Things such as the desire for certain kinds of food or eating in certain kinds of settings can never, in fact, be satisfied in a stable way because once a given eating experience is complete, the desire is sure to return.

Katastematic pleasure, in contrast to kinetic pleasure, is an enduring condition that is best understood as the absence of a pain, and it has a mental element that is largely missing from kinetic pleasure. For example, katastematic pleasure comes from not only being fed, but being what in contemporary terms is referred to as "food secure"—in other words, not having anxiety about where one will get one's next meal. The "pleasure" is characterized by the absence of pain—not only the pain of hunger but also the fear of hunger—but not by any specific positive feeling. While clearly related to a physical condition, it has more to do with a particular mental condition or state of mind (or, more accurately, the absence of a particular mental condition), making it a mental, not a physical sort of pleasure. What this means is that, despite the fact that Epicurus was clearly a materialist in that he held that everything in the universe, including souls and spiritual phenomena, could be explained through the movements of atoms, in its ethics Epicureanism may best be understood, paradoxically, as a profoundly antimaterialist philosophy, both in the sense that material goods are not the primary source of happiness, and that material (i.e., bodily) pleasures are seen as a lesser form.

The difference between kinetic and katastematic pleasure is also reflected in Epicurus's ideas about desire. There are three different kinds of desire, he tells us, based on two distinctions: "Among desires some are natural and necessary, some natural but not necessary, and others neither natural nor necessary."[11] Elsewhere, unnatural and unnecessary desires are referred to as "empty."[12] An analysis of the distinctions between "natural" and "unnatural," and "necessary" and "unnecessary" adds an additional dimension to the difference between kinetic and katastematic pleasure. It is natural to want food; the fulfillment of that desire is the pleasure of satiation, a static pleasure that, as discussed above, is limited by the removal of the associated pain, hunger. But while the hunger may give rise to a natural desire for food, it does not in itself give rise to a desire for a particular kind of food. The particular desire for certain kinds of food is what causes problems, as this involves a kinetic pleasure that not only fades away as soon as the meal is finished, but that is both unstable, in that it may change, and insatiable, as the desire can never be filled in any lasting way.[13] A simple meal made from available ingredients may leave me satisfied, but a fine dinner of lobster leaves me with the desire to repeat the experience as soon as possible, perhaps next time on a bed of rice rather than pasta, and with a different sauce. And were the side vegetables satisfactory? What about dessert? And perhaps the setting could have had better lighting. The varieties are endless, leaving me with an ongoing, unfilled desire. This is the sort of desire that Epicurus considered "empty" and inherently problematic, to be avoided to the greatest extent possible.[14] So, for Epicurus, desire is best understood as the primary source of pain, such that the best route to happiness is the overcoming of these empty desires.

For Epicureanism, then, it is wrong to associate happiness with the fulfillment of desires at all. Happiness based on katastematic pleasure does not arise from any particular activity, so the goal of an activity is neither the experience itself, nor even any particular consequence that arises out of the action. The purpose of any activity is the condition of *ataraxia,* feeling satisfied, at peace.[15] Best suited for this are those activities that are considered virtuous. As Epicurus puts it, "The greatest virtue and the basis for all virtues is prudence ... the art of practical wisdom.... It is not possible to live pleasurably unless one also lives prudently, honorably, and justly; nor is it possible to live prudently, honestly, and justly without living pleasurably. For the virtues are inseparable from a happy life, and living happily is inseparable from the virtues."[16] As he puts it elsewhere, "The happiest men are those who enjoy the condition of having nothing to fear from those who surround them. Such men live among one another most agreeably, having the firmest grounds for confidence in one another, enjoying the benefits of friendship in all their fullness."[17] The greatest value of virtue, then, is that it means that you have nothing to fear. Thus, virtue can be seen as instrumental: not good in itself, but simply the best kind of action because it is most likely to establish the conditions for the kind of pleasure most conducive to happiness.

This ancient, ascetic hedonism based on katastematic pleasure can be contrasted with the modern form of hedonism, which is based on kinetic pleasure. The central tenet of modern hedonism is desire fulfillment. The change occurred over centuries. For the early Church, the afterlife was the inversion of life on Earth: a life of hedonism (that is, desire-fulfillment) would be punished with eternal suffering in Hell, while a life of suffering would be rewarded with the infinite pleasures of Heaven.[18] There could be no happiness on Earth. The happiness of Heaven, however, is characterized by infinite, everlasting pleasure—katastematic pleasure, clearly, as there would be no discomfort or pain. That said, the common use of terms such as "bliss" or "joyousness" seem to suggest that there would be kinetic pleasure, as well, but without the pain of desire. Heaven, indeed.

The reformation of desire is reflected in the work of Thomas Aquinas. Contrary to prior teachings, Aquinas argued that there were two types of happiness: the perfect, eternal happiness that could only be experienced in Heaven, and a lesser sort that could be enjoyed by people on Earth. The true object of desire for life on earth is the infinite pleasure of Heaven;[19] one of the features of Heaven that makes its happiness perfect is that it "excludes every evil, and fulfills every desire." He continues:

> But in this life every evil cannot be excluded. For this present life is subject to many unavoidable evils; to ignorance on the part of the intellect; to inordinate affection on the part of the appetite, and to many penalties on the part of the body.... Likewise neither can the desire for good be satiated in this life. For man naturally desires the good, which he has, to be abiding. Now the goods of the present life pass away; since life itself passes away, which we naturally desire to have, and would wish to hold abidingly, for man naturally shrinks from death. Wherefore it is impossible to have true Happiness in this life.[20]

Modern hedonism, or the idea that sensual pleasure is to be sought for its own sake, firmly enters the scene with the Reformation. Martin Luther argued that "we can be merry with a good conscience," and that one should be "joyful . . . in all things, inwardly in Christ and outwardly in God's gifts; for he gives them that we may have pleasure in them and thank him for them."[21] Misery was a condition to be experienced by those who are not saved; those who are saved should revel in the pleasures God placed on Earth to be enjoyed by man. Luther considered Hell to be a kind of psychological state; the pursuit of happiness was a pursuit of signs of predestination. So, not only was it possible to retain one's dignity in the pursuit of happiness on earth, it was *righteous*.[22] To have one's desires fulfilled was surely a sign of blessedness.

John Locke formalizes the modern perspective on desire, pleasure, and happiness, arguing that human action was driven by two fundamental forces, one attractive and the other repellant: pleasure and pain.[23] In terms that Bentham no doubt had opportunity to consider, Locke writes, "Things then are Good or Evil, only in reference to Pleasure or Pain."[24] Locke argues that what motivates us is not the *experience* of pleasure, but our *desire* for it, which he refers to as a kind of unease;[25] this unease can be understood as a kind of pain.[26] Locke calls happiness that state in which we experience "the utmost Pleasure we are capable of."[27]

The shift in attention from pleasure to desire here is important, in effect elevating the status of desire. For Epicurus, desire was without question an evil to be purged, to the greatest extent possible, from the system. For Locke, it becomes the root cause of action. If pleasure is the removal of pain, and desire is the chief pain to be considered, then if the framework is not based on asceticism the result is that what gets promoted is the fulfillment of desire. So, the antimaterialism and disdain for physical pleasure expressed by the ancient Greeks and early Christians gives way to an emphasis on pleasure and the enjoyment of earthly goods. Left behind is the Epicurean distinction between kinetic and katastematic pleasures. Desire might still have the character of a pain, but the modern solution is to take action to fulfill it (even if that requires subjecting oneself to pain), not to seek to discard it as false or a distraction from happiness.

It has been said that Utilitarianism "was developed in an intellectual atmosphere largely dominated by John Locke."[28] Certainly the similarities between Locke's and Bentham's ideas of the relationship of pleasure and pain to happiness lend support to that notion. Perhaps the primary advance of the Enlightenment was to firmly secularize the idea of happiness. But this was also a period of intense change in the fundamental relations of society, particularly in Britain, where the rapid devolution of the feudal system, the Industrial Revolution, and the transition to an exchange-based, market economy were opening up possibilities that had not previously existed.

Whose Happiness?

Although ancient Greece is famous for its bacchanalian hedonism, perhaps as a reaction to the instability of fate, Greek philosophy as a whole had a skeptical attitude toward sensual pleasure. Happiness might be the *telos* of human life, but that didn't mean it was easy to get.[29] McMahon points to a distinct difference between schools: "Epicureans and Stoics offered their medicine to any who would take it. Whereas Plato and Aristotle restricted happiness to the privileged few, Epicurus and Zeno [the founder of Stoicism] proposed to make gods of many."[30] The harshness of the Stoic view (which denied any connection between happiness and pleasure and held that the basis for happiness was in virtue only) may have limited its popularity, but in the case of Epicureanism, by the third century CE, according to Diogenes Laertius, the Epicurean school in Athens had been in existence for five hundred years, and Epicureans "outnumbered the populations of whole cities."[31]

One important feature of Epicureanism was that the Garden was open to anyone—men, women, even slaves were welcome.[32] However, while membership may not have been restricted, happiness required a very particular and rigorous sort of lifestyle, making it difficult to achieve. Not everyone is suited for the philosophical life, not everyone could achieve the Zen-like focus Epicurean happiness required. If difficult, though, at least happiness in this life was possible. In contrast, the early Christians were faced with a stark choice between profane pleasures of the flesh that might afford a temporal but false happiness that would lead to eternal damnation, or a life of suffering that presented the possibility of eternal bliss.

Part of the radical change brought about by the Enlightenment was the idea that not only was happiness a possibility for everyone, but that there was a general *right* to happiness. This meant that it had immediate political relevance. The Declaration of Independence, along with the French Declaration of the Rights of Man that followed soon after, firmly established the idea that happiness is the primary object of liberty—negative liberty, or the freedom to pursue one's own idea of happiness. Thus, happiness became "the great legitimating concept of national governments and individual lives, pulling across the political spectrum to lead in the direction of a better world."[33] Indeed, the role of the state was seen as paradoxical: At one and the same time, it was both the greatest threat to individual happiness as well as the guarantor of that happiness. Jeremy Bentham was not the first Enlightenment philosopher to suggest that the "greatest happiness of the greatest number" was the principal object of government, nor did he invent the notion of the felicific calculus, having been preceded on these points in one way or another by such figures as Hutcheson, Leibniz, Beccaria, Helvétius, Priestley, and others.[34]

The Temporal Frame

One of the features of kinetic pleasure that distinguishes it from katastematic pleasure is its temporal frame. The latter's stability is contrasted with the inherently unstable, fleeting nature of the former. Kinetic pleasure is in the moment, as it lasts only so long as the experience lasts. As positive entities, pleasure and pain become measurable (at least in theory), so one can tell at any given moment whether their quantity of pleasures exceeds their quantity of pain. One can then measure happiness over any given span of time—in the moment or with the moments all added up into a lifetime. This is qualitatively different, however, from understanding happiness as the quality of one's life. If happiness is understood to be made up of discrete moments, these may be seen as isolated or only thinly connected to one another. Understood in the full frame of a lifetime, the factors that contribute to the quality of our lives take on additional meaning as they relate to one another. While momentary happiness may be recognized as social in the sense that other people are involved, it is easy to see this only as our own happiness, something that we experience ourselves and for which we ourselves are responsible. It is more difficult to individualize happiness when understood in the full frame of life, as it becomes clearer how our relationships with others—our interrelationships—affect our happiness, and our happiness is in fact wrapped up in theirs.

From an economistic perspective, kinetic pleasure is more meaningful because it is more easily measured. The notion of temporally discrete experience-packages containing distinct quantities of pleasure and pain, which can be aggregated and thereby made amenable to intersubjective comparison and analysis, is what enables happiness to be, as some researchers put it, "the ultimate 'dependent variable' in social science."[35] Katastematic pleasure, on the other hand, is not so easily quantified. This does not mean that it cannot be evaluated, but it requires a different set of analytical tools.

Differences with regard to the temporal frame of happiness are important to contemporary research on happiness. Two major categories—similar to those discussed in the foregoing—have been identified: the "Benthamite-subjective-hedonic-individualistic, and the ... Aristotelian-objective-eudaimonic-relational."[36] In simpler terms, the former is often referred to as subjective well-being (SWB), while the latter is called objective well-being (OWB).[37] In fact, within these two categories, the subjective well-being approach is more closely associated with, and makes greater use of, the term *happiness* than is the objective well-being approach.[38]

The use of the term *well-being* here should not mislead anyone into thinking that the two perspectives on happiness have merged, although they have drawn somewhat closer. In general, the SWB literature retains an overall subjectivist and individualistic methodology while acknowledging that happiness is most meaningful when considered as "life-satisfaction" rather than a momentary condition, and paying significant attention to the social conditions of life.[39] But while "life-satisfaction" may be one of the points measured by SWB researchers, note that a common method of determining this involves asking individuals to rate their level of satisfaction at a particular moment on a Likert scale, thus transferring what is a qualitative question into a quantifiable measure.[40] The SWB literature remains largely concerned with individuals' direct experience in terms of the volume of pleasure and pain, although they recognize that happiness/well-being cannot be commodified, which is to say that it cannot be understood in terms of commodities, production, and/or income; and that there are substantial elements that depend on noneconomic factors and, indeed, on factors that may be difficult, if not impossible, to quantify.[41] In contrast, OWB research is more often concerned with assessing the general conditions of people's lives—for example, whether their basic needs are met, and the quality of their social interactions.[42]

Like Bentham, whose work in many ways epitomizes the modern hedonist view of happiness, the scholars working on subjective well-being are generally supportive of free market economics and limited government. Indeed, as will be seen in the next chapter, they have begun to question some of the foundational assumptions of neoclassical economics and, interestingly enough, in some cases return to Bentham to support their arguments. Like Bentham, these researchers recognize the effect that social institutions have in shaping the conditions for happiness, as well as recognizing that well-being means something more than the simple desire-fulfillment.

As far as I have found, no researcher on objective well-being has referenced William Thompson, but they often echo his critiques of the liberal capitalist order. As will be seen in chapter 3, like the Epicureans, Thompson recognizes different kinds of pleasures and, like them, recognizes that happiness in the fullest sense requires the enjoyment of pleasures that stimulate the spirit and the intellect rather than the body—and that the desire for material wealth undermines happiness. Also, like the ancients and the contemporary work on objective well-being, Thompson's view of happiness is deeply rooted in social conditions much more strongly than it is for Bentham.

2
Between Pleasure and Well-being: Bentham

It is a curious feature of the vast secondary literature on Bentham that there has been little exploration of just what he means by the term *happiness*.[1] After all, "the greatest happiness of the greatest number" (later referred to as the "greatest happiness principle") is the central statement of his philosophy.[2] One possible reason for this lack of attention is Bentham's relative silence on the subject—as Harrison notes, Bentham's work on moral philosophy was, for him, secondary to his primary concern with legislative and constitutional reform.[3] Bentham seems to have recognized that while government could not make people happy, what it could do is affect their perception of pleasure—and, at least as important, of pain. As a result, he focused much more attention on pleasure and pain than on happiness per se.

If Bentham's conception of happiness receives little attention, even fewer writers consider what Bentham has to say about well-being, or how it relates to his ideas about pleasure, pain, and happiness.[4] A major point of this chapter is to show the important place that well-being has in his thought. Doing so, however, should not obscure the point that *happiness* is the centerpiece, not only because it establishes a higher standard for the maximization of pleasure and the minimization of pain, but because happiness, for Bentham, is closer conceptually to pleasure and pain than is well-being.

The task of showing how pleasure, happiness, and well-being are related to one another in Bentham's thought is made difficult by Bentham's own inconsistency, but if consistency is not to be found perhaps at least it can be made more or less coherent. What is clear is that pleasure and happiness, in Bentham's work, are closely related: Pleasure, with its constant companion the avoidance of pain, is always the basis for happiness.[5] In similar ways, pleasure and pain are also factors in well-being, which Bentham sometimes equates with and sometimes differentiates from happiness. Where he distinguishes between them, happiness refers to the immediate experience of pleasure without pain (or mostly so), whereas well-being considers the balance of pleasure and pain over a period of time. But because Bentham's "greatest happiness principle" (his alternate name for the principle of utility) emphasizes security and wealth—which require the experience of pain and introduce the passage of time through the deferral of pleasure—happiness in this sense is more like well-being. Happiness, therefore, sits between pleasure and well-being; in some uses it points toward the former; in others it points toward the latter. When Bentham is concerned with the motives of action he focuses on pleasure, and happiness most clearly retains its connection to its fundamental source. But when he discusses the principle of utility as the principal object for legislators to keep in mind as they craft measures that are to lead to the "greatest happiness of the greatest number," then happiness is the means toward well-being, which he recognizes as the great end of human endeavor.

Calculating Happiness

A good starting point for examining Bentham's conception of happiness is the way all motives for human action are boiled down to expectations of pleasure and pain in his famed "felicific calculus," defined in chapter IV of the *Introduction to the Principles of Morals and Legislation* (*IPML*): for any action whose consequences are being considered, each pleasure and pain is prospectively "considered *by itself*"—although it is not clear how we are to distinguish each from the others. A pain that produces a pleasure would be considered an "impure" pain, just as any pleasure that produces a pain would similarly be considered "impure." Spatial and temporal distance are included in the consideration of the "*propinquity* or *remoteness*" of pleasures and pains. Using these criteria (as well as several others, including intensity and duration) to evaluate each individual pleasure or pain resulting from an action, one may sum up the pleasures and pains anticipated from the act in question, subtract the latter from the former, and determine the good or bad "tendency of the act upon the whole."[6] Proper use of the calculus should lead to happiness: the experience of pleasure and the avoidance of pain.

The felicific calculus reveals that happiness might be a difficult condition to attain. Purity is an especially demanding standard, since some pain is involved in most pleasure. Most pleasures require effort—always a pain, according to Bentham—and in some cases the measure of pleasure is in direct relation to the degree of effort, for example, in the pleasure of accomplishment when one has overcome significant challenges. On a more mundane level, if I want to eat I have to work to earn money so I can buy food. Now, the pain I experience in my effort may be near but the pleasure remote: I go to work on Monday but don't get paid until Friday (or worse!—although hopefully I have some money or food stored up so I can last until then). And once I do get paid I can't experience the full measure of pleasure that it might bring all at once—after all, it has to last until I get paid again.

In some ways, what he describes as happiness here has much more in common with his definition of well-being in *Deontology*. There, he distinguishes between happiness and well-being, referring to happiness as a condition that leaves "pain in all its shapes altogether out of the account, but to give it to be understood that . . . the pleasures that have been experienced [are] in a high and . . . superlative degree."[7] Well-being, in contrast, indicates "the *difference* in *value* between the sum of the pleasures of all sorts and the sum of the pains of all sorts, which down to the point of time (suppose the end of his life) a man has experienced"—if positive, well-being; if negative, "ill-being."[8] In *Pannomial Fragments*, the two definitions are merged as happiness, which is "a word employed to denote the sum of the pleasures experienced during that quantity of time which is under consideration, deduction made or not made of the quantity of pain experienced during that same quantity of time."[9] The different definitions are not as different as they appear: well-being (as defined in *Deontology*) is, in effect, happiness writ large. The basis for both of them is pleasures and pains—kinetic pleasures and kinetic pains—understood as discrete experiences, each of which can be measured and included in the calculation.

Although he says at one point that pleasure and pain are "interesting perceptions,"[10] it is unclear whether Bentham thinks that all pleasure amounts to a mental condition, as he expressly avoids the term *physical* in describing pleasures and pains (in favor of "pathological") so as to be sure to *include* the pleasures and pains of the mind.[11] Still, and what matters most to him, is that pleasure and pain, understood as motives, can only be in the mind: "[I]t is no otherwise than through the medium of the *imagination*, that any pleasure, or pain, is capable of operating in the character of a *motive*."[12] While happiness itself requires that we actually experience pleasure, what motivates us is not the experience itself, but our *expectation* that, if we engage in a particular action, we will experience some measure of pleasure or pain; this is, of course, accompanied by a calculation regarding the level of surety as to the results as well as the effort (read: pain) required in order to enjoy the corresponding pleasure (or avoid further pain).

Interest and Interests

At times, Bentham discusses pleasure and happiness using the language of "interests" and "interest." His use of these terms has received some attention in the secondary literature, and working through some of this discussion provides us with some insight into Bentham's conception of happiness and its relationship with pleasure. Bentham's first statement on interest is that it "is one of those words, which . . . cannot in the ordinary way be defined,"[13] although he goes on to say that "[a] thing is said to promote the interest . . . of an individual, when it tends to add to the sum total of his pleasures: or, what comes to the same thing, to diminish the sum total of his pains."[14] In *Deontology,* Bentham refers to different types of interest, including "self-interest" and "extra-regarding interest."[15] In the *Table of the Springs of Action,* however, he refers directly to "interest," and it is here that he most clearly defines what it is that he means. Here, "A man is said to *have an interest in any subject* in so far as that *subject* is considered as more or less likely to be to him a source of pleasure or exemption [from pain]." The "subject" can vary, so this may apply to things, persons, events, or states of things.[16]

Pitkin argues that Bentham's notion of interest suffers because he too easily slips between references to "singular and plural interest(s). Sometimes, self-interest is singular, the total balance of all one's prospective pleasures and pains at a given moment. At other times, Bentham called each of these many, rival, prospective pleasures and pains an interest, so that one's self-interests at any moment are multiple and need to be reconciled before one can act."[17] But the issue here seems to be of a difference in kind rather than an inconsistency in the use of his terms: interest in the singular refers to something different than interests in the plural. Our singular interest is happiness, but we have multiple interests in the specific matters that bring pleasure or exemption from pain. Thus, while it may be difficult for someone to be unclear about her (singular) interest, she may be mistaken about her own (plural) interests because she may misjudge about what will best lead to her happiness. In other words, while Bentham's use of language may be unclear, there is no great ambiguity or difficulty in his argument.[18]

But is Bentham aware of this difference? Engelmann claims that, "Bentham almost always writes 'interest' in the singular rather than the plural"[19] specifically because he is interested in the aggregation of plural interest or, as Engelmann puts it, of "commensurable goods."[20] *Contra* Pitkin, Engelmann argues that Bentham "is not at all confused, just far more subtle than his critics suppose.... [T]here is slippage in Bentham's vocabulary, but this slippage is remarkably systematic."[21] Some of the confusion may arise from the failure to recognize the distinction between pleasure as an *experience,* and the *interest* we have in experiencing pleasure—what Bentham would refer to as a *motive*. Engelmann rightly points to Bentham's shift (rather than slip) from sensation to imagination as crucial for Bentham's theory of government, as a kind of governing of the expectations or the discourse of pleasure and pain. But Engelmann is only partly right when he goes from Bentham's statement, quoted above, that pleasure and pain act through the imagination to produce motives, to the conclusion that "suffered and enjoyed pains and pleasures ultimately don't matter: they are not part of interest."[22]

It may be true that only the expectation of pleasure or pain, and not our experience of them, is important to our motivation. However, our happiness depends on the actual *enjoyment* of pleasures, not merely our expectations of them (expectation might itself be a kind of kinetic pleasure, but that just emphasizes the point). It takes on the characteristics of a positive feedback loop: our experiences of pleasure and pain give rise to expectations that form the basis on which we make decisions about our interests and arrive at our understanding of what is in our interest. This is, of course, subject to manipulation, which I take to be Engelmann's ultimate point. Some of that manipulation, however, comes through the way we feel about the experiences themselves and our recollections of them, which means that our experiences cannot be dismissed altogether.

Bentham clearly distinguishes between pleasure, interest, and motive.[23] Engelmann, however, collapses them all into his conception of "monistic interest." Perhaps the significance for Engelmann lies in what they "matter" for; his argument works if the only object of concern is Bentham's theory of legislation, which is Engelmann's focus.[24] I am not convinced that it is correct to say for Bentham that pleasure constitutes our interest (in the singular) because, as much as he sees pleasure as essential to happiness, he discusses security in similar terms. Bentham would instead argue that our (singular) interest is *happiness,* of which pleasure is the primary—but not the only—component. As he puts it, "My notion of man is, that, successfully or unsuccessfully, he aims at happiness, and so will continue to aim as long as he continues to be man, in every thing he does."[25] *Happiness* is the object, not *pleasure,* although we need pleasure in order to have happiness. If happiness is distinct from pleasure, then our interest in each can be discussed on different terms: pleasures, being multiple, comprise our multiple interests, while our happiness, which is singular, is the subject of our singular interest.

Happiness as the Object of Pleasure

Happiness is composed of—made up of—pleasures, which means that it is, itself, something different from pleasure; it is the whole of which pleasures are the parts, the forest composed of trees, and it is a common error to mistake the forest for the trees. Pleasure is not an end in and of itself but, for Bentham, only the *means* (and, along with avoiding pain, the *only* means) for the larger goal of happiness.

Bentham did not go so far as to argue that government can make people happy (although it may be able to make them *unhappy*), but he clearly thought that it can guide people toward acting in ways that benefit themselves and limit the harm they may do (i.e., the pain they may cause) to others. It can create the conditions necessary for happiness by establishing institutional structures based on the principle of security so people can be sure that they will be able to enjoy the benefits that should accrue to them as a consequence of their actions (and so they will not be harmed by others). It can affect how people think about pleasure and pain; it can even create pleasures and pains in the form of rewards and punishments. *But it cannot make people happy.*[26] As a result, Bentham is much more concerned with investigating the nature and influences of/on pleasure so as to understand how to wield the levers of the law to produce the appropriate results. The goal is the greatest happiness of the greatest number, but the only means the government has to make progress toward that goal is the management of pleasures and pains.

So, although discussions of pleasure predominate in his work, Bentham's primary concern is *happiness* as the end we have in mind in undertaking our actions, not pleasure (even if what he meant by happiness is not always clear). Bentham was concerned to lay out the parameters for a science rooted in basic facts of human nature (as he saw them) in order to set policy, and law and social policy would provide the means for achieving the end of happiness. The reason why one might "point out to a man the *utility*... or the mischievousness" of actions subject to the law is not to convince him of the *pleasure* to be gained, but the ways in which the action would contribute to his *happiness*.[27] In Bentham's view, there was never any need to convince anyone to do anything that would bring them pleasure—they could be expected to seek it on their own—but because happiness has greater requirements, it was sometimes necessary to show how one pleasure might be more conducive to happiness than another, even if its effects might be less immediate.

Bentham and Well-being

While Bentham often elides the difference between happiness and well-being, he also discusses well-being differently from happiness, and the tenor of his discussion here is somewhat different from the terms with which he discusses happiness. Returning to *Deontology*, he expresses the difference between the two as follows:

> What well-being is has been seen: in the instance of the individual in question, for and during the portion of time in question, what balance there has been, if any, on the side of pleasure.
>
> What happiness is has also been seen: any pleasure or combination of contemporary pleasures, considered as existing at an elevated point, though without the possibility of marking it in the scale of intensity.[28]

So, in *Deontology*, at least, it is *well-being*, not happiness, that refers to the balance of pleasure and pain over an extended period of time. The term "happiness" he finds "not... equally suitable to the purpose," because it leaves pain "altogether out of the account" and requires that the pleasures be "in a high and superlative degree." He continues, saying that "few men... would be found who..., the whole length of their lives taken together, have not been in the enjoyment of a measure more or less considerable of well-being. Much fewer, or rather none at all, who during an equal period have been in the possession and enjoyment of *happiness*."[29] In other words, happiness is rare (or at best short-lived), while well-being can be considered the normal state for most people.

Well-being is a larger concept than happiness: it contains more, and takes more into account. Its expansiveness is reflected in Bentham's claim that all the arts and sciences are a branch of what he calls the art and science of well-being, eudaemonics.[30] Eudaemonics he calls "the name for the universally practised *art*—the *pursuit of happiness*"[31] with the rather obvious statement that "*being* in some of its various shapes, will be allowed to be an indispensable *means*." Thus, *being* is a means toward *well-being*: "Eudaemonics is the art of *well-being*. Necessary to *well-being* is *being*."[32]

This recognition that being is essential to well-being leads Bentham to argue repeatedly that, of the four subsidiary principles to utility (security, subsistence, abundance, and equality),[33] "[s]ubsistence can not be placed any where but at the head of the list.... Without actual subsistence [there can be] neither suffering nor enjoyment."[34] However, he also argues repeatedly along the lines that "[s]ecurity... is the pre-eminent object" of law.[35] So what comes first—subsistence or security? Is this a chicken-and-egg kind of problem, or is there a contradiction here in Bentham's theory? In order to answer this question, it is necessary to consider the place of security in Bentham's theory, as well as the related notion of wealth and its connection with happiness.

Security

Alongside pleasure, security stands as an essential element of Bentham's theory of motivation. For Bentham, security is not itself a motive—generally speaking, we do not do things for the sake of security. Rather, it is the degree of assurance we have that our actions will carry the consequences that we anticipate. We do things because we expect them to either bring pleasure or relieve pain, now or in the future; our willingness to endure present pain is entirely based on the security we have that it will bring greater pleasure in the future. Bentham refers to security as the "pre-eminent object" of law because of its future-regarding nature.[36] We make judgments to balance between the degree of security and other elements of pleasure such as intensity, duration, etc., so that we might undertake things for which we have very low expectations if the benefits are great enough—this is part of any cost-benefit analysis. It is clear from Bentham's argument that security is essential to any society: if entirely lacking, the likely result would be the most vulgar sort of hedonism involving actions that immediately bring pleasure or relieve pain, because we would have no assurance that anything we do now would do us any good in the future. "The man who subsists only from day to day is precisely the man of nature—the savage,"[37] Bentham says, and in a Hobbesian tone asks us to "consider the condition of savages. They strive incessantly against famine.... Rivalry for subsistence produces among them the most cruel wars; and, like beasts of prey, men pursue men, as a means of sustenance."[38]

"The care of security," says Bentham, is "the principal object of law," but it is more than that: it is also "entirely the work of law."[39] Security is, in this sense, a social concept, as it has to do with the social infrastructure that may help to maintain the connections between action and consequence, or, from the opposite direction, guard against those factors that may undermine expectations.[40] But its social nature is almost entirely negative: "Security is not to be understood but by its reference to mischief; the chance of which is *danger,* and the expectance *fear,* or apprehension."[41] He makes a similar point in the *IPML,* where he discusses mischief, although we must wade through the brambles of a double negative in order to untangle his meaning:

> When [mischief] is negative, it consists of the loss of some benefit or advantage: this benefit may be material in both or either of two ways: ... 2. By averting pain or *danger,* which is the chance of pain: that is, by affording *security*. In so far, then, as the benefit which a mischief tends to avert, is productive of security, the tendency of such mischief is to produce *insecurity*.[42]

Perhaps the best way to understand security, then, is as a guard against pain. Thus, its relationship to happiness appears to be negative, since it is not itself productive of pleasure. There is, however, a positive aspect to security in the sense that it promotes productive activity: "Nothing but law [security] can encourage men to labours superfluous for the present, and which can be enjoyed only in the future."[43] But it goes beyond that: any activity that requires investment of resources is impossible without security. The conclusion he reaches in a discussion of the "Evils which result from Attacks upon Property" is that

> [p]ower and will must unite for the development of industry. Will depends upon encouragement; *power* upon means. These means are what is called... *productive capital*. When the question relates only to an individual, his productive capital may be annihilated by a single loss, while his spirit of industry is not extinguished.... When the question is of a nation... the evil may infect the will; and the spirit of industry may fall into a fatal lethargy, in the midst of natural resources offered by a rich and fertile soil.[44]

It is because of these economic effects, which affect society as a whole, that Bentham considers the lack of security—or the pains that arise as a result—to be the most important sort of pain. "*Expectation*," he says, "is a chain which unites our present existence to our future existence.... Every attack upon this sentiment produces a distinct and special evil, which may be called a *pain of disappointment*." This is a matter of "extreme importance."[45] In a later discussion of what he calls the "Disappointment-prevention principle," the primary object of the principle is property, which is an element of its fundamental "proposition" or "axiom": "In the distribution made and maintained of the several separable portions of the aggregate subject-matter of property in the state, let the object or end in view be, on each occasion, *minimization,* and so far as possible *exclusion*, of the sensation of *disappointment*."[46] This may not sound much like Locke, but the essence of what he is saying is very much like the idea that the primary function of government is the protection of property. This Lockean tone is quite a bit clearer in the following passage: "What men want from government is, not incitement to labour, but security against disturbance: security to each for his portion of the matter of wealth while labouring to acquire it, or occupied in enjoying it."[47] Without doubt there are differences between what Locke means by property[48] and what Bentham means by it, but the similarity is striking.

And, as will be seen in the next section, Bentham makes clear what he considers to be the primary objects of security: wealth and property.

Money, Wealth, and Property

As a thermometer is the instrument for measuring temperature, money, according to Bentham, is the instrument for measuring pleasure and pain. "Those who are not satisfied with the accuracy of this instrument must find out some other that shall be more accurate, or bid adieu to politics and morals.... [V]aluing everything in money" is the only way "we can get aliquot parts to measure by. If we must not say of a pain or a pleasure that it is worth so much money, it is in vain, in point of quantity, to say anything at all about it, there is neither proportion nor disproportion between Punishments and Crimes."[49] Money is the great equalizer, what enables interpersonal comparisons of pleasure. All things that bring pleasure, and all things that relieve pain, can be assigned a monetary value. A thermometer provides an objective measurement for temperature irrespective of anyone's subjective experience of it: not only do different people experience the same conditions differently, but the same person will perceive the same temperature differently depending on their situation (for example, a hot day will seem much hotter when exiting from an excessively air-conditioned building). Money works somewhat differently, but it is similar. The value of an amount of money is objectively set by what it can be exchanged for in the market. Depending on their situation, however, people will have different perceptions of the amount of pleasure any amount of money represents—something Bentham understood quite well.[50]

Does this also mean that Bentham thinks that money can buy happiness? Yes and no. Money cannot bring happiness in and of itself, because money "in the form of coin is not in itself good for anything except for exchanging against useful things," although it has the advantage of being convertible into "an infinity of uses."[51] A King Midas type might get pleasure from sitting in his counting room counting out his coin, but even here the pleasure that arises from money is really the pleasure of expectation, of the pleasures of what can be bought with that money. "[T]o get money is what most men have a mind to do: because he who has money gets, as far as it goes, most other things that he has a mind for."[52]

Money in the form of coin has little value in and of itself, but the value it represents—wealth—is what matters. Wealth itself comprises "every object which, being within the reach of human desires, is within the grasp of human possession, and as such either actually subservient, or capable of being made subservient, to human use."[53] To increase one's wealth is, Bentham tells us, "with a very few exceptions, the constant aim and occupation of every individual in every civilized nation. Enjoyment is the offspring of wealth: wealth of labour."[54]

Use is essential to understanding wealth; it can be said that an object that has no use cannot be an object of wealth.[55] That is, wealth is used to produce pleasure or relieve pain. As Bentham puts it, "The matter of wealth is not of any value ... otherwise than in so far as the general effect of it is to serve for the attainment of pleasure or for the avoidance of pain."[56] It would be entirely consistent with Bentham's thinking to also say that no articles of wealth would ever be used except as such use adds pleasure or relieves pain.

While the *use* of wealth may be said to pertain to kinetic pleasure and thus to happiness, the *possession* of wealth may be better said to be relevant to katastematic pleasure and well-being. It is not insignificant, then, that Bentham refers to well-being, not happiness, as the "final" cause of wealth.[57] As we saw above, the possession of wealth contributes to happiness in the hedonic sense that at any particular moment we may experience the pleasure of security it may bring. However, the possession of wealth may also lead to feelings of distress or anxiety (clearly pains) if a person does not feel that her wealth is secure[58] or if she feels she has insufficient wealth. But, in a larger sense, the possession of wealth contributes to well-being in the degree to which the possession now (without enjoyment) carries with it the potential value represented by its future use. This is where security comes in.

Bentham recognizes that all four of the subsidiary principles to utility—security, subsistence, abundance, and equality—are directly concerned with wealth.[59] But the notion of wealth carries with it elements that are incompatible with Bentham's understanding of happiness in a hedonic sense, both in terms of the effort required to produce it (the experience of pain) and in the time factor associated with possession for later use (the deferral of pleasure). It is for this reason that Bentham associates wealth with well-being. There are hedonic elements: wealth brings pleasure, we seek to limit the amount of effort required to get it, and we generally want to limit the passage of time before we can convert its stored value into some form of pleasure. But mostly, wealth (given adequate security) is a katastematic pleasure insofar as its primary function is to lessen the pain of anxiety that comes from lack of certainty about the future.

Security, Subsistence, and Basic Needs

Now we may return to the question, raised above, about the possible conflict in Bentham's theory between subsistence and security. On one level, at least, the conflict is more apparent than real. The first point to recognize is that the precedence of subsistence is with reference to the study (and, one might expect, the practice) of political economy. Security, on the other hand, arises as a matter of law, as the best means by which to assure subsistence. In a sense, subsistence is an indirect object of the law, while security is a (perhaps *the*) direct object.

> What can the law do for subsistence? Nothing directly. All it can do is create *motives*... by the force of which men may be led to provide subsistence for themselves. But nature herself has created these motives.... Need, armed with pains of all kinds, even death itself, commanded labour, excited courage, inspired foresight, developed all the faculties of man. Enjoyment, the inseparable companion of every need satisfied, formed an inexhaustible fund of rewards for those who surmounted obstacles and fulfilled the end of nature. The force of the physical sanction being sufficient, the employment of the political sanction would be superfluous.... But the laws provide for subsistence indirectly, by protecting men while they labour, and by making them sure of the fruits of their labour. *Security* for the labourer, *security* for the fruits of labour; such is the benefit of laws; and it is an inestimable benefit.[60]

There is something else that comes across in this passage, however, which is that, as far as subsistence is concerned, all the state should be concerned with is security.[61] Individuals must *secure* their own subsistence; the function of the state is to provide the legal apparatus to ensure that, if they are able and willing to labor, they may do so with the assurance that they will receive the reward appropriate to their efforts.

No one will engage in labor for its own sake, Bentham believed, but only for the sake of some reward. If the reward is unsure, then they will be less likely to labor. So the best means to ensure *both* that people will be able to subsist from the proceeds of their labor *and* that they engage in the productive labor necessary to produce goods for market exchange (rather than for their own benefit) is to provide a high level of security that they will receive the remuneration promised them. The harm, here, that security refers to would include the refusal to pay for labor performed. But while Bentham refers to laborers enjoying the fruits of their labor, when it comes to wage labor it is clear that what he is referring to is no more than subsistence wages, or the going rate.

There is a passing resemblance between Bentham's assertion that subsistence is the first concern of government and the contemporary literature on basic needs, but this resemblance is just that: passing. In fact in Bentham's day it was fairly common to distinguish between "basic" and "non-basic" goods, or "necessities" and "luxuries"; this view can be found in Hume, Smith, Malthus, and others.[62] The types of goods consumed distinguished between social classes: "[T]he consumption of basic goods was mainly attributed to the working classes and the consumption of non-basic or luxury goods to the upper classes."[63] Basic goods are those that satisfy basic needs.

In the contemporary literature, material goods constitute only one part of what is considered "basic." One approach takes as its starting point the idea that the avoidance of harm constitutes the most fundamental need. Harm is defined as "the significantly impaired pursuit of goals which are deemed of value by individuals. To be seriously harmed is thus to be fundamentally disabled in the pursuit of one's vision of the good."[64] Need, then, defines "the preconditions for human action and interaction."[65] Thus, need goes beyond basic survival of the physical self, and even beyond survival for one's self and what is required for reproduction of the species, but it advances to assert that "*physical health rather than mere survival . . . is a basic human need.*"[66] Furthermore, because harm includes the inability to pursue one's vision of the good, autonomy may also be understood as a need.[67] Doyal and Gough argue that society should be structured in order to "optimize" the fulfillment of these needs. Those who follow this approach may then debate about what actually constitutes harm, as well as claims of universality and other issues.[68]

A different approach recognizes a hierarchy of needs, although this does not imply that those at the lower level are any more "basic" than higher-level needs. Rather, they may be understood as "fundamental classes of human need: the needs that must be satisfied to maintain biological existence, the needs that must be satisfied to develop the capabilities distinctive of human life, and the needs that must be satisfied to develop those capacities freely."[69] These are, in other words, "basic physical needs, which are the condition of *life*; socio-cultural needs, including education, meaningful work, and democratic political systems, which are the conditions of *human* life; and a temporal need, for free time, which is the condition for a *free* human life."[70] Although more abstract, and more directly concerned with the specific structure of social institutions, this approach shares with the one outlined above a recognition that human needs extend beyond the merely physical, and that individuals are defined by more than their consumption habits.

While Bentham's discussion of subsistence may carry little resemblance to the contemporary literature on basic needs, it suggests that an adjustment to the prior discussion may be called for in order to take in both subsistence and security together. One way to understand security is as the avoidance of harm: an injury, after all, is a breach of security. Lack of subsistence certainly constitutes harm, so on one level, at least, security could be said to encompass subsistence. In fact, while Bentham places priority in law on security, at the same time he says that security and subsistence are on "the same level" as compared to abundance and equality: "The two first objects are life itself; the two latter, the ornaments of life."[71] As Kelly notes, Bentham is concerned with the "conditions for the realization of individual well-being," which must go beyond simple material concerns. "The absence of harm to possessions, beneficial condition in life, and reputation is a more important source of legitimate expectations then the absence of harm to the person."[72] Arguably, democratic political institutions that at least minimally protect against rulers violating the security of citizens (i.e., tyranny) can be seen as basic need;[73] more broadly, as has been noted, they establish the conditions by which people are able to acquire their subsistence. However, autonomy, meaningful work, and the full development of one's capacity discussed in the contemporary literature could not fit in Bentham's system any place but within the domain of equality (equal civil and political rights),[74] which puts them outside the primary realm of security and subsistence.

Finally, while Bentham asserts that "the protection of the laws may contribute as much to the happiness of the cottage as to the security of the palace,"[75] it is clear that security means something different to each.[76] To the laboring poor, it means hopes for subsistence and little if anything more;[77] to the bourgeois and leisure classes, it means protection for opulence and the means for increase. In fact, Bentham believed that security, fairly and consistently applied, would lead to equality. His belief in "a continual progress towards equality" is based on what he saw as the "opposite habits which are formed in opulence and in poverty. The first, prodigal and vain, wishes only to enjoy without labour; the second, accustomed to obscurity and privations, finds pleasures even in labour and economy."[78] Stark interprets this passage as Bentham saying that "[t]he poor should starve himself into riches."[79] Bentham discusses a variety of measures to promote "self-liberation" and to assist the "self-maintaining poor," including the establishment of "Frugality Savings Banks" by which ordinary laborers could make deposits to accumulate savings.[80] However, the National Charity Company, a kind of private welfare agency, would have the power of "*apprehending* all persons, able-bodied or other-wise, having neither visible or assignable property, nor honest and sufficient means of livelihood" and keeping them in a sort of Panopticon prison for the poor.[81]

The answer to the question posed earlier, then, is that while Bentham values subsistence highly, as a matter of *law* security reigns preeminent. To the degree that he is supportive of any takings of wealth (taxes) as a form of redistribution, this is primarily out of concern that extreme poverty undermines security of property. It would be possible to interpret Bentham's concern for the poor as instrumental to the security of property, although it does seem that he was genuinely concerned that indigence undermines well-being. So, while for Bentham there are reasons to make provisions for the poor, this should not be confused with a right to the means of survival: At least as far as the able-bodied are concerned, he felt that the human drive to survive should be sufficient to ensure it, so security in the produce of one's labor (or security of wages) is all that is needed. For the relative few who are not able-bodied, a small tax on the wealthy would be sufficient to provide for subsistence of those who cannot take care of themselves, and the gain of happiness would offset the pain of the tax. It seems unlikely, on this basis, that Bentham would recognize something like a right to subsistence:[82] given security, people will secure their subsistence for themselves. On that assumption, there is no need for a right to subsistence. So the only "basic need" that the law would need to recognize is the need for security.

Security, then, is the fundamental requirement for subsistence, which is the essential condition for being and, therefore, for well-being. The importance of well-being in his theory is obscured, however, by the focus on pleasure in considerations of Bentham's ethics. In discussing the eudaemonistic elements of Bentham's theory, however, I do not mean to suggest that they are primary: despite his concern for well-being, Bentham's theory retains the focus on the individual that is an essential characteristic of hedonism.

Individuals, Community, and Happiness

In an oft-cited passage, Bentham writes that "[t]he community is a fictitious *body,* composed of the individual persons who are considered as constituting as it were its *members*. The interest of the community then is, what?—the sum of the interests of the several members who compose it." He continues, "It is in vain to talk of the interest of the community, without understanding what is the interest of the individual."[83] This passage is generally taken as an expression of the manner in which individual interests are aggregated in order to arrive at the "interest of the community." However, I want to follow this argument in a somewhat different direction: the (singular) interest of the individual is, as I have already shown, happiness. What this statement does, then, is place individuals directly at the center of Bentham's theory; it is their happiness that is at issue for him. One can refer to the happiness of a community, but the collectivity does not have an existence—or an interest—that is distinct from that of its members. One might refer to the "interest of the community" as a kind of shorthand, but what one is *really* referring to is the individual happiness (or interest) of each member. To suggest that the community has an interest that stands apart or distinct from the interests of the individuals that comprise that community would be, in this view, wrong. The happiness of the community only refers to the aggregate happiness of its members *as individual members of the community*.

Bentham's argument is sometimes referred to as "methodological individualism," which has two primary elements. The first involves the view that the community is best understood as a collection of individuals rather than as a distinct entity with its own character and interests. The second point is that "individuals are the best judges of their own... happiness." This implies that, "Interference with their choices... has to be exceptionally justified."[84] Methodological individualism pertains most directly to the theory of utility, which I examine in chapter 4, but showing how these two points arise from Bentham's conception of happiness will make it easier to recognize how deeply embedded individualism is in his theory of utility.

The Cloak of Individualism

Modern hedonism is unavoidably individualistic because the only pleasure that matters is the pleasure that individuals themselves perceive. The emphasis, then, is on sense perception. Bentham argues that what is real are objects of sense,[85] and it is only individuals—that is, "real" individuals—who may perceive things and have sensations.[86] Only real, existing, and living individuals can experience pleasure and pain; only real, existing, and living individuals can be happy.

The individualism that inhabits Bentham's hedonism runs deep in a way that obscures the functions of social institutions. Communities are fictitious things, entirely constructed either in our imaginations or in our laws, but social relations themselves are real, as is the web of social relations that may be described as "society." In the same sense, the formal and informal structures that may be referred to as "institutions" that produce and are produced by social relations are also very real. When we try to define these things in particular terms and with particular boundaries the result is, in some sense at least, arbitrary (since boundaries tend to be porous) and for that reason creates what Bentham would refer to as a fictitious entity. But while fictitious, it is important to recognize the very real character, function, and effects of power in society.

Bentham is certainly aware of this—after all, the ability of legislators to affect the level of pleasure and pain in a community depends on their ability to wield this kind of power. At the same time, however, while Bentham seems to recognize *political* power he fails to recognize *economic* power. The result is a kind of lacuna in Bentham's theory. For example, with regard to Bentham's claim that money is the measure of pleasure,

John Commons (who as a founder of the field of institutional economics might be expected to be a critic of Bentham's individualism) notes that what is measured by money is not pleasure, but scarcity. Scarcity, in this sense, "is none other than private property itself."[87] His point is that, within the liberal capitalist system, scarcity and abundance are controlled or manipulated through social institutions to which individuals have different levels of access. The degree of access is by and large determined by one's status with regard to private property. More property means more capacity to determine value. Those who have money (which may be understood on some level as the "real" entity underlying both wealth and property) control access to it and determine its value; one who has no or little money can determine the value of nothing. By suggesting that money measures the degree of pleasure much like a thermometer measures the degree of heat, Bentham omits the social institution that regulates the value of money. Unlike temperature, money has no natural value discoverable by scientists; rather, its value is largely determined by the market, and the ability to affect that value depends on the amount of money one can have in play there. In effect, Bentham considers the value of money to be naturally determined,[88] failing to recognize the institutional framework that provides differential access to the thermostat. So, Bentham's individualism obscures not only the different capacity of two individuals at differing levels of accumulated wealth to affect the value of money, but the function of the social institutions within which the determination of value occurs.

Individualism and Liberalism

Now on to the second dimension of Bentham's individualism. In the *Fragment on Government,* his first published work, Bentham claims that pleasure is of great value as the fundamental basis for law: "The consequences of any Law, or of any act which is made the object of a Law, the only consequences that men are at all interested in, what are they but *pain* and *pleasure*?... *pain* and *pleasure* at least, are words which a man has no need... to go to a Lawyer to know the meaning of."[89] But in the *IPML* he took this a step farther to say that "no man can be so good a judge as the man himself, what it is gives him pleasure or displeasure."[90] Furthermore, no one "is so sure of being *inclined,* on all occasions, to promote your happiness as you yourself are."[91] Thus, "The care of his enjoyments ought to be left almost entirely to the individual. The principal function of government is to guard against pains."[92] Not only is the individual the one best able to decide what brings them pleasure or pain, but only they will be sufficiently motivated toward it. Even benevolence is motivated by self-interest: we practice benevolence because it is in our self-interest to do so, for example, to relieve the pain of seeing others in distress (in other words, because we sympathize with them), or because of the positive effect it has on our reputation.[93]

The primary political point here is that Bentham's individualism implies a very strong commitment to liberty. As Bentham puts it, "As a general rule, the greatest possible latitude should be left to individuals, in all cases in which they can injure none but themselves, for they are the best judges of their own interests.... The power of the law need interfere only to prevent them from injuring each other."[94] The exercise of free will is essential to happiness, even in the practice of beneficence. Benevolence may be understood as a kind of motive, one of a set of "natural motives ... derived from our own interest for consulting the happiness of others.... The motive of pure benevolence, a sweet and calm sentiment which we delight to experience ... The motives of private affection ... in domestic life ... [and] the desire of good repute."[95] But such benevolence cannot be legislated, for to do so would deprive the giver of its pleasure, since "it is to individual free-will that benevolence owes its energy."[96] To see civic virtue as a duty is anathema; he is particularly biting in his critique of Cicero.[97]

Bentham's position is, in effect, that of classical liberalism: each should be able to seek their own happiness to the greatest extent. The primary function of the state is to limit the harm they might cause in doing so. This position is surprising, of course, to those who hold Bentham to be more of an authoritarian; indeed, it is difficult to jibe with his apparent willingness to impose rather harsh conditions (via the Panopticon prisons)[98] on those he considered deserving of it—paupers and criminals, whose harm could be either direct, in the case of criminals, or indirect, in the case of able-bodied indigents who would have to be supported by taking money away from productive members of the community.

Bentham's individualism, along with his views regarding subsistence and security, allow us to see why Macpherson argues that Bentham's work reveals a bourgeois attitude that presumes market capitalism and rather hardened class distinctions.[99] While Bentham does appear to have been a very compassionate individual who cared deeply about the well-being of the members of his society, he was also very much a member of his class who believed that the afflictions of poverty were self-imposed by people who preferred leisure to work and that what they needed most of all were clear incentives to productivity. Given the ability to do so, all would gain from the exercise of their liberty (with the minimum of constraints): workers would contribute their labor, for which they would be paid at a rate corresponding to their effort and ability, and capitalists would contribute their funds, for which they would be rewarded based on the degree of risk they were willing to undertake as well as according to their ability in managing their firms. He was certainly, in this way, a Smithian—society works on the basis of individuals acting in their own self-interest through free exchange in the market, and the freer that exchange, the better for everyone involved.

Bentham and Neoclassical Economics

If Bentham was a Smithian who emphasized the individualistic character of Smith's theory, neoclassical economics represents Bentham's modern hedonism *in extremis,* largely stripped of any connection to well-being. Bentham's thought is generally considered to have been transmitted into modern economics through the work of W. Stanley Jevons.[100] A self-described Benthamite, Jevons is credited as one of the founders (with Carl Menger and Leon Walras) of the so-called marginal revolution that launched neoclassical economics, which is premised on the reduction of well-being to happiness and happiness to pleasure.[101] As Warke notes, "Modern economic theory *begins* with an axiomatic presumption that agents can formulate a complete and transitive preference set over all conceivable combination of 'goods' ... thus finessing the index number problem [the idea that we can rank our preferences on a single scale] at the individual level and degrading utility to a one-dimensional indicator of the resultant rank order."[102]

Jevons argued that while pleasure and pain could not be measured directly, our preferences were revealed in our consumption habits, in the "private-account books, the great ledgers of merchants and bankers and public offices"[103] where we sought to "maximise happiness by purchasing pleasure ... at the lowest cost of pain."[104] Our pleasure seeking and pain avoiding, then, can be captured and fully mathematized, expressed in utility functions and the laws of supply and demand. Thus, modern hedonism becomes the fundamental assumption of modern economics.

Veblen articulates something of the psychological profile of hedonic man as expressed in neoclassical economics with this tongue-in-cheek description: "a lightening calculator of pleasures and pains, who oscillates like a homogeneous globule of desire of happiness under the impulse of stimuli that shift him about.... He is an isolated, definitive human datum." Veblen captures in stark terms the determinism that seems to lie in the shadows of hedonism as he continues to describe this "datum" who is

> in stable equilibrium except for the buffets of the impinging forces that displace him in one direction or another. Self-imposed in elemental space, he spins symmetrically about his own spiritual axis until the parallelogram of forces bears down upon him, whereupon he follows the line of the resultant. When the force of the impact is spent, he comes to rest, a self-contained globule of desire, as before. Spiritually, the hedonistic man is not a prime mover. He is...subject to a series of permutations enforced upon him by circumstances external and alien to him.[105]

It is important to recognize that not just happiness is being reduced to pleasure here, but also well-being itself. Gasper writes that, in "utilitarianism and utilitarian-inspired economics" well-being is "reified as a single entity," and that "[m]ost utilitarianism reduced well-being to *well-feeling*...and further reduced well-feeling to a scalar (unitary pleasure, 'utility')."[106] Gasper's criticism (and his characterization of utilitarianism is meant as a criticism) is directed at the reductionism of the hedonistic account, which reduces pleasure to money or, more specifically, income. Citing Amartya Sen, Gasper notes that this "reduced well-being to being well-off, financially or materially; in other words to 'well-having' or 'having much.'"[107]

If happiness is defined as having one's desires fulfilled, and economic activity is the means through which desires get fulfilled, then more economic activity means greater happiness. Thus, the happiness of a society can be measured through its level of economic activity, or GDP. The problem is that elements that are important to well-being—in the sense of pleasures foregone or deferred in the name of security or wealth—are much harder to quantify (they are not captured in what economists call "opportunity cost," which refers merely to options not chosen). What isn't demanded or transacted in the market receives no consideration. In the first place, it means that unpaid work, such as work in the home—work performed mostly by women—is disvalued. Further, while it may be possible to quantify the value of "security" by considering how much people are willing to pay to put up fences or install security cameras, there is no way to measure what it means for a worker to not know if she'll be able to feed her family, or to have to put off needed medical treatment in order to keep a roof over their heads. Besides this, any sort of pain, from a car breaking down that necessitates its repair or replacement, to an illness that brings down a mountain of medical bills, to a natural disaster that requires whole communities to be rebuilt, produces economic activity that would be difficult to classify as so much pleasure.

Furthermore, it turns out that the notion that our economic activity reflects our level of happiness is an illusion, one that takes on the characteristics of an endless upward spiral, since the consumerism at the heart of the capitalist system requires that as desires are fulfilled new ones must take their place, such that there is always unmet desire. "Capitalism, rather than providing for happiness and satisfaction, manufactures an ever-widening field of desire, and innovative ways in which commodities create invidious distinctions, and hence ever-widening gulfs of resentment, dissatisfaction and anxiety."[108] This has recently come to be called the "hedonic treadmill."[109] Its importance cannot be underestimated: Desire sated, economic activity grinds to a halt, and the market—the economic system—collapses. The hedonic treadmill, then, is no mystery or paradox: it exists at the heart of the capitalist system.

Recent work in economics by Layard, Easterlin, and others reflects a reconsideration of the assumptions mainstream economists make about the connection of happiness to economic activity. To the extent that Bentham is cited here it is often favorably.[110] The discovery of the hedonic treadmill is connected to what is called the "income paradox," first described by Richard Easterlin in 1974: despite the tremendous postwar increase in wealth in advanced Western countries, people's responses to questionnaires about their level of happiness indicated that they weren't much happier.[111] After another thirty years (and thirty years' more data) the result is the same: "[H]appiness [in the United States] has not increased since 1950 ... although living standards have more than doubled."[112] However, the level of income in a relative sense *does* have a direct relationship to the level of happiness, both within a country and between countries. The results get muddled again, however, when we see that some countries with relatively low income levels are unexpectedly high in self-reported happiness, and some countries high on the income scale are lower on the happiness scale than one would expect.[113]

Some of the problems may arise from the subjective method of measurement, as what people understand as happiness likely changes depending on their income—with higher income come higher expectations, and what really matters is not the pleasures or pains actually experienced but the degree to which one's expectations are met. But this just goes to underscore that the assumption that greater economic activity reflects a higher level of happiness is false. Indeed, the research finds that once a level has been reached where the basic necessities are taken care of, increased income has little effect on the level of happiness.[114] This would not "come as a surprise to most thinking people. Indeed, Aristotle acknowledged that acquiring anything more than moderate wealth will not result in greater happiness or fulfillment in life. ... But, for neoclassical economic theory, these research findings present a 'paradox.'"[115]

The shift away from assumptions about the immediate connection between consumption and happiness has enabled economists to identify specific problems with the purely hedonistic assumptions of neoclassical economics. The economic (or economistic) accounts remain hedonistic in the sense that the question of happiness is a subjective matter that corresponds to individuals' experience of pleasure and pain. In that sense, this recent work manages to restore some of the eudaemonism that had been stripped from Bentham's theory, making room for the consideration of social conditions and interactions among members of a community, while retaining the individualism common to Jevons and Bentham. While this may be a positive development in terms of rehabilitating Bentham—and the discipline of economics (to say nothing of the society affected by economic thinking)—contemporary economists would likely find a much richer trove of ideas for understanding the social character of happiness in the work of William Thompson, to whose work I now turn.

3
William Thompson's Social Happiness

Earlier, it was noted that Bentham was not the only person thinking, writing, and talking about happiness in the late eighteenth and early nineteenth century—far from it. Happiness was in the air, in a literary sense at least, as a common topic for books, pamphlets, and other writings in both England and on the continent. Bentham's argument that happiness is the foundation of morality can be found in the work of a variety of writers of the time, including Hume, Beccaria, Paley, Godwin, Helvétius, Fourier, Saint-Simon, Priestley, Owen, and others.

To a degree, this attention to happiness is ironic, as it obscures a substantial degree of unhappiness caused by massive economic change in this period. This was, of course, the height of the Industrial Revolution, the period of some of the most extensive enclosures of common lands in Britain and, in the first quarter of the nineteenth century, of war and its aftermath.[1] As will be seen in this chapter and what follows, William Thompson was sensitive to these issues in a way that most other writers of the period were not.

It would be a gross exaggeration to suggest that Thompson articulates a clear philosophy of happiness—certainly nothing on the order of what Bentham provides. So, his philosophy must be constructed from the limited material available. From this, the principal elements of Thompson's conception of happiness are clear, and in many ways they reveal a view that is the mirror image of Bentham's, as he retains much of

Bentham's conceptual framework while reaching the opposite conclusions. Perhaps the most important distinction between them has to do with what they see as the central focus for moral (and, in consequence, political) reasoning: for Bentham, it is the individual, but for Thompson, it is society or, more specifically, the structuring of relations between individuals by social institutions.[2] If Bentham can be understood as arguing that society is made up of or produced by individuals, Thompson can be seen as arguing that individuals are produced by their society, which is to say, through the social institutions that characterize that society.

Bentham considered himself a scientist, working out a "moral science" that would be as rigorous and exact as natural science. Indeed, he compared himself to Francis Bacon, having done, in his own mind, at least, as much for moral science as Bacon had done for natural science.[3] The hedonism that forms the basis for his science means that its subject matter is individuals—the determinants of the experience of pleasure and pain and the manner in which these function as motivations. So the science of happiness is, for Bentham, concerned with individuals. On this basis, it may be called an *individual* science. By extension, the same could be said for all the sciences that have roots in Bentham's utilitarianism, including classical economics and its descendants—including, among their rational choice adherents, political science and sociology.

Here is a fundamental difference, then, between Bentham and Thompson: For Thompson, the science of happiness is concerned with the functions of society and social institutions broadly understood, and how these affect individual happiness. Thus, for Thompson, the science of happiness is a science of society, a *social* science.[4] It is not that he considered the actual experiences of individuals to be unimportant—far from it. But he believed that the experiences of individuals as well as their perceptions of them are powerfully shaped by the social conditions in which they live—which are shaped by social institutions.[5] So, while the object of study might still be happiness, the subject shifts from the individual to the society and, in particular, the social institutions that shape it. Because, in Thompson's view, the presence or absence of material goods (i.e., wealth) necessary for both existence and for comfort were the most important elements for establishing the conditions for individual happiness, he focuses on the institutions concerned with the production and development of wealth—in other words, the economy. Rather than considering the behavior of individuals in a marketplace in which individuals interact with other individuals more or less at their liberty, Thompson is concerned with the ways in which the set of socially structured practices of production and exchange—in a word, economic institutions—affects the individuals interacting within it.

Although Bentham's influence is implicit, manifested primarily through Thompson's conceptual toolbox, Robert Owen's ideas receive more explicit attention than anyone else's in Thompson's work.[6] Thompson cites Owen with regard to two important subjects: cooperative communities and the effects of circumstance on the formation of character. The former will be explored in later chapters. In what follows, I will examine the latter, sometimes called the "philosophy of necessity." After this, with an understanding of the two most significant influences on Thompson's conception of happiness (Bentham and Owen), it will be possible to consider Thompson's thought more directly. At the end of the chapter I will take another look at the contemporary literature on happiness, and see how Thompson's ideas fit in there.

Happiness and the Formation of Character
Tabula Rasa and Social Environmentalism

Thompson cites Owen as an "advocate" of the idea that one's character is formed by the social conditions within which one lives and is raised,[7] but the idea had been circulating in some form or another at least since Locke's discussion of the *tabula rasa* more than a century before.[8] Locke asks, "[S]uppose the Mind to be, as we say, white Paper, void of all Characters, without any *Ideas*; How comes it to be furnished? . . . To this I answer, in one word, From *Experience*."[9] Our experience is shaped by the world around us, so the way we think cannot help but be shaped by that same world. Referring to this as "social environmentalism" and calling it a "hallmark of the ideology of the Enlightenment," Wood points to its political significance, saying, "To make happy, virtuous and cooperative individuals dedicated to the common good, the social context must be rendered amenable to such ends. Social, political and legal institutions and arrangements can be positive instruments in fashioning the human raw stuff according to some ideal model."[10] However, for Locke and the earlier theorists, according to Wood, the idea never developed beyond the question of the development of "true opinion through the reform of education."[11]

It would not be far off the mark to say that Bentham's philosophy represents the epitome of the extension of social environmentalism as Wood describes it, in the sense that Bentham believed in the use of institutional design to affect how people thought about and pursued their interests. Bentham, however, was less concerned with people arriving at some preconceived "true opinion" as much as a more socially conscious notion of their own interest (although Bentham certainly had strong views as to what constituted "true" versus "false" interests), and the vehicles he considered included not just education, but, more centrally, legal institutions. As was detailed in the last chapter, however, Bentham's philosophy remains fundamentally individualistic. As a result, it retains what might be characterized as a bourgeois character that holds that all individuals are equally capable of maximizing their well-being, with the effect that the degree to which any individual is successful (i.e., happy) or not is a matter of the exercise of their free will. This leaves each individual fully responsible for his or her condition.

Philosophical Necessitarianism and Happiness

Although at least one modern writer sees Owen as something of a Benthamite,[12] Owen's "philosophy of necessity" challenges Bentham's emphasis on the individual. He refers to the idea that people "form their own individual characters" as a "fundamental error" that is "impressed from infancy on the minds of all men, and from whence all their other errors proceed."[13] As Owen puts it, "The character of man is, without a single exception, always formed for him ... chiefly created by his predecessors ... they give him ... his ideas and habits, which are the powers that govern and direct his conduct. Man, therefore, never did, nor is it possible he ever can, form his own character."[14]

Character, according to Owen, can be "made entirely *irrational* or *rational*." Irrational character arises from four sources: "In every known region of the earth ... man has been compelled from infancy to acquire the peculiar notions of some sect, some class, some party, and of some country." Generally speaking, all of these are present to some degree for all individuals, although the particulars in each case may differ.[15] None of this is innate: "Man is born in ignorance," but the "seeds of disunion and separation are deeply and extensively sown during infancy and childhood."[16]

Owen uses this argument as a means for explaining the vices of the poor and as a means of critiquing the "governing principle of trade, manufactures, and commerce ... immediate pecuniary gain."[17] He is concerned especially with the effects of the "manufacturing system" on children among the "lower orders," who are "made to labour incessantly for their bare subsistence" and deprived of "innocent, healthy and rational amusements," not to mention education. From such a deleterious upbringing, and surrounded by people in similar circumstances, they are drawn to the "seductive pleasures of the pot-house and inebriation" and become "weak in bodily and mental faculties ... with habits generally destructive of their own comforts, of the well-being of those around them, and strongly calculated to subdue all the social affections."[18]

Note the distinction being made here between "innocent, healthy and rational amusements" and the "seductive pleasures of the pot-house and inebriation." If "amusements" are equivalent to "pleasures," then Owen is not necessarily challenging hedonism. But what makes some pleasures problematic is their "destructive" nature, especially in their effects on social relationships. As is evidenced here, Owen is famously short on detail—he has little to say about how, exactly, certain pleasures harm social relationships or why—but his concern is not simply a matter of reputation or sympathy, which Bentham identifies as the key elements that tie individual happiness to social happiness. Clearly, then, Owen does not endorse a simply hedonistic conception of happiness.

Happiness is at the heart of what Owen calls "the one single principle of action" that can simplify all the rules of morality: "The happiness of self, clearly understood and uniformly practised; which can only be attained by conduct that must promote the happiness of the community."[19] By way of explanation he suggests as a natural law that "man" will "discover, that his individual happiness can be increased and extended only in proportion as he actively endeavours to increase and extend the happiness of all around him."[20] This looks much like the familiar notion of "enlightened self-interest," but with a difference: in Owen's case, the alignment of self- and social interest occurs not through the promulgation of abstract ideals along with Aristotelian or Ciceronian exhortations to the virtuous denial of selfish desires, promises of a more salutary social status, or reminders of the benefits of reciprocity, but in the development of social institutions specifically designed to remove the incentives for selfishness.

Owen's basic premises could have been lifted from Bentham's work, and are articulated as certain "facts" about human nature, starting with the desire for happiness: "[M]an is born with a desire to obtain happiness, which desire is the primary cause of all his actions, ... and ... is called self interest.... [H]e is also born with the germs of animal propensities, or the desire to sustain, enjoy, and propagate life; and which desires ... are termed his natural inclinations." This list continues for several pages, focusing on the sources of true or false knowledge, and how false knowledge leads to errors in reasoning, "hence all the inconsistencies and misery of the world."[21] The list leads to the following conclusion:

> That when these truths are made evident, every individual will necessarily endeavour to promote the happiness of every other individual within his sphere of action; because he must clearly, and without any doubt, comprehend such conduct to be the essence of self-interest, or the true cause of self-happiness.[22]

"True" Happiness

This raises something of a difficulty: If everyone has been surrounded by error all their lives, who can recognize truth? Owen invites "those esteemed the most learned and wise, throughout the various states and empires in the world" to examine his assertions to ascertain their truth; their assent will then constitute proof.[23] Despite the fog of false ideas, Owen argues that truth is still discernible, because "[t]he only certain criterion of truth is, that it is ever consistent with itself; it remains one and the same under every view and comparison of it which can be made."[24] However, special training was required to discern the truth; this was not an activity for the average person. And since most people fail to recognize the truth, they cannot know true happiness.

Owen was not unique in his view of truth, but then again his wasn't the only perspective on it. Bernard refers to a "fundamental epistemological conflict at the heart of the Enlightenment." On the one side were those who, like Owen, saw knowledge as static, "a fixed body of fact that could be applied scientifically to solve social problems." On the other side were those who saw it as subject to a process of development, "constantly changing."[25] In Owen's view, then, human character was plastic, moldable through the careful (or not) design of a social system encompassing every element of a person's environment.[26] William Maclure, Owen's partner in the New Harmony venture,[27] held what Bernard identifies as the opposing belief, that, "human beings [are] rational creatures, and changes in their condition would depend upon political and intellectual freedom."[28] Harrison notes that "[e]ven sympathizers with Owen professed difficulty in reconciling his statement that men were products of circumstances over which they had no control, with his apparent assumption that by acting rationally they could control those very same circumstances."[29] J. S. Mill, for his part, called Owen's argument "a grand error" and sought to restore a sense of agency missing in Owen's account. Mill's intervention to Owen's "fatalistic doctrine" held that, just as others may endeavor to shape our character, "so can we re-mold or re-make our characters according to antecedent causes that include our wish to change who and what we are."[30] However, neither Maclure's nor Mill's positions really undermine Owen's essential point, which is that people's characters are strongly influenced—perhaps that is a better word than "determined"—by their circumstances, which seems to be overlooked or disregarded by advocates of the free-will doctrine Owen was responding to.

Indeed, neither Maclure nor Mill recognize that changing one's circumstances is often quite difficult, precisely because of the conditions in which an individual might find him- or herself. The very condition of political and intellectual freedom is hardly a given, especially for members of the nascent working class in early-nineteenth-century Britain. By the same token, it is fine to suggest that the desire to change one's circumstances can lead to altered circumstances, but a certain minimal level of education, resources, and opportunity are required in order to be able to even recognize the existence of alternative possibilities, let alone seek them out. A benefit of Owen's argument, at least, is that it implicitly recognizes the function of power, of hegemony if you will, and the difficulty this poses for those of the "lower orders." There is no arguing against the view that the poor may pick themselves up by their bootstraps and thereby improve their condition—there are certainly plenty of examples of those who, for whatever reason, are able to do so—but all too often this assertion of one of the basic tenets of individualism is used as an excuse to either ignore or deny the existence of the social conditions that make such changes difficult for most and nearly impossible for many.

There is a further way in which Owen's ideas contrast with those of Bentham. Owen's assertion that most people are brought up with erroneous views, which undermine their ability to seek or enjoy what he clearly thinks is "true" happiness, directly contradicts one of Bentham's most fundamental premises. As was seen in the last chapter, Bentham claimed that no one can know what pleases a person better than they can themselves. But even he recognized that people may be quite wrong about what will lead to their well-being. Owen, on the other hand, seems much more ready to assert that people can be wrong about what brings them pleasure, because of their erroneous ideas about what is pleasurable, and he seems quite certain that, under the given state of society in his time, they haven't a clue about what is best for their well-being.

Owen's most important insight—his central contribution—is that, in order to change people's character, to get them to act differently and to think of their social relationships on different terms, it is necessary to change the conditions in which they live. Education and punishment for contrary behavior are not sufficient. In an important way, this is an example of theory arising from practice: Owen's own experience with the workers at the factory he took over from his father-in-law, David Dale, at New Lanark convinced him that changing the conditions in which people live could change the way that they act.[31] If competition and greed were the primary conditions that led to problems of character, then what was necessary was to design institutions so as to excise these conditions and replace them with more favorable institutions premised on a more benevolent concept: cooperation. The particular institutional structure within which these altered conditions would be manifested, the cooperative or "Owenite" communities, did not take their final shape until at least 1820 in his *Report to the County of Lanark*. The basic elements of these I outlined in the introduction: communities of at least three hundred to at most two thousand persons (men, women, and children, "in their natural proportions"), "founded *on the principle of united labour, expenditure, and property, and equal privileges.*"[32]

Thompson and the Hegemonic Construction of Happiness

Thompson was strongly attracted to Owen's proposal for communities, although, in contrast to Owen, he was more interested in reforming society as a whole than simply ameliorating the conditions of the working class.

But the philosophy of necessity is crucial for Thompson. On the one hand, it is an important element of his critique of the system of individualistic competition (his term for "capitalism," more or less) while, on the other, it is the primary justification for the cooperative communities. In a sense, the effect of circumstance on character adds an important social dimension to his conception of happiness that goes much deeper than is possible for Bentham. Bentham certainly understood that the institutions of government could affect people's choice making by affecting their calculations of pleasure and pain, but he did not think that this would affect their interests in any significant way. That social institutions shape a person's character, however, means that they shape the way people think about themselves and the world around them in a way that does, in fact, shape their interests, or their understanding of their interests.

Thompson's view of the philosophy of necessity seems less deterministic than Owen's. If Owen is understood to be saying that each individual's actions are determined by the circumstances they find themselves in, then Veblen's description of hedonic man seen in the last chapter applies here, too, although acting over a longer span of time—Owen's individual is no more of a "prime mover," no more the master of his destiny, still "subject to a series of permutations enforced upon him by circumstances external and alien to him."[33] Nonetheless, Thompson defends Owen against his critics by saying that those who object do so because they "misapprehend the meaning" or because they cannot bear to part with their notions of free will.[34]

As we might expect from a Benthamite, Thompson focuses on the motives for action more than the abstract notion of "character." Agency is, in fact, an important element in Thompson's view, since "the immediately preceding state of every man's mind is one of the most influential of the circumstances, which, co-operating with those from without, produce his immediate subsequent conduct."[35] Two elements are therefore involved: the mental state of the actor, which is the product of a lifetime of experience, education, and reflection, and the immediate circumstances, or what we might call the environmental conditions.[36] *Both* are essential. Owen gives little attention to the mental operation, but this is the means through which change can take place.

The influence of both Bentham and Owen comes through in the way Thompson brings together the motives (ultimately, pleasure and pain) with the effects of circumstances. It may help to examine a passage, parsed out to make apparent Thompson's particular contribution. We start with a smooth blend of Benthamism and Owenism: "Human actions are produced by *desires* operating on the *will*. What generates, what gives rise to, these desires? The circumstances surrounding the actors." He emphasizes economic condition: "What is meant by these circumstances? The state of plenty or destitution in which they are placed with respect to the comforts and conveniences of life," which is intimately bound up with autonomy: "the degree in which they are dependent on the will of others for pleasures or pains." But Thompson then takes this synthesis a step farther, by specifying the mechanism—social institutions—through which circumstances are manifested: "On what again do these casualties, wealth or poverty, freedom or slavery with respect to voluntary actions, depend? On what but on the *institutions,* the different expedients, devised and upheld by the rulers possessing the public force, to maintain wealth and power so distributed as may best coincide with their particular views?" The political point is then driven home: "It is evident that no mere words, no precepts or commands, as such, can alter these circumstances, can supply any *motives* to action.... Nothing but the relations which a man bears to the persons and things surrounding him can effect this.... [I]n order to change these circumstances, they must change the institutions that give rise to them."[37] Understanding how this works is the task that Thompson gives to social science.

Social science, as Thompson understood it, would be concerned with the study of the relations between people and the things around them. This differentiates him from Bentham's thought, because where Bentham is concerned with the motives and conduct of individuals,[38] Thompson is concerned with the relations themselves. Thus, in his account of the effects of circumstances on character, Thompson is able to consider something missing in Owen and not even possible in Bentham: an account of the function of power through the mechanism of social institutions. This is, in a word, an examination of the principal dimensions and operation of hegemony, although perhaps on different terms from Gramsci's analysis a hundred years later.

For Gramsci, hegemony was a way of explaining how economic power, state power, and social power are mutually supportive. Developed to help explain the lack of revolutionary consciousness among the proletariat and the persistence of capitalism despite the intense economic crisis that followed World War I, hegemony describes the ways in which particular values and ways of understanding the world effectively produce not only the consent of the governed to state power, but also their consent to subordinate social and economic relationships. As one interpreter describes it,

> [H]egemony is a concept that helps us to understand not only the ways in which a predominant economic group coercively uses the state apparatuses of political society in the preservation of the status quo, but also how and where political society and, above all, civil society, [including] the microstructures of the practices of everyday life, contribute to the production of meaning and values which in turn produce, direct and maintain the "spontaneous" consent of the various strata of society to that same status quo.[39]

To be sure, the term *hegemony* never appears in Thompson's work. Nonetheless, by pointing directly to the power held by those who exert control over social institutions through both economic and political means, Thompson identifies the means through which this power can be understood as a unity in its very diversity of forms, as well as the mechanism by which that power is exerted. The kind of power Thompson refers to is generally what we might call a "soft" power, in that it coerces without appearing to coerce: it orders society in such a way as to make its practices seem reasonable, even natural, as opposed to coercing through the rattling of sabers and showing of arms. But though soft in form the effects of this power are no less hard: the threat of starvation has a way of compelling people to do things and accept conditions they might otherwise avoid.

Bentham's autonomous individual, constrained only by the threat of punishment by the state or other unwanted consequences becomes, in Thompson's work, an individual who is clearly situated within a set of social relations that is structured and animated by and for the sake of those who are able to exert dominant influence.[40] That this dominance is largely produced in capitalist society through the accumulation of wealth can clearly be seen in Thompson's arguments.

The contrast with Bentham on this point could not be sharper: the only power Bentham was concerned about was sovereign power. The ability of some men to subordinate other men[41] was a positive attribute of the capitalist system, as they use their "productive capital" as a kind of power to produce wealth.[42] For those who are not enamored of their working conditions, it would act as a spur to get them to better themselves or, as was seen in the last chapter, for the poor to "starve themselves into riches." This Hobbesian strain in Bentham's thought—the competition for power and the need for constant vigilance to maintain and expand it—appears as the underlying motivational force that drives the production of wealth and, for Bentham, the production of happiness. Thompson would have none of this, as he sees no reason why one should assume that individuals whose needs are met would necessarily desire to subordinate others to their own ends. This will be discussed in greater depth later, but for now, it is enough to suggest that the only reason people think otherwise is because those who are the masters work hard to justify their position, and such subordination is seen as natural or just because we have been conditioned to see it that way.

As other elements of Thompson's conception of happiness are discussed below, it may be valuable to keep in mind the extent to which this understanding of the nature of power and its exercise runs through it.

Happiness as Well-being

If it is the case that Bentham's and Owen's ideas had a strong influence on Thompson, it is also the case that he was not limited by them. Happiness, for Thompson, is directly equated with well-being, which means that the emphasis is less on the experience of pleasure than on the conditions of life that constitute or contribute to a sense of well-being, as well as the constancy or stability of these conditions.

Thompson's Hedonism

That Thompson explicitly equates happiness with well-being establishes a clear contrast with Bentham, but there is a kernel of hedonism that resides in Thompson's thought. Like Bentham, Thompson sees pleasures as the "component parts, of which happiness is the aggregate, or result,"[43] and, like Bentham, Thompson is concerned with the relationship between pleasure and pain, and interest and motivation. The difference, however, is that Thompson emphasizes that happiness refers not to any particular experience or sensation, but to the condition of one's life: "Happiness denotes that continued state of well-being which is compounded of the different items of pleasurable feelings, experienced during a considerable space of time."[44] As was seen in the last chapter, this eudaemonistic conception of happiness disconnects happiness from the experience of particular pleasures and pains. This is not to diminish their importance, since the measurement of the degree of happiness or well-being still depends on the balance of pleasure over pain over a period of time.[45] But by placing them within a larger context, the measure of happiness is concerned with the conditions of life more generally.

Like Bentham, Thompson sees the maximization of pleasure and the avoidance of pain as the primary springs of action, and what matters most are their consequences, not their principles or intentions. Thus, all motives "operat[e] sometimes by pain, sometimes by pleasure, sometimes in the shape of a reward, sometimes in the shape of punishment."[46] Furthermore, the ascription of moral value is based on the balance of pleasures and pains that are produced by any action.[47] And, as with Bentham, Thompson argues that the most fundamental motivation, the basis for all interest, is well-being: "Man being . . . essentially a sentient being, it is impossible that any line of action should be followed by him which did not tend in his opinion, directly or indirectly, immediately or remotely, to his well-being."[48] So, on the fundamental questions of human behavior, Thompson accepts Bentham's primary assertions.

Thompson is not as concerned as Bentham with an exact understanding of the "springs of action," so his discussion of pleasures is much less extensive. Dooley picks out four specific forms of pleasure in Thompson's work: "1) of the senses, 2) intellectual, 3) social, and 4) sympathetic."[49] Like Bentham, Thompson says, "In itself, every pleasure is good, and the only rational object of living."[50] However, in contrast to Bentham, who appears not to differentiate between qualities of pleasure (being more concerned with quantity), Thompson clearly states that some pleasures are "of a less value" as compared to others which are "of a superior order."[51] The pleasures of the body may be more fundamental, but they are limited, whereas the pleasures of the mind, of sociality and of intellect are higher pleasures. Ask someone who is "intelligent and . . . moral . . . from what sources their happiness is derived: ask them how much of it proceeds directly from mere wealth [which is associated with the physical pleasures], and you will be astonished at the scantiness of the proportion of their enjoyments arising from that source, beyond the supply of the average comforts of life."[52]

In an important way, the fulfillment of physical pleasures constitutes, for Thompson, the base upon which other pleasures can be experienced. We may enjoy the pun of referring to them here as "base" pleasures, but the point is not to denigrate their importance, rather to demonstrate just how essential they are. Before one can enjoy intellectual pleasures or the pleasures of sympathy or society, one's basic needs must be met.[53] That wealth is mostly associated with the physical pleasures serves to emphasize Thompson's argument that the distribution of wealth is of primary concern in considerations of how to achieve the greatest happiness of the greatest number. The maldistribution of wealth, he argues, undermines the greatest happiness in two ways: first, by denying or reducing the basic means of happiness to the larger group (since, by definition, if few have more, then a greater number will have less), and second, by promoting vice among the wealthy as well as imitative vices among those who aspire to higher status.

Again, this is not to denigrate the physical pleasures. The point is that it is more difficult to appreciate the more esoteric pleasures without "the average comforts of life." Only when one is "raised above the reach of want" do the "compounded motives that lead to superior exertions and excellence" arise.[54] Thus, in his advice for those designing cooperative communities, while he saw agriculture as providing health benefits of outdoor work (he thought two hours a day of outdoor work would be good for people),[55] he advocated for mechanization in the production of finished goods.[56] This was in the interest of expanding leisure time, which is where he expected that most people would be able to enjoy the higher pleasures of association and intellectual pursuits; he anticipated that, once established, most people in these communities would work no more than six hours a day.[57]

In fact, it is evident that he did not think that different pleasures could be considered in isolation from one another. For example, he argues that sexual pleasure, one of the most basic of the physical pleasures, may be "raised in value" when, "[b]y means of true and useful associations [in the] co-operating communities...the sphere of choice is enlarged to both sexes...even to *all* the members of the community"[58] and the members of the community are endowed with the attractive qualities of "health, intelligence, and benevolence" that come from the character of the social arrangements that may only be found in the cooperative community.[59]

Although he does not discuss it much, Thompson does provide us with one way of understanding how pleasure fits into his theory of happiness, as he discusses pleasure as a part of the "means of happiness" (not to be confused with its sources). There are four:

- "*The preservation of health,* bringing in its train the capability of enjoying all the pleasures of sense, sympathy, and intellect in their highest degree." He emphasizes that this "*includes* the greatest pleasures of taste, appetite and of all the senses."
- "*Individual independence,*" which includes the provision of physical space to ensure that each individual may enjoy time alone, free "from the personal intrusion of any human being," and guaranteeing that each may have "entire control over his or her thoughts, words, and actions."
- "*Social and intellectual enjoyment and improvement,*" which is concerned with "enlarging the bounds of knowledge of all sorts, and diffusing it, as well as the means of social enjoyments, through young and old." This also means that members of the community would not be cut off from the outside world, but in "communication . . . with the community at large or with any particular individuals."
- "*Economy of labor,*" the last category, is concerned with not only efficiency as to effort,[60] but also with its quality, as its object is "not only . . . shortening the time, and banishing the intensity of toil, but . . . surrounding, and associating every species of labor, muscular, or mental, with every possible pleasing accompaniment."[61]

Thompson refers to the first three of these as the "most important objects, indispensable to the promotion of individual happiness,"[62] but in many ways they are dependent upon the economy of labor. This last can be understood as "essential" to all the rest, as it "enable[s] the industrious to supply each others' wants."[63] Labor is the means for the production of wealth which, as will be seen below, Thompson recognizes as the form in which we are able to enjoy most of the physical pleasures. Thus, the production of wealth is essential to the enjoyment of all forms of pleasure. The more "economically" wealth can be produced, the more of it there is to be enjoyed and the more the other forms of pleasure can be experienced.

The limit of production is the labor of production. In an autarkic community engaged in production for nothing but its own benefit, the value of wealth will be measured by the willingness of the members of the community to labor to produce that wealth. The profit motive is absent or, at least, substantially curtailed because there is no alienation of labor by some that enables others to accumulate wealth. Efficiency, therefore, loses its primary place of value in production; instead, "The first object in view is to promote the permanent health of the community."[64] The primary value of increasing the efficiency of labor, then, is in the production of leisure time, without which the "higher pleasures" cannot be enjoyed.

Wealth and Happiness

Bentham, as was seen in the last chapter, considered wealth to be "the matter" of happiness, but, as has been discussed, wealth is central to happiness because of the pleasure that derives from its use or from the sense of security that it provides, not for any intrinsic quality that it has. In Thompson's theory, wealth is no less important, although his emphasis is more on security than on pleasure. Thus, for Thompson, the importance of wealth is limited in a number of ways.

Happiness, as Thompson makes clear, is not possible without wealth. Of course this is precisely what he wants to demonstrate in the argument he presents in the *Inquiry*, so it is no mere happenstance that he begins it by defining wealth, after which he defines happiness.[65] The importance of wealth to happiness can be understood from Thompson's definition of what constitutes wealth—which is largely the same as Bentham's.[66] This is the classical labor theory of value: "That portion of the physical materials or means of enjoyment which is afforded by the labor and knowledge of man turning to use the animate or inanimate materials or productions of nature" or, more simply, "any object of desire produced by labor."[67]

Thompson distinguishes between three categories of objects of wealth: "necessaries," "comforts, conveniences," and "superfluities, extravagancies."[68] The first category refers to those goods required "to preserve permanent health thro' the longest life," which are "always worth the trouble of production, be that trouble ever so great."[69] Placement in the subsequent categories depends on the relationship between the value of the labor put into the good and the pleasure derived from it: Comforts are those things that, while not necessary, provide sufficient pleasure such that their use-value exceeds their cost of production. Superfluities, which we might call "luxuries," are those things that provide less pleasure in their use than effort is required to produce them. Thompson does not provide examples to illustrate what he means, but I imagine that a superfluity might include a gilded carriage, which performs the same function at the same level of comfort as a regular carriage that has the same quality seats and suspension system, etc., but the addition of gold trim greatly increases the amount of labor required to produce it.[70] Comforts, then, are reasonable objects of desire beyond what is necessary, while superfluities are irrational.[71]

Exchange, then, plays no part in the determination of value for Thompson, as his categorization is based on use value, not exchange value. He says that the goods produced "should be used by the same persons, or equally by the same association of persons, that produce them." However, because use pertains to happiness more directly than does exchange, Thompson considers use to be a more important concept in economics, so the categories should apply regardless.[72]

A distinction between productive and unproductive labor is common in political economics,[73] but Thompson distinguishes between "*useful* labor" and "*productive* labor," defining the former as "that which affords more pleasure in the use of its products than pain in their production," and the latter as "that which replaces in exchangeable value" as much or more than it uses. For Thompson, "Productive labor, in a mere economical wealth-producing sense, may therefore be utterly useless as the term useful is here applied."[74] So while Thompson is very concerned with the conditions under which exchange occurs in his critique of the capitalist system, the only value that matters with respect to wealth is use value.[75] Exchange has intrinsic value of its own in the development of interpersonal relationships (as will be discussed below), but there is no formal exchange of goods in the cooperative community, as all the products produced and used in the community are freely shared. Members work together "*for each other,* for the mutual supply, directly by themselves, of all their most indispensable wants."[76] So, while exchange occurs in the cooperative community in a kind of informal labor exchange through the division of labor, the goods that are produced are not commodities, and thus cannot be expected to take on the kind of fetish value that Marx discusses.[77] As a result, the benefit derived from their use may be compared directly with the labor required to produce them, understood as a comparison of the aggregate level of pleasure as compared to the aggregate level of pain.[78]

The labor theory of value, which Bentham mentions but doesn't develop in any substantial way, is central to Thompson. To Thompson, "Labor is [the] distinguishing attribute" of wealth, its "*sole* parent;"[79] it is "that ingredient which turns the otherwise useless materials scattered abroad by nature, into the means of happiness to man."[80] Because wealth is essential to happiness, and wealth is produced through labor, then the organization of labor—the institutional structure of production—is an essential component of the happiness of society.

> The only reason that can be given for the *production* of wealth at all, is, that it adds to the means of happiness: the only reason that it should be *distributed* in one way more than another, is, that it tends more to produce, to add to the stock of happiness, the object of its production, by one mode of distribution than by another. The object being happiness, the greater quantity of happiness held in view and attainable, the more completely is that object accomplished, and the greater, of course, the efforts to produce it.[81]

Thompson's assertion only holds, however, if producers enjoy the full fruits of their labor (a topic that will be discussed in greater detail in the next chapter). In articulating something like Locke's labor theory of property rights,[82] Thompson argues that "[t]he motive to ... exertion [is] the *use* of the articles to be produced; and the free use implies the power of free disposal."[83] After all, no one would "engage in voluntary laborious exertion for the mere sake of the pleasure of the exertion, but for some advantage, some means of pleasure beyond, to be derived from it."[84] But above all, labor and the production of wealth confers social benefits: "Where nature would give the means of mere existence to a few individuals ... labor does, out of the same materials, produce all the means of happiness to thousands."[85]

However, the value of wealth is not, according to Thompson, limitless. Bentham does not recognize these limits, arguing that even opulence must be protected on the basis of the principle of security, since "abundance is never so distinct from subsistence, that one can be destroyed without a dangerous blow at the other."[86] Thompson, on the other hand, sees a variety of dangers in opulence, not only for those who, in his eyes, suffer the pains of excess, but also in its effects on members of the lower classes. The wealthy suffer from "positive vices... the peculiar products of excessive wealth."[87] The poor suffer not only from deprivation caused by excessive inequality,[88] but also from the diffusion of vices of the rich through imitation and the "*over-anxious pursuit of wealth.*"[89]

The importance of wealth to happiness is also limited because there are a variety of sources of pleasure, but, Thompson says, "Wealth is limited to the *physical* means or materials of enjoyment. Labor or muscular exertion can be occupied on physical things alone: they only are capable of accumulation. There are numerous means of enjoyment besides those of a physical nature."[90] As was reflected in the threefold categorization of wealth discussed above, the fact that wealth requires labor means that the (rational) desire to accumulate wealth extends only so long as the pleasure derived from that wealth exceeds the pain involved in the labor it takes to produce it.[91] On this basis he argues—again, in opposition to Bentham, although not directly so—that there are what might be called "natural" limits to wealth accumulation.[92] As material needs become sated, other kinds of pleasure begin to increase in value. Since motives arise from the pleasures of the body, of the mind, of sympathy, and from various combinations of these, the idea "that all individual motives [are] centered in those of wealth" must be wrong. "Wealth is only a means of acquiring some of these [pleasures]; and, in society as now constituted, is much more efficient than it ought to be for the acquisition of them."[93] In other words, the desire for leisure time, by which the higher forms of pleasure are enjoyed, restricts, or acts as a brake on, the desire for wealth.[94]

Natural and Factitious Motives

For all their similarity, there is an important difference between Bentham and Thompson with regard to motives. For Bentham, motives are remarkably sterile: they arise in the mind of an individual, perhaps in response to outside stimulus, but they depend primarily on the individual's desires and expectations, with little reference to the outside world. Thompson's attention to the effects of circumstances allows him to bring the outside world into the mental processes that give rise to motives, such that action and the decision-making process that precedes it can be seen within a particular context—a social context—in a way that is largely missing in Bentham's account.

Thompson references the effects of social institutions in another way, in the distinction he makes between "natural" and "factitious" motives. Natural motives are those for which the "consequences follow, as cause and effect, according to what we call the laws of nature, physical and mental." The "contemplation" of those consequences is what serves as a motive to engage in or to abstain from certain actions. These are *natural* motives because the consequences flow "from the acts themselves, without any interference from without."[95] If I enjoy apples, my expected enjoyment of the fruit serves as a natural motive to plant an apple tree: there is a direct connection between the action and the consequences. Factitious motives, on the other hand, do not derive directly from the actions themselves, but are "imposed from without."[96] The source of factitious motives is social institutions, and in particular those institutions that seek to mold behavior through rewards and punishments—both of which are problematic. His argument against punishments is straightforward: an action is evil because it produces more pain than pleasure. To add to the pain by punishing would only aggravate the situation.[97] His argument against rewards[98] is a bit more complicated, although the basic point is the same: reason, freely exercised under conditions of equality, will naturally lead to the best outcome. Evil—action that produces a preponderance of pain—is contrary to reason, contrary to the greatest happiness of the greatest number, and arises from unequal conditions in which one party seeks to gain advantage over others. Rewards are as much a problem as punishments because they produce factitious motives that disrupt the free exercise of reason and obscure natural motives. Thompson points to their explicitly political nature:

> Natural motives will lead an individual to speak truth, as long as a preponderance of good to all affected by the words requires it; and no longer. But political power requires truth to be spoken for its own purposes.... Thus man's interest is placed in opposition to his duty; arbitrarily so placed by political power for its own real or supposed benefit.[99]

Who, asks Thompson, creates rewards and punishments? And who, therefore, can be expected to benefit from them? "[A]ll human regulations tend to the exclusive interest of those who make them."[100] Later: "As soon as the rules of beneficence and justice are violated, factitious motives, factitious rewards and punishments, become necessary to sway human conduct, as a substitute for reason."[101]

The argument could not be more different from Bentham, who relies on self-interested legislators, held accountable by self-interested voters, to craft laws that promote the greatest happiness by using rewards and punishments to guide individuals to act beneficently and avoid causing harm. Instead, Thompson would get rid of all factitious rewards and punishments, replacing them with the broad diffusion of knowledge and awareness of the natural consequences of action that form "the *natural* motive to action."[102] These natural motives are what distinguish "real" interest from "factitious" interest. The key to benevolence, of course, lies in the principle of mutual cooperation, manifested in the cooperative community. Let me point once again to Thompson's underlying point: social institutions based on cooperative relationships will tend to promote cooperative attitudes and beneficence; by implication, social institutions built on competition will tend to promote distrust and indifference, and those built on rapine and the exercise of raw power will tend to promote malevolence and violence.

Security

"Security" might be the most frequently used term in the *Inquiry* after "happiness" and "wealth." Some aspects of security belong to the next chapter, where it will be considered in the context of a broader discussion of utility. Here the focus is on what it means, for Thompson, with regard to happiness, although it may be difficult to completely separate the two.

As was discussed in the last chapter, for Bentham, security is an abstract notion that has to do with expectations. Motivation is one of Bentham's central concerns, and security reflects the degree to which we can be sure that our expectations will be fulfilled. The higher the degree of security, the stronger our motivation will be. The primary function of government, then, has to do with security; despite his antipathy toward notions of natural rights and fictional contracts, Bentham can be understood as taking the Lockean position that government is formed to provide security—which principally, for Bentham, involves wealth and the happiness that wealth brings.

Thompson's view of security is quite different. It is no less important, but much more material—and more broadly political—in its focus.

Thompson uses the term in two different specific contexts: first, in the sense that the product of labor is "secured" to the laborer; second, and related to his conception of happiness, security is still about expectation in a sense, but the expectation that one will be able to eat today, and tomorrow, and the next day and so on, and the object of concern is less on the expectation and more on the actual substance of subsistence.[103] For Thompson, security takes on the characteristics of expectation mostly in its inverse, insecurity, or the *lack* of ability to secure one's subsistence. Security, then, at its most basic level is about meeting one's basic needs. If these needs are not met, happiness is impossible. The problem with capitalist relations of production is the workers' lack of security—they are subject to the will of the capitalist and not only do they not get to enjoy the full fruits of their labor (only that portion deemed appropriate by their employer), but they have little security in their livelihood. Not only are they dependent upon their employer for continuing employment, but they do not have the means to provide for their own subsistence. This is expressed clearly in the following passage, worth quoting at length, in which Thompson demonstrates the multiple levels at which workers' subordination undermines their security:

> The paramount mischief of all systems of insecurity, by whatever subordinate and varying expedients accomplished, is, that by throwing into the hands of a few the dwellings of the whole community, the raw materials on which they must labor, the machinery and tools which they must use, and the very soil on which they live and from which their food must be extracted,—these few, by combining together, seizing on or allying themselves with political power, reserving knowledge to themselves and keeping the mass of the community ignorant, acquire the absolute regulation of the remuneration of all the productive laborers of the community, and possess the faculty of forcing that community or any portion of it to starve, whenever . . . the exercise of their industry does not . . . yield such a return [or] profits on capital, which they have been accustomed . . . to look upon as their due.[104]

Their housing, the means of production and access to their subsistence are all in the hands of the capitalist. But it goes beyond this, as the capitalist also maintains control over the governing institutions of the state and the educational system—and all of these, including the workers themselves, are but instruments that can be discarded at will if they no longer perform as expected. Thompson shows that the workers' relation to the capitalists is not merely the meeting of providers of labor and providers of capital on equal grounds, but a *political* relation whereby the subordination of the workers is more like their *subjection* to the will of the capitalists.

Thompson also demonstrates how, for women in particular, the lack of security undermines even the apparent happiness of a comfortable life. Thompson's feminism will mostly be examined in the next chapter, but part of his argument for political rights for women is that, absent these rights, they lack security, and this lack of security necessarily undermines their happiness in a variety of ways. For example, even if they were to be granted civil rights denied to them under the laws of coverture,[105] they would remain at risk of having those rights taken away as long as they still lack political rights.[106] In Thompson's time, women (especially married women) had little in the way of legal protection; the principle of security not being extended to them, "*The law excludes her from protection* against the vices and violences of her husband."[107] Certainly a woman might be fortunate enough to have a benevolent husband, but, Thompson asks, can she be secure in her enjoyment of his benevolence? "If we were but sure that [these] good masters would never change their minds, no other wish would remain for us. We might then give way to all the security of joy!"[108] But, lacking such security, real happiness must be lacking, as well.

Individual Happiness and Social Happiness
Capacity for Happiness as the Basis for Fundamental Equality

The next chapter will consider some of the points of congruence and divergence between Bentham and Thompson on the notion of equality, its importance, and its extent, but a discussion of the issue in this chapter cannot be avoided in its entirety. Bentham and Thompson essentially agree on the principle of fundamental equality. In Bentham's words, each person has an equal "sensibility ... to suffering."[109] Thompson says that, "All members of society (cases of mal-conformation excepted), being similarly constituted in their physical organization, are capable, by similar treatment, of enjoying equal portions of happiness."[110] Their differences, however, extend beyond the fact that Bentham refers to suffering and Thompson refers to enjoyment.

In Bentham's case, what we have is little more than an assertion. Thompson, for his part, ends up making a kind of negative argument. In fact, he admits to a lack of knowledge as to whether people do or do not have equal capacity for happiness. Certainly, different people have different tastes, and so will react differently to the same stimulus; in the aggregate, each person's capacity, he suggests, is more or less the same. But this is not the point. It may in fact turn out that some people have greater capacity for enjoyment than others. However, there is no way to determine who or how much: "[W]hat mode, what measure, have we to ascertain where or by *whom* this superior aggregate of pleasures ... is enjoyed? ... We have no means of weighing or measuring them, even if their existence ... were as demonstrable as the light of the mid-day sun."[111] The question is not an abstract one to Thompson. The issue here is whether there is a moral basis for the justification of particular economic and political arrangements for the distribution of wealth: "The fact of their inequality is one thing, the possibility of measuring the degrees of this inequality, so as to make them serve as the basis of distribution, is another."[112]

A further problem Thompson identifies with assumed inequality of capacity is the impossibility of a purely objective measurement. Just suppose, he says, that differences existed, and that these differences could be measured: "Who are to be the *measurers* of these susceptibilities? The rich or the poor, the young or the old, the studious or the illiterate? Are we to institute a court, and to impanel a jury, in the case of every individual ... label every man's neck, to say nothing of the women, with tickets of susceptibility of one to one hundred ... ?"[113] To engage in this kind of measurement, he points out, is itself an exercise of power. As long as individuals are able to exercise power in such a way that will benefit themselves, those who have power will tend to exercise it for their own benefit. Furthermore, the exercise of that power will reflect the particular character of the person who exercises it—which will come from the circumstances in which they live. Thus, all such measurement will be subjective, shaped by the measurer's own social position. What Thompson does, then, is once again point our attention to the fact that happiness is something that takes place within a social context, within the context of institutions that structure power, such that even something as seemingly personal and individual as the relative pleasure we get from different things may interact with those structures.

The Inherently Social Character of Eudaemonism

The argument that Thompson's conception of happiness is necessarily social in a way that Bentham's is individualistic rests to a certain extent on an intuition that hedonism is individualistic while eudaemonism references a social condition. I would like, however, to get behind the intuition to make the argument explicit. This is challenging. For example, there is no necessary reason why Robinson Crusoe could not have made a judgment about his degree of eudaemonia, or well-being, during the entire time he was alone on his island any less than he could have made a hedonistic judgment at any particular point during his stay there. Still, the very condition of being alone, which is a kind of social condition marked by the absence or lack of social interaction, would necessarily be an element of his evaluation of his whole time on the island (at least before his rescue of Friday), while it might or might not be a part of the evaluation of a particular moment. The pain of loneliness is something we experience over time, and it depends in an essential way on the condition of being alone over a significant expanse of time. By the same token, the nature of our social relationships is an important element of the condition of our lives. Whether these relationships contribute or detract from our happiness is something that we can only really consider over a long period of time—even though at any given moment a particular relationship we have with someone may or may not be conducive to happiness. We may even maintain a relationship that detracts from our happiness because we expect that it is better than loneliness, or because we expect that eventually it will get better such that the balance will end up being positive. Because of the importance of our social relationships to our happiness—including in a negative sense in the lack of them, and over an expanse of time that takes in both positive and negative experiences—the eudaemonic conception of happiness is necessarily social.

There is another way to see the social character of eudaemonism, in a way that brings us back to the circumstances in which we live. It is true that with regard to the formation of character, the effect of circumstances on happiness is relevant in the hedonistic sense, because this has a significant effect on how we perceive pleasure. In fact, this reveals a social characteristic that is latent in hedonism. But circumstances are central in eudaemonism in a different way, in the way that a society organizes its productive activity and the distribution of resources and wealth. Thompson articulates two different ways in which this is the case. First, if production is inefficiently organized, less wealth will be produced, and to the extent that wealth is conducive to happiness, there will be less overall happiness.[114] But while those who live in poverty amidst a wealthy society may be able to experience happiness in a hedonistic sense, they cannot be said to be happy in a eudaemonistic sense (at least as Thompson sees it), first because of their lack of security, but also due to the presence of inequality itself. To be poor in an impoverished society is one thing; to be poor in a wealthy society quite another.[115] Thus, Thompson's *Inquiry* about how to distribute wealth so as to maximize happiness is also concerned with how to arrange production so as to ensure the greatest possible production, which involves seeing how the distribution of what is produced affects productivity.

The Social Character of Interests and the Voluntary Society

The social nature of Thompson's theory is also evident in his view of interests. Thompson accepts Owen's argument that the effects of circumstances leads to the claim, *contra* Bentham, that individuals are not always the best judge of their own interests. This is, in a curious way, reflected in the central position voluntarism occupies in his theory, particularly in his discussion of the idea that all exchange must be voluntary. Within the system of individual competition, the test for whether an exchange is truly voluntary is whether the producer freely consents to it.[116] This is similar, in a way, to Smith's argument that the butcher, the baker, and the brewer engage in exchange because it is in their interest to do so; if an exchange is not in their interest, then they will not do it. Benevolence plays no part in the market system.[117] It may happen, Thompson argues, that a producer does not agree to an exchange; if so, the person who wants to make the exchange, thinking it to be fair, must "enlighten the ignorance, to explain the truth, to show his own interest to the person whom his proposed exchange would serve."[118] What produces this misunderstanding, Thompson asserts, is that one or both parties suffer from a lack of knowledge or understanding about their true interest: "The simple and obvious remedy for those cases where both exchanging parties are mistaken as to their real interest, is to show them their mistakes, to give them *knowledge*."[119] Interest, here, is the same as it is for Bentham, and what motivates the desire for exchange is an expectation regarding pleasure and pain. However, the social conditions within which the parties live, or more simply the lack of sufficient education, may give rise to false interests that are based on a misunderstanding of their "true" interests. If this is the case, then one cannot simply rely on the actions of possibly ignorant individuals to determine either levels of happiness or people's "true" preferences.

Thompson makes numerous references to "false" and "true" interests in a way that carries strong associations with the kind of Enlightenment universalism that has come under sharp criticism.[120] But while he may be guilty of making universalist assumptions at times, there are important differences between Thompson's discussion of self-interest and the familiar notion of "enlightened self-interest." There is little in Thompson that is anything like an appeal to virtue—not that he's opposed to the idea, mind you, or that he doubts the capacity of humans to be virtuous. But there is little use to exhortations to virtue from within a social system that promotes selfishness:

> Tell [a person] to be virtuous, to be beneficent, to promote the happiness of his fellow-creatures; you must show him it is his *interest* to do so. Tell him to be virtuous, and surround him with such circumstances as make the virtues you recommend contrary to his *apparent* interest; his conduct will unhesitatingly follow in the line of what seems to him his interest, and all exhortations in opposition thereto, will be unheeded and inoperative.[121]

Virtue does not simply "spring up" by itself, but through people engaging in networks of social interaction that are premised on mutual support. In this regard, Thompson discusses the many positive effects produced by exchange of a truly voluntary nature. Note that Thompson considers any system of labor cooperation or the division of labor to be a system of exchange.[122] The important question is whether those who are engaged in it are doing so voluntarily (in the interest of mutual benefit) or whether they are compelled (for example, because they lack the means to produce on their own and must therefore exchange their labor for wages). Exchange that comes about through mutual cooperation

Thompson considers "indispensable for the evolution of morality, of beneficence."[123] These benefits may be felt even in a simple barter system (involving individual production), which enables a person to see that, "the co-operation of his fellow-creatures with him, and of him with them, is necessary to their mutual happiness: he becomes *interested* in the success of their *joint* labors; he feels a sympathy in their exertions; his feelings are carried out of himself... mutual satisfaction is produced, mutual sympathy is excited... a pleasurable *association* is formed, and the discovery is made that the happiness of others is not necessarily opposed to our own, but is frequently inseparably connected with it." As a result of *voluntary* exchange, people become "more social... more benevolent."[124]

The cooperative communities are premised on just this sort of benevolent exchange. The communities are intended to be large enough to take advantage of the division of labor in order to maximize the members' productive efficiency. This represents a kind of informal exchange of labor as, for example, you work in the fields to produce flax, among other things, which I use to produce linen to make clothes that will clothe the community, while others grow food, or make furniture, or whatever else the community needs. The sort of "exchange" envisioned within the communities, then, is not of commodities—especially not commodities produced explicitly for exchange. Everyone in the community contributes in their own way to the benefit of the community, and everyone enjoys those benefits. Thus, it is a social process where each individual may see him- or herself as acting within a network of interaction, as opposed to either a series of individual exchanges or a magical process of reciprocation governed by an invisible hand. This is similar, in a sense, to Marx's idea of the social process of production or the "social division of labour,"[125] but instead of being a secret process that "goes on behind the backs of the producers,"[126] it is direct, open, and apparent to all the members of the community.

The capitalist system, however, is not a system of voluntary exchange. Rather, it performs a political function as the inheritor of the "feudal and theological systems" of institutionalized "force and fraud" that dispossess the producers in favor of the powerful.[127] Thompson offers a long list of examples of systems that support involuntary exchange:

> All public and local revenues of almost all countries, are levied by mere force, in contempt of the consent of the producers. In all transactions

in which monopolies . . . or any species of unequal law favoring the rich, have any share, force, the ultimate supporter of the laws, is a partner in the transaction. Ecclesiastical dues, when voluntarily paid . . . are founded on fraud, the abused credulity and fabricated ignorance of the payers . . . from the intricacies of production, the difficulties of ascertaining value and quality, from the inequalities of knowledge and skill, there is scarcely a transaction of barter or exchange in which the over-reaching spirit of competition does not mingle fraud. . . . By unjust *exchanges*, then, supported by force or fraud, whether by direct operation of law, or by indirect operation of unwise social arrangements, are the products of the labor of the industrious classes taken out of their hands.[128]

These involuntary exchanges are extremely damaging to society, as they "annihilate industry and virtue," and constitute the most serious threat to security.[129] The effect of this is positively Hobbesian: from the worker's perspective, the lack of security represented in involuntary exchange steals all motives to industry. "The productive laborer has toiled, and the fruit of his labor is taken from him. Why should he work again?"[130] The harm extends to the person who seizes the produce of his workers, as it "renders *less* probable his future supply by discouraging production."[131] The force used need not be direct. If a laborer has no choice but to accept the wages offered or watch his family starve, then the effect of this coercion is little different than if he was a slave. Coercion is an exercise of power, and can only be exercised by the powerful, but the exercise of coercion is a marker that the person being coerced is being made to do something that violates their interest. Coercion and volition are dichotomous: "There is in fact no intermediate principle between the principle of 'voluntary exchanges' by means of equivalents satisfactory to each of the exchanging parties, and the empire of 'brute force.' The *degree* of force employed, and the *direction* in which it is exerted, may vary; but the *principle* is the same."[132] Furthermore, the practice has been "to deceive and induce, to terrify and compel, the productive laborer to work for the *smallest possible portion* of the produce of his own labor."[133]

But, while involuntary exchange is just so much "brute force and robbery,"[134] voluntary exchange is "the most useful and beneficent of social operations,"[135] requiring as it does the recognition of others' interests and attention to mutual benefit. As is evident in the passage quoted above, exchange in the spirit of cooperation connects people together, enabling them to recognize "their mutual happiness" and the common interest they have in their "*joint* labors." In stark contrast with involuntary exchange, in cooperative exchange we feel the pleasure of association: "The more of these mutually convenient exchanges that take place, the more man becomes dependent on man, the more his feelings become sympathetic, the more social he becomes, the more benevolent."[136] As Thompson sees it, this introduces an automatic, "immediate *restraint* on the selfish desires of the party demanding the exchange."[137] Voluntary exchange is, therefore, "the most useful and beneficent of social operations."[138]

The key to the benefits of exchange lies in its voluntary nature. Voluntariness is, for Thompson, the test of benefit: a person will consent to exchange only if it is in their interest, in other words, if it will lead to their benefit—in short, if it will contribute to their happiness. It is worth noting that voluntariness is also the key to justice: if there is a question about whether or not some exchange is just, Thompson suggests the proper response is, "*Is it voluntary?*"[139]

As was noted above, Thompson considers it possible for people to be mistaken about their true interest, and he expresses great confidence in the ability of all parties in an exchange to arrive at a mutually beneficial conclusion once given full knowledge and freed from all forms of coercion and factitious motive. This is not the place for a thoroughgoing critique of Thompson's faith in rationality. Certainly we have reason to be dubious about people's ability to recognize the difference between their "true" and "false" interests, just as we may have reason to question the value of the categories themselves. Furthermore, people's ability to use knowledge-claims and interested (as opposed to disinterested) rationality as a kind of club by which to bludgeon an unwilling would-be partner should not be underestimated.

Thompson's reaction to this doubt would be, I think, to point us toward its underlying assumptions: we assume that individuals, given the opportunity, will seek their own advantage over that of others. But there is nothing in the basic principle of seeking pleasure and avoiding pain that implies coercion or the subjugation of others. To the extent that such coercion or subjugation occurs, it is a product not of the basic drive for benefit, but of a defect in social institutions. Social institutions that promote personal over mutual gain will tend toward coercion and subordination as a means toward gain. What is the object of gain?

"Now it would appear that the possession of individual property, the consequence of individual competition... renders [the] perfect union of interests as to wealth impossible."[140] Eliminate private property, and one eliminates the motivation for selfishness: "All their property is in joint possession, and indissolubly linked up with the happiness of each other."[141] In his view, if self-interest and mutual interest are not aligned, then this is because the social institutions make it so.

An essential point to remember, however, is that this alignment cannot be forced, and that, ultimately, it is a matter of individual motives, individual expectations, and experiences of pleasure and pain.

> All enjoyment must be individual enjoyment: all motives to produce individual action must be brought home to the individual to be acted upon.... [A] motive not individual... is no motive: a social motive, if you please, and not a selfish motive; but selfish or social, it must be individual, must come home to the real or supposed interest of the agent, or he cannot act.[142]

Pleasure, Happiness, and Well-being: Thompson and the Contemporary Literature on Happiness

In the last chapter it was noted that the "Back to Bentham" movement in the contemporary literature on happiness is somewhat ironic, given that Bentham asserts that happiness and well-being are distinct while the contemporary literature holds that they are the same. On this point, at least, there is greater congruity with Thompson. The question that needs to be considered is whether this congruity is simply apparent, or whether it goes beyond an affinity of language. What might a greater understanding of Thompson add to the contemporary discourse on well-being?

One point differentiates the discussion here from that at the end of the last chapter: I make no claim whatsoever that the contemporary literature is in any way derived from Thompson. There is no evidence that any of the contemporary authors has ever read Thompson or is otherwise familiar with his work.[143] A weak argument could be made that some part of the contemporary argument is derived from Thompson through Marx, but this is a very attenuated relationship, since although Marx may have been more strongly influenced by Thompson than his own citations reveal, there is no question that Thompson was only one among many. In any case, only a few of the writers on these subjects refer to Marx, so although their arguments could in some way be said to emanate from the Marxist tradition of social criticism and critiques of capitalism, their connection to Marx is no clearer than Marx's connection to Thompson.

Like Bentham, Thompson predates the recent separation between the subjective and objective approaches and does not fit neatly into either one.[144] As will be seen, Thompson's thought bridges the two camps in a way that provides linkages between the two approaches. Subjective well-being was discussed in some detail in the last chapter; here the focus will be on the objective side, followed by a general discussion.

Objective Well-being

Where the subjective approach is largely empirical in its methodology, the objective approach is more conceptual and philosophical and less directly associated with happiness. Where SWB represents an empirical approach that attempts to measure happiness directly, based (usually) on respondents' own understanding of the term, the objective approach is, as Gasper points out, more explicitly "a normative concept"[145] that asserts particular requirements for well-being. Objective theories often begin with foundational principles, that of justice in particular, and they arise from two directions: out of a concern with the failure of either liberal capitalism or state socialism to ensure any measure of distributional equity, as well as in considerations defining development objectives with regard to underdeveloped economies. This has given rise to a variety of distinct theoretical models. Two of the most prominent are the basic human needs approach[146] touched on in the last chapter, and the capabilities approach.[147] While these two approaches differ in substantial ways, there are also strong similarities.

Both of these approaches can be said to arise out of a common Aristotelian core that asserts that to "be human" carries certain particular meanings and requirements, and that it is possible to articulate these in a way that is generalizable across all social and cultural categories. The human needs approach is more concerned with the basic requirements of life (or, more specifically, the "good life," although there is plenty of room for a variety of interpretations of what that might mean), while the capabilities approach might be considered more aspirational in the sense of establishing what the requirements are for individuals to be able to realize the kind of life they wish to lead.

Both of these make use of what Gasper refers to as "objective lists,"[148] although the basic needs approach builds its list from the bottom with the basic physical requirements of life, while the capabilities approach tends to start at a higher level with notions of liberty/freedom or human dignity. The value of these lists is that they offer specificity, but this is a double-edged sword, as this same specificity tends to detract from their claims to universality.

The basic premise of the basic human needs literature is that, as needs are met, well-being increases; indeed, one cannot be considered to have attained a measure of "well-being" unless and until basic needs have been met. Importantly, then, it is not concerned with the potential for limitless increase in the material stuff of pleasure, but in the presence of basic conditions for people to achieve fulfillment in their lives. This literature could, on its face, be accused of a kind of minimalism, as it presents not a continuous scale but a dichotomous condition: either the minimum conditions have been met or they have not. But its demands are, in fact, far from minimal, as its normative stances lead to radical conclusions that go well beyond the provision of food and shelter. In a review essay, Doyal notes that "[t]he problem of discovering what humans really need and the creation of a social programme to meet these needs is central to socialist theory [as a] yardstick... to assess the success of social practice,"[149] although the question is by no means limited to socialism, having been debated through the ages, as Springborg shows.[150]

Springborg notes that the concept of needs, while appearing unproblematic, is in fact very complex and open to interpretation, as it touches on fundamental questions of human nature.[151] Beyond this, the development of civilization has given rise to social structures that intercede between individuals and the fulfillment of their needs, so that even where basic biological needs are concerned these cannot be separated from questions of the structure of social institutions and the organizational premises of society. The fact that different societies are structured in different ways then gives rise to a significant problem for the objective approach, as claims to universalism become very difficult to sustain. Further, it raises important issues of responsibility, especially as regards international, intersocial or even interpersonal claims.

While the basic needs literature is generally quite concrete, maintaining a focus on people's lived experiences, the capabilities literature tends toward the abstract.[152] In Sen's words, "The approach is based on a view of living as a combination of various 'doings and beings', with the quality of life to be assessed in terms of the capability to achieve valuable functionings."[153] The normative basis for this literature is the question of egalitarian justice, reflected in the title of Sen's 1980 Tanner lecture to which it owes its origins: "Equality of What?"[154] In arguing that the leading conceptions of equality—of outcome (welfare) or of opportunity (resources)—are insufficient, Sen argues instead that what is required is that all have equal ability to act on the basis of values they choose, or, in other words, the freedom to *do* or to *be* as one chooses.

Although Sen avoids specificity in articulating his theory, he does recognize that there might be a category of "well-recognized, urgent claims" that could be referred to as "basic capabilities"[155] in a way that deploys the logic if not the form of the basic needs literature. Nussbaum, in her work, does identify what she refers to as the "central human capabilities."[156] The list she offers shares important features with the needs articulated by Doyal and Gough.[157]

Of Subjective and Objective Happiness

In his overview of the field, McGillivray tells us that "the term 'well-being' is a concept or abstraction used to refer to whatever is assessed in an evaluation of a person's life situation or 'being'. In short, it is a description of the state of individuals' life situation." He notes that many terms have "appeared in the research literature to label this situation," including welfare, utility, empowerment, capability, development, and several more. Only "recently," however, has happiness joined this list.[158]

In one way, at least, SWB can be understood as positive, in that it seeks to understand happiness as a definite object that can be acquired and quantified, while OWB can be understood as negative, in that it seeks to understand the character of harm or the primary barriers to happiness. That said, SWB, and the hedonistic perspective it is associated with, have greater affinity for the kind of negative liberty associated with liberalism, while OWB is closer to a positive liberty position that seeks to ensure that all members of society have what they need in order to fully participate in their self-governance—indeed, one of their basic criteria is the capacity to be full participants in society.[159]

One feature of the new literature in general is that well-being has a less direct association with pleasure. The contemporary literature on well-being treats it as a "multidimensional concept," whose dimensions include "knowledge, friendship, self-expression, affiliation, bodily integrity, health, economic security, freedom, affection, wealth and leisure."[160] This list is not unfamiliar to a reader of Thompson, except that in his work many of these dimensions are referred to simply as different kinds of pleasures—pleasures of the body, of the mind, and of association. The question is whether anything is gained from the added detail.

Despite the general consensus in the SWB literature that happiness or well-being is properly measured over the span of a lifetime, the fact that researchers in this area seek to measure the subjective experience of happiness makes significant the question of whether a given individual is "happy" at any particular point in time, since their evaluation of their life experience may be strongly affected, if not determined, by their current state of mind. But the question of short-term feelings of happiness is also significant because of the desire to identify the determinants or "causes" of happiness by testing hypotheses about correlations between state of mind and certain conditions or activities.[161] Indeed, their survey methods ask people directly whether they feel they are happy[162] without specifying just what they mean by the term—this is deliberately left to the respondent's interpretation.[163] So, although such a prominent researcher as Veenhoven may dismiss hedonism as an important category,[164] pleasure has a way of creeping back in, albeit in more formal terms such as "hedonic experience."[165]

The objective approach reflects a distrust of the stability of language, rejecting the idea that interpersonal comparisons of happiness are possible as long as the term itself can mean something different for each person.[166] Those writing in the OWB field posit that happiness is not something that is experienced directly, but is the result of the presence of certain conditions and, in particular, the presence of those conditions over an extended period of time. Some, in fact, question whether "happiness" is an important category at all.[167] The question here is about determining, and then establishing, the necessary conditions for well-being, and less about whether people actually experience (or say they experience) happiness. We may have reason, on this basis, for wondering whether the OWB literature can really be considered a part of a larger genre of writing on happiness—although it could also be said that the association of happiness with purely subjective well-being is a new phenomenon, and that what is needed, politically, is for happiness to be reconnected with objective well-being.

Thompson: The Objective Happiness of the Individual

Thompson does not equivocate with respect to the subject of his investigations: it is happiness. However, the relationship of pleasure to his ideas about happiness is not nearly so clear, for two reasons. One of these has to do with the hedonistic aspects of his theory. The other has to do with his identification of different kinds of pleasure, each of which has a different role in happiness. One value of naming different kinds of pleasures, and of holding that these pleasures are not all the same, is to avoid the sort of reduction of well-being to pleasure or desire-fulfillment as was seen in Jevons's work in the last chapter. It could be said that Thompson also reduces the various pleasures into his categories of physical, mental, and associational, but this is very different from what Jevons does. The reduction of happiness into a single, distinctly measurable quantity (and, more especially, measurable through activity in the marketplace) is not possible with Thompson, for two reasons. Thompson rejects the idea that all pleasures are fundamentally equal, but he also rejects the idea that anyone's particular sensitivity to pleasure is objectively measurable, which means that pleasures—especially what we might call the "higher pleasures"—cannot be measured through market mechanisms.

However, while it is important to reject the reductionism represented by Jevons and the neoclassical economists, on a theoretical level I question the efficacy of developing seemingly endless and necessarily incomplete, competing lists of criteria for happiness, as seen in both the SWB and OWB literature. Such an approach would tend to obscure similarities and divert attention from the principles behind the list itself. From a practical perspective, such a list can be seen as an important tool for the establishment of specific policies regarding the means by which the items on the list may be fulfilled, but then this is a political discussion that must take place in some sort of deliberative manner.[168]

I return, again, to Thompson's most basic point: Happiness, or well-being, cannot be thought of in isolation from the social institutions that shape the lives of the individuals that are a part of that society. It is not uncommon in this literature for writers to consider the nature of social institutions—it is, for example, an important part of Doyal and Gough's work. But what Thompson does is look beyond the distributional question and the issue of the efficiency or efficacy of these institutions in fulfilling people's needs, to consider the character of the institutions themselves. What he sees is that we cannot judge the value of institutions based on how well they perform the role they are meant to play, but we must also be concerned with the principles on which the institutions are based and how well they adhere to those principles. This goes back to the idea that people's character is socially constructed through the institutions with which they interact throughout their lives. Institutions have effects that go beyond their direct purposes, and we must be as attentive to those additional effects as well as the institution's ostensive purpose. Ultimately, Thompson reminds us that the question of need fulfillment or people's development of their capacities is not an abstract question, but a *practical* and a *political* question that has to do with the structure of the institutions through which we fulfill our needs and exercise our abilities.

The institution that Thompson is most directly concerned with is one that few of the writers on well-being are willing to address, at least not so directly: Private property and what he refers to as the system of individual competition—the basic outlines of what we now call capitalism. As will be seen in the discussion of Thompson's political economics in the next chapter, as far as he is concerned, these constitute the primary barrier to happiness. As the discussion from the last chapter showed, the institution of private property not only inhibits people from experiencing happiness, it generates unhappiness; in fact, it depends on it.

But if happiness cannot be considered apart from the institutional structures that shape it, it is also the case that happiness is about the experience of individuals, real people, many of whom face significant struggles simply to fulfill their basic needs. Thompson reminds us that "[t]here is no such thing as a general, abstract, happiness. All happiness is made up of that of individuals."[169]

Where Bentham's conception of happiness emphasizes the individual experience of pleasure, Thompson's eudaemonism emphasizes the social conditions of individual happiness. Bentham understood that social institutions affect individual happiness, but what Thompson's theory reveals, in a way that Bentham's theory misses, is the way that social institutions structure social relationships (for example, in the form that exchange takes) and the effect this has on happiness. Thompson is also attentive to the character and functions of power within these social institutions, understanding the political nature of those relations in a way that is not captured in Bentham's theory, even though Thompson is less directly concerned with the direct practices or functions of governmental institutions and law. The political implications of their different conceptions of happiness come to the fore in their respective theories of utility, to which I now turn.

PART II
THE POLITICS OF HAPPINESS

4
Happiness and Utility

In the more than 175 years since Bentham's death, utilitarianism has developed without having given much thought to just what is meant by "happiness." As the previous chapter demonstrates, however, there are different ways of understanding what is arguably utilitarianism's central concept. This chapter shows how those differences become manifested within the context of Bentham's and Thompson's respective theories of utility. The next chapter considers its significance within the more specific context of their democratic theory.

Although both Bentham and Thompson conceive of utilitarianism as a social philosophy, the individualism inherent in Bentham's hedonism produces a theory of utility that is ultimately individualistic, as it is centered on the independent activities of individuals relating to one another as individuals, even as they act within a social context that, in effect, conditions their actions. In this way, his political theory is very much a liberal theory that seeks to ensure the ability of individuals to seek their own happiness with the support of state institutions that provide security yet at the same time interfere with individuals' actions as little as possible. Bentham understands that the behavior of individuals within the private sphere is to some degree regulated by law, but while a legislature (which is accountable to the people) may establish particular institutions for the regulation of behavior (such as Panopticon prisons or poorhouses), its primary function is more remote. Bentham's utilitarianism is broadly liberal, then, as it is concerned with the ways in which political institutions affect individual behavior, and the "greatest happiness of the greatest number" means that the maximum number of individuals is able to achieve the maximum quantity of happiness.

Thompson offers a social theory of utility—even, it can be said, socialist. For his sake, Thompson would reject the distinction between a public and a private sphere. His focus is on the means through which individuals relate to one another, which is to say social institutions understood broadly. Thompson's utilitarianism is concerned with the way social institutions establish the conditions within which people live and interact with one another. It should be clear that Thompson is concerned with the way *individuals* interact within the context of these social institutions, but while it is true that the institutions do not act on their own, Thompson also recognizes that individuals are always acting from within an institutional context.. Because the relations of individuals within institutional structures are always conditioned in some way through or as power relations, social institutions are always—or, to use the Marxian term, *always already*—political. So, for Thompson, the "greatest happiness" is always a political question that is concerned with the structure of the social institutions within which people act.

One of the most significant elements of their theories has to do with the principles that are subsidiary to utility, which may be understood as intermediary principles for the operationalization of the principle of utility. There are significant differences, both in terms of their content and in the principles' relation to one another. Bentham's subsidiary principles—security, subsistence, abundance, and equality—can be understood to some degree as a lexicographical ordering such that one follows the other, determining relative importance. Thompson, on the other hand, offers a different set that includes security and equality, taking subsistence and abundance as assumed, and adds voluntarism, united effort/common property,[1] and democracy. The most important difference has to do with the relative positions of security and equality. Bentham, who considers equality to be one of the "ornaments of life,"[2] sets these at odds, creating a tension that Thompson resolves. The key for Thompson is to structure social institutions in such a way as to remove those elements that give rise to inequality and coercion—competition and private property—and replace them with institutions based on cooperative effort and the communal ownership of property within a democratic system.

The main focus of this chapter is Thompson's theory of utility and the political economics and social theory that arise out of it. However, because Thompson himself never directly presents a theory of utility, or certainly not as directly as Bentham does, drawing its outlines requires a careful consideration of his economic and social theory. As was evident in the discussion of happiness, although their ideas are very different, Thompson draws on Bentham's logic and his terminology. So, in order to understand Thompson it is necessary to go through Bentham.

Bentham: The Pursuit of Pleasure and the Greatest Happiness

It should be noted at the outset that there is a difference between *happiness* and *utility*. Like pleasure, utility is closely associated with happiness, and again the terms seem interchangeable, or nearly so. It doesn't help that when he went to republish his primary exposition of the principle of utility (the *IPML*), Bentham indicated that he thought a better term for what he had called the "principle of utility" would be the "greatest happiness principle."[3] Of course, to say that the principle of utility is equivalent to the greatest happiness principle is not the same as saying that it is equivalent to something that might be called the "principle of happiness," *greatest* happiness being distinct from simple happiness. Furthermore, just as a distinction may be made between simple happiness and the greatest happiness principle, so Bentham distinguishes between utility and its principle. In his second edition of the *IPML* Bentham also added a footnote to the effect that in his initial articulation of utility he failed to establish "a sufficiently manifest connexion between the ideas of *happiness* and *pleasure* on the one hand, and the idea of *utility* on the other."[4] Note that "happiness and pleasure" are on one hand, while "utility" is on the other. So, while connected, they are different.[5]

Utility and the Principle of Utility

What is utility? Here is Bentham's most direct definition:

> By utility is meant that property in any object whereby it tends to produce benefit, advantage, pleasure, good, or happiness ... or ... to prevent the happening of mischief, pain, evil or unhappiness to the

party whose interest is considered: if that party be the community in general, then the happiness of the community: if a particular individual, then the happiness of that individual.[6]

In this passage, Bentham identifies two separate levels of utility—one in the aggregate, which is the concern of the legislator, and one at the level of the individual, where considerations of utility are directly manifested. The former can be referred to as utility operating at the "macro" level and the latter as "micro" utility.

Bentham's definition is at once both personal and political. In one of his most frequently cited passages, he begins the *IPML* by arguing that all human action arises out of our desire to experience pleasure and avoid pain, and he refers to pleasure and pain as man's "two sovereign masters."[7] Pleasure and pain are clearly personal, but this is a political claim in the sense that, as far as Bentham sees it, pleasure and pain constitute the *only* rule people will follow. If state authority wishes to affect the actions of the people, it can only do so by affecting people's experience or (what may be more important) expectations of pleasure and pain.[8]

Notice that utility here is merely a way of describing a "property" of "any object." Bentham then defines the *principle* of utility as the feeling of approval or disapproval that we have for anything depending on its tendency to produce or inhibit pleasure or pain for the person making the judgment (who may be the actor, the recipient, or an observer of an action).[9] It is at this point that utility becomes the foundation for morality, as by "principle" Bentham means, essentially, a starting point for a system of law and morality;[10] more specifically, it is "a sentiment of approbation...which, when applied to an action, approves of its utility, as that quality of it by which the measure of approbation or disapprobation bestowed upon it ought to be governed."[11]

What isn't clear, however, is how we get from what must be an individual "sentiment of approbation" to the central tenet of Bentham's political system, the idea that "*it is the greatest happiness of the greatest number that is the measure of right and wrong.*"[12] Although the principle of utility is often understood as the desire to maximize happiness, Bentham is referring here to a kind of judgment, one that approves or disapproves of actions on the basis of whether they contribute to the happiness of "the party" being considered. The micro/macro distinction is useful here: If the party here is an individual, then the principle is operating at the micro level. If, however, the party is a community or society, then it is functioning at the macro level. The distinction is valuable because the principle functions somewhat differently at the two levels. At the micro level it is something that we as individuals engage in all the time with respect to ourselves and others around us: we approve of actions that contribute to happiness and disapprove of those that do not. But it isn't immediately clear how this works at the macro level. How is the judgment made, and to what does it apply?

There are, I think, two answers to this question. On the one hand, it can be seen as the micro principle writ large, in terms of considering the broader impacts of specific actions. How do specific actions affect members of the community or the broader society? Do they make for a better society (higher level of well-being, with greater opportunities for happiness), or not? The alternative perspective requires a recognition that Bentham was writing as a legal philosopher concerned with the moral implications of government and law. Here, the principle acts less as an ethical judgment of individuals' actions than as a political judgment about the nature of the institutional conditions within which action occurs.

As Bentham sees it, social relations are structured through law, which sets the boundaries within which social institutions operate. The sense of approbation or disapprobation cannot be determined by law (he did not assume that legislators could tell people how or what to think) but can be influenced by the absence or presence—and degree of—punishment for acts understood by legislators as detrimental to the general happiness (or rewards for acts seen as beneficial). Where the state has criminalized or designated punishment for some act, it is a clear signal of disapprobation; likewise, if it subsidizes or protects particular acts, then this is a sign of approbation.[13] As a political principle, utility is the end of government in the sense that government sets the parameters within which individuals may pursue the maximization of their happiness; if all are able to maximize their happiness without causing harm to others, the result will be the greatest happiness of the greatest number.

Principles Subsidiary to Utility: The Opposition of Security and Equality

In and of itself, the principle of utility provides little guidance for legislators in the development of a legal system. It is in this context that Bentham offers the four principles "subsidiary to utility" discussed in chapter 2: subsistence, security, abundance, and equality.[14] As seen in chapter 2, Bentham separates them into two sets, one essential and the other ornamental, but they can, in fact, be understood as an ordered set, with security and subsistence more or less co-equal at the head, followed by abundance and equality.[15] As was discussed earlier, Bentham argues that while subsistence may seem to take precedence over security, as a matter of law and social policy, security is the preeminent concern: Given security, people will take care of their subsistence themselves.[16] Bentham sees abundance as, in effect, an extension of subsistence, something we are naturally motivated to pursue such that law need do nothing to promote it.[17] Equality, however, is different from the others, because it is the only one of the subsidiary principles that may come into conflict with the rest—notably, abundance is not seen as being in conflict with either subsistence (for example, the idea that one person's abundance may undermine another's subsistence) or equality. If the demand for equality requires the taking or redistribution of property, then it undermines security. By undermining security it undermines subsistence and, by extension, abundance. Therefore, he argues, "Equality ought not to be favoured except in the cases in which it does not interfere with security."[18] So, with respect to law, they can be put in order of importance: security, subsistence, abundance, equality.

Although it may be the last of the subsidiary principles, this is not to say that Bentham was unconcerned about inequality.[19] Stark argues that "the great idea of human equality... though unexpressed, underlies all Bentham's philosophy."[20] Rosen argues that "the greatest happiness principle meant an 'equal quantity of happiness' for every member of the community in question... a substantive goal which aimed at an equality of condition."[21] In fact, Bentham articulated a theory of marginal utility precisely to reflect and to justify equality, which rests on the assumption that each person has equal "sensibility... to suffering," so "the part which their happiness constitutes of the universal happiness" is equal, as is "their right to have as much regard shown to their happiness as to that of... other persons."[22] The theory of marginal utility goes like this:

(1) Each portion of wealth has a corresponding portion of happiness.
(2) Of two individuals with unequal fortunes, he who has the most wealth has the most happiness.
(3) The excess in happiness of the richer will not be so great as the excess of his wealth.

(4) For the same reasons, the greater the disproportion is between the two masses of wealth, the less it is probable that there exists a disproportion equally great between the corresponding masses of happiness.

(5) *The nearer the actual proportion approaches to equality, the greater will be the total mass of happiness....*
Fortunes being unequal, the loss of happiness produced by a given loss of wealth will become less in proportion as the distribution of the loss shall tend towards the production of an exact equality.[23]

From this, it can be seen that the principle of utility must take distributional questions into account. The question remains as to how central these questions are to Bentham.

While Bentham may have believed that the greatest happiness of the greatest number ideally meant an equal quantity of happiness for everyone, it seems that he considered the possibility to be extremely remote, so much so that it should take a back seat to all other concerns. More specifically, he argued, security trumps equality: "When security and equality are in conflict, it will not do to hesitate a moment. Equality must yield. The first is the foundation of life.... Equality produces only a certain portion of good." Security is the source of stability, while equality "will never be perfect; it may exist a day; but the revolutions of the morrow will overturn it. The establishment of perfect equality is a chimera; all we can do is to diminish inequality."[24] It is here, in fact, that his commitment to liberal principles stands out most clearly, and his antipathy toward proposals for what might today be thought of as communitarian redistributive principles. "[I]f property should be overturned with the direct intention of establishing an equality of possessions," he warns, "the evil would be irreparable. No more security, no more industry, no more abundance! Society would return to the savage state whence it emerged."[25]

Equality is not absent, and Bentham insisted strongly on the sort of formal or legal equality that is one of the foundation stones of liberalism. His theory may even have been, as Postema puts it, "equality-sensitive."[26] But his commitment to equality rested on the faith that, should a legislature enact a system of laws completely conformable to the principle of utility, this would tend toward equality of outcome. "*Security*," Bentham argues, "leads indirectly to *Equality*."[27] But the goal of equality, while not unimportant, should not be a principal guide in policymaking.

Utility and Private Property

In chapter 2, it was argued that Bentham considered wealth, specifically in the form of property, to be the primary object of security, and in a Lockean tone that the principal function of government is the protection of property. Here the argument will be carried forward to consider its implications with regard to the principle of utility. My discussion involves, in part, an examination of Kelly's argument that Bentham presents a theory of distributive justice, which he ties closely to Bentham's conception of private property and which has clear implications for the principle of utility in the macro sense.

Both Locke and Hume argue that justice is principally a matter of property. As Locke puts it, "*Where there is no Property, there is no Injustice.*"[28] But abstract notions of justice are not meaningful to Bentham, who has no patience for what he considers meaningless ideas with no positive basis. What matters to Bentham are pleasure and pain, and justice or injustice is a matter of whether or not expectations regarding these are fulfilled. If someone experiences pain—for example, through engaging in some sort of labor—with the expectation of some pleasure to follow from it, the denial of that pleasure is an injustice. If a man is wealthy and his children have grown up with the expectation that upon his expiration they will be able to inherit and enjoy their father's wealth, then to deny them that pleasure is also an injustice. Really, if anyone has any property that they have acquired by legal means—even slaves[29]—then it is an injustice to take any portion of it that they may have expected to be able to enjoy (so, for example, a tax is fine so long as it is a part of their expectation).[30] Bentham argues that the principle of security, or the "disappointment-prevention principle," provides "for the first time, a clear idea to the denominations *justice* and *principle,* say rather *principle* of *justice.*"[31] From a Benthamite perspective, then, this is the basis for property and the underlying reality of the connection between property and justice. It is also the connection between security and justice, as what must be secured is that expectation.

Kelly claims that Bentham "was concerned to emphasize that property was a fictitious term which only derived a determinate sense from a particular theory,"[32] although if he was so concerned there isn't much evidence of it, as Kelly provides no citation and I have not found any discussion by Bentham on this point.[33] But while property could be considered a fiction associated with security, it is most clearly a construct of the law[34] and the mechanism through which the law is able to affect the security of wealth.

Bentham acknowledges Beccaria's concern that, because of the ways in which it has been abused, "[t]he right of property... is a terrible right, which perhaps is not necessary,"[35] but Bentham defends property, saying that "the right itself presents only ideas of pleasure, abundance, and security. It is that right which has vanquished the natural aversion to labour;... given man the empire of the earth;... brought to an end the migratory life of nations;... produced the love of country and a regard for posterity." The problem is not with the right of property itself, but with man's "desire to enjoy speedily... without labour. It is that desire which is terrible; since it arms all who have not against all who have."[36] The issue raised here is not a concern with the presence of inequality, but with its effect. He is not concerned that idle landowners may take advantage of their wealth and status to engage in perfectly legal activity so as to perpetuate and even improve their status, gaining wealth at the expense of those worse off. Rather, the concern he expresses is much like Smith's, that "the affluence of the rich excites the indignation of the poor, who are often both driven by want, and prompted by envy, to invade his possessions."[37] It seems that, given a choice between an "equality of misery" and a condition in which most may be miserable but at least some few are not, Bentham would choose the latter.

This reveals a deep tension in Bentham's theory between property and the greatest happiness that derives from the conflict between security and equality. The greatest happiness requires the greatest possible level of equality, but it also requires the kind of security of expectation that comes about through property. The distribution of property, however, is unequal, and it would be a grave violation of security to attempt a transfer of wealth in order to bring about greater equality.[38] The trick, then, is to implement measures that will promote a more equal distribution of property while respecting the demands of security. This is a difficult task. Kelly suggests that, in all his work, Bentham is only able to identify three methods of addressing this problem: limited taxes, as long as they are not excessive and not imposed without due notice (so that individuals may engage in activity with the full awareness of them); the "sacrifice of security to security," where legislators may engage in some redistribution in order to avoid civil unrest, although this must be used with great caution and only in extreme circumstances; and by changing the laws of inheritance, eliminating primogeniture, allowing women to inherit (and retain) property on an equal basis with men, and allowing that the property of people who die intestate and without a clear successor would revert to the state for the purpose of redistribution. Of these, the last was to be preferred.[39]

In a curious way, with an understanding of Bentham's ideas about property as security of expectation, his rejection of the redistribution of wealth and his defense of opulence,[40] the principle of security appears to be quite conservative, and his theory of diminishing marginal utility could be interpreted not as an argument for equality but as an argument for the perpetuation of *inequality*. After all, since a person of great means derives less pleasure from the same portion of wealth as does a poorer person, the one who is wealthier requires a greater income just to maintain their status and their expectations for the pleasure to be derived from their wealth. Kelly argues that "[t]he pattern of rights which embodies equal spheres of personal inviolability is that which maximizes social well-being," and that Bentham's articulation of "rights to protect the person, condition in life, and reputation . . . are equally necessary for all individuals to form and realize their own interests and projects."[41] This may be true, but what is required to maintain the condition of life and reputation for someone of great wealth is clearly much greater than what is required for someone who is impoverished. The direction the argument points to is that because a poor person expects less, they should have less. So the idea of distributive justice one finds in Bentham may have little to do with substantive notions of equality; rather, that Bentham considered the existing distribution of wealth to be just—or, if not just, that the damage to security of measures to correct the injustices would generally outweigh the benefits gained.

The implications of Bentham's concern for the security of property are starkly present in his argument against emancipation. It is not that he supported slavery—indeed, he refers to "the evil inherent in the very nature of the thing" and offers a number of arguments against it[42]—but he opposed a sudden emancipation because he believed that it would have to be accomplished by "a violent revolution, which, by displacing all men, by destroying all property, by putting all persons into situations to which they had not been educated, would produce evils a thousand times greater than all the immediate good which could be expected from it."[43]

Rather, Bentham argues, "When it regards the correction of a species of civil inequality, the same attention ought to be paid to the rights of property; the operation should be gradual, and the subordinate object should be pursued without sacrificing the principal object."[44] In other words, measures need to be developed that will induce slaveowners to relinquish their property. He suggests several.[45] But his opposition to abolition, despite his clear opposition to slavery, reveals much about the strength of his commitment to the principle of security.

Self-Interest and Social Interest

The priority placed on security reflects the importance of self-interest in Bentham's theory. To be sure, that he considered self-interest the only "rational" basis for human action should not be construed as an endorsement or even a sanctioning of self-interested behavior. Like Smith, Bentham clearly understood that self-interest was the great engine of progress. But there is a paradox at the heart of his views on self-interest, because at the same time it was also the greatest threat to the greatest happiness, on two levels. First, "[S]elf-regarding interest is predominant over all other interests put together,"[46] and, "That the uncoerced and unenlightened propensities and powers of individuals are not adequate to the end without the controul and guidance of the legislator is a matter of fact of which the evidence of history, the nature of man, and the very existence of political society are so many proofs."[47] Thus, the need for government to utilize legislation to affect individual calculations of self-interest to guide individuals toward the greatest happiness. The second—and more serious—threat posed by self-interest is what Bentham calls "sinister interest," which arises when a minority (for example, rulers) has an interest that is contrary to the greatest happiness and the ability to pursue it at the people's expense.[48] The answer to sinister interest Bentham refers to as the "junction-of-interests prescribing principle," although there appears to be some circularity in his argument, as he says that the means for instilling the junction of interests is by "destroying the influence and effect of . . . sinister interest."[49]

Baujard argues that this paradox reveals, in fact, "an inner contradiction in Bentham's theory."[50] There is no problem when individual and community interests coincide. This may happen when there is a "sympathetic fusion of interests," or a "natural identification of interests." But, she points out, "Bentham devotes the principal part of his work to developing the third approach embedded in his philosophy of law: the artificial identification of interests," which requires "outside intervention."[51] The existence of sinister interest means that, if the "greatest happiness" is understood simply as the aggregation of individual, unmodified interests, the result is a condition that falls short of the collective welfare, because the normative value of collective welfare is something outside of the individuals of which it is composed. This normative value may be enforced by various means (for example, through the four sanctions noted above), but, she argues, it "implies modification of the definition of individual interest." Bentham's argument that the "interest of the community [is] the sum of the interests of the several members who compose it"[52] implies, in Baujard's words, that "'what is good for the individual (premise) is good for the community (conclusion).'" However, if, in fact, a normative standard exists that may come into conflict with individual interests, then what Bentham really means is, "'What is good for the community (premise) is what is good for the individual (conclusion).'"[53] So, while the intention of Bentham's utilitarianism is to articulate a "bottom-up" notion of the greatest happiness, to achieve the end of the greatest happiness requires the "top-down" imposition of an ethical criterion.[54]

Bentham's effort to align self-interest with social interest through the coercive mechanism of the law might be characterized as a kind of sleight of hand (not to be confused with the "invisible hand"), getting people to act or restrain themselves in a socially positive manner without their even realizing it.[55] The alignment of self-interest and social interest is one crucial element of the differences between Bentham and Thompson. Rather than Bentham's sleight of hand, Thompson addresses the issue head-on. As with happiness, however, while many contrasts can be drawn between Bentham's and Thompson's utilitarianism, there are a number of similarities, as well.

William Thompson: Security, Equality, and the Political Economy of Happiness

"Utility, calculating all effects, good and evil, immediate and remote, or the pursuit of the greatest possible sum of human happiness, is the leading principle constantly kept in view, and to which all others are but subsidiary, in this inquiry." So begins Thompson's *Inquiry*. He leaves no doubt as to the source of his statement, as he adds, "In Bentham's 'Introduction to the Principles of Morals and Legislation,' and the first chapters of the celebrated 'Traités de Legislation,' this principle, recognized by Helvetius, Priestley, Paley and others, is developed and established for ever, to the exclusion of all other pretended tests of morals."[56] However, given the significant difference between Thompson and Bentham in the way they think about happiness, we have good reason to wonder whether Thompson's idea of "the greatest possible sum of human happiness" means something different from Bentham's "greatest happiness of the greatest number." While the "utilitarian" label would be difficult to avoid for Thompson, it will be clear from what follows that his theory is based on a set of principles that, while they intersect with Bentham's at various points, also diverge widely.

The difference between Thompson and Bentham can be seen most clearly in the principles they consider subsidiary to utility. He argues, *contra* Bentham, that security and equality are not only not opposed to one another, but are in fact mutually constitutive. Further, there is no need to specifically include subsistence and abundance because, with the reconciliation of security and equality, these follow as consequences, not as separate principles. The voluntarism discussed in chapter 3 constitutes a third principle making up the essential core of the subsidiary principles. This is not, however, sufficient, as a further set of principles, democracy and united effort/common property, are required to put the others into practice.

Unlike Bentham, Thompson is not satisfied to assert that equality is an important goal, subordinate to other, more important concerns, and he is much less concerned with violating security if it maintains a social order that protects a small minority yet produces injustice for a substantial majority—although it should be noted that, rather than undertake a revolution to enforce radical change, Thompson advocated evolutionary change through the establishment of alternative, egalitarian institutional structures (the cooperative community). It should be no great surprise that someone who holds that happiness is a social condition, and that people's character is a product of their circumstances, would be critical of a "system of individual competition" that turns all the members of a society against one another as potential rivals in the pursuit of accumulated wealth. A critic of all forms of subordination as incompatible with the greatest happiness, Thompson articulates one of the most substantial early attacks on an emerging liberal capitalist order premised on wealth inequality and class domination but also characterized, especially in his time, by slavery and racial domination and the oppression of women by men.[57]

Thompson argues that the opposition of security and equality are a product of the system of individual competition, which is, in effect, a system of insecurity for workers. But systems of subordination and inequality don't only harm those on the losing end of a sort of Hobbesian war of each against all.[58] Not only do the poor suffer from destitution, from poverty in the midst of plenty, but the idle rich themselves suffer from various vices that result from their own condition. Moreover, to the degree that the development and dissemination of knowledge is considered a valuable asset advantageous for all members of society, Thompson argues that in the system of individual competition, those who wish to protect their advantages will seek to limit the educational opportunities of the rest of society—the majority—and thereby limit the advancement of knowledge. Further, workers' lack of security acts as a limit to their productivity, meaning that less wealth is generated, making the society as a whole less wealthy—and, by extension, less happy.

Thompson's answer to all this is an endorsement of Robert Owen's proposal for cooperative communities in which all property is owned in common and the products of the collective labor are distributed equally, although he went well beyond Owen's proposals for relief for the lower classes. Thompson meant for his communities to be open to members of all classes, and indeed he argued (as Owen himself later did) that the cooperative model, as a more rational system, would eventually predominate (or, as we might say now, achieve hegemony) over one based on competition. The removal of the desire for the private accumulation of wealth manifested through the institution of private property, and the establishment of attitudes of cooperation manifested through the institution of united effort/common property, would enable the members of the community to enjoy both equality and security to the greatest possible extent and, thereby, the greatest happiness. In what follows I shall explore all of these various pieces of Thompson's theory.

Surplus Value and the Premises of Political Economy

Thompson considered himself a political economist and both the *Inquiry* and the shorter work *Labor Rewarded* are meant as interventions in debates about political economy. Thompson is often referred to as a "Ricardian Socialist,"[59] although since he never mentions Ricardo (or Smith for that matter)—a better term would be to refer to him as an "Owenite political economist." In fact, a discussion of the "competitive school of political economy" that encompasses the main body of *Labor Rewarded* fails to identify a single individual author.[60] The much more extensive discussions in the *Inquiry* provide little additional insight into his sources, as he only briefly mentions James Mill's *Elements of Political Economy,* and he discusses Godwin and Malthus[61] in the *Inquiry* only to dismiss them.[62] His critiques of bounties (subsidies), monopolies, and tariffs[63] could be taken from Smith, Ricardo, Bentham, or Mill. So, while Thompson clearly draws from his peers, the only way to identify their influence is by inference. Since they clearly dominated the discussions of political economy of his time, the discussion that follows focuses mostly on Smith and Ricardo (Mill, who was also important at the time, is largely derivative of Smith and Ricardo).[64]

Smith's primary concern in the *Wealth of Nations* is the aggregate level of wealth. Ricardo, in his *Principles of Political Economy* raises this issue but is more concerned with the distribution of wealth.[65] In the *Inquiry,* Thompson examines the effect of distribution on the total level of wealth. "The only reason that it [wealth] should be *distributed* in one way more than another, is, that it tends more to produce ... happiness.... If it could be proved that more happiness on the whole would accrue to society by centring the whole sum of wealth in many or a few individuals, such should be the distribution of wealth, in full accordance with this first principle."[66] One of the central problems he identifies with the existing system of distribution is that, by relying on coercion to induce laborers to produce and then denying them the full produce of their labor, the workers' productivity, and thereby the level of wealth, is reduced. As it turns out, he argues, "the quantity of production will depend on the stimulus to production: and the strongest stimulus is necessarily security in the entire use of the products of labor" by the laborer.[67] Note that this is not just a problem of *production,* but also of *distribution,* and the problems of production are linked to the problems of distribution. These problems arise from the conflict between capital and labor, and he develops the theory of surplus value to analyze it.

Smith understood that capitalists and laborers would have conflict over the level of wages, but he saw wages, rent, and profit all as various deductions from the produce of labor. "The produce of labour constitutes the natural recompense or wages of labour," Smith says, but, "this original state of things, in which the labourer enjoyed the whole produce of his own labour, could not last beyond the first introduction of the appropriation of land and the accumulation of stock." Appropriation of land (private property, controlled by landlords) gives rise to rent, and the accumulation of stock (private property in the form of capital, controlled by capitalists) gives rise to profit. Wages are, in effect, an advance to the workers for the sake of their subsistence as they produce the goods that will return that advance to the capitalist, who "would have no interest to employ him, unless he was to share in the produce of his labour, or unless his stock was to be replaced to him with a profit."[68] The capitalist provides the stock to pay the wages, so the capitalist decides the amount of those wages and whatever is left after paying for rent and the means of production is added to his stock. This is as far as Smith takes the notion of surplus value: "He shares in the produce of their labour, or in the value which it adds to the materials upon which it is bestowed; and in this share consists his profit."[69]

Ricardo criticizes Smith for a lack of precision in his discussion of the relationship between labor and value, and is more insistent than is Smith that labor is "really the foundation of the exchangeable value of all things."[70] Regarding the relationship of wages to prices, there is little difference between Smith and Ricardo, although the latter provides more detail in arguing that the level of fixed capital (for example, machinery) can significantly alter this relation—indeed, he argues, an increase in wages can even produce a *reduction* in price.[71] Like Smith, Ricardo argues that the "natural price of labour is that price which is necessary to enable the labourers ... to subsist and to perpetuate their race," although this does not depend on the "quantity of money" but on the "quantity of food, necessaries, and conveniences ... which that money will purchase." The natural price of labor, according to Ricardo, depends on the price of securing their subsistence,[72] and the level of wages will vary on the basis of supply and demand of labor and the cost of subsistence.[73] This, of course, introduces some problematic circularity to Ricardo's argument, as the cost of subsistence depends, in part, on the cost of labor. What Ricardo's theory does, however, is point more clearly to the importance of a "web of exchanges" that reflects "the institutions, customs and social structure of the society under consideration."[74]

So, for both Smith and Ricardo, labor is the determinant of value: I will only exchange for something if its value to me is equal to or greater than the value of the labor I would have to expend in order to either produce the same thing or produce something I can exchange for the object of my desire. That makes sense for an independent producer engaged in direct exchange of use-values. But how does it work under the principles of commodity exchange? Specifically, how does this produce profit—*surplus* value? This is how Engels explains the problem:

> Whence comes this surplus-value? It cannot come either from the buyer buying the commodities under their value, or from the seller selling them above their value. For in both cases the gains and the losses of each individual cancel each other, as each individual is in turn buyer and seller. And yet we find that in each country the capitalist class as a whole is continuously enriching itself before our eyes.[75]

Engels, of course, attributes the answer to Marx, but Marx may have picked it up from Thompson, who wrote,

> There can be no other source of this profit than the value added to the unwrought material by the labor guided by skill expended upon it. The materials, the buildings, the machinery, the wages, can add nothing to their own value. The additional value proceeds from labor alone. The spade may as well be called the parent of the grain instead of the laborious arm that wields it, as any of these articles constituting capital, can be called the parents of the manufactured article. 'Twas labor that gave to all these their value as wealth, before they came into the hand of the mechanic; and by his additional labor alone can their value be still further increased.[76]

The laborers, he says, are "deprived of" the excess value that they create and he cites "[a] universal and always vigilant conspiracy of capitalists ... to cause the laborers to toil for the lowest possible, and to wrest as much as possible of the products of their labor to swell the accumulations and expenditure of capitalists."[77] Thompson recognizes that landlords need to be compensated for the use of their land, and that those who provide capital need to be compensated for the use of their stock (to use Smith's term): "Doubtless the laborer must pay for the use of these, when so unfortunate as not himself to possess them: the question is, *how much* of the products of his labor ought to be subtracted for their use?"[78]

In answering this question, Thompson does not take the default position of the political economists critiqued by Marx in the *Economic and Philosophical Manuscripts*, which is to take private property as a "presupposition."[79] Rather, he offers two ways of measuring the amount to be subtracted: That of the laborer, for example a "mechanic at woolens or cottons" who has "no other fund out of which to pay [his] rent than the produce of his labor," and a capitalist "who owns the buildings ... the unwrought materials which he [the laborer] is to fabricate, and the machinery (the tools) with which he must operate, as well as the wages to be advanced until the wrought article is exchanged." The laborer "would replace the waste and value of the capital by the time it would be consumed, with such added compensation to the owner and superintendent of it as would support him in equal comfort with the more actively employed productive laborers." The "measure of the capitalist," however, would be "the additional value produced by the same quantity of labor in consequence of the use of the machinery or other capital; the whole of such surplus value."[80] So, Thompson accepts Smith's and Ricardo's separation between wages, profit, and rent, but instead of giving the capitalist the residual after deducting shares for the laborer and the landlord, he gives the residual—the surplus value—to the producer of value, giving determinate compensation to the capitalist and landlord.[81]

The advantages of voluntary exchange (and the disadvantages of involuntary exchange) were discussed in the last chapter, and Thompson directly connects this to surplus value through his discussion of the "forced abstraction of the products of labor." Marx, of course, prefers the term *alienation,* and while Marx articulates a much richer theory of alienation, Thompson clearly lays the groundwork for Marx's theory. In addition, what could be the seedling of a theory of species-being as connected to the issue of abstraction (alienation) may be found in the context of Thompson's discussion, in his reference to "the pleasure of skill, of perseverance, of success," which is "included in the pleasure of employment, of having some *fixed purpose in life,* which fills up all the voids of existence."[82] Besides the alienation of labor and the theory of surplus value, Marx would have found much of interest in Thompson's critique of the capitalist system.

Private Property and the Disutility of the System of Individual Competition

Thompson does not refer to "capitalism," as the word was not yet in use in his time (although he has frequent references to "capitalists"),[83] but what he calls the "system of individual competition," characterized by competition between individuals in the pursuit of private property, comes reasonably close. As has already been noted, Thompson is quite critical of this system, arguing that it is an impediment to achieving the goal of the greatest happiness.

One of the features of this system is class conflict. "The object of capitalists, is not to increase the general capital of the community, but to make most productive of profit to themselves, what is absolutely in their possession: the real interest of the capitalist, as such, is always and necessarily opposed to the interest of the laborer."[84] Indeed, in language echoed by Marx and Engels in the *Communist Manifesto,* he claims that "[t]he whole system of human regulations hitherto, has been little more than a tissue of restraints and usurpations of one class over another."[85] In effect, capitalism is not a natural outgrowth of social relations. Rather, it is the intentional product of those who see this manner of producing and distributing wealth as beneficial to their interests and a manifestation of the social (or sociopolitical) power of wealth: "The object of those who instituted and maintained such a state of things ... possessing mostly the wealth and the ruling powers of society, have uniformly established their subordinate objects as ultimate ends of pursuit; such as the support and continuance of their order, the continuance of the system of rule, whatever it might be, which they had introduced; the continuance, at all events, and increase of their own superiority in wealth, power, and happiness."[86] The state is part and parcel of this, as it is, in effect, the means for the maintenance of the system and the enforcement of rules that ensure the continued dominance of the "superior" class. Again, in this respect Thompson anticipates Marx, who, with Engels, says, "The executive of the modern State is but a committee for managing the common affairs of the whole bourgeoisie."[87]

In capitalism, wealth becomes inseparable from its particular form as private property, and the private accumulation of property leads to coercive labor and exchange and the loss of equality, but not just in the sense of living standards. That the owners of property retain security in the produce of their investments, while laborers lose security in the produce of their labor, reflects an inequality of security. Thus, capitalism is a system of security for the ownership class and a system of *insecurity* for the working class. For Thompson this inequality of security is fundamental, one of the primary causes of other forms of inequality.[88] Thus, inequality of outcomes can be said to derive from an inequality in the application of rights (specifically, the right to security).

It is in this context that Thompson attacks Bentham's argument regarding the abolition of slavery.[89] Security, if a meaningful principle equally applied, must apply to the produce of labor. But, under conditions of slavery, while the *master* may be said to enjoy security in *his* labor and to enjoy the principle of voluntary exchange consonant with that, all this is denied to the slave. But it is not just that the slave is denied the produce of his or her labor: "In the security of the slave are comprehended *all his rights,* all *his means of happiness,* not just those arising from wealth, but from all other sources; all compromised and annihilated by slavery." The master may believe that he gains in happiness through the wealth produced by the slave, but, Thompson argues, the slaveowner in fact loses, because the productivity of the slave is so much lower than the productivity of "voluntary labor." Further, the master suffers in a myriad of ways, in the "disquietudes, precautions, and efforts necessary to uphold forced labor. The security of the master consists in the preservation to him of a *very doubtful* balance of enjoyment in *one item* of all the numerous sources of happiness incident to human beings." Against this must be considered the "security of the slave [which] consists in the preservation to him of *every item of all possible sources of happiness,* of which slavery robs him, and lodges in the caprice of another person." Thompson goes on to say, "*The security of acquired property, the produce of labor, is only a branch of the security of labor:* and *the security of labor is only a branch of general security, guarntying equal rights to all sentient and rational beings.* . . . Where two masses of security are incompatible with each other, the sacrifice of the smaller mass is to be preferred." Thus, he argues, the principle of utility requires that the slaves be emancipated, with compensation given to the owners by the state that "sanctioned and upheld" the practice.[90]

Thompson does not refer to capitalism itself—that is, competition in a system of private property—as a form of slavery, yet his argument reveals that it undermines utility in several ways. Competition works hand in hand with private property to allocate resources and define social functions and roles. In this system, some people own capital; use that capital to finance production, including purchasing material, tools, and labor; and then claim ownership of the produce of the hired labor. Others have nothing to offer but their labor. Private property, in establishing separate, "private" spheres for individuals, separates people from one another, and, within a competitive environment in which the object of competition is the accumulation of wealth in the form of property, sets them against one another. Even if everyone started out on an equal basis (a utopian idea if there ever was one), in a system of competition and private property, inequalities would soon arise. Where everyone does *not* start out on an equal basis (i.e., the real world), competition and private property only serve to perpetuate—even worsen—the existing inequalities. Further, wage labor violates the principle of security in the sense that workers are not secured the produce of their labor, since the output of their labor is not theirs but belongs to the person who pays their wages, and it is the capitalist, not the worker, who determines the rate of exchange (i.e., the level of their wages). Again, this cannot be considered voluntary exchange (with all of the implications of involuntary exchange), as long as "the laborer is *compelled,* by the necessity of living" to accept the capitalist's terms.[91]

Although Claeys asserts that Thompson "retained some elements of ambiguity" with respect to his views on competition,[92] Thompson seems quite clear in his major works that a system based on competition can never produce a benevolent society. "Competition," he says, "makes us regard from birth the interests of every one as opposed to and incompatible with the interest of every other person because it really puts all interest in opposition to each other. In every happy face, we now see a successful rival."[93] This opposition is an unavoidable feature of a system that encourages the private accumulation of property:

> The object of all the exertions of individual competition as to wealth, is to acquire for immediate enjoyment or accumulation, individual property. Every individual, striving for *self* at the ultimate peril of want, destitution, and death, there is a constant motive operating to regard the interests of others as opposed to his own.[94]

Competition is a problem not only because of the inequality of wealth it engenders, but because it depends on the establishment of social relations in which individuals see their interests as opposed to the interests of everyone else. If the character of individuals is shaped largely by the society in which they live, then a competitive society would produce people bred for competition: "The very gathering together by every one of an individual heap of wealth, necessitates individual as opposed to general feelings, selfishness as opposed to benevolence."[95] Even under the most favorable circumstances, competition would be problematic:

> [A]fter all that can be done under the best arranged system of perfect equal security, with the undeviating observance of the natural laws of distribution, there will still remain evils inherent in the very frame of society, arising out of that very healthful, active, competition of individual interests put into motion by security for individual well-being.[96]

The lack of security for producers and the subsequent reduction in productivity were not, he believed, the only ways by which the capitalist system undermined utility. Enormous disparity of wealth he saw as the source of all vice: "For what, in the ultimate resort, on almost every occasion, is the great contest between morality and immorality, between law and crime?—for what, but for the possession of the objects of wealth?" Besides the problem of crime on the part of those denied legitimate means for subsistence, it "engenders *positive vices*" on the part of the wealthy and concomitantly through "admiration and ... imitation ... diffuses the practice of those vices of the rich in the rest of the community."[97]

Finally, competition also undermines utility by producing a kind of perverse justification for limiting educational opportunities. He argues, in effect, that knowledge itself becomes separated from labor in a kind of division of labor, ultimately becoming *opposed* to labor, as its antithesis rather than its aid, as it becomes a means by which those who have been successful can maintain their position for themselves and their progeny.[98] Thompson was an advocate of universal education, as all "sentient rational beings ... should be educated for their own sakes [and] for *their own sakes alone*,"[99] because it is important to their happiness, not in order to produce more efficient, more complaisant workers.[100] While he did believe that people should receive a practical education that would enable them to engage in productive activity, in his view intellectual activity constitutes a particular kind of pleasure in and of itself, within an "intellectual culture" that contributes to happiness by enabling individuals to engage in "interesting conversation" and exercise their "curiosity, judgment, anticipation."[101] "The vacuum of an unemployed mind," on the other hand, "is not simply the absence of happiness; it is a state of positive torment."[102] However, where access to a meaningful education constitutes a competitive advantage for those with access to it, for the rest, education will be more like training for subordination: "Under bad institutions, what is called the teaching of morality is nothing more than the inculcating *habits of submission to oppression.*"[103] To the degree that the progress of human society requires the development and diffusion of knowledge, the competitive system is an impediment to it: "It is on the diffusion, by individual effort, of moral knowledge, that all hopes of human improvement and happiness must be founded. From existing institutions the most that can be expected, is a mitigated hostility."[104]

So, to sum up, the system of individual competition undermines utility in a number of ways. Competition in itself is inimical to utility because it promotes conflict. The important principle of security is violated for individuals because the produce of labor, understood as surplus value, is allocated on the basis of the ownership of capital (private property) instead of on the basis of labor (production). Although labor is the source of value, that value is secured to the owner of capital, not to the owner of the labor. The result is a lack of security for workers who, as a result, are less productive than they would otherwise be. The system itself is based on inequality manifested in a number of ways, including in the standard of living of workers and capitalists, but also in the ability of capitalists to control the political, economic, and educational systems, directing them in their own interests. Thompson provides something of a summary here:

> As long as that force-supported organization of things continues, by which one set of men possess the productive powers alone, and another possess the physical means of putting those productive powers into operation, so long will the latter, the capitalists, use the means in their power to render the labor and the happiness of all laborers subservient to their greatest interests; so long will the happiness of the whole human race be sacrificed, if necessary in the estimation of capitalists, to produce an additional quarter per cent profit.... As long as two hostile masses of interest are suffered to exist in society, the owners of labor on one side

and the owners of the *means* of laboring on the other, as long as this unnatural distribution is forcibly maintained... so long will perhaps as much as nine-tenths of attainable human productions never be brought into existence, and so long will ninety-nine hundred parts of attainable human happiness be sacrificed."[105]

Selfishness and Self-Interest

Part of the problem with competition, to Thompson, is that it promotes selfishness, which he distinguishes from self-interest. "Self-interest," he says, "implies a general desire to promote our own individual well-being, without reference to any particular means." This is to be distinguished from selfishness, which "implies a desire to promote by all *immediate* and *direct* means in our power our well-being, without calculating the effects of our conduct on the feelings and conduct of those whom it may affect, nor... their reflect operation on ourselves." Both have the same object: "well-being, happiness" to the greatest possible degree. "The difference is in the *means* by which [it] is sought. The one seeks it by direct, short-sighted means, ignorantly disregarding the surrounding interests of other sentient beings; the other seeks it on an enlarged calculation." While "[t]he general pursuit of self-interest, is only... the general pursuit of happiness,"[106] selfishness is self-interested behavior that is contrary to, or fails to consider, mutual interest. But while selfishness can be seen as having undesirable social consequences, there is no reason why, given the appropriate sort of social institutions, self-interest should not be completely conformable to the common interest.

Like any good Benthamite, Thompson argues that self-interest is the only rational form of motivation. But rather than seeking to contain self-interest, to direct it in the way Bentham does by establishing rewards and punishments to limit the harm the pursuit of self-interest might cause to others, Thompson argues that true liberty consists in the pursuit of self-interest such that social interests are furthered at the same time. The key is to align self-interest with social interest through the structuring of all social institutions—and not just the narrowly political institutions of the state, as Bentham would have it. These may be organized in such a way that they either promote antagonistic relationships that lead people to pursue their self-interest in a selfish manner (as they are in systems based on individual competition with the aim of accumulating private property), or to promote social cooperation and the pursuit of self-interest in a way that is compatible with—even advances—social interests: "Here private interest and public interest, here private virtue and public virtue, both as to the individual and the community, are one and the same: here interest and duty are united."[107] To the extent that Bentham saw self-interest as a kind of a problem such that it required that careful restraints be placed on its pursuit either through direct legal prohibitions or more indirect means, Thompson might say that these are required only because of Bentham's commitment to the system of individual competition, which is premised on individual pursuit of self-interest without regard for social interest. With the reform of social institutions so as to firmly align individual and social interest, those restraints would no longer be necessary. Those restraints are, as he puts it, the "restraints of insecurity," and their removal would "give fair play to human exertion."[108]

The Evils of Subordination

As has been said, one of the problems of competition for property is that it produces inequality. Where there are inequalities there is bound to be subordination. And subordination is inimical to the greatest happiness. It should be noted that Thompson's critique of subordination is most directly articulated in the context of an argument for the rights of women, but his arguments clearly extend to all forms of subordination, or the personal subjection of one individual to the will of another. He refers to it as "one of the greatest sources of human helplessness and misery."[109]

Thompson clearly recognized that subordination takes on different forms within different social institutions, and he did not reduce, as Marx later did, all forms of subordination to different facets of economic subordination. He understood that women's struggle against subjugation by men had a different basis from that of workers' struggle against the forces of capital in that it required political equality that was being denied them on a basis different from that of workers, yet at the same time both were part of a broader fight for a social system based on the establishment of equal relationships. Like Wollstonecraft, he refers to marriage as a kind of slavery; although as Ferguson quite reasonably asserts, Thompson's arguments for sexual equality went beyond those of Wollstonecraft and other feminists of his time.[110] Indeed, he goes so far as to equate the condition of women in marriage with the sort of slavery found in the "foul Slave States" of the American South.[111] His radical (allowing, for example, that young children might be treated differently) argument that equality should be extended as far as reasonably possible (so, for example, young children could be excluded) without discrimination or relationships based on subordination arises from his perspective on what it means to pursue the greatest happiness of the greatest number: "The happiness of *every individual,* and of course of *all classes, of the human race,* ought to be promoted for the sake of such individual or individuals, and not in subserviency to the happiness of any other individuals or classes whatever. When every individual is made happy, the happiness of the whole is promoted."[112]

Thompson's arguments for equality and against subordination come out most clearly in his *Appeal of One Half of the Human Race, Women, Against the Pretensions of the Other Half, Men, To Retain them in Political, and thence in Civil and Domestic, Slavery; In Reply to a Paragraph of Mr. Mill's Celebrated "Article on Government."* Mill's article, which originally appeared in the 1820 edition of the Encyclopedia Britannica, proved to be quite popular and was extracted and distributed fairly widely. Much of the article is a discussion of various aspects of the "system of representation," which he refers to as "the grand discovery of modern times."[113] In a discussion of the appropriate extent of the franchise—he was an advocate of universal male suffrage—Mill explicitly asserts "that all those individuals whose interests are indisputably included in those of other individuals, may be struck off without inconvenience." Included in this group are children and "women ... the interest of almost all of whom is involved either in that of their fathers or in that of their husbands."[114] These claims are the focus of Thompson's *Appeal.*

In his essay, Mill does not explain why he thinks that it would be better to have fewer voters rather than more. If it were the case that he was thinking in terms of households—that each household would correspond to one electoral unit—then he may have had reason to be concerned that the household of a married couple would have two votes, which would give them an advantage of sorts over single people. But he does not explain why, of the two members of a married couple, the law should stipulate that the female member of the relationship is the one to give up her right to vote, nor why single women should be excluded. He also provides no explanation of how the supposed identity of interests between a man and his wife (to say nothing of that between a *woman* and *her husband*!) arises, what its basis is, or how it functions. These are all issues that Thompson takes up in various ways in the *Appeal*.

Thompson does not argue against the exclusion of children from political rights, but points out that the exclusion of women means the exclusion of "one-half of the human race" or any defined group thereof (e.g., a nation). If, on Thompson's estimation, children make up about half the population (possibly true in his time, if not in ours), and women are half of the remaining adult population, then Mill is saying that "one fourth of the human race...is the greatest number whose interests ought to be directly consulted in the making of laws."[115] If, as Mill asserts, a "grand governing law of human nature" is that all men "desire...that power which is necessary to render the persons and properties of human beings subservient to our pleasures,"[116] and that the interests of any aristocracy (rule by a group greater than one but less than a majority) will be to "take from the rest of the community as much as they please of the objects of desire,"[117] then, argues Thompson, Mill's claim that the "ruling quarter is necessarily benevolent toward the three fourths," while ignoring its own interests, is incoherent.[118]

Mill argues that, if we assume self-interested individuals, then we may also assume that these individuals will, if given the chance, subjugate others to their will. As Thompson points out, if this is the case, then *any* relationship of subordination will follow the same logic: the interests of the persons subjugated will be subordinated to those who have control. In the case of a British woman in Thompson's time (and until the late nineteenth century) who upon entering marriage was stripped of her rights as an individual under the laws of coverture, her subordination to her husband's will was complete, at least by law. Thompson argues that, according to Mill's political logic, the husband's relationship with his wife will be purely instrumental, and since he has complete control, her happiness will be subordinated to his.[119] The situation of one who works for wages is similar: the worker's interests are subordinated to the interests of the person for whom they work or who pays their wages. In other words, the worker is not working for their own happiness, but for the happiness of the employer; thus, the worker's own happiness can be said to be diminished in favor of the owner's. Women's subjugation to men means that the happiness of half the adult population is subjugated to the happiness of the other half. Of this other half, if we then add all the men who work for wages, clearly the vast majority of the (adult) population finds themselves in subordinate relationships of one sort or another.

In fact, Thompson recognizes the connection between the subjugation of women and other forms of oppression: "The penalty of injustice to women is...the justification...of similar injustice from men to men."[120] Where one person or group both asserts and effects superiority over another group, who will be the ones to exercise judgment about the rightness of their actions? "Such are to be the judges in the last resort of the political rights of women—*men!*"[121] So it is with workers, colonial subjects, and slaves. Thompson draws an interesting parallel between women's condition and that of slaves and colonial subjects in his discussion of the marriage contract. He begins by noting that a contract is understood to be a voluntary agreement between the parties. He notes, "As little as slaves have had to do [with] the enacting of slave-codes, have women...had to do with...that most unequal and debasing code, absurdly called the *contract* of marriage." Against the view that women freely enter into marriage, and therefore voluntarily accept the terms of the contract, he points, in a tone dripping with irony, to "happier times of East India monopoly" when, "under the shield of mercantile political power, the poor people were kindly told, 'They were at liberty to buy or not to buy.' But if they did not buy, the trifling inconvenience of the alternative was, that they must starve." So it is with the marriage contract: "[T]he great majority of adult women must marry on whatever terms their masters have willed, or starve."[122]

That women might benefit in some superficial ways from marriage Thompson does not deny. He notes that

> [t]he ox is better fed when the master is rich—so far the common interest extends—but wherefore? Because it is the interest of the master that the ox should be fattened as speedily as possible.... The *permanent* interest of the ox, that of health and long life, is sacrificed. So with respect to all other beings.... The interest of each of them, is promoted, in as far only as it is coincident with, or subservient to, the master's interest.[123]

On the other hand, if a true "identification of interests" did exist, there would be no need for laws to assign control to one of the parties; neither would require power over the other.[124]

Thompson continues on to reject Mill's basic premise that people are by nature exploitative. While Mill, one of Bentham's most ardent disciples, deploys a version of the theory of utility that highlights the self-interest of rulers (what Bentham calls "sinister interest") as the problem that must be overcome in any system of government, Thompson argues from Bentham's fundamental psychological principle that the basic rule of human nature is "simply the desire of happiness and aversion to misery," which, in its pure form, comes "without any wish, kindly or malignant, to others.... It is neither an original, nor an universal principle of human beings to trample on, any more than it is to promote, the happiness of others."[125] To argue, as Mill does, that Bentham's hedonic principle is egoistic is to conflate self-interestedness with selfishness, but (as was discussed above) Thompson rejects this conflation. For one group of people to abuse or misuse their power over others, they must be "shut out from the moral knowledge requisite to show them the identity of their real comprehensive interest with that of their fellow creatures and ... divested of those dispositions or habits of sympathy necessary to enable to act according to their knowledge."[126] The opposition of interests is a product of the conditions within which we live and an instance of the ways in which our character is shaped by social institutions. So Thompson admits, "*Under the existing and all past circumstances of society,* Mr. Mill's proposition is doubtless correct as applied to the immense majority of men."[127] However, "Were knowledge and benevolence so increased and improved ... that all men saw their interest in tracing the consequences of their actions on the happiness of others as well as on their own, and that they were disposed to regulate their actions by this knowledge ... men would not wish for power over each other."[128]

The pain of suffering that must be endured in subordinate relationships is not, in Thompson's view, the only way in which this form of inequality undermines utility. Indeed, he argues that, in marriage, "The happiness of both [husband and wife] is sacrificed."[129] The husband's mastery over his wife means that,

> He surrenders the delights of equality, namely those of esteem, of friendship, of intellectual and sympathetic intercourse, for the vulgar pleasure of command.... [T]he whole moral structure of the mind of *man* is perverted.... He has been rendered incapable of considering the effects of his actions on all whose interests they may reach. He calculates their effects with reference to himself alone.[130]

The exercise of this nearly unlimited power "necessarily hardens the heart and destroys sympathy for those subjected to it."[131] Thus, he says to women, "As your bondage has chained down man to the ignorance and vices of despotism, so will your liberation reward him with knowledge, with freedom and with happiness."[132]

Conditions for a Real Identity of Interests

Despite his condemnation of Mill's assertion of an identity of interests between women and men, Thompson argues that the conflict of interests arises not due to any natural opposition between individuals, but because of the nature of the institutions within which they must relate to one another. Freed of institutional constraints and given "perfect wisdom and benevolence, the interests of all individuals... are involved in or identified with those of others." However, given the actual state of society, "individuals are not perfectly wise or benevolent," instead considering it to be in their interest to seek their own benefit even if it is at the expense of the greater good.[133] In fact, Thompson argues for a universal identity of interest "between all human beings of all nations, were they enlightened enough... to perceive it." The same could be said of a "political community." Indeed, the smaller the grouping, the stronger the identity of interests. However, he argues that we should not be misdirected by the easy assertion of this identity at a superficial level. "It is the *general* happiness of the family, as it is of the town, the province, the nation, the universe, that [there is] as great a quantity of the articles of wealth and all other means of happiness as possible.... But this general interest attained, a second question springs up as to the *distribution* of these means of happiness." So, in considering the economics of happiness, mere aggregate measures are meaningless if they do not reflect distribution. A passage quoted in the last chapter deserves to be repeated (and extended) here: "There is no such thing as a general, abstract, happiness. All happiness is made up of that of individuals.... Let wealth and all other means of happiness exist in ever such profusion... little is done as to happiness, until these *means* are rightly *distributed*."[134]

This idea, that any reference to the general happiness must take into account the happiness of individuals, is very similar to Bentham's passage in the *IPML* that reminds us that the community is a fictitious entity composed of individuals, although the point seems somewhat different.

Bentham is isolating the members of the community, insisting that their interests as individuals need to be considered separately from the interests of all other individuals in the aggregation of interests by legislators. Thompson, on the other hand, is reminding us that the community is composed of individuals who cannot be considered in isolation from one another.

The argument cited in the foregoing, from the *Appeal*, is primarily a response to Mill's claim regarding men's subordination of women. But Thompson extends this to argue that an identity of interests is impossible in capitalist society: "[T]he object of capitalists, is not to increase the general capital of the community, but to make most productive of profit to themselves... the real interest of the capitalist... is always and necessarily opposed to the interest of the laborer."[135] Identity of interest *is* possible, however, once the institutional structures of power that create and enforce division are removed. In the context of the *Appeal*'s argument about the lack of identity of interests between women and their male overseers he says, "To produce a real identity of interest between any two individuals; first, all power to injure or molest must be taken away equally from both; next, benevolence and reason must have been so comprehensively cultivated by both, that they shall both perceive that it is in their mutual interest to promote in every thing the real happiness of each other."[136] In the context of society as a whole, this means the elimination of private property, competition, and the unequal distribution of wealth (and the political power that comes with it). Eliminating these should produce a true identity of interests, as opposed to the supposed identity that James Mill refers to between women and the men who control their lives. Any condition under which one person is able to exercise power over another is a condition in which it is impossible to speak of an identity of interests. As Thompson puts it, "if [an] identity existed, there would be no need of power to enforce obedience."[137] The only benefit that comes from the subordination of one person to another is the latter's:

> For if the interests were identical, what could be gained by either party by reserving the power of control over the actions of the other? Subjection to such controlling power being itself one of the greatest sources of human helplessness and misery. The mere reserving the use of the exercise of such a power... is a demonstration, that... there

necessarily must arise occasions when views of interest of the parties must differ, and when of course the interests of the subjected party must in the opinion of that party suffer.[138]

The primary cause of this division is the private accumulation of property, so the elimination of private property—in other words, collectivizing property—and removing the division enables interests to be collectivized: "All their property is in joint possession, and indissolubly linked up with the happiness of each other."[139]

The Natural Laws for the Distribution of Wealth

Ultimately, Thompson's point in articulating his critique of subordination and the system of individual competition is not simply to point out its flaws, but to lay the basis for his argument for the system of mutual cooperation that would be superior in all respects. The first step in doing this is to lay out what he sees as the natural laws for the distribution of wealth—natural in the sense that no coercion, whether direct or indirect, is required to support them.[140] "By natural laws of distribution," Thompson says, "enlightened political economists do mean, or ought to mean, those general rules or first principles, on which all distribution of wealth ought to be founded, in order to produce the greatest aggregate mass of happiness to the society ... producing it."[141] In his preface to the *Inquiry* he notes that James Mill, in his *Elements of Political Economy*, argues that if these "*natural laws* of distribution were allowed to operate freely" it would produce circumstances such that "Society would ... be seen in its happiest state,"[142] but Thompson notes that these natural laws are "no where developed," in Mill or elsewhere.[143] His attempt to do so takes up the 178-page first chapter of his *Inquiry*, about one-quarter of the book, and is the centerpiece to his political economics.

Thompson's natural laws (there are three) should be easily recognizable from the discussion thus far. The first of these is that workers must have the full produce of their labor secured to them. This contributes directly to utility on the assumption that workers will be more productive if they enjoy all of the benefits of their labor. It is also indicated by the principle of security, as Thompson understands it: since labor is the source of value, then the surplus value should belong to the laborer. It is also based on the principle of equality, as all people have equal right to happiness, thus to the means of happiness, thus to wealth. "Whatever right, founded on its tendency to produce happiness... any one individual has... every other adult individual ought to have, for exactly the same reasons, the same right."[144]

The second law is that all exchange must be truly voluntary, for reasons discussed in the last chapter. To briefly restate those arguments in this context, this contributes directly to utility because Thompson assumes that people will be inclined to pursue their self-interest, and will only refuse to engage in exchange if they do not consider it to be in their interest. If an exchange is not voluntary, then it must be coerced in some way, and coercion is always damaging to utility, first because it reflects dissatisfaction with the terms of the exchange by the party being coerced, second because people are less likely to be as productive as they can be if they are being coerced, and last because the person doing the coercing will themselves lose out on the social benefits of voluntary exchange, in positive communication with a fellow-being. It again is connected to security, because involuntary exchange is always an affront to security, and equality, because in order for someone to be induced to act against their interest assumes that they are under someone else's power, who is dominant, which means that they do not have an equal relationship.

Finally, all labor itself should likewise be voluntary—that is, not coerced, whether by lack of access to capital or by destitution. This could be considered an extension or restatement of the mandate that all exchange be voluntary, since forced labor is, in effect, an exchange of labor for some good, whether wages or some other good. These three points Thompson calls "the *natural laws* of distribution [of wealth]... by which security, impartially applied to all, and not exclusively and hypocritically applied to a few, may become the firmest guarantee, instead of being the eternal opponent, of rational and healthful equality." Thompson claims that "[t]he literal and impartial execution of these laws of distribution, will produce... the greatest happiness to a community... and will ensure the greatest reproduction of wealth."[145] It is through these natural laws that Thompson is able to "*reconcile equality with security* [and] *reconcile just distribution with continued production.*"[146]

The natural laws for the distribution of wealth, Thompson asserts, will not only "produce to a *numerous class,* intellectual and moral culture, with the comforts and conveniencies of life, and therefore happiness: [they] would even produce these blessings to the *community at large.*"[147]

However, as he makes clear, they cannot function under the system of individual competition. Instead, they require a system of mutual cooperation.

The System of Mutual Cooperation

With the natural laws for the distribution of wealth established, Thompson has a clearly delineated set of principles subsidiary to utility: voluntarism, security, and equality. As noted above, these principles can only be realized within a system of mutual cooperation. The primary features of the system of mutual cooperation—in effect, an additional set of principles that operationalize the principles subsidiary to utility—are united effort/common property and democracy, established within the context of cooperative communities of between five hundred and two thousand persons. The community would collectively produce all the materials of its subsistence and comfort, with each individual contributing to the best of their ability (provision made for children, the elderly, and infirm whose ability to contribute is limited), and each taking from the collective produce what they require.[148]

The elimination of private property might seem contradictory given the requirement of ensuring security of the produce of labor to the worker. Thompson's answer to this is in the particular form for the collectivization of property. For Thompson, the elimination of private property does not imply its transfer to the state. Rather, property is to be held in common within the context of the cooperative community. Eliminating private property therefore does not constitute the further alienation of property—or what might be a more apt term here, wealth—from individuals. In the capitalist system wealth is alienated from those who produce it by the owners of capital; in a state-ownership model wealth is alienated from the producers to the state. In neither case do the producers exercise anything like direct control. In the cooperative community, however, the members of the community own the assets of the community and the produce of their collective labor is also owned by the community.[149] All members of the cooperative retain control on an equal basis with all the other members. No one's labor in the community serves to benefit any other specific member—rather, it benefits all of the members, and all members are involved in the labor of the community (with the proviso noted above). No one member retains complete control over any part of the "wealth" (explicitly avoiding the term *property* here) of the community against or even on behalf of any other fully vested member, but each retains an equal degree of control over all of it in its entirety. Each member can be said to retain full security in the produce of their labor, as they have full political rights within the community to participate in all decision making with respect to the common property.[150]

In Thompson's cooperative socialism, then, property is owned in common by the community. This is not to say that there would not be any possession of personal items. Thompson distinguishes between these and capital: personal items, or objects for consumption, are those which are used or held "*without any view to any further exchange.*" On the other hand, an object that is held not for consumption or use by the owner but is "capable of being made the instrument of profit" is considered capital.[151] Capital itself does not entirely go away under the system of mutual cooperation, but instead of being held by non-laborers for the purpose of increasing its value through the exploitation of labor, laborers use it to control the conditions of their labor—i.e., they control the means of production. Thus, when Thompson says, on the one hand, that there would be "capital without capitalists,"[152] and on the other that "all productive laborers should become capitalists,"[153] he is not contradicting himself, but arguing that there would not be a capitalist class distinct from a laboring class. In Marxian terms, the working class would be the universal class, except that Thompson is concerned first and foremost with relations within the cooperative community. Capital would not be held privately in the sense that individuals hold it. Rather, each group or cooperative community holds it collectively, such that no one member of the group can be thought of as having a greater interest in the enterprise than any other member. Net proceeds from the operation of an economic enterprise, then, would not be claimed by an individual or a small defined group of people who provide the capital and take as much as they can in profit, but by the producers themselves (who provided the capital themselves). Capital, rather than standing in opposition to and controlling labor, is an agent of and controlled by the community, in which all labor together.

One problem that Thompson never effectively addresses is the economic relationship among communities and with the society beyond. For the most part he anticipates that each community would be self-sufficient and autarkic, but he has little to say about what would happen under conditions of shortage or surplus. On the whole, he is rather sanguine about the communities meeting their subsistence needs.[154] In the *Inquiry* he shows a strong faith in the wisdom of the people to make the correct decisions about how to run their communities; the publication, six years later, of *Practical Directions,* a manual of sorts for starting communities, suggests that his faith was weakened if not lost. In any case, he doesn't consider the possibility of crop failures or other calamities that would undermine the viability of a community. He recognizes that communities may produce a surplus, of either agricultural or manufactured goods,[155] but he presents a fairly weak argument as to why the communities would not engage in competitive practices against each other, let alone with other producers in the market. As he sees it, the members of the communities would have beneficence so thoroughly ingrained in their character that they would only consider exchange on the basis of a direct exchange of labor value.[156] But he claims that surplus production in any great quantity is unlikely, because of "the inconvenience of production"[157]—in other words, given a choice between leisure time and the production of a surplus, most producers would choose leisure time. Therefore, there would never be more than minimal exchange either with other communities or the larger society.[158]

It could reasonably be argued that Thompson does not fully address the problems of private property because the community, considered as a "corporate" entity, claims exclusive rights to its property—in other words, the assets of the community are its private property. It differs from traditional notions because in this case the property of the community is not strictly divisible as in, say, a joint stock corporation. The community is not necessarily isolated from the community at large, but although he doesn't suggest that it should be isolated, at the same time Thompson never really addresses the question of the nature of the relationship between the cooperative community and the rest of society. Even if the cooperative communities would be predisposed to act benevolently toward one another, there is no reason to assume that they would not seek to improve their own welfare at the expense of those with whom they might exchange on the outside, for example by raising prices in order to reduce the amount of work they have to do to maintain a given standard of living, or to increase their level of comfort, or any of the other kinds of things a capitalist might want to do by raising their profit margins. In this sense, competition might be seen as valuable to keep these desires in check, but Thompson seems to think they simply would not be able to take hold, mostly because the benevolence cultivated within the community would prohibit it. Nonetheless, a critical perspective would reveal that his argument is rather weak in this respect.

Thompson's Utilitarianism

If Jeremy Bentham was the father of utilitarianism, then Thompson's theory might be seen as more of a nephew than a direct descendant. Both hold "the greatest happiness" as a bedrock principle, but while there are important similarities, the difference between their perspectives on happiness is reflected in the subsidiary principles, and in particular the relationship between security and equality. This connects, in turn, to their ideas about political economy and the nature of social institutions.

In Bentham's view, the greatest happiness is the product of individuals independently pursuing their self-interest, although their doing so is conditioned by the political institutions of the state, which may set particular conditions for the functioning of social institutions. In general, Bentham's emphasis is on these individuals, understood either separately or, for example in his discussions of political economy, in the aggregate. Of course, he understood that for various reasons—feelings of sympathy and benevolence, for example—people would seek the well-being of others besides themselves, but even these were fundamentally rooted in self-interest. Part of the function of law was to put some limits around the pursuit of self-interest in order to inhibit (although it could not entirely prevent) one person from causing excessive harm to other people. Understood in this way, Bentham's political economics has to do with the mechanics of people seeking their self-interest and the role of the state with respect to the conditions within which they do that. The subsidiary principles, then, are meant as a guide to legislators to assist them with decision making at the macro level, not as a guide to citizens in pursuing their self-interest at the micro level.

Thompson's political economics is much more deeply rooted in his utilitarianism. The greatest happiness, not the individual pursuit of self-interest, is the first premise of his approach. Also, unlike Bentham, Thompson is focused first and foremost on the institutions that structure social relations, understood broadly. The institutions of daily life, through which people are engaged in production, distribution, and exchange, are every bit as important—maybe even more important—than the institutions of the state. Thompson's political economics, then, are concerned with the way social institutions may be structured so as to ensure the greatest happiness. Like Smith, Ricardo, and other political economists of his day, Thompson is interested in the means by which national wealth might be maximized, because he saw this as vital for happiness, but unlike Smith, Ricardo, and the rest he does not presume market exchange and private property, so he is not interested in the determination of price and its relation to (exchange) value, because, unlike the others, he sees individuals who are always already social pursuing their self-interest from *within the context* of social institutions that structure their relationships, as opposed to independent individuals who interact with other individuals *through* social institutions.

For Thompson, the subsidiary principles of equality, security, and voluntarism, along with united effort/common property and democracy, form the basis for a set of social institutions that, in contrast to the institutions of the system of individual competition, establish relationships founded on cooperation and benevolence, which may therefore promote greater happiness in their effect on individuals' character and attitudes toward others. That democracy must be the basis for decision making in these institutions may be obvious, but it deserves closer exploration.

5
The Politics of Happiness and Democratic Principles

"'Democracy,'" as someone has pointed out, "is a relative term."[1] It comes in a variety of forms, some of which are, from one perspective or another, unrecognizable as democracy: one person's unruly mob may be another's democratic movement, while the United States, often held up as a paragon of democratic practice, has recently been referred to as an example of "inverted totalitarianism."[2] Underneath this plurality of forms is a basic division between the idea of democracy as a kind of institutional structure and democracy as a kind of action.[3] Theorists of the first type—who occupy the mainstream of democratic theory—are concerned with questions of governance, particularly (even exclusively) at the level of the state. The second type, which most often goes by the name of radical democratic theory, is concerned with the interactions between individuals and groups within society. These two perspectives are not mutually exclusive, as mainstream theorists may be concerned with social interaction, and radical democrats are often concerned with the function and effects of democracy at the level of the state.[4]

Bentham, as we will see, is firmly in the mainstream.[5] His attitude toward democracy is strongly shaped by his consequentialism: it is not an end in and of itself, but a means to secure "good government." Indeed, he was not always an advocate of democratic practices. It wasn't until the latter part of his career—the late 1810s at the earliest[6]—that he became committed specifically to the idea of representative democracy as the best form of government. But even then the basic structure of the political system never changed in his mind: There were rulers, and there were the ruled, and what was important was to ensure that the interests of the former were aligned with (or subordinated to) the interests of the latter. The best means by which that could be accomplished, he came to believe, was by enabling the ruled to hold the rulers accountable through a system of representative democracy with "universal suffrage."[7] Only in this way could the individual interests of the electorate be aggregated and reflected in the political system. Once he came to those conclusions he was a forceful advocate of representative democracy. Still, democracy is always only a means to an end, and given the emphasis in his late constitutional writings on what he called "securities against misrule," he retained no small measure of distrust even for the products of a representative system.

Although Thompson was concerned with the structure of institutions, he clearly belongs in the radical camp. As we saw with regard to utility, he makes use of some of Bentham's concepts but produces a theory that is substantially different. The central position accorded to equality and the recognition of the crucial role played by social institutions in establishing the living conditions of the community means that all social institutions—indeed, all social relationships—can be understood on political terms. These relationships can be understood as authoritarian where one party is subordinate to another, or as democratic where the two parties interact on the basis of equality. As a result, democracy is an integral part of Thompson's theory, and democratic practices are seen as embedded in or essential to the structure of social institutions at every level. While Thompson does not exclude the use of representative bodies even at the level of the cooperative community, these only serve to formalize the deliberation and decision making that is a regular part of community life.

To some extent, the difference between Bentham and Thompson can be explained by reference to their primary object of concern or what might be called the level of analysis: Bentham's work begins with his interest in reforming the British legal system and proceeds from there to the reform of the political structure of the state. Thompson is primarily concerned with the conditions in which people live, or more broadly with political economics, so he is more interested in the structure of social institutions. As with his conception of happiness and his theory of utility, Thompson provides no direct statement of his theory of democracy that one can refer to, so the elements must be drawn out and pieced together.

Because Thompson was already committed to democratic ideas prior to his association with Bentham, he is not so dependent on Bentham's conceptual framework; still, there exist some important parallels, as will be seen in what follows.

Bentham and Representative Democracy

In some ways, what is referred to as Bentham's theory of democracy is really a theory of governance with representative democracy as the preferred form of selecting rulers. There are two principal aspects to Bentham's mature theory: first, that rulers act in their own interest and cannot be trusted to act in the best interests of their subjects (so-called sinister interest), and second, that the people must be sovereign—in other words, that the people themselves must be seen as the ultimate political authority. These can be seen as extensions of Bentham's theory of utility operating at the macro level: as the fundamental basis for moral judgment, the greatest happiness of the greatest number must be the primary objective or goal of any system of government. If it is the people's happiness that is to be maximized, then clearly the state must be managed, or administered, in the people's interest. The legislature must be subordinate to the will of the people, even as it acts, indirectly, to shape that will. Put another way, in Bentham's view, good government requires that the sovereign power (legislative, executive, and judicial) be dependent upon—and therefore accountable to—the people. The only means to ensure this is representative democracy.

Bentham was equivocal about democracy in his early work. In the early phase of the French Revolution he quite actively promoted democratic governance and universal suffrage, including for women, with literacy the only requirement.[8] However, his thoughts were explicitly directed at France: he was, as he put it, "a royalist in London...a republican in Paris,"[9] and he felt that "such radical measures [were not] necessary in England,"[10] where "equal representation has already been accomplished, more or less,"[11] and its political institutions already incorporated the elements he saw as necessary: "Liberty of the press, the absence of arbitrary executive power, and the impartial administration of justice."[12]

By the time of the regicide and the French declaration of war on Britain in 1793, Bentham had begun to express views that are clearly antidemocratic. Simply put, he felt that the people could not be trusted to exercise the judgment necessary to be participants in government.

In Bentham's words, "The people are all *will*—they have no reason, no understanding," and democracy only worked in America because, as most men were farmers, "their business keeps them separate and quiet."[13] The British system, which had showed over the years the capacity to reform when necessary and that it could be responsive to public opinion, ensured that, by strictly limiting suffrage, government was in the hands of the "well-informed classes."[14] Eventually, however, his own experience and his ongoing pursuit of legal reform led him to become a supporter of radical parliamentary reform, even in Britain.[15] The first step of this was the discovery of sinister interest.

Sinister Interest and the Sovereign

A fairly common principle of political theory is the idea that governors must govern in the interests of the people, or in other words, that the sovereign must rule in the interest, or for the benefit of, the people.[16] The fiduciary duty of the sovereign should not be confused with popular sovereignty. There is nothing inherently democratic about the idea that sovereign power must be exercised for the benefit of those who are subject to it, as the idea of a trust may hold true as much of a monarch or a dictator as for an elected official. In fact, it can be seen as largely paternalistic: the subjects are to be taken care of by the rulers, an arrangement that always leaves the former subordinate to the latter.

Initially, Bentham was content to argue that the sovereign power "can never be other than fiduciary,"[17] and, while he saw the need for legal reform, as long as the regime kept its fiduciary responsibility in view, there was no need for constitutional reform. Over time, and with the repeated failure of his reform efforts, he began to suspect that there was a sinister power at work—what he came to call "sinister interest."[18] Technically, the term refers to the idea that the promotion of some people's happiness could only come at the expense of the rest—that is, of the greater part of the community.[19] In practical terms, sinister interest is the antithesis of fiduciary duty, as it means that powerful elites—both those in government and, in a restricted electoral system, the people who vote to put them there—will tend to put their own self-interest ahead of the interests of the general public.

Bentham's discovery came in an essay, *The Elements of the Art of Packing*, in which he considered how public officials were able to pack juries in libel cases in order to win convictions, thereby silencing their critics. Since reform required the exposure of corruption in order to move public opinion and enable the people to hold its government accountable, this kind of jury packing constituted a serious barrier to change. While his immediate concern was the legal system, he recognized that sinister interest could exist in "any or all" of the "several departments of government, howsoever carved out and distinguished," wherever "*abuses* exist, from which the persons, or some of the persons, by whom those departments are respectively filled, derive... in some shape or other, a sinister advantage."[20] Sinister interest, then, was a force that could affect its corrupting influence at all levels of government.

Bentham draws a distinction between the "right and proper" and the "actual" end of government: the government should properly be concerned with the "greatest happiness of all the individuals of which [a political community] is composed" as opposed to its actual functioning, corrupted by sinister interest, which promotes the "greatest happiness of those... by whom the powers of government are exercised."[21] Clearly, the only force capable of exposing the actual ends of government, the free press, was of great importance in revealing the workings of sinister interest. But what Bentham came to realize was that a people could not hold its government accountable if it could not see or hear of abuses kept hidden by a government able to quash the voices of its critics. So, if Bentham had earlier believed that fundamental reform of the British political system was unnecessary because of "[l]iberty of the press, the absence of arbitrary executive power, and the impartial administration of justice," his recognition of sinister interest at work in the packing of juries (not to mention the activity that led to the underlying legal action) undermined this faith.

In response to sinister interest, Bentham came to argue for what he called, in one context, "securities against misrule." Of these, he considered official aptitude to be the most important, made up, as it were, of three parts: moral, intellectual, and active. Moral aptitude he sees as a negative quality, the absence of motivation to pursue one's own self-interest before that of others. While recognizing the presence of fellowship and social concern, he felt that constitutional law must presume the predominance of sinister interest. Moral aptitude, then, must be forced by organizing the institutions of government so as to produce it—in other words, by making it so that those in power are not capable of using that power in a way that would further their own interests at the expense of the common interest, or rather, the pursuit of their own interest *requires* that they further the common interest. The difficulty is getting them to see this, which is where "intellectual aptitude"—the knowledge and judgment necessary to recognize their fiduciary duty—comes into play. Finally, "active aptitude" simply refers to the conscientious performance of duty.[22]

The next question, of course, is how to guarantee official aptitude. Important here is a second security against misrule, popular sovereignty. Apparently, the assignment of fiduciary duty is insufficient to ensure that the sovereign would act in the interest of the people—especially if the people are not themselves sovereign. While in his early work he placed both sovereignty and sovereign power in the hands of the government,[23] Bentham came to understand that official aptitude required that sovereignty itself be held by the people, and in his later writing, he was very clear: the people are sovereign, and they are to exercise their sovereignty in a democratic fashion. He articulates his view in the *Constitutional Code*: "The sovereignty is in *the people*. It is reserved by and to them. It is exercised, by the exercise of the Constitutive authority.... To the Constitutive Authority [the people acting in their capacity as the sovereign] it belongs ... to depute and *locate* [i.e., elect] ... the members composing the Legislative [i.e., the legislative authority, or legislature]; and eventually ... to dislocate [i.e., recall] them."[24] The specific features by which representative government should be constituted were through "*Secrecy* [of the ballot], *universality* [of suffrage], *equality* [of the vote], *and annuality of suffrage* [one-year terms of office, or elections held annually]."[25] However, while the people may be sovereign, their direct exercise of sovereign power itself was to be very limited, extending only to the constitution of the legislative body. The people are "not to give direction, either *individual* or *specific*, to [the legislature's] measures."[26] As will be seen below, this did not mean that between elections they must be silent. But before I discuss the informal political role of the public, it is worth considering the implications of the formal structure he articulates.

Bentham's Instrumental Theory of Democracy: Elite Rule and Official Aptitude

What is significant about Bentham's turn to a representative system is that he clearly did not consider it to be a good of and by itself. To be sure, he thought that representative democracy was the only means by which government could be ensured to pursue the happiness of the people in general.[27] But democracy in his theory is clearly instrumental, based not on democratic principles but on what I referred to in the last chapter as the macro principle of utility.

While Bentham's theory may be democratic, in many ways it is more a theory of governance than a democratic theory. It is, as Rosen says, "a theory of elites." Rosen continues, "A major thesis underlying his argument is that all rulers, however they are chosen, form a class apart by virtue of their wealth and political power and are potentially at odds with the people whose happiness they are supposed to secure."[28] Democracy, in the form of periodic elections, is a mechanism that links the ruled to the rulers and makes the rulers dependent upon, and accountable to, the ruled. The sovereign (the people) does not exercise its sovereign power except in a very limited sense. It is not a system by which the people can be said to rule themselves; it is democratic only in the sense that the people, understood fairly broadly, are the ones who determine who the rulers will be. Elite rule, however styled, is not rule by the people.

A consequence of the instrumental character of Bentham's theory is that the design of the system of representation is based not on democratic principles but on Bentham's ideas about what had the greatest utility value. The issue of suffrage provides an important example. Bentham argues that there is no need to exclude criminals and the insane, because the former would not be released from confinement in order to vote, and the latter would be too small in number to affect the outcome.[29] However, while he argued for the inclusion of women at one point early in his career, at least with regard to France,[30] their exclusion is a more consistent theme. In the *Theory of Legislation,* he argues that women should be excluded because they could not be presumed to have "a sufficient degree of knowledge"[31]—although apparently this was not a concern with regard to men. By1809, when he began to advocate parliamentary reform in Britain, he argued for suffrage rights based on the "payment of direct taxes," which Schofield points out was "in effect the equivalent of householder suffrage."[32]

By 1817 in the *Radical Reform Bill,* Bentham began to argue for what he calls "virtual universality"—which explicitly excluded women as well as children.[33] But while he excoriated Mill for his failure to provide an argument to support his claim that women could be excluded from the franchise,[34] not long after this, Bentham himself excluded women from the "Constitutive Authority" in the *Constitutional Code*. Despite a spirited argument for their inclusion, he ultimately rejects the idea for fear that it would derail the possibility of other reforms being implemented: "There is no political state that I know of in which, on the occasion of any new constitution being framed, I should think it expedient to propose [suffrage for women].... The contest and confusion produced...would entirely engross the public mind, and throw improvement, in all other shapes, to a distance."[35]

On this account, it seems that the exclusion of women arises not from any defect in his theory but from practical political considerations. Essentially, Bentham justifies his position by saying that the greatest happiness requires constitutional reform that expands the franchise and makes legislators accountable to the electorate. If it is necessary to exclude half the adult population to accomplish it, so be it, since some expansion is better than none at all. What matters is official aptitude, which is the consequence of a democratic system, not the principle of democratic participation. Democratic principles are not the point. The principle that matters is the greatest happiness of the greatest number. He comes to believe that representative democracy is the only means for achieving that end, and that it is incumbent upon the architect of the constitution to design the system in such a way as to produce the intended effect.

It may be said, then, that democracy in Bentham's political theory amounts to a third- or even fourth-order concern: the first concern is the greatest happiness of the greatest number, which requires good laws. To get good laws requires establishing a system for good governance, which requires maximizing official aptitude and minimizing expense. Democracy, then, is instrumental to good governance—and to the ultimate end, the greatest happiness—only insofar as it ensures official aptitude and minimizes expense. Schofield admits that "[t]he system of representative democracy was not an end in itself—the end was the greatest happiness—but it was an indispensable means to that end, in that it was only under such a system of government that effective measures could be implemented to secure the appropriate aptitude of officials and minimize the expense of government."[36] There may be no question that by the later part of his career Bentham wholeheartedly embraced the idea of representative democracy. However, this should not be confused with the acceptance of democratic principles for their own sake.

The Role of the Public: The Public Opinion Tribunal

While the people might not have a direct role in the legislature, they are not absent from Bentham's theory of governance. Schofield describes "a dynamic process, whereby open communication or dialogue between legislators and people would benefit both parties" as the people gain confidence in the capacity of their legislators, and the legislators learn the "real wishes of the people."[37] This takes place through what Bentham refers to as the "Public Opinion Tribunal." In his early *Essay on Political Tactics,* a treatise written primarily for the French Estates General, he says:

> The public compose a tribunal, which is more powerful than all the other tribunals together.... [T]hough this tribunal may err, it is incorruptible;... it continually tends to become enlightened;... it unites all the wisdom and all the justice of the nation;... it always decides the destiny of public men; and... the punishments which it pronounces are inevitable.[38]

By the time of the *Constitutional Code* the idea was much more formalized. The tribunal includes not only those who wield constitutive power (i.e., voters), but "[a]ll those classes, which... stand excluded from all participation in such supreme power," including women and even members of "other political communities" who might have some interest in the question under consideration. Not considered merely an outlet for the release of social tensions, Bentham refers to public opinion as "a system of law, emanating from the body of the people," not unlike the common law, which is "not sanctioned by the Legislative authority otherwise than by tacit suffrance." Although it may have no formal presence, its importance cannot be overstated: "To the pernicious exercise of the power of government it is the only check; to the beneficial, an indispensable supplement. Able rulers lead it; prudent rulers lead or follow it; foolish rulers disregard it."[39]

Bentham recognizes that the Public Opinion Tribunal is an amorphous object, a "purely fictitious and verbal entity" that nonetheless "possesses the substance of reality." Unlike the legislature, the opinion of the tribunal, which is made up of the public as a whole, will always reflect the wishes or interests of the people, or at least the majority of the people. Thus, it can only ever lead in the direction of the greatest happiness.⁴⁰ The tribunal functions primarily through the power of reputation: a public official condemned by it will lose whatever benefits they might have otherwise expected to receive from the public, and might instead experience positive pains.⁴¹ Beyond what he refers to as the "moral sanction" entailed in the loss of reputation itself, Bentham isn't very clear about the nature of these consequences, but we might imagine that it would entail a loss of authority and, for elected officials, the possibility of not being reelected.

Given its stated importance, the Public Opinion Tribunal seems underdeveloped in Bentham's work. Although he does consider some particular "disadvantages," in particular the existence of the "two intestine sets of enemies [of the greatest happiness] . . . the ultra-indigent class of malefactors . . . and the ultra-opulent," he considers their capacity to undermine the tribunal to be fairly limited, and in any case "the body politic" can be expected to "outgrow" the disease.⁴² Beyond this, he does not discuss why those people excluded from the constitutive authority (e.g., women who are denied the franchise) would receive any attention from public officials, except as they might be able to influence the men who are able to vote. The issue of women's voice is, in fact, only a part of a larger problem, which is that Bentham does not recognize the existence of power differences within the society at large that amplify the voices of some while tending to silence the voices of others. It seems that Bentham is as willing to accept inequality in the institutions of politics (including the tribunal) as he is in economic institutions.

Thompson: Democracy as a Social Practice

Arguably, democracy also plays an instrumental role in Thompson's theory to the degree that it supports the fundamental premise of his theory of utility: that the moral measure of any principle, premise, act, or system is the degree to which it contributes to the greatest happiness of the greatest number. To suggest that democracy is instrumental to utility in a utilitarian theory of democracy is, in a way, tautological, since every element in a utilitarian theory should be instrumental to the end of the greatest happiness. To suggest that democracy is not instrumental to utility in this way is to suggest that the greatest happiness is not the fundamental premise of Thompson's theory and that he is not, in fact, a utilitarian.⁴³ Indeed, this sort of instrumentality is not exclusive to utilitarianism, since the same could be said of a liberal theory of democracy that emphasizes individual rights, where democracy is justified as the best protection for those rights.

Thompson doesn't use the word *democracy* all that much, although *self-government* appears with some frequency in the *Inquiry*. In his discussions of representative systems he does not use the terms *democracy* or *democratic,* simply referring to representation. His discussions of "self-government" rarely refer to representation; he uses it in some places to draw a contrast with, for example, systems of "arbitrary regulations and involuntary obedience."[44] "Self-government" is used to apply both to individuals as well as to the cooperative communities. In many ways, Thompson's most significant contribution to democratic theory can be seen in the way he situates individual self-government within the specific context of the cooperative communities, such that democracy becomes a principle of social interaction as much as an institutional mechanism for decision making.

The examination of Thompson's democratic theory begins with a look at the ways in which democracy plays an instrumental function in Thompson's theory. This is most strongly reflected in the way he discusses the educative effects of democratic practice, especially with regard to national governance. He also argues strongly for universal suffrage, although his arguments in this area mostly appear in the form of a critique of restricted suffrage, especially with regard to women but by extension to the vast majority of men. More of my attention, however, will be given to Thompson's argument for self-governance in the cooperative communities and the particular manifestation or mechanisms of self-governance. Finally, public opinion comes up in a way that is both quite similar and quite different from the role it plays in Bentham's theory.

Democratic Participation in Government as an Instrument for the Greatest Happiness

In a discussion of "the political evils of forced inequality of wealth," Thompson expresses his view of the primary object of government, which could have been lifted directly out of Bentham's work: "The object to be aimed at in legislation, to which every political as well as economical regulation should tend, is, to promote the greatest happiness of the community, i.e., of the greatest number of the community." But rather than Bentham's argument that members of the political elite must be held accountable to the electorate, Thompson argues that "the makers of these regulations should have a sympathy, a fellow-feeling, an identity of interest, with the community, that is to say, with the greater number of the community, for which the regulations are formed." Lacking this, leaders must be "under the real and bona-fide control of those whose interests they represent." Better yet, there should be both: "[I]s it not necessary for the security of the community that this *double* guarantee should be imposed? That *sympathy* and *accountability* should both . . . be required from those intrusted with the solemn charge of making laws and exercising the judicial and executive powers?"[45]

This "double guarantee" sets a fairly high standard. It should be noted that the sort of "sympathy" Thompson is referring to is not an abstract, paternal sympathy, but one that arises from an "identity of interest," the kind of identification that can only come from being a member of the group an elected official putatively represents.[46] Another way to put it is that all of the varying interests of the various groups of which a community is comprised should be represented in some way. It may help to explain his point by referring to a recent work with respect to what the authors call the "personnel" dimension of democratic representation, which, they say, "is important because the more demographically representative a political system is, the more likely it is that the interests of the basic groups of the social structure will be adequately and substantively represented. It is highly unlikely, for example, that a group of business leaders will accurately represent the interests of workers."[47] The basic requirement for this kind of representation is universal suffrage which, in Thompson's view, includes *all* members of the society, with the exception of children, but including all men and women, and of all races. In fact, Thompson goes so far as to suggest that within the context of the cooperative communities, even "children capable of forming an opinion" should be asked for their consent, at least in the community's developmental stages.[48]

Even with universal suffrage, Thompson expects little social improvement to come from its effects on legislators. The contrast with Bentham could not be stronger: The most significant changes would come about not from affecting elite attitudes, but through the educative effects of democratic practices:

A *very small part* of the blessings of just (universally elective and representative) government, will be found comprised in the amelioration of the characters of the national agents for matters of government, or even in the utility of regulations they make. By far the greater portion of these blessings will be found in the salutary effects produced by the exercise of political rights by the individuals of the community, *on their own characters,* in that acquisition of *knowledge, security,* and *enlarged sympathy* with indefinite numbers of their fellow-creatures . . . which the constant exercise of political rights has a necessary tendency to produce.[49]

It is not without reason, then, that Thompson's major discussion of political participation occurs in the *Inquiry* in a chapter on education. Thompson's arguments against inequality in education echo Smith's concern that where the division of labor is advanced it will make workers "as stupid and ignorant as it is possible for a human being to become."[50] As Thompson puts it, "the *general intellectual power*" of the working class is "enfeebled. His judgement, never exercised, pines and perishes."[51] Effectively, the opportunity to enjoy the intellectual pleasures that Thompson considers to be "higher" pleasures is diminished, as is the happiness of society.

Unlike Smith, however, Thompson extends his discussion to political institutions. He begins by noting that "men wielding the public force" have access to institutional means "to generate motives for the guidance of the actions of their fellow-creatures in subserviency to their wishes."[52] Similar to Bentham's notion of sinister interest, Thompson argues that "all human regulations tend to the exclusive interest of those who make them . . . no regulations tending to the *benefit of all* can be expected except where *all interested* are concerned in the formation of them." Using the division of labor as an analogy, he points out that just as machine operators need have no knowledge of the principles that underlie the work they perform, "So with a perfect system of laws made by other hands than those whose actions and interests they are to regulate. The laws may produce a mechanical effect, and the people may be drilled to act their particular parts of subordination." Thompson asks, "What is it that renders the lawmakers . . . statesmen, as they are called, men of more comprehensive views, of more improved intellectual power, than other men . . . ? What but the habit of exercising these powers? of exercising their judgement on these measures? of learning in the school of legislation and public action... what others are excluded from learning?" If we wish that all members of society be able to exercise such public judgment, be able to be "as intellectual as these few," there is but one method: "Give them a share in the making and the executing of the laws which concern their own welfare."[53]

In the *Appeal,* many of these same arguments are repeated. For example, he says that "the exercise of political rights afford the best opportunity for the exercise of the intellectual powers and enlargement of the sympathies of human beings." Without political rights, people "can never have enlargement of mind, they can never have expansive benevolence; because without them they can never pass through those *incidents* which are necessary to the unfolding of such qualities."[54] Certainly there exists some similarity between this and Wollstonecraft's argument that "it is a farce to call any being virtuous whose virtues do not result from the exercise of its own reason."[55]

Intellectual aptitude, which for Bentham is a part of official aptitude, is invoked by Thompson but, in contrast to Bentham, he applies it to the public at large, arguing for broad rights for political participation based on its educative effect. Intellectual aptitude, then, is seen as valuable because it tends directly toward the greatest happiness:

> Here then, by extending to the utmost possible degree the faculty of co-operating in the power of making, applying, and executing laws, we not only improve, nay create, intellectual aptitude in that department as well as in every other which the mind can exert itself, but give that intellectual power a necessarily favorable direction; while the basis of morality is laid by, showing the tendency of co-operation to produce universal good and happiness.[56]

He draws a contrast here with what goes on in systems based on subordinate relationships, where it is necessary to "keep the living part of the machinery ignorant of the secret springs which [regulate] the machine and... repress the general powers of their minds, lest by searching they should find out that they were made to toil for others, and that the fruits of their own labors were... taken away from them." But under conditions where those who work at the machines have the produce of their labor secured to them and have the opportunity to participate in the governance of the organization, "motives to exertion, instead of being diminished, would be increased," because the workers would see "that industry was as necessary to production as production to happiness, and obedience to the public regulations... was but obedience to what he had contributed to establish as most conducive to general good, meaning thereby the mass of individual good."[57] In other words, the best means for ensuring obedience to rules is to involve the people in the devising of those rules.

While Thompson's arguments seem to lead toward a very participatory, even direct system, it should be noted that in these passages he is specifically discussing the value of "political institutions... founded on the basis of self-government, by means of representation and election." The benefits of such a system would be most strongly felt by "widening and rendering local the basis of representation."[58] To this end he suggests the creation of local legislative assemblies, such that "every legal, general, act [would require] the approbation of a majority of these, besides the concurrence of the general representatives, one from each county or department, convened at the capital." Although he refers to these assemblies as representative, he also suggests that "[p]art of the unemployed portion of every seventh day... would be appropriately, peacefully, delightfully, and morally, employed, by all the people, in their share of these political and most interesting duties."[59] It is unclear whether he means that this discussion would be in the character of the Public Opinion Tribunal we saw above in the description of Bentham's theory, or if these assemblies would be somehow open to participation by all members of the community.[60]

The argument regarding the educative effects of democratic practices is circular in a sense, because participation requires a certain amount of educational attainment. Thompson argues strongly for universal education: "The very object is to enable a community to manage its own affairs, to make men equal to the task of self-government."[61] Thus, education is necessary in order to participate in government, and the act of participating in government provides the people with further education. Perhaps "circular" isn't the right term—perhaps an upward spiral is more appropriate, since education enables people to participate in government, from which they learn to use their judgment, which helps them recognize the importance of the acquisition of knowledge, which encourages them to learn more, which encourages their participation in public affairs. The purpose of education, Thompson says, is "to give the great majority of the community the requisite *knowledge* to discover the means, as they have already the *interest,* to pursue and attain their own greatest possible happiness."[62]

This circularity makes democracy in Thompson's theory less instrumental than Bentham's—if it can be said to be instrumental at all—because the end toward which it moves supports it in that movement. It is also less instrumental to the degree that, as means, it is more strongly associated with its end than in Bentham's theory. Where democracy is at least twice removed for Bentham (democracy being necessary for good government, which is necessary for the greatest happiness), in Thompson's theory it can be understood as a necessary condition, as its absence would break the cycle and undermine the whole system.

The Limited Value of Representation

In the *Inquiry,* Thompson makes some positive references to the American representative system, although always qualified by a condemnation of slavery and the political exclusion and subordination of women. For example:

> *There* was the only sound principle of just social institutions first solemnly proclaimed and acted upon.... [E]xcept in the iniquitous case of slaves ... and in the degradation of women ... [e]very exchange, either directly from the productive laborer himself or indirectly from his representative whom he has deputed to act for him, is there *voluntary.* Force is excluded. Representative and elective agents in every department of the state, and nothing but representation and election—such is the simple and vivifying principle of all just government, having the greatest possible sum of happiness of the whole community in view.[63]

In *Labor Rewarded,* published three years later, Thompson again praises representative systems, saying that "those who are friendly to the principles of co-operation, cannot reason consequentially, if they are not also friendly to equal political institutions."[64] But now his views of the American system have changed:

> But we are not to suppose, as did the simple French people at the time of their (as yet) abortive revolution, as do now the equally simple American

people, that the mere naming, by the industrious classes, of men to make public regulations to promote their happiness, would necessarily secure that object, or would even in any material degree secure to them the use of the products of their labor. In some parts of the United States of North America,—the Non-Slave States,—the industrious classes have for a great many years *almost* entirely named their representatives.... Yet the North American edition of representation (wretchedly imperfect no doubt... with its... upper house nest of oligarchy... its president king... its limitation of the rights of men to *white* men; its exclusion of women... from the rights of humanity...) has not secured to the American industrious classes, a much greater portion of the products of their labor than the English system of privileged classes, and law-making and office-holding in contempt of delegation, has procured for the best-paid of the English Industrious classes.[65]

Part of the problem Thompson identifies is that "knowledge [is not] equally diffused and the representatives [are] of the idle or lawyer classes," but more fundamental is that "the principle on which the labor of their industrious classes... is conducted, being that of individual competition, the root of inequality and wretchedness remains."[66] The competitive system breeds inequality, and this inequality undermines democracy. Much of his explanation for this can be found in the *Inquiry*.[67]

Thompson makes the now-common observation that with great wealth comes great power, and those with wealth use this power to exert control over the political system, particularly with the goal of protecting their wealth. Thompson's version of this is somewhat different from most: "It is one of the strongest and most unavoidable propensities of those who have been brought up in indulgence, to abhor restraint, to be uneasy under opposition, and therefore to desire *power* to remove these evils of restraint and opposition. How shall they acquire this power?... [T]hey endeavour every where to seize on, to monopolize, the *powers of government*."[68] It seems almost involuntary, as Thompson describes it: "The necessity of their condition forces on them this career in preference to every other, as well to preserve what they have, by whatever means, acquired, as to fence themselves round with new securities against the jealousies and intrusions of the mass of the community."[69] Government, then, turns into just so many "expedients for perpetuating property... to perpetuate their superior *power* to command the means of happiness, and to repress the equal and just competition of the rest of the community."[70]

The problem with representative institutions, then, is that they place power in the hands of one group of people, whose object it becomes to protect and perpetuate their power. "The radical defect in the constitution of society, that which must necessarily engender every other evil, is the excessive inequality of wealth. Wherever this radical evil is permitted to exist, no free institutions, no just laws can be made."[71] In other words, he is concerned about the ability of the wealthy to control the political system—a problem that was even more pronounced in his day, when all others were excluded, than in our own.[72] Another part comes from the separation of the rulers and the ruled, and the recognition that it is in the interest of the rulers to devise rules in order to perpetuate their rule. This can be seen by revisiting his argument against James Mill's claim that men alone should have the franchise, shifting the argument to consider representative government more generally.

Mill argues that men, in Thompson's words, "are necessarily inclined to use for their own exclusive advantage whatever power they can acquire over the actions of their fellow-men."[73] Thompson argues that this premise is, in fact, false, because by the principle of utility men (and women) are only really concerned with their own happiness, and that this does not imply that they will seek to control others—if they recognize that the best means for achieving happiness for themselves involves seeking the happiness of others, then they will do so. That they subordinate others to their own interests, and the degree to which they do so, is a product of their circumstances: "*Under the existing and all past circumstances of society,* Mr. Mill's proposition is doubtless correct as applied to the immense majority of men: while these or similar circumstances operate upon them, men will, almost universally, use power for their own exclusive, obvious and immediate, benefit."[74]

This argument can be brought together with Thompson's argument regarding the destructive effects of competition to show that systems that rely on the competitive election of representatives may be problematic on two levels: First, to the extent that economic inequality translates into political power, those with greater wealth will be inclined to use their economic power to capture and exercise political power to their own benefit, which means, effectively, ensuring the maintenance of those institutional structures that protect and perpetuate—even increase—their wealth. Call it "sinister interest" if you like, but it is a structural feature of the system. If this were all there was to it, then under a system of perfect competition, which could theoretically lead to a "natural distribution of wealth" and something like perfect equality, representative systems could work effectively to the benefit of all, assuming a universal franchise. Thus, he points to the United States as a positive example, where (at least at the time of the *Inquiry*), as far as he could tell there was near-universal (male) suffrage and greater economic equality. By the time he wrote *Labor Rewarded*, however, his views had changed. There, he cites problems of insecurity for labor as undermining the representative system, but we might also recognize that the problem lies with the competitive system of election *itself,* because it becomes a competition for power, and it is in the nature of competition that those who win—those who gain power—will seek to perpetuate their power, whether or not it contributes to the greatest happiness, turning the notion of a level playing field into little more than a rhetorical strategy.

Thompson certainly saw representative institutions as a great step forward from monarchy and feudalism, but he also saw that they were not immune from the problems of force and fraud. However, as has already been seen, for Thompson the greatest happiness has steep requirements: chief among them are security, voluntarism, and equality. These could not be realized under a system based on competition. Where they could be realized is within the cooperative communities, founded on the principles that utility requires. So, while members of these communities might elect a governing board, self-governance means much more than that.

Equality and the Context of Democracy

In many ways, the most important of Thompson's contributions to political theory, and democratic theory in particular, come not from his critique of representation, but in his extension of democratic principles to the specific setting of the cooperative community, *outside* of—and alongside—the formal political institutions. To explore this, some groundwork must be laid using contemporary political theory before returning to Thompson.

Within mainstream democratic theory, those who consider democracy to be more than a matter of the presence of particular procedures (and even some who don't) generally consider equality to be a condition of democratic self-government.⁷⁵ Generally, the primary concern is formal equality, although it is a fairly common point of critique of late modern liberal capitalism that the inequality it engenders undermines democracy, where the advantages of wealth (and the disadvantages of poverty) enable some to have greater influence than others, or even most.⁷⁶ In the radical democracy literature, equality is a central concern, especially in the form of a critique of subordinate relationships such as those in the workplace, along with other forms of social subordination (for example, as arise in racial or sex-based hierarchies).

Equality comes in many different forms: formal (legal), economic, social, etc. Mainstream and radical democracy theorists generally agree that political equality is a necessary condition for democracy. In fact, democracy can be understood as the enactment of political equality: political equality put into practice is democratic practice.⁷⁷ A major difference between mainstream and radical democracy, then, is the scope of the domain of the political: for mainstream theorists, it is usually limited to the formal institutions of government, or what we might refer to as the civic domain, and political equality usually is limited to the formal political act of voting to elect representatives (ballot measures—direct democracy—are generally treated with suspicion). In radical democracy, the domain is expanded to include the social arena, particularly in the spaces where individuals interact on a regular basis: social institutions. As Mouffe puts it, radical democracy calls for "the radicalization and deepening of the democratic revolution—as the extension of the democratic ideals of liberty and equality to more and more areas of social life."⁷⁸ Another way of putting this is to say that mainstream theorists tend to—although by no means do they all—maintain respect for a strict division between public and private realms, while radical democrats challenge that division.⁷⁹

The radical democratic project can be understood as an attempt to extend the notion of equality as broadly as possible through the society. In terms that Thompson would clearly understand, Laclau and Mouffe propose that the "proliferation of antagonisms and calling into question of relations of subordination should be considered as a moment of deepening of the democratic revolution."⁸⁰ Referring to what the Greeks called *isonomia,* or political equality, Euben argues that "we must look below the state level in order to find ways and places to maximize the democratization of power."⁸¹ So, just as Foucault referred to all sites of the assertion of power as potential sites of resistance,[82] these may also be understood more positively as sites or spaces for democratization: where the relationships between individuals are shaped in some sense by dynamics of power, there exists the potential for the participants to be recognized as equals in a political sense. To be political equals means that each may have equal opportunity to affect—in other words, to participate in decision making about—the conditions of that space.

The nature of that space—the context of politics—then becomes a central question for democratic theory. If this is understood as some sort of "public" or "collective," then the determination of the public involved in that decision making determines the context being referred to. The question of "the people" is a familiar one in democratic theory,[83] and it can be understood very broadly and flexibly: a "collectivity" can be as small as two people. This means that we can even understand something like an intimate relationship on political terms: if its members relate to one another on the basis of equality, then it is democratic; if not, then "autocracy," "tyranny," or "slavery" become valid descriptors.[84] Also, the particular collectivity in question changes depending on the particular context of decision making or the set of interests being considered.

In effect, Thompson proposes the cooperative community as just such a democratic space, where its members are recognized as equal across as many domains as possible: political, social, economic, sexual, racial, religious, etc. He contrasts the cooperative community with capitalist society. Despite powerful arguments in the *Appeal* for political equality for women, he ultimately argues that the granting of political rights is insufficient for equality given social conditions that are premised on competition and inequality. Early in the *Appeal*, he says that the granting of political and civil rights "would not raise women to an equality of happiness with men: their rights might be equal, but not their happiness, because unequal powers under free competition must produce unequal effects."[85] Later, he argues that "it is only under the system of voluntary associated labor and exertion and equal distribution, that justice can have free scope, that the equal rights of all can prevail, and that women can become in intelligence, virtue and happiness, the equals of regenerated men."[86]

In the cooperative community, people relate to one another as equals, and the institution of the community is structured so as to ensure that equality. Because all hold membership on an equal basis, each with an equal ownership stake in the assets of the community, the landlord/tenant relationship doesn't exist; neither does the capitalist/worker relationship; men and women are considered equal partners, no one is subordinate to anyone else, and no one's happiness can be subordinated to anyone else's. The practice of equality—in other words, democratic practices—is, in a sense, free-floating, in that equality is present as a structural condition in each interaction between members of the community. This is quite different, however, from Wolin's idea of democracy as fugitive,[87] which seems to imply that it is on the run, that it needs to hide, and perhaps it only appears when called upon. Here it is ever-present. But while free-floating, equality and democratic practices are a part of the institutional structure, contained specifically within the institution of the cooperative community, and there is no guarantee that they will exist, at least in the same form, outside of the confines of the particular institution.

Self-Government, Public Opinion, and the Principle of a Virtuous Disposition

Democratic governance in Thompson's proposal for co-operative communities, in contrast to Owen's, is included as an inherent element: "[T]he government of the community shall be inherent in itself, in all its adult, male and female, members." In context, it is a statement about the community establishing committees "by election, or rotation, or seniority, or any other manner that may be proposed," with the membership entirely made up of the members of the community.[88] Thompson believes that individual members of the community will be self-governing in the sense that they will, even in the absence of "factitious" motives, undertake such actions as will tend to the benefit of the community, through what he calls the "principle of a virtuous disposition":

> [O]bstacles withdrawn, knowledge within their reach, and the greatest sum of happiness to all, the sole and avowed end of their association; is it within the scope of any rational probability, that such associated members should not perceive that the same motives which led them to mutual co-operation in essential matters, demand that in every minor pursuit they should seek the happiness of all by mutual kindness and good offices?[89]

Although it is only mentioned once in this brief passage, the operation of this principle is evident throughout his work. He argues, "The operation of the institutions of insecurity, ceasing, or being evaded, under the system of voluntary equality, the natural motives of sympathy, benevolence and public opinion, resume their empire." In fact, of the higher pleasures—sympathy, benevolence, and intellectual pursuits—the first two are "if possible, cheaper and more abundant than those arising from the exercise of the intellectual faculties. They are within the reach of all, and of every degree of intellectual power."[90] Within the context of the cooperative community, at least, the motives for selfish action are replaced by self-interest aligned with the community's interest. "Here private interest and public interest, here private virtue and public virtue, both as to the individual and the community, are one and the same: here interest and duty are united."[91] There is no need, therefore, for formal political institutions providing "factitious" motives either to promote pro-social action or to prevent antisocial action. Governance becomes little more than a way of solving coordination problems. In Thompson's view, no coercion would be required at all—although it is difficult to see "the power of expulsion" as anything other than a coercive threat.[92]

The self-governing nature of the cooperative community is also expressed through Thompson's ideas about the role of public opinion, which plays a similar sort of role as that played by the Public Opinion Tribunal in Bentham's system, while differing in the way it functions and in its effect. In Bentham's theory, the tribunal regulates the actions of political leaders via the mechanism of publicity. For Thompson, public opinion acts to regulate the actions of the members of the community themselves. In Thompson, as in Bentham, public opinion is open to all, although Thompson offers what might be a subtle critique of Bentham as he notes that "in these united communities, every member has a real available voice, and forms a part of that public opinion," while in "general society, the opinions of one class are rejected and ridiculed in mass by another."[93]

If Bentham's tribunal performs a democratic function whereby the people influence political leaders, then public opinion can be said to have a vertical, upward, and unidirectional operation from public to officials.[94] In the cooperative communities, on the other hand, its operation is horizontal, as it acts among the members of the community, all of whom interact with one another on an equal basis. As Thompson puts it, each person "has a daily and equal opportunity of influencing the formation of this opinion: he is one of the jury that compose it.... [I]n respecting the public opinion of the majority of the community, he does in fact no more than respect his own opinion" in the case where he is in the majority; where he disagrees with the majority opinion his consideration and respect for his companions in the community, his "habit of respectful sympathy with the moral sentiments of the great mass of the community, in whose happiness his own is bound up and included" will make him no less likely to comply.[95]

Thompson's ideas about public opinion could be interpreted as endorsing a kind of tyranny of the majority á la Tocqueville and Mill. Indeed, Thompson could be describing a situation in which, as Mill puts it, "the 'self-government' spoken of is not the government of each by himself, but of each by all the rest."[96] It is important to recall, however, that Thompson is describing the conditions within the particular context of the cooperative community, in contrast to Mill, who is discussing democratic governance at the national level, where "[t]he 'people' who exercise the power are not always the same people with those over whom it is exercised."[97] One of the reasons why Thompson limits the size of the community to two thousand persons is because this is, in his view, the largest size compatible with a high level of familiarity of each with all. The attitude of benevolence goes both ways: As much as those in the minority are expected to acquiesce to the majority, so the majority is expected to take the minority's views into consideration and involve them in their deliberations. "Voluntariness is the life principle of these associations, compulsion their death-warrant."[98]

Thompson also expects conflict to be limited in the cooperative community because of the absence of its principal causes, private property and competition among members. Further, ensuring an equal distribution of the fruits of the community's labor allows an identity of interests to form among the members.[99] This identity of interest is best understood as the opposite of sinister interest. As Thompson puts it, "'Tis sinister interest and the force and fraud by it engendered, that corrupt and brutalize public opinion." Sinister interest and its handmaidens force and fraud would have no place in the cooperative community.[100] Identity of interest engenders a high level of trust among the members of a community, which frees them from many of the restraints suffered under conditions of subjugation to sinister interest. Public opinion itself would be the only real enforcement mechanism: "The only guards, the only enforcing power is *public opinion,* the public opinion of the community. If this public opinion be formed of a very small majority, its force will be weak... and the expression of [opposing views] will but give rise to friendly discussions."[101] In some ways, this might appear to be the very epitome of a deliberative democratic system, where deliberation is understood as an integral element of the decision-making process of the community. "[I]n order to command usefully and permanently the voluntary actions of rational beings, fraud (or delusion) as well as force, must be excluded. The real interests of the agents must be sought out; a true statement or picture of things must be laid before them; and through their understanding, the deliberate assent of the will must be obtained."[102]

Thompson's Political Theory

Thompson's political theory can, perhaps, be summarized in his statement, "Hitherto mankind have been governed by the unreflecting *habits* formed by *institutions,* with the necessary supplement of *force* always at hand to restrain their aberrations. Henceforth, rational beings must be governed by reason."[103] The question is, how to remove the institutional factors that impose force and constrain or distort reason. While it may be said that this is not necessarily the basis for a democratic system, it is for Thompson, with his emphasis on equality, voluntarism, and self-government. The "reason" by which people should be "governed" must be their own. The elimination of the causes of social division—property and competition—creates the conditions whereby, under the principle of a virtuous disposition, an identity of interests can develop among the members of a community such that they may be self-governing both individually and collectively through the mechanism of public opinion. This is clearly "rule by the people"—the people ruling themselves and the institutional context within which that rule takes place.

In considering these cooperative communities as democratic institutions it is important to keep in mind the voluntarism that is one of Thompson's central principles. The fact that members of the community are free to join (subject to an admission process that would ensure that new members share the values of the community), means that in joining they make a commitment to the community and to its values. That they are free to leave means that at least a general level of consensus must be maintained, although there could be disagreement on some particulars. This is another way by which the tyranny of the majority may be avoided, as no part of the community, even if they constitute a majority, could exert tyrannical control for fear of an exodus that would threaten the community's viability.[104]

But while the governing of a small community must be considered separately from that of a nation, Thompson does not advocate the abandonment of politics at the national level by the members of the community. As he puts it,

> [L]et not... these proposed arrangements be charged with *excluding* national or provincial affairs from the consideration of the individual members.... They have not ceased to be members of the great general community in which they live. They take no monastic vows of voluntary seclusion from the world. They cease not to be men and to have a country.[105]

Two points might be raised here: First, that in Thompson's view members of a community, schooled as they are in reasoned deliberation and expansive in their views, would be well positioned for political engagement within the larger political context. "By reason, by generosity, they will always seek to promote the public good" even though, "Different members will necessarily take different views of public affairs."[106] Second, by not withdrawing from the larger society, the cooperative communities make themselves into vehicles for social change through demonstration. "[B]y the proposed arrangements, an expedient is devised, as profound as it is benevolent, for *evading* many of the evils of the institutions of insecurity, instead of calling on political power to *abolish* them.... The co-operating societies, if successful in a few instances, would rapidly defuse themselves, till economy of labor, co-operation in producing, and equality in distributing, would by degrees supersede, wherever such advantages could be procured, the present waste of labor and happiness."[107] Thompson's view of social change, then, could be said to be evolutionary, proceeding through persuasion by way of practical example. Indeed, he explicitly argues that it is antithetical to revolution: "A more important and more extensive change in human society was never contemplated by the mind of man. Reason is the only agent worthy of effecting such a change."[108]

Utopia and the Cooperative Communities

Thompson might reasonably be accused of having an overly optimistic view of life in these cooperative communities. As one writer describes it, the sort of society Thompson envisioned "would eliminate the causes of most vices, miseries, and moral failings, would promote human love and benevolence, would eliminate the social origins of extreme selfishness, competitiveness, and pugnacity, would increase economic productivity, and would eliminate all forms of economic insecurity."[109] Perhaps that is a bit much to expect. Considering the prominence given to books and articles on conflict resolution provided on the Web sites of associations of intentional communities,[110] it might be recognized that the process of operationalizing the identity of interests and distilling public opinion is more complicated than Thompson thought it was—or perhaps it is testimony to the strength of his argument that intentional communities have found ways to address these problems.

It is true, however, that Thompson does not consider issues of differentials of power within the cooperative communities, perhaps assuming either that an identity of interests will overcome any such differences, or that the communities would be large enough so that no one person or small group would be able to take over—or that they would be small enough that no factions or conspiracies could form.

Thompson offers a ringing critique of power relations under capitalist institutions, but he doesn't consider the ways in which power imbalances might become significant or problematic within the cooperative communities. While it is certainly true that the competitive accumulation of private property is an important cause of social inequality, it is not the only one. What might be considered "natural" causes of inequality such as age or physical or mental capacity cannot simply be ignored. Thompson does not ignore these entirely, if only to raise them in a positive mein:[111] at one point he considers the possibility that some workers would be more productive, suggesting that "[t]he mere praise of being the best workman, is sufficient to keep alive the superior efforts of the superior men . . . regret will be on the part of those, whose powers of . . . usefulness will be the least. On the part of the superior workmen, there will be a constant effort to improve these."[112] But might these "superior" workers also have greater influence in the community, with regard to its self-governance? And what might be the consequences of this? Thompson doesn't consider the possibility.

It turns out that it is fairly impossible to entirely eradicate all forms of politically meaningful inequality. As Rothschild and Whitt note, "Inequalities in influence persist in the most egalitarian of organizations.... Because authority resides in the collectivity as a unit, the exercise of influence depends less on position and more on the personal attributes of the individual. Members who are more articulate, responsible, energetic, glamorous, fair-minded, or committed carry more weight."[113] There are also problems, as Mansbridge notes, with "conflict management." Indeed, the very sorts of close personal relationships that might make a consensus-based, nonhierarchical model highly egalitarian, participatory, and deeply democratic can also serve to limit and even distort participation. In particular, "Face-to-face assemblies provoke anxieties and tensions that rarely arise when a citizen simply walks into a voting booth and pulls a lever... that subtly influence the way decisions are made."[114] These factors lead some to argue that systems of formal representation that involve secret ballots and the like may be more effective at overcoming identity-based inequalities in a democratic system than do systems that rely on face-to-face encounters.[115]

If Thompson does not consider the challenges and potential downsides of the attempt to remove all forms of inequality, he does think that when it comes to mental capacity, some inequality may be a good thing: "In no community have the wise and good ever enjoyed such ample opportunity of directing aright public opinion."[116] Perhaps he believes that, given the identity of interests and a rational consideration of whatever issues might be involved, these "wise and good" individuals would always agree, and that they might "direct" public opinion is apparently seen as unproblematic. Thompson recognizes the "possibility of the public opinion... being altogether misdirected," although he argues that "under the original and fundamental stipulation for freedom of opinion on every possible subject, all real evils from this source are obviated" because, over time, any misdirection will undoubtedly be corrected.[117] This, however, seems to indicate that while everyone will technically be equal, some individuals might have more influence than others—they may become the leaders of the community. This points to a problem that has long posed difficulty for democratic theorists with regard to the nature and role of leadership within an egalitarian framework.

As fate would have it, the practical difficulties in Thompson's theory never got a chance to play out in the context of cooperative communities.

Despite the detailed plans laid out in *Practical Directions,* no community based on that model was ever founded, and Thompson's sisters made sure that his bequest would never be used to start one. Nevertheless, after some years his ideas did take shape in a different form from what he had anticipated, in the cooperative movement that dates its own beginnings to the Rochdale cooperative store that opened in 1844. Some elements of his theory did not translate into the enterprise model that evolved—cooperatives today are rarely so participatory, for example—but important parts survived. The chapter that follows explores both the historical and theoretical linkages between Thompson and the modern-day cooperative movement, and what recognizing this connection might mean for cooperatives today.

6
From Theory to Practice
Cooperatives, Happiness, and Democratic Social Change

On its face, the question of the nature of happiness is very abstract and conceptual. The intent of the last chapter was to demonstrate that it has implications for political theory. In this chapter, I finish building the bridge from philosophy to theory to practice by examining what is, in both a historical and an ideological sense, a particular manifestation of Thompson's ideas: the cooperative movement. Given its immense size and global extent as an actually existing alternative model to liberal capitalism, this may be Thompson's most important legacy. But while Thompson laid a rich theoretical foundation that articulated a vision of deep social change, the cooperative movement's connection to his ideas has largely been lost sight of over the course of nearly two centuries. This, then, is an attempt to reassert first principles as the basis for a new political theory of cooperatives.

One cannot escape the fact that, like More's fictional island, the cooperative communities Thompson promoted turned out to be utopian in both senses of the word: *eu-topian* in that they would have been very good places, but *ou-topian* in that they turned out to be nowhere. Although he offered his own land for the establishment of a community near Cork in 1830,[1] nothing ever came of it, and no community based on the plan he laid out in *Practical Directions* appears to have ever been attempted. Thompson was not alone in his failure: none of the communities actually started or planned in this period (Ralahine, Orbiston, Owen's New Harmony) lasted more than a few years. After Thompson died in 1833, the movement for cooperative communities declined substantially, partly because many of its principals were caught up in an effort to secure Thompson's estate from his sisters, who had contested his will, and partly because working-class energies shifted to Chartism, the movement to gain working-class male suffrage through the People's Charter. Even Owen, the great visionary of cooperative communities, moved on to other projects.

The idea of cooperation, however, did not die. Today, Owen and Thompson's cooperative community ideas may be considered a kind of "prehistory" in the development of the modern cooperative movement. It is not uncommon for the community idea to be left out entirely in this history, even though Owen is often considered the "father" of the idea of cooperatives.[2] As was discussed in the introduction, Thompson's role, while not entirely ignored, is not often recognized.[3] The original members of the Rochdale Society of Equitable Pioneers that in 1844 opened up the famous store on Toad Lane from which the modern cooperative movement dates its origins may have called themselves "Owenites," but a close reading of the historical record reveals that they had at least as much reason to call themselves "Thompsonians."

It would be very reasonable to ask what difference it makes whether Owen or Thompson is more prominent in the history of cooperatives. The difference is this: where Owen offered vision and passion (if not persistence), Thompson provided much of the theoretical grounding, including solid arguments for basic principles. Owen certainly took on the cause of the working classes with gusto, and there is no question that he gave it his fortune. However, after he was fairly clearly rebuked at the 3rd Cooperative Congress in 1832 (by Thompson and others) and he was unsuccessful in raising the funds he considered necessary to establish a community, he moved away from the idea of cooperative community[4] and toward other grand schemes to improve the lot of the laboring classes and, thereby, repair the problems of society. In fact, Owen was opposed to the establishment of retail stores and the kind of gradualism that led, ultimately, to the Rochdale model and the modern cooperative movement.

The cooperative movement that exists today, which generally dates its origins to the Rochdale Society, is, in many ways, significantly different from what Thompson envisioned. One effect of the historical development of the cooperative movement is that the basic principles that he articulated have become attenuated, such that it is reasonable to ask whether the movement today can be understood, in any real sense, as based on Thompson's ideas. The primary concern of this chapter is to demonstrate that those principles remain at the heart of the cooperative system.

An examination of both the theoretical and historical development of the cooperative movement, and Thompson's role in it, will occupy the first part of this chapter. That will be followed by an examination of the state of the cooperative movement today, linking the principles that govern the global movement—known simply as the Cooperative Principles—to Thompson's work.

The Historical Development of the Cooperative Movement

Understanding how Thompson's conception of happiness and the political theory he derives from it relate to the cooperative movement is not simply a matter of looking for correspondence between his ideas and the principles espoused by cooperatives today. Cooperatives are actually-existing institutions, which have undergone a process of development that has been continuous at least since 1844, although the Rochdale Pioneers themselves and the principles they adopted reflect a historical development from the previous two decades. Thompson was a central character in that history.

Rochdale: Creation Myth and Historical Context

Every movement has its founding myths, and this is no less true of cooperatives. As one historian recently suggested, "Creation myths are essential to the cultures of co-operatives generally and of each of them in particular."[5] Central to the creation myth of cooperatives is that they are autonomous, self-sufficient enterprises that were created by socially minded entrepreneurs who brought people together to deal with specific, mostly local, market or social problems. These myths arise because histories of individual cooperatives are institutional biographies that focus on the growth and success of their subject and are little concerned with the larger context. The effect is to isolate the cooperative not only from other similar institutions, but also from the ideological and theoretical currents of which it is (or was originally) a part.[6] This means that an understanding of the ideological and political basis for their founding is often lost and forgotten.[7]

The basic outline of the Rochdale myth has it that the cooperative movement began when the Rochdale Society of Equitable Pioneers established a retail store for members in Rochdale, England (near Manchester) in 1844. A group of twenty-eight desperate, impoverished hand loom weavers, influenced by Owenism[8] and Chartism, driven to destitution by industrialization and victimized by unscrupulous merchants, bands together and adopts a set of principles and objectives that reflect the failures of similar prior efforts—for example, requiring cash payment for all sales—but including one key innovation that becomes the foundation for their success where others had failed: the dividend, a payment to members of net revenue after all expenses had been deducted, paid in proportion to members' patronage. Contributing a few pence a week over the course of a year or so, they open their own retail operation which, when it opens (initially two evenings a week), offers a very limited range of goods for sale to members. Within a short period, demand requires that they open more often and carry more goods, and before you know it similar operations based on the Rochdale model are springing up all over England and beyond. By the 1930s cooperatives based on the Rochdale model are well established throughout the industrialized world.[9]

It goes without saying that the story is much more complicated than this romanticized version, although it has, of course, a basis in truth. I will focus here on the beginnings of Rochdale. In the first place, the founding group was more diverse than it appears. While at least some of them were, in fact, weavers, Fairbairn argues that "the role of weavers in setting up the Rochdale Pioneers has been exaggerated by many casual writers.... [M]ost of the founding members were not starving and desperate," but were skilled artisans who were comparatively well paid. This may be due in part to the fact that those who were desperate would not have been able to afford the weekly subscription fee. "The Rochdale Pioneers did not rise spontaneously from need, but were organized consciously by thinkers, activists, and leaders who functioned within a network of ideas and institutions." Fairbairn suggests that "[t]he creation of the Pioneers is better seen as a kind of partnership between a group of Owenites, the weavers, some ex-Chartists, and some temperance campaigners."[10]

The relative importance of the Owenites and Chartists, as well as some other important figures, in terms of their ideological influence on the Rochdale Pioneers will be examined below. The important point at this juncture is that all of these groups were actively working for broad-based social change. "The driving forces in the [Rochdale] cooperative were...people with years of experience in the labour movement, in other organizations, and in social and political causes."[11] They saw themselves as working from within an extended tradition of activism among the laboring classes, one that had a history that was fairly well known to the people at the time.

The early nineteenth century was, in fact, a period of extensive experimentation in various forms of collective organization, responsive to local conditions and opportunities, in some cases prior to Owen's agitation for cooperative development. For example, a flour mill founded in 1795 in Hull called the Hull Anti-Mill Co-operative Society continued in operation for more than one hundred years.[12] Estimates of the number of cooperative societies inspired by the work of Owen, Thompson and others in the late 1820s and 1830s vary; Cole reports that there were "over 250 societies" which "we know by name" that "formed between 1826 and 1835."[13] Mercer says that Holyoake was "more picturesque than accurate" when he claimed that all that was left by 1840 was "the wreckage of 'a dead movement,'" as "[a] considerable number of societies had an unbroken existence from the early eighteen-thirties until the end of Queen Victoria's reign."[14] During this period, many societies opened retail stores to serve their members and as a way of accumulating funds toward the eventual goal of starting up an Owenite community—a goal the Rochdale Pioneers shared, as can be seen from their Law the First (discussed below).[15] Indeed, a number of the members of the Pioneers had been members of the Rochdale Friendly Co-operative Society, founded in 1830, that operated a store from 1833 to 1835 just up the street from the location on Toad Lane where the Pioneers opened their store in 1844.[16]

The language of happiness is common among advocates of the working class in this period, so its appearance in the literature of the cooperative movement cannot be attributed directly to Thompson.[17] Nonetheless, the presence of language remarkably similar to Thompson's is evident, including references to happiness and a strong dislike for the capitalist system. For example, the Introduction to the Laws of the First Armagh Co-operative Society, established in 1830, specifically condemns "individual appropriation" and "the impossibility of the great mass of mankind reaching any other condition than that of being the *servants of those who live upon their labours,* and, consequently, the continuation of ignorance, vice and misery."[18] Similarly, the "Principles, Objects and Laws" of the First Salford Community state that "[c]o-operation should do away with competition; and, of course, with all the evils that arise from it."[19] The London Co-operative Association (which may have included Thompson as a founding member) gives as its Object that "[t]he object of this Association of persons of both sexes, is to co-operate, in promoting the mutual happiness and common wealth of all its associates, and in securing and affording to them all equally, the means of satisfying their physical and intellectual wants."[20] The address given at the opening of the Birmingham co-operative society in 1828 also opens with the language of happiness, clearly articulating it as a social concern[21]—and William Pare, one of the founders and leaders of the society, offered a toast to Thompson at the Birmingham Society's anniversary dinner in 1829, specifically citing the *Inquiry* as his inspiration.[22]

Thompson was not only a theorist, but also an important activist in the early movement. At the 1st Cooperative Congress in 1831, a resolution was passed to take steps toward the formation of a cooperative community "upon the plan laid down by Mr. William Thompson"—a reference, no doubt, to his *Practical Directions,* which had been published the year before. [23] We may note that the resolution was moved by Thompson and seconded by Owen. However, it appears that little or nothing was done toward that goal, as at the 2nd Congress six months later a committee was formed—which included both Owen and Thompson—to move the process forward and draft a "Prospectus of the Objects and Nature of a Community."[24] The Articles of Agreement for the Formation of a Community adopted at the 3rd Cooperative Congress in 1832 is clearly based on Thompson's work, beginning with the statement that "[h]appiness is the true object of human exertions, and the real and permanent improvement of Society must be founded on the happiness of its individual members." The agreement also argues that the evils of society are due to the "system of *Individual Competition and Private Accumulation,*" and refer to "the *excessive inequality of wealth*" as the end product of that system. It is also of note that the society is to be "*self-governed*; all its internal regulations will be formed, and its proceedings conducted by the adult members themselves." A later section on the "Rights of Women" specifically refers to women as "half the human race, equally capable with men of contributing to the common happiness, and equally capable of individual enjoyment." Finally, a section on the "Principles of Exchange" renounces "*profit, which implies living on the labour of others.*"[25] All of these provisions clearly have Thompson's stamp on them.

The Rochdale Principles

It is within the context of this tradition that we can best understand the founding principles of the Rochdale Pioneers. What is referred to as the Rochdale Principles don't really look very much like what we think of as principles. Rather, they perform two functions: An articulation of the goals and objectives of the group (the "Law the First"), and a set of detailed bylaws or articles of incorporation that lay out the functioning rules of the association. Their principles are embedded in their goals and in the rules they laid down for their governance and operation.[26] Included in the Law the First are such ideas as that the purpose of the group is "to form arrangements for the pecuniary benefit, and improvement of the social and domestic condition of its members"; to open a store; to build housing, establish manufacturing and agricultural operations to employ members who are un- or underemployed; to establish a "self-supporting home-colony of united interests" (essentially, a cooperative community); and, "for the promotion of sobriety," the establishment of a "temperance hotel."[27]

There is little here that stands out, to a modern reader, as evidence of the social movement discussed above: there are no grand statements about changing the basic character of society or even of the individuals who join. In fact, in many ways the Principles taken in isolation seem to support the romantic history of a group banding together as a way of dealing with the enormity of the social and economic changes facing them, a modest measure of self-help to deal with the failure of the market and other social institutions to address their needs. Its character as a social movement organization is more subtle, coming across in the objectives and operating rules themselves: that a group of working-class citizens would take it upon themselves to establish their own enterprise to serve their own needs, and that they would run it themselves, democratically.[28]

The principles became more explicitly articulated over time as the Rochdale cooperative grew and the Pioneers considered means to ensure its ideological stability and, at the same time, flexibility as they adapted to new realities. Revisions to their basic statement of principles were adopted at various points in the succeeding years, leading up to more substantial changes as more cooperative societies formed and merged into large-scale federations and, finally, the establishment of the International Cooperative Association in 1895. I will examine more of this development below, after a consideration of a persistent historical debate concerning the role of another important working-class movement of the time, Chartism.

Chartism and Owenism

The Industrial Revolution, coupled with the removal of peasants from the land through enclosures, fundamentally altered class relations in England, creating a great class of people who were free, in Marx's words, "in the double sense that they neither form part of the means of production themselves as would be the case with slaves, serfs, etc., nor do they own the means of production, as would be the case with self-employed peasant proprietors."[29] But as industrialists (Owen among them) were enjoying astounding increases in wealth, working conditions and pay for those who toiled in their factories were abysmal.[30] Both Chartism and Owenism were, in different ways, attempts to address these conditions.

Chartism was, in itself, a fairly short-lived movement with a specific goal: winning the franchise for all adult males. In this, however, it was part of a much longer history. Radical movements calling for universal (or near-universal) male suffrage date at least back to the rise of Parliamentary supremacy in the English Civil War. For the so-called Levellers (not a name they gave themselves), who were arguing on behalf of the men who fought in support of the Parliamentarian cause to overthrow the monarchy, it was a matter of right: The men who had sacrificed so much clearly had earned the right to participate in the election of Parliament, and they questioned "whether any person can justly be bound by law, who does not give his consent that such persons shall make laws for him?"[31] However, their arguments largely fell on the deaf ears of aristocratic leaders who argued that to give the vote to those who were not "freed from dependence upon others"—that is, who did not have property and could not provide their own subsistence—would "put it into the hands of men to choose, not of men desirous to preserve their liberty, but of men who will give it away."[32]

Calls for universal male suffrage died down for a while, but, according to Stedman Jones, "In England, radicalism first surfaced as a coherent programme in the 1770s, and first became a vehicle of plebeian political aspirations from the 1790s."[33] However, the 1832 Reform Bill, championed by Bentham and other Philosophical Radicals such as James Mill, among others, fell short of the Radicals' hopes for an expansion of the franchise to all adult males. While workers were recruited to support the bill by the capitalists with whom they were "fighting day by day," they found to their dismay that "the moment of victory would also be the moment of betrayal," as the bill only continued their disenfranchisement.[34] Its failure to expand voting rights to the working classes in effect established new class divisions in British society, defining a "lower class" that was denied the vote while placing "the government... in the hands of the middle classes" and launching a period of "political hostility between the middle and working classes."[35] First published in 1838, the People's Charter, like the Levellers' movement before them, was an attempt to wrest from Parliament political rights for a class that had been denied them. In contrast to the Levellers, however, whose cause was mostly advanced by soldiers during the course of the Civil War, Chartism was a broad-based social movement that circulated petitions and held rallies and marches. The belief of the Chartists was that the conditions that served to oppress the working class could be addressed when the working class had representation in Parliament. As one Chartist leader put it, "[Y]our poverty is the result not the cause of your being unrepresented."[36]

The content of Owenism is, in some ways, more difficult to pin down, mostly because of its association with Owen, who rarely stuck with a project for more than a few years.[37] Nonetheless, Harrison offers something of a synthesis, incorporating the ideas of people, such as Thompson, who picked up and expanded on Owen's ideas. Harrison identifies three primary elements—communitarianism, political economics, and social science—each of which may be associated with Owen's ideas in different ways and to different degrees.

All three of these aspects of Owenism have been evident through much of the discussion of Thompson in this book, because in fact they come at least as much from Thompson as from Owen. Owen's communitarianism, as was discussed at the beginning of chapter 3, is his primary contribution, as its basis is philosophical necessitarianism, or the idea that a person's character is formed by their circumstances. But Owen's statements on political economics and social science are themselves rather vague and not infrequently contradictory,[38] and Harrison describes Owen as "sometimes reluctant to see social institutions as infrastructures [whereas] the Ricardian socialists accepted economic relationships as the basis of social institutions."[39] Rather, it was Thompson who gave Owen's economic ideas a degree of rigor and definition, and it is with respect to political economics that Harrison refers to Thompson as "the most influential of the Owenite socialists."[40] The notion of social science has a somewhat stronger association with Owen himself, first because a kind of Enlightenment rationalism pervades his work,[41] and second because a central element of his early work on the formation of character focused on the "laws of social dynamics."[42] But again, where Harrison notes that "[i]n Owen's writings the formulation of these concepts is partly obscured by his terminology" he goes on to say that "in Thompson the matter is put more plainly."[43] And, of course it was Thompson, not Owen, who directly referred to the effort to analyze social institutions in order to arrive at a better arrangement as "social science." It would seem, therefore, that the moniker "Owenism" is somewhat misleading, as much of its content comes, in fact, from Thompson.[44]

Owenism owes much to Owen, of course, and in particular its popularity in England in the second quarter of the nineteenth century. Older than Thompson when they met and already well known as a social reformer, Owen lived for another twenty years after Thompson's passing, and for much of this time he was quite active in pursuing various plans for social change. Of his various activities, his development of the Universal Community Society of Rational Religionists (generally known as the Rational Society) had the most significant impact, particularly on the development of the cooperative movement. Indeed, from 1838–1842 the Rational Society regularly employed a number of "social missionaries," led by the Thompsonite William Pare, who were expected to study both Owen's and Thompson's works. As a kind of precursor to the development of Owenite communities, Halls of Science were built in a number of cities in which to hold educational and social events (although few of these survived for more than two or three years).

Owenism attained such broad reach that in 1840 the Bishop of Exeter was moved to attack it before the House of Lords, detailing its extensive organization throughout the kingdom, its publication of a monthly journal that reached perhaps four hundred thousand people as well as a weekly paper with a circulation of forty thousand, and supporters in various official positions.[45]

It is not clear whether Owen's Rational Society had a Hall of Science in Rochdale, although nearby Manchester was one of its most active centers.[46] Chartism in Rochdale was, however, according to Cole, "a very powerful force."[47] The original Pioneers are described as a mixture of Chartists and Owenites; a roster that includes their "Persuasion" shows nine "Chartists" and fifteen "Socialists,"[48] and the Pioneers' meetings started out in the Chartists' meeting room. Apparently, such mixing between the two groups was rare, and their appearance on the roster together should not be taken as evidence that the two groups got along well. In fact, Holyoake says that those in Rochdale who supported the Pioneers were "treated as apostates," but that after the store became successful the Chartists tried to take credit for it.[49] A local Chartist leader, who joined the Pioneers in 1846, later said in an interview, "It all started with the Chartists."[50] Holyoake notes that, to outsiders, it was impossible to determine to whom credit was due for the establishment of the Society. However, he says, for people who were actually there, it was perfectly clear: "[T]he Socialists were the persons who first thought of starting co-operation, who counselled it, who originated it and organised it, kept it going, and carried it out. The fact is, the Chartists were impediments in the way of it. They were the most troublesome opponents the co-operators had to contend with."[51] Indeed, after a point the group was kicked out of the Chartist meeting hall.[52]

Discussing the two movements as a whole, Stedman Jones argues that "the fundamental incompatibility between Owenism and radicalism [the Charter movement] should not be underestimated."[53] The class antagonism that was at the heart of Chartism did not exist in Owenism, and the Chartists were overtly political in a way that Owenism avoided. While the Owenites did produce their own appeals to Parliament at the 2nd and 3rd Congresses, there was little emphasis on this, and Thompson, for one, considered it a waste of time and effort.[54] The Chartists were also more willing to engage in the use of force than were the Owenites; the former were a kind of mass social movement, relying on civil actions to press for significant and immediate change (if short of revolution, although they may have been seen that way by their opponents), whereas the latter believed in slow, developmental change. The Owenites were a product of the Enlightenment, arguing for a removal of constraints against the dispersal of knowledge and the application of reason—what Stedman Jones calls the "rationalist and scientific strand of enlightenment thinking"[55]—whereas the Chartists saw themselves in more romantic terms, as participants in a battle between two forces in competition for power.

Stedman Jones's point taken (that the conflict between Owenism and Chartism undermines the idea of a unitary, cohesive working class), the conflict between Owenism and Chartism *can* be overstated. After all, both were, essentially, working-class movements that sought to address the horrific conditions of the vast majority of the British people. The rank and file members of the two groups were likely mostly the same people. As Harrison notes, "When a working man declared himself a cooperator he did not necessarily cease to be a trade unionist nor give up the struggle for the vote."[56] In fact, William Lovett, who was one of the leaders of the London Cooperative Society, was the author of the Charter,[57] and he was not the only one of the Chartist leaders who could be described as an Owenite. Harrison notes that both Henry Hetherington and James Bronterre O'Brien were active in both worlds. Hetherington wrote, "[L]et the Radical take the Owenite by the hand, and the Owenite do the same by the Radical, for both parties are the *real,* and only *friends* of the working people."[58]

In fact, one of the positions of the Chartists was that, "[c]o-operation could only become a real possibility once the people had obtained their political rights."[59] In 1845, after the Charter's second and final defeat in Parliament, one of its leaders, Feargus O'Connor, started the Chartist Cooperative Land Society to develop "Chartist colonies."[60] Finally, there may have been a kind of tidal movement of popular working-class activity from the cooperative societies to Chartism and back again. The decline of cooperative societies in the 1830s may have simply been a reflection of the problems of leadership: not long after Thompson's death Owen abandoned the cooperative movement, starting up his Association of All Classes of All Nations; Cole suggests that the Owenites "had ceased to be the leaders of a mass movement and had become a sect."[61] On top of the lack of leadership, the repeated failure of cooperative communities (and the loss of assets as a result) may have soured people on what had been held out as the ultimate objective of the cooperative societies. Because the retail stores were established to accumulate funds for the purpose of establishing communities, the enthusiasm of the public for the stores (which mostly sold at market prices in order to assure a profit that could be retained to purchase land for a community) may have waned, and management problems—such as too-easy credit terms—may have led to the failure of retail stores that had been established. In the meantime, the Charter movement grabbed the attention of many, who turned their energies to Chartist societies. After two defeats in Parliament, however, people may have decided they'd had enough of mass actions and that locally based activities that could help them address their immediate needs would be a more effective means for improving their condition, turning them back to the cooperative idea.[62]

This dispute between the Chartists and the Owenites is not terribly important except in one respect: as Stedman Jones makes clear, they represent a classic opposition between two very different approaches to social change, the Chartists' efforts to open up the existing system to greater participation while maintaining its overall structure, versus the Owenites' development of entirely new alternative institutions.[63] The Charter movement may have been seen as wildly radical (especially by the upper classes who felt threatened by it), and some Chartists may have seen the expansion of the franchise as the lynchpin for greater economic and social change, but in fact the movement was fairly narrow in its goals, limited to the expansion of the franchise to working-class males. In this way their demands had scarcely advanced from those of the Levellers.[64] But their methods were also narrow: as their objective was constitutional change, their only avenue was through popular appeals to Parliament. Thus, they can be seen as an effort to bring about change by working within the general constraints of the political system, much like the American civil rights movement more than a century later—citizens excluded from the political process petitioning their government for inclusion (although "petitioning" does not reflect the intense passion and even violence associated with that process, as the powerful never seem willing to accede to such demands without a fight). The Owenites, on the other hand, sought to develop alternative institutions that could benefit members of the working class—or, as they argued, of any and all classes—with only limited interaction with existing political structures. In this evolutionary model of change, over time the alternative would attract the majority, especially the majority of the working class, such that the capitalist system would simply collapse. Contrary to the Chartists, then, for the most part the Owenites worked on the outside of the political system, only interacting with it when necessary to their interests.

Development of the Cooperative Principles

While Chartism did invoke principles of equality and inclusion (for men, at least), it was the ideas of Thompson and the Owenites that formed the basis for the development of the cooperative movement. The principles that guide the movement today evolved from those adopted by the Pioneers in 1844. Two particular phenomena can be identified as the primary drivers for change: the transition of the original cooperative societies from the community-based model into an enterprise model, which on the one hand led to their consolidation in Britain as retail operations but on the other hand led to a diversification in form; and the internationalization of the cooperative system through the founding of the International Cooperative Alliance (ICA), which resulted from the global spread of the Rochdale model.[65]

From Cooperative Communities to Cooperative Enterprise

The Rochdale principles themselves evolved over the years, particularly as they came to form the basis for larger societies of cooperatives, then for the British national Co-operative Union (founded 1873), and ultimately as they became adopted as the guiding principles—referred to formally as the Rochdale Principles—for the International Cooperative Alliance at its founding in 1895. A significant step taken at some point before 1860—the exact timing is unknown—came with the Pioneers' abandonment of the idea of forming a cooperative community.[66] We may consider the effect of this: the idea of forming a community had been the driving force of most cooperative societies for much of their history to that point. Although some societies managed to buy some land, no communities succeeded. But one of the key features of the communities was that they incorporated both production and consumption, thereby fulfilling all the needs of their members.

For Thompson, the productive aspect of the communities was one of their key elements. In *Practical Directions,* Thompson refers to "Want of Employment" as the primary concern of the "great majority of the industrious classes," the principal cause of which was the "want of a market" for manufactured goods that would induce employers to offer steady, and sufficient, employment. The remedy he offers is the formation of intentional communities in which the division of labor is organized in a system of internal exchange such that the members "afford *a market to each other,* by working together *for each other,* for the mutual supply, directly by themselves, of all their most indispensable wants."[67] In the capitalist system, working people found themselves pressed from both sides: on the one hand, they were dependent upon employers who wanted to exploit their labor at as low a cost as possible, and on the other hand they were dependent upon merchants and landlords who wanted to sell them the necessities of life at as high a price as possible. They were in this condition because they were unable to produce the means of their own subsistence. Thompson's answer was to bring the full cycle of production and consumption, with the advantages of the division of labor and large-scale production through industrialization, including access to land for agricultural production, all together within a single community. The producers *were* the consumers: in this respect the community was a microcosm of the larger society, except that it was organized around mutual support rather than individual competition and exploitation.

At first, at least, letting go of the community ideal did not mean abandoning the notion of united production and consumption. As is evident from the Law the First, part of the Rochdale model was the development of production facilities for the express purpose of affording employment for members. Further, productive members were considered to be contributing to the cooperative through their work just as consumers contributed through their purchases. So, just as consumers received a dividend based on the amount of their purchases, workers received a share of the profits. Fairbairn refers to "a movement away from the 'home colony' idea, and toward, instead, a federalist system and a second tier of productive enterprises owned by local co-operatives."[68] A Rochdale Co-operative Manufacturing Society was started up in 1854; workers received a share of its profits in proportion to their wage earnings. However, because the enterprise was funded through shares sold openly in the town, a group that Holyoake bitterly refers to as "anti-co-operators" led by "orators of greed" managed to agitate to discontinue the profit-sharing plan.⁶⁹ This marks a turning point: "Through to the 1890s the British co-operative movement had many projects in worker ownership and profit-sharing with workers, some quite successful. But these were gradually abandoned."⁷⁰

Letting go of the idea of autarkic communities gave the Rochdale group some important advantages, as it enabled them to do something other societies had been unable to do: expand horizontally and vertically. Its horizontal expansion came in the form of opening branches: by 1859 there were six.⁷¹ Vertical expansion came not only in the development of production facilities but also in the formation of a federated wholesale society owned by the local cooperative societies themselves. Fairbairn notes that the movement expanded in non-economic directions as well, as the Pioneers decided to put 2.5 percent of their surplus revenue to education, offering lectures, a library, and a reading room for members.⁷²

Over time, cooperative societies in Britain became more and more focused on retail operations, and more and more consumer-oriented. Two primary causes contributed to this: first, the development of centralized distribution through the Co-operative Wholesale Society (CWS)⁷³ became a powerful engine of growth, which gave the CWS a great deal of economic power. This success served as a kind of legitimation, but the CWS was "a conservative influence, stifling experimentation," with the result that "part of the Pioneers' vision fell away as the movement grew and narrowed."⁷⁴

A second reason for the shift was the rise of the notion of consumer cooperatives as the central element in what came to be called the "cooperative commonwealth," on the basis of arguments put forward in Britain by the Fabian socialists (particularly Sidney and Beatrice Potter Webb) and in the United States by J. P. Warbasse, head of the consumer-oriented Cooperative League of the USA. The essential point the Webbs made was that worker cooperatives were still "capitalistic" as they produced goods for profit, even though in their case all profit was for the benefit of the workers themselves and not outside investors. Consumer cooperatives, they argued, were more socially oriented, as any positive net revenue that was not used either to strengthen the cooperatives' finances (to pay debt, for example, or kept as retained earnings) or for socially oriented purposes (such as education) would be returned to the members—i.e., the patrons of the cooperative. In that sense, there was no "profit" in the traditional sense, only excess revenue that would be returned to the consumers themselves.[75] In effect, as the Webbs point out, this was a debate between "the idea of manufacture organised by groups of producers, *for exchange* with the rest of the world [as opposed to] manufacture organised by the whole democracy of consumers, for their consumption or service [and] therefore *for use*."[76]

With all consumption (and, therefore, production) organized around cooperatives, the "cooperative commonwealth"[77] would lead to the withering away of the state.[78] Local societies would unite to form national societies; these then would be coordinated through the International Cooperative Alliance, forming a global network of cooperatives through which all production and consumption could be organized. With cooperatives coordinating and addressing distributional issues, the political frameworks would be recognized as superfluous and would simply fade away.[79]

With the rise in influence of the CWS and the development of the cooperative commonwealth idea, the objects and motives of the Rochdale movement—and the movement it grew out of—become inverted in the shift of focus from workers to consumers. This amounted to a "consumers' revolution in the co-operative movement, [in which] the traditions and principles of co-operatives were remade in the interests of consumers."[80]

In a formal sense, the abandonment of the cooperative community model meant that, instead of seeking to establish a self-contained, self-sufficient egalitarian alternative to capitalist society one small community at a time, the cooperative societies became independent economic enterprises that benefit their members through the redistribution of surplus revenue. While this clearly came at the loss, or at least moderation, of some of its ideals, it also enabled the expansion of the cooperative model on a vast scale. The economic enterprise model is not limited to small-scale retail stores providing basic goods to local populations. In fact, it became possible for any kind of economic activity to be organized as a cooperative—as, indeed, has happened.

Cooperatives Today

Two features of the cooperative movement today stand out: Its size and its diversity. The ICA bills itself as "the world's largest non-governmental organization,"[81] with 233 member organizations representing more than a billion people in over one hundred countries worldwide. The ICA reports that "[t]he United Nations estimated in 1994 that the livelihood of nearly 3 billion people, or half of the world's population, was made secure by co-operative enterprise."[82] Cooperatives are well integrated into all of the world's leading economies, for example in the United States, where a recent report found that "[n]early 30,000 U.S. cooperatives operate at 73,000 places of business.... These cooperatives own >$3T[rillion] in assets, and generate > $500B[illion] in revenue and >$25B[illion] in wages."[83] According to the National Cooperative Business Association (NCBA), an estimated 120 million Americans are members of a cooperative.[84] In other parts of the world cooperatives are even more significant: one out of every three families in Japan is a member of a cooperative; in Singapore fifty percent of the population belongs to a cooperative. In Quebec, 70 percent of the population is a member of at least one cooperative.[85] They are also important parts of the economies of developing nations: for example, cooperatives account for 45 percent of the Kenyan economy, according to a recent report by the UN.[86]

Cooperatives have also attained substantial diversity of form. As the ICA points out, "The co-operative model of enterprise can be applied to any business activity."[87] The three most significant types of cooperative are distinguished based on the type of membership: consumer cooperatives, owned by those who purchase the goods or use the services of the cooperative (including credit unions, as well as retail, service, and utilities such as electrical and telecommunications cooperatives); producer cooperatives, which are typically primarily engaged in distribution and marketing, are owned by people or enterprises that produce similar goods (this includes agricultural cooperatives, as well as independent craftspeople and artisans); and worker cooperatives, owned and governed by the people who carry out the functions of the enterprise—i.e., the workers.[88] Of these three types, consumer cooperatives are the most directly descended from the Rochdale model, and, having attained the largest size in terms of numbers of members, in Europe and the United States especially, these are the "face" of the cooperative movement.[89] That said, some of the best-known cooperative brands are producer cooperatives (such as Sunkist, Ocean Spray, and Land o' Lakes), including some very large companies.[90] Finally, while worker cooperatives may best fulfill the original intent of the early British cooperative movement in that they address the problem of the subordination of labor to capital,[91] they have had the least success in the developed economies.[92]

What sets all of these different forms apart from traditional capitalist forms of organization is that they describe types of enterprises that are explicitly based on a particular set of egalitarian and democratic principles and values. Different kinds of cooperatives may implement these principles and values in different ways, and in some cases may fail to honor them almost completely, but there remains a fundamental core that nonetheless sets them apart from traditional capitalist firms.

The Cooperative Principles Today

In recognition of the 150th anniversary of the opening of the store in Rochdale, in 1994 the ICA undertook a new revision of the Principles.[93] In a departure from tradition, the Rochdale name was dropped, and the revised principles are called, simply, the Co-operative Principles. These were adopted as part of a Statement of the Cooperative Identity, which also includes a formal definition of cooperatives and a defined set of values. A cooperative is now formally defined as "an autonomous association of persons united voluntarily to meet their common economic, social, and cultural needs and aspirations through a jointly-owned and democratically-controlled enterprise," which essentially means that they are socioeconomic enterprises organized as voluntary associations, collectively owned and democratically operated. The seven principles adopted are, in brief: [94]

1. Voluntary and open membership
2. Democratic member control
3. Member economic participation
4. Autonomy and independence
5. Education, training, and information
6. Co-operation among co-operatives
7. Concern for community

Much is changed from the original Laws and Statutes agreed upon by the Pioneers. In fact, they serve a fundamentally different purpose from those adopted in 1844: the Pioneers were setting out the basic operating rules for their Society, whereas these offer general guidance and are meant "to explain how co-operative principles should be interpreted in the contemporary world."[95] Whereas the Pioneers were concerned with identifying the nature of their organization with respect to a particular group of individuals, and with setting out the procedures for a particular enterprise, the ICA Statement seeks to define a class of enterprise that must be flexible to address many different kinds of groups of individuals. Thus, the Pioneers' document is practically oriented, while the ICA's is much more conceptual. In fact, to refer to the Pioneers' document as a statement of principles is somewhat misleading: it is only as the rules become generalized that the principles reveal themselves.

These principles and values are implemented somewhat differently in different kinds of cooperatives; indeed, with the adoption of the new principles each of five cooperative sectors formally recognized by the ICA (consumer, worker, credit, agricultural, and service) were to develop their own set of operating principles to accompany the general Principles. The function of the adopted principles, then, is to provide "a common framework" in order to foster "understanding, joint activities, and expanded horizons for all kinds of co-operative endeavor" toward the goal of the "harmonization of interests among groups of people organised as consumers of goods and services, as savers and investors, as producers, and as workers."[96] In providing this framework, the Principles clearly show what cooperatives are *not*: They are *not* closed or exclusive organizations, nor may people be coerced into joining them. They are *not* controlled on the basis of the provision of capital. They are *not* subsidiary organizations, nor are they state-run enterprises.

Although the principles are meant as standards to be adhered to, they function, more or less, as ideals to be aspired to.[97] As a former president of the ICA has noted, cooperatives have struggled throughout their history to retain their commitment to their principles in the face of competitive pressures, particularly within the advanced capitalist economies. The temptation is always strong to jettison principle in the interest of developing and maintaining an ongoing enterprise, and to take on more of the character of the capitalist mainstream, especially as the articulation of principles and ideals becomes more distant.[98] The temptation becomes stronger as management becomes professionalized—schooled not in the ways of cooperation, but in the ways of business, which generally means the capitalist model of business.[99] Birchall discusses a number of the ways in which present-day cooperatives fall short of their ideals, including problems of democratic participation, the failure to effectively include women as equal partners,[100] the exploitation of workers, failure to engage in educational programs, insufficient economic participation (i.e., members' contribution to capital is not meaningful),[101] the trading of control for capital, lack of attention to members' interests in favor of managerial interests (or, in the case of credit unions and agricultural cooperatives, larger members over smaller members), interference by the state, and tensions between centralization and localization—to name just a few.[102]

Taken individually, the Cooperative Principles and values are not unique to cooperatives. For example, any enterprise can espouse ethical values of the sort listed above (and many do, although, like cooperatives, in practice many fall short of their ideals). Additionally, it is not unusual for traditional companies to implement democratic practices among various levels of their work force (so-called shop floor democracy); by the same token, a common complaint with regard to cooperatives is a lack of opportunities for meaningful democratic participation, especially for nonmember employees. Also, the values of self-help and self-responsibility are espoused by many voluntary associations (for example, Alcoholics Anonymous). The uniqueness of cooperatives, then, comes from the whole set of values and principles. The significance lies in the very structure itself, and in the ideological framework that underlies that structure—the framework laid out by William Thompson.

Ideology and the Cooperative Principles

There is no consensus on the ideology behind the cooperative principles. Indeed, it is often remarked that the cooperative movement owes much of its success to the lack of ideology, including its stated neutrality on religious and political questions.[103] Political and religious neutrality, however, should not be confused with a lack of ideology. There must be some ideological basis for the principles; this could take the form of a "central" principle, or a principle that unifies the set. Three competing perspectives, based on economic, associational, and democratic principles, have been suggested over time.

Cooperatives' Practices: The Economic Principle as Primary

Fairbairn notes that "the divi," or patronage refund, is the best known of the cooperative principles.[104] Indeed, for some cooperatives, the dividend seems to be the only part of the principles directly discussed in their literature.[105] However, the dividend itself is not a principle, but a practice that arises out of the principle that profits are distributed to members, not to capital. Lambert refers to this as a negative principle, because there is nothing in the principles that says that a dividend *must* be paid, only that it *shall not* be used as a reward to capital investment.[106] In fact, in their rules adopted in 1854, the Pioneers referred to the dividend as a distribution of "the residue" left after deducting from net revenue: (1) management expenses, (2) interest on loans, (3) depreciation of fixed assets, (4) a fixed percentage paid as interest to capital invested, (5) funds set aside for a reserve or for expansion, and (6) two and a half percent set aside for "educational purposes."[107]

Ironically, while it appears to have been considered as the least important thing to do with the cooperative's funds (by the Pioneers, at least), it may have been the primary factor in the rapid acceptance and growth of consumer cooperatives, for two principal reasons: The first is that, even if the cooperative charged market prices, members knew that at the end of the term (for Rochdale, quarterly) they would receive something back for their patronage, which encouraged them to do as much of their shopping there as possible. But another reason has to do with the Chartist principle of exclusive dealing, or only patronizing merchants who supported the Charter. While the Charter movement was mostly relegated to the past by the time the Rochdale-led movement picked up steam, the idea of shopping as a political act had already been well ingrained among the working class. Thus, the political implications must have been quite clear—when shopping at the cooperative they really were shopping at *their own store*,[108] and the divi only served to emphasize and remind them of the real economic implications of that fact.

Here, then, is where the revolutionary potential of consumers' cooperation lies: if the people who make their living through wages (as opposed to investment) were to shift all or even much of their shopping to cooperatives, capital would be effectively starved of its profits, and the "residue" that would otherwise have gone to investors would go to the member-patrons of the cooperatives instead. Lambert refers to this as "a silent revolution."[109] This is their common property, they own it together, and, when all is said and done, they enjoy the financial benefits of that ownership.

However, as Lambert points out, the dividend itself cannot be the measure of whether an enterprise is a cooperative or not. There are two problems with giving the dividend the primary position: first, to require it would be to doom many cooperatives to failure. There are many good reasons why cooperatives may not pay a dividend in any given year, whether from insufficient revenue to cover expenses or because other interests, such as expansion or education, take priority. But Lambert also notes that while one of the fundamental ideas of cooperatives is to address social inequalities, the dividend itself may perpetuate them, because "they would be proportional to each individual's capabilities and efforts: the highest income would automatically give a right to the highest purchases and return."[110] So, while the principle of rewarding patronage rather than capital is of great importance, it cannot be the most important one.

Association as the "First Principle": William Watkins

Former ICA director William Watkins,[111] one of the architects of the 1966 revision of the ICA Cooperative Principles, notes that "the word 'principle' has different meanings for different people." He argues (prior to the 1994 revision) that what the ICA refers to as principles are, in fact, operating rules or practices that are only principles in the sense that they are the basic set of rules that define cooperatives, to which cooperatives must adhere in order to be considered as such. He offers a set of what he sees as principles in the sense of "general ideas which inspire and govern the application of the Co-operative technique of social organisation [which] result from inductive reasoning upon experience of fundamental and universal social realities. They lay down lines for the Co-operative solution of social problems to which those realities give rise." He enumerates six such principles: "Association (or Unity); Economy; Equity; Democracy; Liberty; Education."[112] Association/Unity is, in his view, the most important.[113]

Watkins argues that the importance of Association can be recognized because at the simplest, most ostensive level, the formation of a cooperative is an instance of people coming together to, in his words, "satisfy common needs, achieve common ends, or derive mutual advantage."[114] "Association" represents the coming together of individuals in a way that counteracts the increasing individualism of liberal capitalism, in some senses similar to labor unions, although the two seek to address the problems of capitalism from opposite sides of the economic equation. It is, in effect, an exercise of economic power. In that sense, then, size matters: the larger the organization, the greater the influence it can bring to bear on producers and suppliers. Ultimately, local cooperative societies must take their association to a higher level by establishing federations; these federations then may achieve sufficient size to be able to take over the functions of distribution and, finally, finance and production.[115] This horizontal and vertical integration brings important cumulative benefits, according to Watkins, as greater control over the supply chain enables the profits to be reinvested to continue expansion (not unlike in capitalist firms) or returned to the members. Thus, the principle of Association is primary, Watkins argues, because it is through association that cooperatives are able to exercise sufficient power in the market to make a difference in their members' lives—and, by extension, in society as a whole.[116]

There are problems with assigning primacy to Association, however. The first of these is that increasing size has a weakening effect on association itself. The larger the society, the less connection its members are likely to feel with it, the more alienated it becomes from them, the less it must rely on member involvement, and the more it must rely on professional management. In other words, the bigger it is, the less it understands its members and their needs as individuals. If it is the case, as Watkins argues, that "in many branches of distribution today the true operational unit has ceased to be the local society and can be nothing smaller than the whole national movement,"[117] then it would seem that the associational aspect of the cooperative has been lost. This may not be a fatal problem if methods are implemented in order to maintain and enhance the local character of a larger society by, for example, establishing a local council for each retail branch, but it clearly represents a challenge that must be addressed.

A second problem with considering Association to be the most important principle is that it may undermine other principles. For example, increasing size can have a negative effect on democratic practices. Watkins recognizes this when he notes that the application of democratic principles "to large-scale enterprises is beset with difficulties."[118] The problem of increasing professionalization in management may have positive aspects with regard to ensuring the long-term viability of an enterprise (although professional management can also make mistakes with disastrous effects), but it also has problematic tendencies as it leads to a class of officials whose interests, focus, and concerns may come to be different from those of the membership.[119] Greater professionalization can also undermine Responsibility, another of the principles Watkins outlines. Part of what makes the cooperative a different sort of enterprise is that it alters the relationship between its members, such that they are no longer alienated from one another but are engaged with one another in an enterprise. As Watkins argues, this engagement gives rise to an important sense of responsibility with regard not only to the enterprise but to one's fellow members.[120] Professionalization, however, implies professional control, which will tend to undermine members' participation and sense of responsibility. Finally, while not confined to large organizations, the bigger the group the greater the likelihood of factions developing that may undermine the functioning of the whole.

To enumerate these problems is not to suggest that Watkins's Association principle is unimportant. In fact it is clearly fundamental. The point, rather, is to show that it cannot stand alone as the primary principle.

Democracy as Cooperation's Core: Paul Lambert

Watkins recognizes the importance of democracy as a cooperative principle. Indeed, he recognizes that it is "the major feature which distinguishes Co-operation as a system of economic organization" and that "more than a few" theorists of cooperatives consider democracy to be primary.[121] Paul Lambert, whose work is frequently cited in this regard, refers to democracy as the "true yardstick of co-operatives."[122] One of the reasons why it should be considered primary, he argues, is that it applies across the full spectrum of cooperatives, regardless of size or type. Of all their characteristics, it is the feature that most clearly distinguishes them from traditional enterprises. Indeed, the lack of democratic practices—in particular, the failure to implement the one-person one-vote rule—is what sets an enterprise outside of the sphere of cooperatives. In this regard, Lambert discusses the large agricultural producer cooperatives, where "a few big landowners employing farm workers combine to form a purchasing or marketing co-operative," calling this a case of "superficially a staunch adherence to the Rochdale principles but in the last resort an absence of democracy" because the people who are most directly involved in the activity of the cooperative—the workers—are excluded from any participation in the cooperative's decision-making. The point of cooperatives is to improve the well-being of people, but in cooperatives made up of independent enterprises it becomes not one *person* one vote but one (member) *company* one vote.[123]

Lambert's critique of agricultural cooperatives could apply to consumer cooperatives with a hired workforce where no mechanism exists to involve them in decision making, but there are some important differences. It may be true that, for the most part, employees do not have a role in the governance of consumer cooperatives.[124] The point has to do with the nature of the "involvement" that constitutes the cooperative. In a consumer cooperative, the involvement is that of consumption—that is, buying the products sold by the cooperative. The individuals who are engaged in this activity are the ones who generate its capital, benefit from it, and, in the end, are the ones who run it. In a worker cooperative, the form of involvement is labor, or producing the products sold by the cooperative. In this case, too, the individuals who provide the labor generate its capital, benefit from it, and govern it on the basis of one person one vote. But in an agricultural cooperative, the members are companies, not individuals. If the definition of a cooperative is that it is "an autonomous association of persons," an agribusiness does not meet this definition. While many agricultural cooperatives may be made up of family farms, it is still the *farm,* not the individuals who actually perform the labor to produce the goods, that is a member. However, this remains a substantial gray area in cooperative theory.

Democracy is generally accepted as an essential element of cooperatives, but while it cannot be said to undermine other principles, it is not without its problems. Principally, however, these are problems of translating theory into practice. On the one hand is the problem of exclusion, as noted above. While Lambert argues that workers in consumer cooperatives must be able to participate in governance,[125] Watkins raises concerns about employees organizing themselves into a faction and taking control from the consumer-members.[126] Another concern for consumer cooperatives arises when a major portion of the business is conducted with nonmembers. Lambert goes so far as to say that no cooperative can be considered genuine in such a case, because then a minority (the members) would benefit from the activity of a majority (the nonmember consumers), which would be "contrary to the co-operative spirit."[127] This may be true, but at worst it suggests a challenge for cooperatives to convince nonmembers of the value of joining, and it means that the cost of membership cannot be so high that it constitutes a barrier (although, as discussed above, it should be meaningful). But in the absence of an effective means for limiting sales to nonmembers, and as long as membership is open to all, the objection is not a strong one.

More significant are problems associated with size. Some of these have been discussed above. Lambert raises a concern with very low participation rates in annual general meetings by members of large cooperative societies—as low as 0.14 percent in one case in 1954; one can imagine these rates have only gotten worse.[128] This reflects the alienation and apathy that arise as cooperatives grow large. Lambert discusses a variety of mechanisms whereby members might be encouraged to participate more directly (including the use of smaller local and regional meetings that would feed into a larger general meeting), but he concludes that this is not a great concern, because what he calls the "essence of democracy" is the possibility for the expression of opposition. As long as that possibility exists, even when "the members may appear to be sunk in apathy," the cooperative has not lost its democratic character.[129]

The Unifying Principle

There is no question that cooperatives are a very particular sort of enterprise, although what makes them particular is not their content (i.e., the sort of business they are engaged in) but their form. Unlike traditional capitalist enterprises, cooperatives adhere (at least in theory) to a set of principles. Underlying these principles is an ideology. The key to understanding the ideology is understanding the principles, and in particular identifying a unifying principle that holds the set together. I have examined three of the principles—the economic principle of member involvement and member benefit, the association principle, and the democratic principle—and found that while each is of central importance, each also comes with problems that to some degree represent conflicts with the other principles. For this reason, none of these three can be the unifying principle. It turns out, then, that the unifying principle may be something that stands outside of the set enumerated by the ICA.

At this point we may return, at last, to William Thompson. If the three principles discussed above are given slightly different names that nonetheless reflect their content—equality and common property, voluntary association, and democracy— it is immediately apparent that these are none other than the principles subsidiary to utility in Thompson's utilitarianism. It is certainly true that cooperatives today look very different from what Thompson had envisioned, but it is clear that they embody his principles. Thus, the unifying principle that is at the heart of what we might call the cooperative ideology is clear: the greatest happiness of the greatest number.

Happiness, Thompson, and the Cooperative Principles

Today's cooperatives—autonomous voluntary associations, collectively owned and democratically run—are a more limited version of the autonomous voluntary communities, collectively owned and democratically run, that Thompson advocated. Collective ownership as practiced in cooperatives can be recognized as ensuring that cooperatives function in the interests of all members rather than in the interest of a few major shareholders. The "one-member-one-vote" rule ensures formal political equality,[130] although the Cooperative Principles could say more about making sure that all members have equal opportunity to participate in the decision making of the cooperative, and most cooperatives (at least, of the consumer and producer type) fail to address issues of distributional equality. And, just as Thompson emphasizes the importance of both education and participation in the life of the community for the development of each person's rational faculties,[131] education has been a part of the Cooperative Principles since the days of the Rochdale Pioneers—although many cooperatives, at least in the United States, fail to follow through on the fifth Cooperative Principle's call for them to "inform the general public—particularly young people and opinion leaders—about the nature and benefits of co-operation."

Although limited in practice, at the heart of the Principles is the idea that cooperatives change the nature of the relationship between their members, giving them the opportunity to see that their own interests are best served when they work with others to meet the collective interests of the members of the community. In other words, the happiness of each member is related to the well-being of the membership as a whole, something that is reflected in the notion of "mutual self-help."[132] As

Thompson argued, this notion can only be embodied in institutions that are voluntary, democratically run, and collectively owned. And it is through the union of interests that the greatest happiness of all members of the community can be most effectively pursued.

It would be a vulgar interpretation of his work to suggest that Thompson believed that simply forming cooperatives would make people happier, and I doubt that anyone today would suggest that there is an inverse relationship between membership growth in cooperatives and sales of antidepressants. Still, it is an inescapable conclusion that Thompson believed, as do today's advocates of cooperatives, that the growth of cooperatives could make for a better society.[133] In fact, there is no question that cooperatives *have* affected the well-being of people around the world, from working-class families in Britain in the nineteenth century to craftspeople in impoverished communities in many parts of the Global South today, if only by helping to improve their standard of living.[134] But, as has been argued repeatedly throughout this work, wealth is only one part of happiness, and this is certainly only one part of the political significance of cooperatives. As is noted in the Background Paper published with the Cooperative Principles, "helping to provide a better way of life—cultural, intellectual and spiritual—may become one of the most important ways in which the co-operatives can benefit their members and contribute to their communities."[135]

In a formal sense, cooperatives are political in their potential to affect the political attitudes and sense of efficacy of their members. As was seen in the last chapter, Thompson argues that, schooled in the democratic environment of the cooperative community, cooperative members may be expected to have a more expansive, benevolent attitude when it comes to larger political questions. Pateman presents both normative arguments and empirical evidence to support the claim that we "learn to participate by participating" and that there is a direct link between the feelings of political efficacy and what she describes as a "participatory environment."[136] More recent research demonstrates that those who have opportunities to engage in participatory decision-making systems are more likely to become involved in formal political practices—thereby providing further explanation beyond socioeconomic status as to why those who are employed in managerial positions are more likely to be active participants in electoral politics.[137] This is reflected in the ICA's elaboration of the value of self-help, where it is argued that this requires "association with others," and that, "Individuals . . . develop through co-operative action by the skills they learn in facilitating the growth of their co-operative; by the understanding they gain of their fellow-members; by the insights they gain about the wider society of which they are a part."[138]

Self-help, in this sense, also points to additional political effects where cooperatives provide people with a means for empowering themselves, not simply as individuals but within a collectivity, such that individuals are empowered from within the community rather than against or in contrast to it. This empowerment effect has been noted in contexts where rural poverty meets traditional power structures. Empowerment in this sense refers not only to the ability of individuals to exert control over the conditions of their lives with regard to formal structures of power, but also to informal economic and social institutions. At the same time it points to some of the challenges that arise in the face of well-established forms of domination, especially when it comes to the subordination of women,[139] as well as the dangers of state-sponsored cooperative development where empowerment comes with strings attached.

The Cooperative Principles, then, serve as a remarkable example of the application of political theory to produce real and meaningful change in people's lives. One attractive element is that significant political, economic, and social change can come without the disruption and violence associated with capturing state power. After all, nothing in the Cooperative Principles is unfamiliar from the perspective of liberal capitalism. But while cooperatives are able to exist within the dominant framework, their implementation leads to institutional structures that are radically different from those that dominate liberal capitalist society. While there are certainly cooperatives that make every effort to blend into the capitalist system, as well as those that consider themselves to be vanguards for far-reaching social change, certain fundamental features are common to all cooperatives, and are required in order for them to be thought of as cooperatives, even if they don't adhere terribly well to the Cooperative Principles. These features, which are entirely consistent with Thompson's arguments, are that they are owned in common and controlled by their members, for whose benefit they explicitly exist, not for people whose sole connection to the enterprise is the fact that they have invested some of their money in it. Cooperatives *do* exist for the benefit of a particular group of people, and it is true that what distinguishes those people is the fact that they have an ownership stake in the cooperative, but they benefit from it as *users* of the cooperative, not as shareholders whose only interest is in the maximization of profit.

Thompson's theory does raise questions about the structure of cooperatives today and how they may affect the alignment of self-interest with social interests. Thompson clearly argues that one of the most important means for this alignment is through the collective ownership of property. But he also makes clear that this alignment depends on regular interaction among member/owners. This would seem to imply that cooperatives come closest to fulfilling both the spirit of Thompson's vision and the Cooperative Principles when they are able to develop a strong ownership and participation ethic among their members. Clearly, this may have implications for the size and type of the cooperative: Smaller cooperatives will have an easier time of this than larger ones, and although it is not impossible for large cooperatives, neither is it guaranteed for small ones. But the more that members interact with other members, the more they can see and experience the mutual character of the cooperative, and the closer they approach Thompson's vision. Also, the type of cooperative may make a difference: this mutuality may be particularly difficult for the large agricultural distribution cooperatives (such as Sunkist and Ocean Spray). It may also be a challenge for consumer cooperatives generally (especially the larger ones, such as REI in the United States or The Cooperative Group in the UK), where the domain of shared interests of consumers as consumers is likely to be more limited in scope than the domain of interests shared by producers as producers in worker's cooperatives. Then again, for worker's cooperatives the challenge is to retain a strong sense of the enterprise as part of a larger community and avoid the perception of the worker's interests as being in opposition to or in competition with the interests of the larger community.

By the same token, given the rapacious nature of late-modern capitalism, survival may require consolidation and federation. This points in the opposite direction, to increased size, more bureaucratic structures that resist member control, and greater organizational distance from individual members. This is not necessarily the case, however, as horizontal and vertical integration may in fact present opportunities for the forging of stronger connections between different communities in networks of interaction that, for example, connect producers with consumers or people in different regions in systems of mutual benefit.[140]

One of the conclusions we can draw from this discussion is that the elements of what I am calling the ideology of cooperatives interact with one another and cannot be understood in isolation from one another. Thompson's subsidiary principles—voluntary association, equality, united effort/common ownership, and democracy—depend on the greatest happiness principle from which they draw their meaning. At the same time, they are specific elements by which social institutions can be measured, and the greatest happiness, as Thompson understood it, can best be promoted with the maximization of all of the principles.[141]

Cooperatives and Social Change

The cooperative movement has achieved a level of success that Thompson may have only dreamed of, but it also seems to have left important elements of his vision behind. I am not referring here to the shift from the cooperative community to the more limited form of a specific economic enterprise, but to the sense of cooperatives as a movement for social change. Certainly that sense exists for many who participate in small cooperatives, and it may exist for at least some of the people who are in leadership positions in the movement. But the move into the economic mainstream has led many cooperatives to avoid discussion of principles or progress. Certainly, cooperatives have none of the trappings of what we have come to expect in a social movement: there are no inspirational slogans, no rallies or marches, and only rarely vocal demands for some sort of state action.[142]

Cooperatives represent a model for social change that is generally less visible than the typical social movement because it is social change by social action, through people carrying out the regular functions of their lives, rather than through episodic demands for state action. But for many cooperatives, the notion of social change is not just less visible, but invisible. For example, when cooperatives' monthly newsletters to members include nothing but announcements for upcoming events and special benefits for members, and are silent about cooperative principles and values or cooperative history or the broader social vision they embody, then it is difficult to see how this promotes social change or furthers the movement. Similarly, if a cooperative's Web site fails to provide even the most basic information about what a cooperative is—such as the ICA's definition and the Cooperative Principles—then it would seem that the idea that this is a part of some kind of "social movement" seems dubious at best.

I have argued elsewhere that it would be difficult to consider the cooperative "movement" in the United States as a movement for social change.[143] At the same time, I agree with Huet's argument that to work for the development of cooperatives constitutes important work for social change.[144] Considering the challenges of the future and the role of cooperatives in helping to address them, MacPherson concludes, "In the final analysis, the co-operative promise is that it is possible and ultimately necessary that economic and social affairs be conducted democratically and responsibly for the present and long-term benefits of the members and their communities."[145] Clearly, there is great potential.[146] But for that potential to be realized, cooperatives must celebrate their difference, not hide it. They should take advantage of opportunities to remind people of the advantages of association and of owning the enterprise together, so that their democratic nature is meaningful. Members of a cooperative form a kind of community, but oftentimes there are few markers to designate it as such. These need to be established and reinforced. As Thompson argued, "A more important and more extensive change in human society was never contemplated by the mind of man."[147] Those who are interested in bringing about the kind of change reflected in the Cooperative Principles should keep in mind that in order to contemplate a change, the markers of that change must be evident.

Conclusion

The Concept of Happiness

Happiness, it appears, belongs in the set of "essentially contested concepts" as the term is defined by Gallie: it is used as a means of appraising some object or condition; it can be described in a variety of ways, none of which may make a prima facie claim to precedence; it cannot accept a specific value of measurement; and it gets used both to defend particular arrangements and to attack arrangements supported by those who hold a different conception.[1] It may also be considered a confused or hopelessly vague concept,[2] especially when it relies on such an indeterminate, subjective quality as pleasure—although this simply points back to its nature as a contested concept, as some might argue that the vagueness or confusion is only evidence of the weakness of the subjective hedonistic conception of happiness.

A historical perspective makes the significance of this contestation abundantly clear. The ancient Greeks held that happiness was something that only had meaning when considered over the course of a life span, whereas the dominant philosophy in contemporary economics considers it to be a fleeting experience, experienced in the moment and difficult to capture. For the better part of two thousand years, happiness was associated with the abnegation of desire; only in the last two hundred years or so has the emphasis been on the pursuit of pleasure and the fulfillment of desire. The emphasis on virtue that was a central feature in classical theory clearly connected individual happiness to the well-being of others. This connection has been lost with the invention of the modern, self-interested, hedonistic individual who seeks nothing other than the maximization of his or her pleasures and the minimization of his or her pains—along with the assertion that pleasure is morally good, and pain morally evil. The moral character of happiness is, of course, deeply connected to its political character, as our ideas about it affect what we do and how we relate to other people and the world around us.

The two concepts of happiness that underlie modern social science have been examined here: the idea that happiness is a purely subjective matter, and the objective view that holds that a standard or more context-sensitive set of standards can—and should—be used as a basis for measurement. Bentham's idea that happiness is the experience of pleasure and the absence of pain, and that "*pain* and *pleasure* at least, are words which a man has no need . . . to go to a Lawyer to know the meaning of,"[3] place him firmly in the subjective camp, so there is good reason for Bruni and Porta to refer to this group as "Benthamite-subjective-hedonic-individualistic." Thompson, on the other hand, with his assertion that happiness is a matter of the conditions in which one lives one's life and despite his agreement with Bentham that pleasure is constitutive of happiness, clearly is a member of the group Bruni and Porta call "Aristotelian-objective-eudaimonic-relational."[4] This fundamental difference serves to explain the very substantial differences between the conclusions they reach and the kinds of social and political institutions they promote, despite the similarities in their language and in their shared commitment to "the greatest happiness."

The Hedonic Heart of Bentham's Conception of Happiness

For all the simplicity of Bentham's view of pleasure, his view of happiness turns out to be quite a bit more complex than he lets on. Admittedly, it would help if he were more consistent in his usage. It would also help if he were clearer about the relationship between pleasure, happiness, and well-being. Alas, these questions are left to his interpreters to consider and, while they seem quite fundamental to an understanding of his work, they have mostly been overlooked in favor of close examinations of the functions of pleasure and pain and the requirements for utility, usually either at the level of the individual, or in terms of its use as a tool for legislators, although the distinction is rarely noticed. One result of this has been the rise of a vulgar Benthamism, embodied in neoclassical economics, that reduces well-being and happiness to pleasure, and fails to put happiness, or the pursuit of pleasure (and avoidance of pain) for that matter, into its proper perspective with regard to well-being, ignoring the subsidiary principles of subsistence, security, abundance, and equality that Bentham considered essential.

Bentham, of course, knew full well what he was about, and he was a powerful advocate for social and political change to promote his vision. He believed that the fundamental basis of all human activity was self-interest, but that, in pursuing it, people left to themselves might undermine the happiness of others (and, quite possibly, their own), so it was up to legislators to establish laws to affect individual calculations of self-interest so as to guide people away from actions that would tend to harm others. Another way of putting this is to say that the principal role of government is to provide people with a sense of security, principally in the form of private property rights, so they would know that they could enjoy the fruits of their labor or that they would be rewarded for taking financial risks. Government need do little to encourage people to seek their own subsistence, he thought, but if it did its job well, the people might enjoy abundance. Further, government policy should promote equality to the greatest extent possible (without undermining security) to ensure the widest distribution of happiness.

None of this would be possible, however, without a government that was committed to adopting policies that would promote the greatest happiness of the greatest number. The only way to ensure that kind of government was to make it accountable to the people it supposedly served. For this there were two basic requirements: representative democracy with frequent secret ballot elections and a wide suffrage (removing exclusion based on class or status but retaining those based on sex and age) and a free press. Beyond this, individuals should be assured the greatest degree of liberty, limited only by the fear of punishment should they cause avoidable harm either directly or indirectly to others (for anything ranging from positive crimes to failing to succeed at supporting themselves through their labor). While a firm believer in the role of government to ensure honesty and fair dealing, Bentham was also a firm believer in the power of the free market to set prices at the correct levels, so that labor is compensated at the proper rate, and business and finance function efficiently. He was, therefore, both an authoritarian in the sense that he felt that the civil code could be used to shape people's behavior, and a libertarian in the sense that the imposition of limits was itself a kind of harm that should be avoided to the greatest possible degree.

Thompson and Happiness as a Condition of Life

That Bentham could be considered Thompson's mentor is evident from Thompson's own proclamations of fealty, but it comes across in the similarities in their language. Both are concerned with happiness and with ensuring that all members of society are able to enjoy it to the greatest possible degree. Both consider subsistence, security, abundance, and equality to be essential to this end, although in different ways and to different degrees. But the parallels end there: where Bentham is a proponent of private property and competitive, free markets, Thompson argues that these are all productive of great evils and that achieving the greatest happiness requires reconciling security and equality. Thompson solved the dilemma Bentham faced—that measures to promote equality might undermine security—by organizing production and consumption into relatively small (by our measure; large by his), autarkic communities in which all share equally in the production of and the consumption of its produce. This, he felt, was the only way that what he called the "natural laws of distribution," voluntary production, voluntary exchange, and securing the full produce of labor to the laborers, could be realized. So, Thompson's political economy is fundamentally different from Bentham's. But why, if they seem to have the same goals and use the same language, would they arrive at such radically different conclusions? The answer, I have argued here, is that the difference in their political economics is related to the difference in their views of happiness.

Thompson agrees with Bentham that pleasure is a necessary basis for happiness, since no one could be said to be happy who did not experience pleasure, but the essential difference between them lies in Thompson's claim that happiness is equivalent to well-being (in contrast to Bentham's argument that they are distinct). Where happiness for Bentham is a kind of experience, for Thompson it is more of an ongoing condition of life, more a general feeling than a temporal state. But if happiness is not associated with any particular experience, then pleasure loses its status as the primary source of motivation.

As it turns out, the condition of a person's life must be more fundamental to his or her happiness than any direct experience of pleasure, because, Thompson argues, while it may be the case that people seek pleasure and avoid pain, what they consider to be pleasure or pain is not predetermined, but a product of their society. Building on Robert Owen's "philosophy of necessity," Thompson argues that there is a direct and necessary connection between the character of the institutions that make up a society and the character of the people in it. On the one hand, institutions that rely on competitive relationships will cause people to see themselves as being at odds with the people around them: "In every happy face, we now see a successful rival."[5] On the other hand, a benevolent society will arise where its institutions foster cooperative relationships. Thus, for Thompson, the alignment of self-interest and social interest may still be a political process, but rather than being produced by the machinations of public servants, as it is for Bentham, it comes about through the interaction of people within social institutions that are designed specifically to promote that alignment. Democracy, then, is integral in Thompson's theory where it is instrumental in Bentham's, because it is a principle of social interaction that describes a dimension of the way people relate to one another—democratic if on the basis of equality, or authoritarian (or at least nondemocratic) if otherwise.

Thompson's analysis of political economics leads him to a powerful critique of the "system of individual competition," or what we would refer to as liberal capitalism. Unlike his contemporaries, Thompson did not accept as a presupposition that those who provide the capital have the right to the surplus value produced by those who provide the labor; rather, he argues, the surplus value belongs to those who produce it. The only reason laborers accept less than the full value of the produce of their labor is because they have no choice: they must accept the capitalist's terms, or starve. This, Thompson argues, is a form of coercion that undermines the greatest happiness, for two reasons: first, because of the existence of coercion, which always indicates that a person is being required to do something they see as being against their interests, and second because workers will be less productive, and produce less wealth, when a portion of it—the greater portion, in many cases—is "abstracted" from them against their will.

So, the system of individual competition, with the accumulation of private property as its principal object, undermines the greatest happiness because competition is antithetical to mutuality, and because competition produces inequality, which produces subordination, which means that the production and distribution of wealth are organized to benefit not the great masses of people, but the few who control capital. In addition, those who benefit from inequality are able to use their superior wealth to ensure that the power of the state is exercised in such a way as to protect their privilege and property—not to ensure the security of the workers.

The enjoyment of wealth is not, however, the only kind of pleasure. Wealth is associated with physical pleasures, which are essential, but where Bentham argues that all pleasure is, in its essence, the same, Thompson argues that other forms of pleasure—those which involve the mind and the social pleasures—are what we might call "higher" pleasures (though he does not use the term himself). In a society where security and equality are reconciled, where private property and competition are abolished, and where people do not suffer insecurity in their subsistence, their desire for wealth will be modest, balanced by their desire for leisure time in which they can enjoy the greater sources of pleasure: learning, discussion and debate, producing and enjoying art, etc. Compared to a society focused on the "rat race" and the competitive accumulation of property, where hedonism can be seen as one of the markers of insecurity, such a society would, in Thompson's view, experience a much higher degree of happiness, which would also be much more equally distributed, leading not only to "the greatest happiness," but "the greatest happiness of the greatest number."

With his endorsement of the view that the greatest happiness is the yardstick for moral and political reasoning, Thompson can be considered a utilitarian, but of a very different sort from Bentham. In Thompson's work, five principles take the place of Bentham's subsidiary principles of subsistence, security, abundance, and equality. These are security, equality, voluntarism, democracy, and united effort/common property. Like Bentham's subsidiary principles these can be understood as the means by which the greatest happiness of the greatest number can be brought about, but although the first three may be seen as the basis for the latter two, this is not a hierarchy as is Bentham's.

Thompson became a powerful advocate of the development of cooperative communities based on a version of Robert Owen's plan for self-sufficient communities of between five hundred and two thousand members. While Thompson's own detailed plan to combine housing, consumption, and production into one democratic community never came to fruition,[6] his ideas are at the ideological foundations of the modern cooperative movement, which usually traces its founding to the establishment of the Rochdale cooperative society in 1844. The Rochdale model of autonomous enterprises is very different from Thompson's vision of autarkic community, and as it has grown—it now claims more than a billion members in more than one hundred countries—and addressed the challenges of survival in the face of ever-expanding global capitalism, the Rochdale model has become farther distanced from Thompson's theory. Nonetheless, Thompson's fundamental principles—specifically, equality, voluntarism, democracy, and common property[7]—remain at the heart of the cooperative movement.

As the weaknesses of the global economy have become increasingly evident, the cooperative movement has received greater attention. Given the recent global economic collapse, it is neither ironic nor mere coincidence that the UN named 2012 the International Year of the Cooperative (IYC). More generally, important new directions in economic theory have opened up over the past thirty years in response to the kinds of problems associated with the assumptions of neoclassical theory. Those who study happiness seem to have reached conclusions that, on some level at least, are more in line with Thompson's arguments than with Bentham's—most particularly the point that happiness should be understood as a life condition, better seen as well-being than as pleasure. For example, the Stiglitz Commission report is quite clear in emphasizing not only the relevance of social institutions to well-being, but the importance of equality and the distribution of wealth.[8]

From Cooperative Community to the Cooperative Movement

Although Thompson did not succeed in establishing cooperative communities on the model he outlined, his ideas were not merely swept into the dustbin of history. Although they look little like the self-sufficient, autarkic communities Thompson envisioned, cooperatives today can be seen as a kind of embodiment of his theory, in an ideal if not always a practical sense. Equality, democracy, voluntarism, and common property are present to the extent that cooperatives are governed on democratic principles and all members have an equal voice (one member, one vote); people may join or leave of their own free will, and where there are limits to membership due to capacity (such as agricultural or worker cooperatives) there is no discrimination in accepting new members; and the cooperative belongs to the members in common, meaning that no one's ownership stake is greater than anyone else's, and no one has a greater say—in a formal sense, at least—than do others.

In practice, cooperatives fall short of Thompson's theory in a variety of ways, for example where they fail to provide meaningful opportunities for member participation and where democracy is limited to annual elections for members of a board of directors. In her day-to-day interactions, a member may have no less of a sense of alienation from a huge consumer cooperative federation than she does from, for example, a supermarket chain. Indeed, she might feel a closer connection to the mom-and-pop grocery store on the corner than to other members in her three hundred thousand member credit union. In their defense, one might argue that in contrast to the failed notion of communities, these are real, existing institutions that have had to survive in a highly competitive environment. Size may not only be a sign of success, but in a society that remains dominated by traditional capitalist enterprises, where access to resources can make the difference between success and failure, it can also be valuable as a survival mechanism. Indeed, size in and of itself may not be a problem where members have opportunities to participate, for example in local or branch councils.[9] However, increasing growth and the professionalization of management has tended to impede, rather than promote, the involvement of members.

These practical questions are political issues that test the true democratic nature of cooperatives: for those cooperatives that fail to provide opportunities for participation, it might reflect a general level of satisfaction by members who don't consider it important to make use of the democratic procedures that do exist to express opposition and effect change, or it could reflect an exercise of power within the cooperative to effectively exclude members, perhaps in the name of efficiency, stability, or growth. This is an empirical question, however; from a theoretical perspective, the potential for democratic participation, at least, remains a feature of cooperatives that clearly sets them apart from traditional capitalist enterprises. But the issue points to a more fundamental concern, that, where these issues of inclusion and participation exist, cooperatives have lost any sense of their fundamental character as mutual associations, of people coming together to address common concerns. Something important is lost in the mainstreaming of cooperatives and their distance from their origins as a movement for social change—indeed, it makes it difficult to understand cooperatives as a "movement" at all.

Despite the difficulty of recognizing cooperatives as a social movement, it remains the case that they have made a significant difference in the lives of billions of people around the world—a fact recognized by the United Nations' 2012 IYC designation. But while they may have affected the well-being of billions, the language of happiness is no longer an explicit part of the cooperative movement in the way it was during Thompson's time. Indeed, one clear distinction between the earlier, "Owenite" phase of the cooperative movement (prior to 1844) and its current phase is that the mutual pursuit of happiness is no longer deployed as the primary motivation for the formation of cooperative associations. It is difficult to attach too much meaning to this, as the reference to happiness could be seen as nothing but a convenient rhetorical device. On the other hand, at the center of Thompson's ideological system—which, as I have argued, provides the basis for the cooperative movement—is his alternative conception of happiness. This is the basis from which a system arises that has a fundamentally different structure than that of liberal capitalism. At its heart, the political ideology of cooperatives is based on the notion that they change the nature of the relationship between their members, giving them the opportunity to see that their own interests are best served when they work with others to meet the collective interests of the members of the community—in other words, to see that the happiness of each is inseparable from the happiness of all. Where this fundamental idea is articulated, cooperatives retain their political salience and their ability to be perceived as agents for social change. Where they fail to articulate it, they become little different from traditional capitalist firms.

Conclusion

The conditions in which we live our lives are very different from those which Jeremy Bentham and William Thompson confronted, at least in the advanced industrialized societies. There is, generally speaking, a consensus in favor of the democratic governance of states with universal suffrage, secret ballots, and reasonably frequent elections (if not annual, as Bentham proposed). In most places, legal rights are established that enable a free press to hold the powerful to account (should they choose to do so), that ensure that most people have their daily bread and a roof over their heads, and that they will be remunerated for their labor. Slavery has been outlawed (if not eliminated) and debtors' prisons abolished. The rise of the middle class has brought a measure of economic equality and affluence for a substantial portion of the population.[10] While there is no question that perfection has not been achieved on any of these measures, the promises of liberal capitalism of an improving standard of living for everyone[11] have not proven empty: life for most people in the "advanced" nations of the world is much improved from what it was two hundred years ago. That this has come about as a result of an intense and difficult (and continuing) struggle against entrenched power, and that much of the advance, especially in the last half of the twentieth century, came on the backs of people in other parts of the world, are important points that should be remembered, although they do not lessen the nature of the contrast. Much of the abject misery and insecurity under which the vast majority of people lived in Britain in the early years of the nineteenth century, as well as the absolute impunity of those who enjoy wealth and power, has been eliminated for most—but not all—people across the Western world. It might cautiously be suggested, in the absence of any firm empirical evidence, that a greater level of happiness has been achieved.

Does this suggest that we have reached some sort of magical "end of history," our institutional structures organized so as to produce the best possible results? We can reject the idea on many—or any—terms. The first problem is that to suggest that this is the best that we can do is to ignore the fact that even with all of the improvements that have been made, great inequalities still exist, and large numbers of people—even if no longer the majority—live in miserable conditions made worse not only by the contrast with the increase in living standards for the rest, but in order to *produce* that increase, as the so-called "resource wars" over oil in the Middle East or minerals to make cell phones in central Africa, might attest. Despite political and social advances the rich and powerful still enjoy a high degree of control over social institutions, as well as an immense amount of privilege and a great deal of impunity (as reflected in the slogans "Too Big to Fail" and "Too Big to Jail"). And the Industrial Revolution, having provided so much wealth to so many, is beginning to take its toll in the degradation and destruction of ecosystems, the depletion of natural resources, and the alteration of the climate.

At the same time, from the perspective of liberal capitalism itself, the answer must also be "no," because if it were the case that society had achieved its maximum level of advancement, then the game would be over and the system would collapse. The capitalist economy depends on the endless stimulation of desire, which means that it requires that people be, in a fundamental sense, dissatisfied as much of the time as possible.[12] Perhaps this is the ultimate paradox of capitalism, underlying or going beyond the income paradox and the hedonic treadmill: that its basic premise is that the driving force of human nature is a desire for happiness that can never—*must* never—be met. It might be suggested, after Marx, that antidepressants are the modern-day opiates of the masses, even more so than religion, as the permanent sense of dissatisfaction that is a consequence of the hedonistic conception of happiness that has been driven into Western minds over decades of capitalist hegemony finally takes its psychic toll, and people find that they would rather sedate themselves than deal with its implications.

The politics of happiness is reflected in the recognition that there are different ways of conceptualizing happiness, and that these lead to different sets of fundamental principles for the structuring of social institutions—including not only the institutions of government, but also of those with which we interact on a regular basis: where we work, where we live, and where we obtain the material that sustains us. The hedonistic conception of happiness that has dominated political and economic discourse for much of the past two hundred years—first systematically articulated by Jeremy Bentham, although his ideas have been largely vulgarized and corrupted over that time—has produced a highly competitive society concerned with the accumulation of wealth that reduces individuals to their instrumental value in their productive and consumptive relationships, where power is expressed largely through the ability to extract value from others and democracy has a very limited place as the means to hold political leaders to account, and where politics has more to do with winning and losing than with promoting a vision of the common good.

A different conception of happiness—called here "eudaemonistic"—is evident (although not so directly articulated) in the work of William Thompson. This conception emphasizes the interaction of individuals within a community with well-being as the goal, while people are still assumed to be self-interested in the sense that they wish to be happy, and the physical pleasures, fulfilled mostly through consumption, are considered less important (assuming basic needs are met). Relationships are based on equality and shared interests, and politics is an element of those relationships as the interested parties work out their differences with respect to what is recognized as a common goal. Democratic practices are recognized as an essential element in all social institutions, reflected not only in formal structures of governance but in the regular interactions between those who are a part of them.

While this work has explored a number of facets of Thompson's work, specifically relating it to the development of the cooperative movement, further exploration may offer much of value to debates on various social questions—understanding "social" in its broadest sense, as incorporating matters that touch on all aspects of the various institutional structures that order our world and through which we interact with the world that lies outside of those structures, the "natural world" (what some call the "given environment"). Valuable perspectives on some of the questions that economists such as Sen, Stiglitz, and Layard are exploring, having to do with the connection between happiness and economic productivity, might be found in Thompson's work. Debates over the shape of our political institutions might also gain from the perspective Thompson brings, particularly with respect to the effects of competition. For example, the American political system seems to have produced parties that seem to function largely as instruments of those with great wealth; at the same time, the competition between them takes on the character of sport, a strategy game in which the object is simply winning, not securing the greatest happiness of the greatest number. Finally, this work cannot go farther than simply to suggest new directions for a political theory of cooperatives, one that brings together Thompson's insights with that of contemporary democratic and social movement theory. The Occupy movement of 2011 demonstrated a great deal of interest in a new approach to politics and economics—one that, as this exploration of Thompson's work demonstrates, isn't really so new. In considering the shape of a new movement for a refashioning of our social institutions, Thompson's work offers an interesting and valuable place from which to start.

Appendix 1

Laws and Objects of the Rochdale Society of Equitable Pioneers, adopted 1844 (abridged)

Law the First (excerpts)[1]

The objects and plans of this Society are to form arrangements for the pecuniary benefit, and improvement of the social and domestic condition of its members...;

The establishment of a store for the sale of provisions and clothing, etc.;

The building, purchasing or erecting a number of houses, in which those members desiring to assist each other in improving their domestic and social condition may reside;

To commence the manufacture of... articles... for the employment of... members who are unemployed or under-paid;

[T]he society shall purchase or rent an estate or estates of land, which shall be cultivated by the members who are unemployed or under-paid;

As soon as practicable, this Society shall proceed to arrange the powers of production, distribution, education, and government, or in other words to establish a self-supporting home-colony of united interests, or assist other Societies in establishing such colonies;

[F]or the promotion of sobriety, the establishment of a temperance hotel.

Further statutes (selected)

2. The society is to be governed by officers and trustees to be elected at the general meeting held in January, the directors to be elected at the July general meeting, any of them being eligible for re-election

10. The property of this society shall be vested in the trustees [who] shall hold such property for the benefit of the society
13. Membership is open by election, requiring that new members be proposed and seconded by two members; upon election, an entrance fee is due; shares may be paid for in weekly three-pence installments
15. Members can withdraw with one month's notice
21. [No person] shall be allowed to sell any article or articles except for ready money
22. Profits to be distributed quarterly as follows: 3.5% interest on value of shares to members, the remainder distributed as a dividend to members in proportion to the amount of money expended at the store
26. That all purchases be paid for on delivery

Appendix 2

International Co-operative Alliance Statement on the Co-operative Identity, adopted 1995[2]

Definition

A co-operative is an autonomous association of persons united voluntarily to meet their common economic, social, and cultural needs and aspirations through a jointly-owned and democratically-controlled enterprise.

Values

Co-operatives are based on the values of **self-help**, **self-responsibility**, **democracy**, **equality**, **equity**, and **solidarity**. In the tradition of their founders, co-operative members believe in the ethical values of honesty, openness, social responsibility, and caring for others.

Principles

The co-operative principles are guidelines by which co-operatives put their values into practice.

1. Voluntary and Open Membership

Co-operatives are voluntary organisations, open to all persons able to use their services and willing to accept the responsibilities of membership, without gender, social, racial, political, or religious discrimination.

2. Democratic Member Control

Co-operatives are democratic organisations controlled by their members, who actively participate in setting their policies and making decisions. Men and women serving as elected representatives are accountable to the membership. In primary co-operatives members have equal voting rights (one member, one vote) and co-operatives at other levels are also organised in a democratic manner.

3. Member Economic Participation

Members contribute equitably to, and democratically control, the capital of their co-operative. At least part of that capital is usually the common property of the co-operative. Members usually receive limited compensation, if any, on capital subscribed as a condition of membership. Members allocate surpluses for any or all of the following purposes: developing their co-operative, possibly by setting up reserves, part of which at least would be indivisible; benefiting members in proportion to their transactions with the co-operative; and supporting other activities approved by the membership.

4. Autonomy and Independence

Co-operatives are autonomous, self-help organisations controlled by their members. If they enter into agreements with other organisations, including governments, or raise capital from external sources, they do so on terms that ensure democratic control by their members and maintain their co-operative autonomy.

5. Education, Training, and Information

Co-operatives provide education and training for their members, elected representatives, managers, and employees so they can contribute effectively to the development of their co-operatives. They inform the general public—particularly young people and opinion leaders—about the nature and benefits of co-operation.

6. Co-operation among Co-operatives

Co-operatives serve their members most effectively and strengthen the co-operative movement by working together through local, national, regional, and international structures.

7. Concern for Community

Co-operatives work for the sustainable development of their communities through policies approved by their members.

Notes

Introduction

1. "Le bonheur est une idée neuve en Europe." Louis Saint-Just, "Sur le mode d'exécution du décret contre les ennemis de la Révolution," http://www.royet.org/nea1789-1794/archives/discours/stjust_decret_ennemis_revolution_03_03_94.htm.
2. Hedonism is a moral philosophy concerned with the pursuit of pleasure, identifying pleasure as the sole intrinsic good. Bentham himself represents the paradigmatic case, although other modern philosophers before and since, including, most significantly, Locke, expressed similar ideas. See John Locke, *An Essay Concerning Human Understanding* (Oxford: Clarendon Press, 1975), Bk II ch XX.
3. Eudaemonism is a moral philosophy concerned with well-being, or the quality of life understood in a very broad sense. Eudaemonism is often associated with Aristotle and ancient Greek notions of happiness, as will be discussed in chapter 1.
4. One of the strongest and most persistent voices in this has been Gar Alperovitz, *America Beyond Capitalism: Reclaiming Our Wealth, Our Liberty, and Our Democracy* (Takoma Park, MD, and Boston: Democracy Collaborative Press and Dollars and Sense, 2011); *What Then Must We Do?: Straight Talk About the Next American Revolution* (White River Junction, VT: Chelsea Green Publishing, 2013). The number of such works has increased in recent years, including Robin Hahnel, *Economic Justice and Democracy: From Competition to Cooperation, Paths for the 21st Century* (New York: Routledge, 2005); David Schweickart, *After Capitalism* (Lanham, MD: Rowman and Littlefield, 2002); Erik Olin Wright, *Envisioning Real Utopias* (London, New York: Verso, 2010).
5. Claeys, for example, refers to Thompson as the "most analytical and

original thinker to contribute to the Owenite tradition." Gregory Claeys, *Machinery, Money, and the Millennium: From Moral Economy to Socialism, 1815–60* (Cambridge: Polity Press, 1987), 90. Harrison calls Thompson "the most influential of the Owenite socialists." J. F. C. Harrison, *Quest for the New Moral World: Robert Owen and the Owenities in Britain and America* (New York,: Scribners, 1969), 64.

6. For a brief, pointed expression of this view, see Martin Buber, "Comments on the Idea of Community," in *Martin Buber: On Intersubjectivity and Cultural Creativity*, ed. S. N. Eisenstadt (Chicago: University of Chicago Press, 1992).
7. Wendy Brown, "At the Edge," *Political Theory* 30, no. 4 (August 2002): 561.
8. Ernesto Laclau and Chantal Mouffe, *Hegemony and Socialist Strategy* (London: Verso, 1985), 163.
9. Brown, "At the Edge," 563–64.
10. Two pieces of evidence may be offered for this: First, that in the 2009–10 debate over healthcare, the original proposals of the Obama administration were derided by the Right as "socialist" and the more "moderate" alternative offered involved the development of large-scale cooperatives. Second, in 2011, the U.S. Senate, in one of its most partisan periods in history, *unanimously* approved a resolution that supported adopting 2012 as the United Nations–designated International Year of the Cooperative.
11. See, e.g., J. S. Maloy, "Real Utopias in a Gilded Age: The Case of American Populism," *New Political Science* 34, no. 3 (2012).
12. http://www.geo.coop/.
13. Steven Deller et al., "Research on the Economic Impact of Cooperatives" (Madison: University of Wisconsin Center for Cooperatives, 2009).
14. See, e.g., J. R. Dinwiddy, *Bentham* (Oxford and New York: Oxford University Press, 1989); Ross Harrison, *Bentham* (London and Boston: Routledge and Kegan Paul, 1983); Philip Schofield, *Bentham: A Guide for the Perplexed* (London: Bloomsbury Academic, 2009).
15. There exists one biography: R. K. P. Pankhurst, *William Thompson (1775–1833): Britain's Pioneer Socialist, Feminist, and Co-operator* (London: Pluto Press, 1991); one book-length treatment that is focused specifically on his feminist philosophy: Dolores Dooley, *Equality in Community: Sexual Equality in the Writings of William Thompson and Anna Doyle Wheeler* (Cork, Ireland: Cork University Press, 1996); and one journal essay specifically dedicated to his political economics: E. K. Hunt, "Utilitarianism and the Labor Theory of Value: A Critique of the Ideas of William Thompson," *History of Political Economy* 11, no. 4 (Winter 1979).
16. There are chapters or extended discussions of Thompson in several works on socialist history and the history of economics, including Max Beer, *A History of British Socialism,* One Volume Edition (New York: The

Humanities Press, 1940); Claeys, *Machinery*; G. D. H. Cole, *A History of Socialist Thought: The Forerunners 1789–1850*, 2 vols, vol. 1 (London: Macmillan, 1953); E. K. Hunt, *History of Economic Thought: A Critical Perspective*, 2nd ed. (Armonk, NY, and London: M. E. Sharpe, 2002); Esther Lowenthal, *The Ricardian Socialists,* (New York: Columbia University, 1911); Anton Menger, *The Right to the Whole Produce of Labour*, ed. H. S. Foxwell (New York: Augustus M. Kelley, 1962); W. Stark, *The Ideal Foundations of Economic Thought: Three Essays on the Philosophy of Economics* (Fairfield, NJ: Augustus M. Kelley, 1976). He is most often discussed as a "Ricardian" socialist, a classification that Marx suggests in *The Poverty of Philosophy,* trans. H. Quelch (Amherst, NY: Prometheus Books, 1995), 74. The idea gets more fully articulated by H. S. Foxwell in his introduction to the 1899 English translation of Menger's book, *The Right to the Whole Produce of Labour*. This then gets cemented by Lowenthal in her work. The association of the early British socialists with Ricardo has been challenged in recent years. For example, Claeys notes that "this association of ideas [of the Ricardian socialists with the ideas of Ricardo] . . . suffers . . . from the embarrassing omission of any evidence that the early socialists ever read Ricardo." While that may not be a fatal flaw, Claeys continues, the fact remains that this supposed association was "severely overburdened by its purported explanatory capacity," as it in fact does little to explain the (limited) similarities among the members of the group. Claeys, *Machinery*, xxii–xxiii.
17. In addition to Dooley's book, cited above, Thompson's radical feminism is discussed in Susan Ferguson, "The Radical Ideas of Mary Wollstonecraft," *Canadian Journal of Political Science / Revue canadienne de science politique* 32, no. 3 (September 1999); Eve Taylor, *Eve and the New Jerusalem* (New York: Pantheon Books, 1983); Carole Pateman, *The Sexual Contract* (Stanford: Stanford University Press, 1988).
18. G. J. Holyoake, *The History of Co-operation in England: Its Literature and Its Advocates* (New York: AMS Press, 1971); T. W. Mercer, *Towards the Co-operative Commonwealth: Why Poverty in the Midst of Plenty?* (Manchester: The Co-operative Press, 1936); Taylor, *Eve*; Gregory Claeys, *Citizens and Saints: Politics and Anti-politics in Early British Socialism* (Cambridge: Cambridge University Press, 1989).
19. Brett Fairbairn, "The Meaning of Rochdale: The Rochdale Pioneers and the Co-operative Principles," *University of Saskatchewan Centre for the Study of Cooperatives Occasional Paper Series* (1994), http://www.usaskstudies.coop/pdf-files/Rochdale.pdf; David Thompson, *Weavers of Dreams: Founders of the Modern Co-operative Movement* (Davis, CA: Center for Cooperatives, University of California, 1994); Robin Thornes, "Change and Continuity in the Development of Co-operation, 1827–1844," in *New Views of Co-operation,* ed. Stephen Yeo (London: Routledge, 1988).
20. I say he would deny it because, as will be evident from what follows,

he felt that the political economic system that meant that some were wealthy while others were poor worked to the detriment of all involved.
21. Claeys, *Machinery*, 90.
22. Pankhurst, *William Thompson*, 3.
23. Ibid., 15.
24. Dooley, *Equality in Community*, 15.
25. William Thompson, *Practical Education for the South of Ireland, in Letters addressed to the Proprietors of the Cork Institution, etc.* (Cork: West and Coldwells, 1818).
26. This letter has apparently been recently lost. Although Pankhurst cites it and Dooley includes it in her bibliography (Dooley, *Equality in Community*, 413), it does not appear in the relevant volume of Bentham's correspondence. Jeremy Bentham, *The Correspondence of Jeremy Bentham: January 1817 to June 1820*, ed. Stephen Conway, vol. 9 (Oxford: Clarendon Press, 1989). However, Bentham's reply six months later does. Ibid., 329–30.
27. William Thompson, *An Inquiry into the Principles of the Distribution of Wealth Most Conducive to Human Happiness, Applied to the Newly Proposed System of Voluntary Equality of Wealth* (New York: B. Franklin, 1968 [1824]), 1.
28. In contrast to the standard model of exploitive absentee landlords in south Ireland, Thompson was quite involved with his tenants, promoting advanced agricultural techniques and providing long-term leases on generous terms to his tenants. The beneficial effects of his efforts, detailed in an 1834 report to a House of Commons Select Committee on drunkenness, were such that the local magistrate's office was closed due to the nearly complete lack of crime on his estate. Over a hundred years after his death, Pankhurst found him still remembered fondly by locals, with stories of his benevolence passed down through generations. Pankhurst, *William Thompson*, 4–6.
29. Thomas Hodgskin, "Labour Defended Against the Claims of Capital; or, The Unproductiveness of Capital Proved with Reference to The Present Combinations amongst Journeymen," and William Thompson, "Labor Rewarded: The Claims of Labor and Capital Conciliated: or, How to Secure to Labor the Whole Products of its Exertions," in *Ricardian Socialism*, ed. David Reisman, *Democratic Socialism in Britain: Classic Texts in Economic and Political Thought, 1825–1952* (London: Pickering and Chatto, 1996 [1827]).
30. "Labor Rewarded," 108–14.
31. See, e.g., Anon., "Lecture on Cooperation," *Manchester Times & Gazette*, 4 June 1831; William Thompson, "Correspondence," *The Register for the First Society of Adherents to Divine Revelation at Orbiston*, Dec. 13, 1826; "To the Members and Managers of the Mechanics Institutions in Britain and Ireland," *The Co-operative Magazine and Monthly Herald* 1, no. 1 (1826); "To the Industrious Classes of Britain and Ireland; Particularly

to our neighbors, the distressed Spitalfields Weavers," *The Co-operative Magazine and Monthly Herald* 1, no. 11 (1826).
32. "Lease of an Estate for Ever, With Liberty to Purchase the Fee at Convenience," *The Weekly Free Press and Co-operative Journal* V, no. 239 (1830).
33. Pankhurst, *William Thompson,* 135–36.
34. Holyoake, *History of Co-operation,* 278. Holyoake criticizes Pare for never providing an accounting of the costs of the litigation or the final distribution of funds.
35. Fintan Lane, "Review," *Irish Economic and Social History* XXX (2003).
36. Peter Berresford Ellis, *A History of the Irish Working Class* (London: Pluto Press, 1985), 86.
37. Karl Marx, *Capital: A Critique of Political Economy*, 3 vols, vol. II (London: Penguin Classics, 1992), 397–99.
38. For example, the text cited in the prior note. It is possible, but seems unlikely, that Marx worked from the original edition of Thompson's *Inquiry* when writing *Capital, vol. I*, but the abridged version when he was working on volume II.
39. Frederick Engels, *Socialism, Utopian and Scientific*, trans. Edward Aveling (Chicago: Charles H. Kerr, 1910), 93.
40. His assessment of Thompson's theory of surplus value as compared to Marx's is that "[i]n all these respects Marx is far inferior to Thompson." Menger, *Right to the Whole Produce,* 101–102. Although he may be alone in placing Thompson above Marx, he is not the only one to suggest that, as Harold Laski put it, Thompson "laid the foundations" for Marx and Engels. Ellis, *A History,* 86.
41. John Stuart Mill, *Autobiography* (London and New York: Penguin Books, 1989), 106.
42. See, for example, the debate reflected in Terence Ball, *Reappraising Political Theory: Revisionist Studies in the History of Political Thought* (Oxford: Clarendon Press, 1995); Jim Jose, "Contesting Patrilineal Descent in Political Theory: James Mill and Nineteenth-Century Feminism," *Hypatia* 15, no. 1 (2000).
43. Hunt, "Utilitarianism"; *History of Economic Thought.*
44. Claeys, *Machinery; Citizens and Saints.*
45. Lowenthal, *The Ricardian Socialists,* 42.
46. Hunt, "Utilitarianism," 571.
47. Claeys, *Machinery,* xxix.
48. Lowenthal, *The Ricardian Socialists,* 42–43. Lowenthal suggests that "Thompson's real kinship is to Godwin," ibid., 43, but it should be noted that while Thompson praises Bentham repeatedly, he says little about Godwin—and what he says is mostly critical. Thompson, *Inquiry,* iii–v.
49. John Minter Morgan, *Hampden in the Nineteenth Century, or, Colloquies on the Errors and Improvement of Society*, 2 vols. (London: E. Moxon,

1834), vol. II, 301–302 fn. It is notable that Minter Morgan refers to Bentham as Thompson's "friend." Ibid., 320. Unfortunately, little in the way of correspondence between the two men—which would do much to reveal the character of their relationship—has been found. Of what has been published (through June 1828), the last mention of Thompson is in a letter from May 1827 in which Bentham refers to a pending visit from "a friend from Ireland"—whom the exceedingly careful editors of the *Correspondence* think is "Possibly William Thompson"—"with whom I have a good deal of business to settle which I must settle by the earliest opportunity." Jeremy Bentham, *The Correspondence of Jeremy Bentham: July 1824 to June 1828,* ed. Luke O'Sullivan and Catherine Fuller, vol. 12 (Oxford: Clarendon Press, 2006), 366–67. We have no idea what that urgent "business" might have been. No letters between them appear in this volume of the *Correspondence,* and the records of Bentham's financial dealings—if the business involved here was of a financial nature (perhaps having to do with the business Thompson inherited from his father)—apparently were not retained with his papers.
50. See, for example, Villa's essay and the subsequent debate between him and James Johnson in the pages of the *American Political Science Review* in the early 1990s. Dana R. Villa, "Postmodernism and the Public Sphere," *The American Political Science Review* 86, no. 3 (1992); James Johnson and Dana R. Villa, "Public Sphere, Postmodernism and Polemic," *The American Political Science Review* 88, no. 2 (1994).
51. Jeremy Bentham, "Method and Leading Features of an Institute of Political Economy (including finance) considered not only as a Science but as an Art," in *Jeremy Bentham's Economic Writings: Critical Edition Based on his Printed Works and Unprinted Manuscripts,* ed. W. Stark (London: George Allen and Unwin, 1952), 3 vols., vol. III, 308. The text in brackets reflects emendation by Stark.
52. The classic statement of this is, "The community is a fictitious *body,* composed of the individual persons who are considered as constituting as it were its *members.* The interest of the community . . . is . . . the sum of the interests of the several members who compose it" *An Introduction to the Principles of Morals and Legislation* (Oxford: Clarendon Press, 1996), 12. A good recent discussion of this is Antoinette Baujard, "Collective interest versus individual interest in Bentham's felicific calculus. Questioning welfarism and fairness," *European Journal of the History of Economic Thought* 17, no. 4 (2010).
53. I am not certain whether or not Bentham would have considered the economy to be an institution as such. He discusses political economics as an important function of the state with respect to the economy, but in general he saw economic relations as discrete interactions between discreet individuals bounded, of course, by legal constraints.
54. Jeremy Bentham, "Constitutional Code, Vol. 1," in *The Collected Works*

of Jeremy Bentham, ed. F. Rosen and J. H. Burns (Oxford: Clarendon Press, 1983), 25–36.
55. Thompson, then, would agree with Brown, who suggests that "the political is signaled by the presence of any human relations organized by power." Brown, "At the Edge," 569.
56. A longstanding claim that Thompson's usage was its first appearance in English is not entirely correct. Gregory Claeys, "'Individualism,' 'Socialism,' and 'Social Science': Further Notes on a Process of Conceptual Formation, 1800–1850," *Journal of the History of Ideas* 47, no. 1 (Jan.-Mar. 1986): 83. Poets, including Milton, had used the term previously, but it did not gain traction until the 1820s. Sismondi—whom Thompson likely knew—uses it in a way that is similar to Thompson's, albeit with little elaboration. Sismondi, "On the History of the Middle Ages—No. 1," *The New Monthly Magazine and Literary Journal* II (1821). So Claeys may be correct in the sense that Thompson provides the first real discussion of the notion of a social science in English.
57. Thompson, *Inquiry,* viii.
58. Ibid., xiv.
59. Thus, Menger argues that Thompson, not Marx, is properly seen as "the most eminent founder of scientific socialism." Menger, "Right to the Whole Produce," 51. Lowenthal disputes this, however, arguing that Thompson is far too utopian to be considered a "scientific" socialist. Lowenthal, *The Ricardian Socialists,* 45–46. However, given the advantage of a longer view of history, it would seem difficult to support a claim that Marx was not, himself, quite utopian in his outlook.
60. As Stark puts it, "[T]he *Wealth of Nations* was Bentham's economic bible and he assimilated it until he thought in its terms and spoke in its tongue." W. Stark, "Introduction," in *Jeremy Bentham's Economic Writings: Critical Edition Based on his Printed Works and Unprinted Manuscripts,* ed. W. Stark (New York: Burt Franklin, 1952), 3 vols., vol. I, 14.
61. Thompson, *Inquiry,* 178.
62. In particular, an excellent recent work by Philip Schofield, *Utility and Democracy: The Political Thought of Jeremy Bentham* (Oxford: Oxford University Press, 2006).

Chapter 1: The Two Faces of Happiness

1. At least, this is what comes across in most of his writing. Late in life—following Thompson's visit—he changed his position to something much closer to Thompson's, as will be seen in the following chapters.
2. I refer here to the secular literature. There is a vast literature from many perspectives, from Christianity to Zen Buddhism, but these are not

of concern here. In excluding them I do not mean to denigrate the importance of these views—historically, politically, or personally—but the social scientific literature is entirely concerned with secular understandings of happiness.
3. While non-Western perspectives may have much of great value to offer, this account is only concerned with the Western tradition. Given that Bentham and Thompson were British and Irish, respectively, this review is limited to Europe. For an interesting take on some of the non-Western traditions, see McCready's edited volume of essays, *The Discovery of Happiness* (Naperville, IL: Sourcebooks, 2001). Absent even here, however, are any perspectives from Sub-Saharan Africa or indigenous communities in the Americas or Australia. A challenge for any researcher who undertakes such a task is to avoid the imposition of familiar Western categories and concepts on ways of thinking that bear little resemblance to the Western tradition—all the more reason to keep the topic outside of the scope of the current work.
4. Plato, *The Republic,* trans. Tom Griffith (Cambridge: Cambridge University Press, 2000), 113 (421b).
5. The *locus classicus* of ancient Greek discussions of happiness is Aristotle's *Nichomachean Ethics,* written as a companion to his *Politics*. Aristotle argues that happiness is the ultimate purpose of human life, its "chief end," something that is "complete" and "self-sufficient." Aristotle, *Nichomachean Ethics,* ed. and trans. Roger Crisp (Cambridge: Cambridge University Press, 2000), 10–13. While there might be different "substantive conceptions of happiness," he holds that pretty much everyone understands "being happy as equivalent to living well and acting well." Ibid., 5. Aristotle argues that the measurement of happiness is the lifespan, because "there are many vicissitudes in life, all sorts of chance things happen, and even the most successful can meet with great misfortunes in old age." One attains happiness by living a virtuous life, or through "activities in accordance with virtue," precisely because these sorts of activities have the greatest degree of permanence—in other words, they are least likely to lead to misfortune, and most able to withstand challenge. Ibid., 16–17.
6. See, e.g., Frederick Rosen, "Epicureanism and Utilitarianism: A Reply to Professor Lyons," *Utilitas* 18, no. 2 (2006): 183; Geoffrey Scarre, "Epicurus as a Forerunner of Utilitarianism," *Utilitas* 6, no. 2 (1994): 219–31.
7. Stephen E. Rosenbaum, "Epicurean Moral Theory," *History of Philosophy Quarterly* 13, no. 4 (1996): 393.
8. It is a mild sort of asceticism, as will be seen, but it is ascetic nonetheless.
9. Julia Annas, *The Morality of Happiness* (New York: Oxford University Press, 1993), 188. Rosenbaum notes that, despite "scholarly controversy" with respect to the relationship between kinetic and katastematic

pleasure in Epicurus, "it is widely agreed that Epicurus took the good for people to be katastematic *hedone*." Rosenbaum, "Epicurean Moral Theory," 395.
10. Epicurus, "Principal Doctrines," Epicurus.info, http://www.epicurus.info/etexts/PD.html.
11. Ibid.
12. "Letter to Menoeceus," Epicurus.info, http://www.epicurus.info/etexts/Lives.html#I40. Annas explains that "[t]here is an established idiom in Greek in which 'empty' is used for what is futile or pointless," so the pursuit of an "empty" desire reflects not simply a "factual error but a mistake which renders your efforts pointless, sidetracking your life away from the right way to happiness" and therefore harmful. Annas, *The Morality of Happiness,* 190.
13. *The Morality of Happiness,* 195.
14. All this said, Epicurus admits that "[t]here is also a limit in simple living. He who fails to heed this limit falls into an error as great as that of the man who gives way to extravagance." Epicurus, "Vatican Sayings," Epicurus.info, http://www.epicurus.info/etexts/VS.html.
15. Annas, *The Morality of Happiness,* 348.
16. Epicurus, "Letter." Virtually quoting this passage, Cicero has his Epicurean interlocutor refer to this as the "royal road to happiness." Cicero, *De Finibus Bonorum et Malorum,* trans. H. Rackham, 2nd ed. (Cambridge: Harvard University Press, 1931), 61–62. This accords well with Aristotle's position, that "happiness is activity in accordance with virtue." *Ethics,* 194.
17. Epicurus, "Doctrines."
18. Alain Caillé, Christian Lazzeri, and Michel Senellart, *Histoire Raisonnée de la Philosophie Morale et Politique: Le bonheur et l'utile* (Paris: La Découverte, 2001), 123.
19. Thomas Aquinas, "The Summa Theologica of St. Thomas Aquinas," http://www.newadvent.org/summa/, 1a 2æ Q3 1.
20. Ibid., 1a 2æ Q5 3.
21. Quoted in Darrin M. McMahon, *Happiness: A History* (New York: Grove Press, 2006), 165.
22. Ibid., 164–75.
23. Locke, *An Essay,* 128–31.
24. Ibid., 229.
25. Ibid., 230.
26. Ibid., 251.
27. Ibid., 258.
28. A. P. Brogan, "John Locke and Utilitarianism," *Ethics* 69, no. 2 (1959): 79.
29. McMahon, *Happiness,* 64–65.
30. Ibid., 58–59.

31. Quoted in Pamela Gordon, *The Invention and Gendering of Epicurus* (Ann Arbor: University of Michigan Press, 2012), 1.
32. McMahon, *Happiness,* 59. There is evidence (albeit not conclusive) that some early Epicurean leaders were women. Gordon, *Invention of Epicurus,* Ch. 3.
33. McMahon, *Happiness,* 266.
34. Ibid., 212.
35. John F. Helliwell and Robert D. Putnam, "The Social Context of Well-Being," *Philosophical Transactions: Biological Sciences* 359, no. 1449 (2004): 1435. The quantification of happiness in neoclassical economics is discussed at the end of chapter 2.
36. Luigino Bruni and Pier Luigi Porta, "Introduction," in *Economics and Happiness,* ed. Luigino Bruni and Pier Luigi Porta (Oxford and New York: Oxford University Press, 2005), 20.
37. In the chapters that follow, my usage of the terms *happiness* and *well-being* differs somewhat from that of the contemporary literature, which uses well-being as its central concept and then considers "happiness" to be a way of understanding well-being. Gasper notes that "the 'in' term is well-being, not happiness," and he cites writers who "define the conception of well-being as happiness or pleasure the *hedonic* conception; versus the *eudaemonic* conception of well-being as well-considered fulfillment." Des Gasper, "Human Well-being: Concepts and Conceptualizations," in *Human Well-being: Concept and Measurement,* ed. Mark McGillivray (New York: Plagrave Macmillan, 2007), 24–26. Eudaemonic conceptions of happiness (or well-being) often emphasize that they refer to a span of time such as a lifetime; the term *well-living* has been suggested as a "superior term ... for eudaemonists." Ibid., 26.
38. Mark McGillivray, "Human Well-being: Issues, Concepts and Measures," in *Human Well-Being: Concept and Measurement,* ed. Mark McGillivray, *Studies in Development Economics and Policy* (New York: Palgrave Macmillan, 2007), 10.
39. See, e.g., Richard Layard, *Happiness: Lessons from a New Science* (New York: The Penguin Press, 2005). Fowler has a very different take on the social nature of happiness. James H. Fowler and Nicholas A. Christakis, "Dynamic spread of happiness in a large social network: longitudinal analysis over 20 years in the Framingham Heart Study," *BMJ* 2008; 337:a2338(2008). This also may reflect that what is being examined here is the *social science* literature, which no doubt implies more of an interest in the social implications of happiness, as compared to the psychology or neuroscience literature.
40. See, e.g., Ruut Veenhoven, "Subjective Measures of Well-being," in *Human Well-being: Concept and Measurement,* ed. Mark McGillivray (New York: Palgrave Macmillan, 2007).
41. Some of these noneconomic elements have to do with psychological or

emotional factors that are purely individual, but many are related to the structure of social institutions, including issues of autonomy and participation. Ibid.

42. These two approaches are not mutually exclusive (although their adherents may beg to differ, for example, Richard Layard, "This is the greatest good," *The Guardian*, 14 Sept. 2009.), as the kinds of conclusions that may be drawn from them are not necessarily in conflict. For example, the recent report of the Commission on the Measurement of Economic Performance and Social Progress, formed by former French president Nicolas Sarkozy and chaired by former World Bank chief economist Joseph Stiglitz, argues directly that *both* objective and subjective measures are important. Joseph E. Stiglitz, Amartya Sen, and Jean-Paul Fitoussi, "Report by the Commission on the Measurement of Economic Performance and Social Progress," (Commission on the Measurement of Economic Performance and Social Progress, 2009), 15.

Chapter 2: Between Pleasure and Well-being

1. I wish to note up front that my exposition of Bentham relies, in part, on the *Theory of Legislation,* a collection of Bentham's writings translated into French and edited by Etienne Dumont into the three-volume work *Traités du Legislation* in 1802, and translated back into English in 1864 by an American, Robert Hildreth (London: Routledge and Kegan Paul, 1931). Bentham scholars now consider the *Traités* to reflect more of Dumont's understanding of Bentham than an accurate reflection of Bentham's thought. But while Bentham himself was critical of Dumont's work (C. K. Ogden, "Introduction," in *The Theory of Legislation,* ed. C. K. Ogden [London: Routledge and Kegan Paul, 1931], xlvii), he also praised it. Bentham, *Correspondence,* 9: 360. More to the point is that Bentham published little of his own work and, during his lifetime, the *Traités* was considered the most complete exposition of his ideas. Because the exposition of Bentham's thought here is intended in large part to consider the way his work was appropriated (as is discussed later in this chapter) and to present a contrast with Thompson, what is needed is not so much an *accurate* Bentham but the historical one. David Lieberman discusses the issue of the "accurate" versus the "historical" Bentham in "From Bentham to Benthamism," *The Historical Journal* 28, no. 1 (1985).
2. As Burns points out, considering its importance, the phrase has a curious history, as it is introduced as his "fundamental axiom" in his first work, the *Fragment on Government,* but does not reappear for another forty years. J. H. Burns, "Happiness and Utility: Jeremy Bentham's Equation," *Utilitas* 17, no. 1 (2005): 46–47. After its reappearance in

1820, however, it appears quite extensively, a fact Burns attributes to Bentham's growing radicalism (54–55). See also R. Shackleton, "The Greatest Happiness of the Greatest Number: The History of Bentham's Phrase," *Studies on Voltaire and the Eighteenth Century* 90 (1972).

3. Harrison refers to Bentham's more philosophical concerns as "a relatively peripheral part of his work." Harrison, *Bentham,* 4. Or, as Lyons puts it, "Bentham was never much concerned with strictly private ethics." David Lyons, *In the Interest of the Governed: A Study in Bentham's Philosophy of Utility and Law,* 2nd ed. (New York: Oxford University Press, 1991), 51.
4. David Collard, "Research on Well-Being: Some Advice from Jeremy Bentham," *Philosophy of the Social Sciences* 36, no. 3 (2006) is an exception.
5. Unlike Epicurus, however, Bentham does not define pleasure as the absence of pain; the absence of pain is, rather, a condition for *happiness* (although he seems to have modified his view on this toward the end of his life).
6. Bentham, *IPML,* 38–41.
7. "Deontology," in *Deontology; Together with A table of the Springs of Action; And the Article on Utilitarianism,* ed. Amnon Goldworth, *Collected Works of Jeremy Bentham* (Oxford: Clarendon Press, 1983), 130.
8. Ibid.
9. "Pannomial Fragments," in *Selected Writings/Jeremy Bentham,* ed. Stephen G. Engelmann (New Haven: Yale University Press, 2011), 245–46.
10. *IPML,* 42.
11. "A Table of the Springs of Action," in *Deontology,* 89.
12. Ibid., 90.
13. *IPML,* 12 fn c.
14. Ibid., 12.
15. "Deontology," 195.
16. "A Table," 91.
17. Hannah F. Pitkin, "Slippery Bentham: Some Neglected Cracks in the Foundation of Utilitiariansim," *Political Theory* 18, no. 1 (1990): 117.
18. "Interests," as the term is being used here, are like kinetic pleasures in that they are specific to particular desires. However, "interest" is not like katastematic pleasure, because the former refers to a goal, and the satisfaction of various interests can be seen as means toward that goal. In contrast, there is no such instrumentality in kinetic pleasure with respect to katastematic pleasure.
19. Stephen G. Engelmann, *Imagining Interest in Political Thought: Origins of Economic Rationality* (Durham: Duke University Press, 2003), 3. Bentham does, however, use the plural form at key passages, such as when he refers to the means by which one might categorize the motives of others, "according to the tendency which they appear to have to unite,

or disunite, his *interests* and theirs." Bentham, *IPML,* 116; emphasis added.
20. Engelmann, *Imagining*, 3.
21. Ibid., 49–50.
22. Ibid., 51.
23. See, for example, the way each of these is indicated separately in the *Table of the Springs of Action*.
24. Engelmann says the collapse of these terms is "at the heart" of his argument, but because my interest (no pun intended) here is different, I may reject his claim without rejecting his overall argument.
25. Jeremy Bentham, *A Comment on the Commentaries and A Fragment on Government*, ed. J. H. Burns and H. L. A. Hart, *The Collected Works of Jeremy Bentham* (New York: Clarendon Press, 2008), 67.
26. Bentham does not state this directly, but it is implicit, for example in his assertion that legislators ought not compel people to act either for the sake of their own happiness or of the community, at least not in every case. *IPML,* 285.
27. *A Fragment on Government*, ed. J. H. Burns and H. L. A. Hart, New authoritative ed. (Cambridge and New York: Cambridge University Press, 1988), 25–26.
28. "Deontology," 135.
29. Ibid., 130.
30. *Chrestomathia*, ed. M. J. Smith and W. H. Burston, *The Collected Works of Jeremy Bentham* (Oxford: Clarendon Press, 1983), Table V.
31. This appears to suggest that well-being and happiness are the same. Below I will show why this is not the case.
32. Bentham, *Chrestomathia*, 181. To point out Bentham's argument here may serve as an answer to critics of utilitarianism who argue *ad absurdum* that the injunction to avoid pain is most securely met through the destruction of all sentient species.
33. In this chapter I focus mostly on subsistence and security, with a brief discussion of equality. Equality and, to a limited extent, abundance, will be discussed in greater depth in chapter 4.
34. Bentham, "Institute of Political Economy," 309.
35. *The Theory of Legislation*, 97.
36. Ibid.
37. Ibid., 113.
38. Ibid., 109.
39. Ibid.
40. However, security as Bentham has it is not *necessarily* social, since due to environmental factors even Robinson Crusoe was concerned about whether he would be able to reap the crops he sowed.
41. Bentham, "Institute of Political Economy," 309.
42. *IPML,* 148.

43. *The Theory of Legislation*, 110.
44. Ibid., 115–16.
45. Ibid., 111.
46. *Official Aptitude Maximized; Expense Minimized*, ed. Philip Schofield (Oxford: Clarendon Press, 1993), 342.
47. "Institute of Political Economy," 324. Compare to John Locke, "Second Treatise of Government: An Essay Concerning the True Original, Extent, and End of Civil Government," in *Two Treatises of Government*, ed. Peter Laslett (Cambridge: Cambridge University Press, 1988), II. §124: "The great and *chief end,* therefore, of men's uniting into common-wealths, and putting themselves under government, *is the preservation of their property*."
48. There is considerable debate over what "property" means for Locke, and most likely it means many things, but it is certainly more expansive than the narrow economic conception Bentham is working with, as (depending on the passage in question) it may include such things as property in the person and natural rights.
49. Quoted in Charles W. Everett, *The Education of Jeremy Bentham* (New York: Columbia University Press, 1931), 36. The passage is from an undated manuscript in the Bentham collection at University College London; it may date from as early as 1763, when Bentham was a student at Oxford.
50. Harrison, *Bentham*, 157–58. As we will see in chapter 4, Bentham argues this point with an early version of what is now familiar to economists as the theory of marginal utility.
51. Bentham, "The True Alarm," 70–71.
52. "Defence of Usury," 157.
53. "Manual of Political Economy," 226.
54. "Institute of Political Economy," 323. The colon here makes the meaning somewhat ambiguous (the use of punctuation has changed since his time). He does not mean that wealth is a kind of labor, but that, as enjoyment springs from wealth, so wealth springs from labor.
55. As I understand it, what Bentham considers "use" may be quite broad, since any object that brings us pleasure can be said to have a "use." Art objects, for example, can be understood to have a use in this sense.
56. Bentham, "Deontology," 152.
57. "Institute of Political Economy," 324.
58. This can be seen in Bentham's emphasis on security of property, and on legally established and ensured rights of property as a kind of security. *The Theory of Legislation*, 111–13.
59. "Pannomial Fragments," 267.
60. *The Theory of Legislation*, 100.
61. With some exception for indigence. Bentham supported taxation for the support for those who "are in want of what is absolutely necessary,"

arguing that since the "pain of death, which would presently fall upon the starving poor, would be always a more serious evil than the pain of disappointment which falls upon the rich when a portion of his superfluity is taken from him." This should be limited to "what is simply necessary. To go beyond that would be taxing industry for the support of idleness." Ibid., 132–33.

62. Stravos Drakopoulos and Anastasios Karayiannis, "Human Needs Hierarchy and Happiness: Evidence from the Late Pre-classical and Classical Economics," in *Handbook on the Economics of Happiness,* ed. Luigino Bruni and Pier Luigi Porta (Cheltenham, UK, and Northampton, MA: Edward Elgar, 2007).
63. Ibid., 62. Bentham does note that the poor have their luxuries, referring specifically to "tobacco (the luxury of the great body of the people)." Bentham, "Institute of Political Economy," 326.
64. Len Doyal and Ian Gough, *A Theory of Human Need* (New York: The Guilford Press, 1991). 50. We might translate *one's vision of the good* as one's own well-being.
65. Ibid.
66. Ibid., 56.
67. Ibid., 59–69.
68. See, e.g., Len Doyal, "Comment: Thinking about Human Need," *New Left Review* no. 201 (1993); Kate Soper, "Review: A Theory of Human Need," *New Left Review* no. 197 (1993).
69. Jeff Noonan, *Democratic Society and Human Needs* (Montreal: McGill-Queen's University Press, 2007), 54.
70. Ibid., 58.
71. Bentham, *The Theory of Legislation,* 98. In one sense, however, equality is on a par with security, in the formal sense that the security the law provides should apply to all equally.
72. P. J. Kelly, *Utilitarianism and Distributive Justice: Jeremy Bentham and the Civil Law* (Oxford and New York: Clarendon Press/Oxford University Press, 1990), 154–57.
73. Stephen G. Engelmann, "'Indirect Legislation': Bentham's Liberal Government," *Polity* XXXV, no. 3 (2003).
74. See Kelly, *Bentham and the Civil Law,* 167.
75. Bentham, *The Theory of Legislation,* 114.
76. As Anatole France famously remarked some decades later, in a rather different tone, "The law, in its majestic equality, forbids rich and poor alike to sleep under bridges, beg in the streets or steal bread."
77. One might ask what sort of happiness might come from the decision of a late-eighteenth-century laborer to agree to work in a factory fourteen or more hours a day six days a week under death-defying conditions for wages barely sufficient for subsistence, especially since the "pleasure" to be got from such a continued existence is little more than survival to

work another day and enable one's family to survive so the children might be able to take their positions at the factory (E. P. Thompson provides an account of why this might be so, that we need not explore here. E. P. Thompson, *The Making of the English Working Class* [New York: Pantheon Books, 1964]). As was discussed earlier, Bentham thought the fear of death was quite important as a motive. That said, Bentham supported the Factory Acts, which were meant to improve working conditions, or at least limit the worst abuses of workers. Michael Quinn, "Subsistence, Security, Abundance, and Population in the Political Economy of Jeremy Bentham," in *ISUS-X, Tenth Conference of the International Society for Utilitarian Studies* (Berkeley: 2008). But I digress.
78. Bentham, *The Theory of Legislation*, 123.
79. W. Stark, "Liberty and Equality or: Jeremy Bentham as an Economist," *The Economic Journal* 51, no. 201 (1941): 76.
80. Jeremy Bentham, "Tracts on Poor Laws and Pauper Management," in *Works of Jeremy Bentham,* ed. John Bowring (Edinburgh: William Tait, 1843), vol. VIII, 406–10.
81. Ibid., 370.
82. In any case, what would be the basis for such a right? Bentham was famously opposed to the notion of natural rights. See "Nonsense upon Stilts, or Pandora's Box Opened, or The French Declaration of Rights Prefixed to the Constitution of 1791 Laid Open and Exposed—with a Comparative Sketch of What Has Been Done on the Same Subject in the Constitution of 1795, and a Sample of Citizen Sieyès," in *Rights, Representation, and Reform: Nonsense upon Stilts and Other Writings on the French Revolution,* ed. Philip Schofield, Catherine Pease-Watkin, and Cyprian Blamires (Oxford and New York: Clarendon Press, 2002).
83. *IPML,* 12.
84. John Bonner, *Economic Efficiency and Social Justice: Development of Utilitarian Ideas in Economics from Bentham to Edgeworth* (London: Edward Elgar, 1995), 12.
85. Bentham, "Fragment on Ontology," in *Works of Jeremy Bentham,* ed. John Bowring (Edinburgh: William Tait, 1843), vol. VIII, 196–97.
86. This includes nonhumans as well as humans. *IPML,* 44. As he famously notes, "The question is not, Can they *reason*? nor, Can they *talk*? but, Can they *suffer*?" Ibid., 283.
87. John Commons, *Institutional Economics: Its Place in Political Economy,* vol. 1 (Madison: University of Wisconsin Press, 1934), 234–38.
88. See Bernard E. Harcourt, *Illusion of Free Markets: Punishment and the Myth of Natural Order* (Cambridge: Harvard University Press, 2011), ch. 5, for a defense of the idea that Bentham held a naturalist perspective in his political economics.
89. Bentham, *A Fragment on Government,* 28.
90. *IPML,* 159.
91. Ibid., 244.

92. *The Theory of Legislation*, 95.
93. "Deontology," 193–94.
94. *The Theory of Legislation*, 63. In determining how best to do this, it is necessary to recognize that law, of itself, necessarily works through the mechanism of pain. "Every law is an evil," he asserts, "for every law is an infraction of liberty." Ibid., 48. Thus, the use of the law to limit harm is itself limited by the fact that doing so is necessarily a source of harm in the restriction of liberty.
95. Ibid., 64.
96. Ibid., 65.
97. "Article on Utilitarianism (long and short versions)," in *Deontology; Together with a Table of the Springs of Action; And the Article on Utilitarianism,* ed. Amnon Goldworth, *Collected Works of Jeremy Bentham* (Oxford and New York: Clarendon Press/Oxford University Press, 1983), 300–301. However, Cicero would agree that virtue must be an act of free will. Cicero, *On Duties,* ed. M. T. Griffin and E. M. Atkins (Cambridge: Cambridge University Press, 1991).
98. Harsh, at least, according to our own standards. By the standards of his day the Panopticon would have been a great improvement in quality of treatment.
99. C. B. Macpherson, *The Life and Times of Liberal Democracy* (Oxford and New York: Oxford University Press, 1977), 33–34.
100. Jevons certainly had help with this, particularly from F. Y. Edgeworth, but Jevons was the principal figure in the incorporation of Bentham's theory—or some parts of it—into neoclassical economics. Alessandro Roncaglia, *The Wealth of Ideas: A History of Economic Thought* (Cambridge: Cambridge University Press, 2005), ch. 10.
101. It is curious to note that W. Stanley Jevons's son, H. Stanley, published a book after his father's death on cooperatives and economics, and that Anton Menger, who as noted above praised Thompson over Marx, was Carl's brother. H. Stanley Jevons, *Economic Equality in the Co-operative Commonwealth* (London: Methuen, 1933).
102. Tom Warke, "Multi-Dimensional Utility and the Index Number Problem: Jeremy Bentham, J. S. Mill, and Qualitative Hedonism," *Utilitas* 12, no. 2 (2000): 177 fn 2.
103. W. Stanley Jevons, *The Theory of Political Economy*, 5th ed, Reprints of Economic Classics (New York: Augustus M. Kelley, 1965), 11.
104. Ibid., 23.
105. Thorstein Veblen, "Why Is Economics not an Evolutionary Science?" *The Quarterly Journal of Economics* 12, no. 4 (1898): 389.
106. Gasper, "Human Well-being," 25.
107. Ibid., 26.
108. Grant Duncan, "After Happiness," *Journal of Political Ideologies* 12, no. 1 (2007): 95.
109. Layard, *Happiness,* 48–49.

110. See, e.g., ibid.
111. Richard Easterlin, "Does Economic Growth Improve Human Lot? Some empirical Evidence," in *Nation and Households in Economic Growth: Essays in Honor of Moses Abromowitz,* ed. P. A. Davis and M. W. Reder (New York and London: Academic Press, 1974).
112. Layard, *Happiness,* 29.
113. Ibid., 30–32; David Leonhardt, "Money Doesn't Buy Happiness. Well, on Second Thought...." *New York Times,* April 16, 2008.
114. As of the late 1990s, it was found that "When the $20,000 point is passed, the regression line is almost flat, which suggest[s] that the law of diminishing returns applies." Ruut Veenhoven, "Advances in Understanding Happiness," *Revue Quebecoise de Psychologie* 18, no. 2 (1997): 12.
115. Duncan, "After Happiness," 91.

Chapter 3: William Thompson's Social Happiness

1. Pauline Gregg, *A Social and Economic History of Britain: 1760–1980,* 8th ed. (London: Harrap, 1982), ch. 1–4.
2. As was discussed in the Introduction, Thompson's consideration of social institutions is broad, as it includes everything from the political institutions of the state to economic institutions to more intimate institutions such as marriage.
3. Bentham, "Article on Utilitarianism (Long Version)," 294–95.
4. Or, as he puts it, the "application" of "social science" is the "art of social happiness." Thompson, *Inquiry,* viii.
5. Bentham would not have disagreed, but he focused on how the institutions of the state—political institutions—affected individual decision making. Thompson takes a much broader view, with a broader conception of social institutions, as was discussed in the Introduction.
6. That is, if we don't count James Mill, who is the subject of a sustained attack in the *Appeal*. I discuss Thompson's attack on Mill in some detail below, in chapter 4.
7. Owen lived a long life in which he wrote a great deal. The focus in this section, however, will be on Owen's early writings, prior to his association with Thompson. The reason for it is that we want to get a sense of Owen as Thompson knew him and was influenced by him. Owen's later writings may reflect Thompson's own influence, which would only serve to confuse rather than illuminate. With the possible exception of his *Autobiography,* Owen's best work came prior to 1824 (when Thompson's *Inquiry* was published); his last major work in this period, the *Report to the County of Lanark,* was published in 1821. One commentator says of his later works, those published after 1834, which "make up

the great bulk of his writings, by far the larger part is valueless." G. D. H. Cole, "Introduction," in *Robert Owen: A New View of Society and Other Writings,* ed. G. D. H. Cole (London and New York: Everyman's Library, 1927), vii.
8. Neal Wood, "Tabula Rasa, Social Environmentalism, and the 'English Paradigm,'" *Journal of the History of Ideas* 53, no. 4 (1992). Wood notes that Locke did not invent the idea, but calls the Lockean version the "archetypal expression" of it. Ibid., 649. It is worth noting that the Owenite John Minter Morgan puts the Lockean individual, who begins life with a mind "like a sheet of blank paper," at the center of his "diagram illustrative of the formation of the human character" (which appears as a series of concentric circles). Morgan, *Hampden,* vol. I, 133.
9. Locke, *An Essay,* II.I.2.
10. Wood, "Tabula Rasa," 647.
11. Ibid., 665.
12. E. P. Thompson refers to him as "in one sense the *ne plus ultra* of Utilitarianism, planning society as a gigantic industrial panopticon." Thompson, *The Making,* 781.
13. Robert Owen, "A New View of Society, or, Essays on the Principle of the Formation of the Human Character, and the Application of the Principle to Practice," in *A New View of Society and Other Writings,* ed. Gregory Claeys (London: Penguin Classics, 1991 [1813–16]), 55.
14. Ibid., 43; italics removed. Owen's idea was not original, however, as he would have found it in the writings of Godwin and Helvétius. Paul R. Bernard, "Irreconcilable Opinions: The Social and Educational Theories of Robert Owen and William Maclure," *Journal of the Early Republic* 8, no. 1 (1988): 25.
15. Robert Owen, "A Sketch of Some of the Errors and Evils Arising from the Past and Present State of Society," in *Robert Owen: A New View of Society and Other Writings,* ed. Gregory Claeys (London: Penguin Classics, 1991 [1817]), 161.
16. Ibid., 163.
17. "Observations on the Manufacturing System," in *Robert Owen: A New View of Society and Other Writings,* ed. Gregory Claeys (London: Penguin Classics, 1991 [1815]), 95–97.
18. Ibid., 97–98.
19. "A New View of Society," 14; italics removed.
20. Ibid., 14.
21. Ibid., 53–55.
22. Ibid., 56.
23. Ibid.
24. Ibid., 50.
25. Bernard, "Irreconcilable Opinions," 22.
26. Owen's epistemology points to the basis for autocracy in at least some

strands of socialist thought, although an examination of this lies outside the scope of the current work.
27. New Harmony was a cooperative community Owen founded in southern Indiana in 1825. It failed within three years.
28. Bernard, "Irreconcilable Opinions," 21–22. Bernard refers to their differences on this point as the basis for the "irreconcilable opinions" that contributed to New Harmony's disintegration.
29. J. F. C. Harrison, *Quest for the New Moral World: Robert Owen and the Owenities in Britain and America* (New York: Scribners, 1969), 82.
30. Terence Ball, "The Formation of Character: Mill's 'Ethology' Reconsidered," *Polity* 33, no. 1 (2000): 30–31.
31. At least some of the reforms Owen claimed to have initiated were already present at New Lanark when he took it over, nor were they unique to New Lanark. Nonetheless, Owen did implement a number of important reforms, including limiting the use of child labor and increasing their education. Harrison, *Quest*, 51–52.
32. Robert Owen, "Report to the County of Lanark," in *A New View of Society and Other Writings*, ed. Gregory Claeys (London: Penguin Classics, 1991 [1820]), 271–72.
33. Veblen, "Why Is Economics," 389.
34. Thompson, *Inquiry*, 491.
35. Ibid.
36. We might also include the future here, although as we already know from Bentham that can best be understood as part of the mental state in the form of expectations as to consequences.
37. Thompson, *Inquiry*, 289–90.
38. Exemplified most clearly, perhaps, in his *Rationale of Evidence*. As he says in the introduction: "As to the faculty called *will*, its act, *volition*, has on each occasion, for its causes, *interests*, acting in the character of *motives*. In what way these springs of action ... give existence everywhere to the law of evidence" is the primary question examined in the work. Jeremy Bentham, "Introductory View of the Rationale of Evidence; for the Use of Non-lawyers as Well as Lawyers," in *Works of Jeremy Bentham*, ed. John Bowring (Edinburgh: W. Tait; London: Simpkin, Marshall: 1843), vol. VI, 6.
39. Renate Holub, *Antonio Gramsci: Beyond Marxism and Postmodernism*, ed. Christopher Norris, Critics of the Twentieth Century (London: Routledge, 1992), 6.
40. Bentham, using the terms *sinister interest* (which will be discussed in chapter 5) and *interest-begotten prejudice*, shows that he is not unaware of this tendency on the part of some to dominate others in their own interest. See, for example, Bentham, "A Table," 111–12. Quinn, saying that "Bentham might have referred instead to the corruptive influences of power," notes that Bentham considers this a disadvantage of morality "as against natural philosophy." Michael Quinn, "Post-modern Moments

in the Application of Empirical Principles: Power, Knowledge and Discourse in the Thought of Jeremy Bentham vs. Michel Foucault," *Revue d'études benthamiennes [En ligne]*(2011), http://etudes-benthamiennes.revues.org/245#article-245. However, while Bentham seems to be concerned with the moral weakness of rulers, Thompson is concerned with the social effects of the exercise of power.

41. I am specifically excluding women here to avoid the complicated question of Bentham's perspective on women's rights. This issue will receive some attention in chapter 4.
42. Bentham, *The Theory of Legislation*, 116.
43. Thompson, *Inquiry*, 17.
44. Ibid.
45. This way of thinking about happiness approaches the Epicurean model, as it comes closer to associating happiness with katastematic pleasure. However, it is different because, for Thompson, kinetic pleasures are still an important part of one's happiness, as will be discussed below. Nevertheless, Thompson comes closer to Epicureanism than does Bentham.
46. Thompson, *Inquiry*, 449.
47. Ibid.
48. Ibid., 49.
49. Dooley, *Equality in Community*, 157.
50. Thompson, *Inquiry*, 555.
51. Ibid., 554–55.
52. Ibid., 26.
53. This, for Thompson, is the essence of security, which will be discussed in detail below.
54. Thompson, *Inquiry*, 515.
55. *Practical Directions for the Speedy and Economical Establishment of Communities on the Principles of Mutual Co-operation, United Possessions, and Equality of Exertions and of the Means of Enjoyments* (London: Strange, and E. Wilson, 1830), 98.
56. It should be noted that this was specifically in the context of cooperative communities:

    > Thus only, by co-operative industry, can domestic manufactures be rendered compatible with machinery ... thus only can they be rendered compatible with increased & increasing knowledge, thus only will they be rendered compatible with universal intercourse, and include a thousand times more than all the advantages, avoiding all the evils, of that supposed happy and simple state of human society when domestic manufactures, carried on by hand labor, prevailed. Ibid., 138.

57. Ibid., 39.
58. The point about choice being opened "to both sexes" clearly refers to the lack of choice most women had in their partners. The mention here of

"*all* the members of the community" could be an oblique reference to the possibility of same-sex relationships, but nowhere does Thompson discuss it directly.
59. Thompson, *Inquiry*, 555.
60. Although it may be open to interpretation, "economy" here appears to refer primarily to the efficient employment of labor.
61. Thompson, *Practical Directions*, 26.
62. Ibid., 27.
63. Ibid.
64. Ibid., 97.
65. Perhaps this is of no great moment. After all, the work is called an "Inquiry into the Principles for the Distribution of *Wealth* most Conducive to Human *Happiness*," so lexicographically this ordering makes sense: he is interested in the effect of wealth on happiness, not the effects of happiness on wealth, so wealth must be defined first. It could be said that the subject of the book is wealth, and happiness is its object.
66. It may be noted that Bentham emphasizes *use* in his definition, whereas Thompson emphasizes *production*.
67. Thompson, *Inquiry*, 6. Thompson surrounds his definition with quotation marks but does not indicate who, if anyone, he is quoting. It may be that he just wanted to set the text apart to indicate that this was the substance of the definition.
68. *Practical Directions*, 2.
69. Ibid.
70. Thompson rejects the term *luxury* because it is too vague, generally used as a term of moral disapprobation to describe expensive objects. *Superfluity* has a more specific meaning because it compares use value to the value of the labor required to produce it—the assumption being that the only reason these things are produced is because the people using them are not the same as the people producing them. In his view, no one would make these things for their own use, because of the effort required. Ibid.
71. Thompson offers a specific definition of rational in this context: "Those desires which, besides being attended with preponderant good, are also worth gratification at the expense of the trouble of producing the articles necessary to gratify them." Ibid., 5.
72. Ibid., 2. The context of this discussion is important: Thompson is describing ideal conditions within the autarkic cooperative community, though it reflects his orientation toward political economics that he felt that these categories should be the basis for economic reasoning.
73. See, e.g., Adam Smith, *An Inquiry into the Nature and Causes of the Wealth of Nations* (Chicago: University of Chicago Press, 1976), bk II ch III.

74. Thompson, *Practical Directions*, 1–2. It should be noted that Thompson's definition of productive labor is fully consistent with Smith's.
75. As will be seen below, his concern regarding the conditions of exchange constitutes part of his critique of the system of individual competition. Exchange will mostly be discussed in the next chapter.
76. Thompson, *Practical Directions*, I.
77. Karl Marx, *Capital: A Critique of Political Economy*, trans. Ben Fowkes, 3 vols, vol. I (London: Penguin Classics, 1990), 163–77. Thompson could be said to be following the distinction between natural and unnatural exchange in Aristotle, where natural exchange is that in which "things which are useful are exchanged themselves... for similar useful things.... Exchange simply serves to satisfy the natural requirements of sufficiency." Aristotle, *Politics*, trans. Sir Ernest Barker (Oxford: Oxford University Press, 1995), 25.
78. Thompson is not strictly opposed to trade—including foreign trade—although he is certainly opposed to the presence of a competitive marketplace that primarily serves to force down worker's wages. But for a community in which all receive the same level of benefit from their labor, and no one exploits the labor of others for their own sake, the calculation is somewhat different: "If the articles to be prepared to purchase any quantity... of foreign sugar, require more labor than the growth and... preparation of the sugar at home of equal sweetening quality... then it would be more prudent to make sugar at home... without any regard to the comparative prices in the market of the two species of sugar, the home and the foreign made." Thompson, *Practical Directions*, 105.
79. *Inquiry*, 6–7.
80. Ibid., 89.
81. Ibid., 19–20.
82. "In the mere effort of seizing and appropriating what had before been seized and appropriated by no one, as in taking water from a common well, it is the application of labor alone that turns that into property which before belonged to no one." Ibid., 94. One might notice, however, that Thompson does not explicitly say here that the claim of right belongs to the person who performs the labor. This can, however, be surmised from his argument: no one would by right claim the produce of someone else's labor as their own—unlike Locke, who famously assigned property rights to the master for "the turfs my servant has cut." Locke, "Second Treatise," II §28.
83. Thompson, *Inquiry*, 94. This includes exchange. At this point in the *Inquiry*, Thompson is not yet discussing arrangements within the cooperative community, but considering what he calls the "natural laws of distribution," which will be discussed in the next chapter.
84. Ibid., 38. It could be objected that at least some people engage in some

forms of labor at least as much for the sake of the pleasure of the work as for the ends—for example, gardening or crafts. But these are pleasures of a most bourgeois sort, since their first requirement is leisure time that was hardly available for the laboring classes in Thompson's day.

85. Ibid., 8.
86. Bentham, *The Theory of Legislation*, 118. Indeed, Bentham offers a positive defense of opulence. "The True Alarm," 85–86. In the version of his principles subordinate to utility that appears in the *Institute of Political Economy* he explicity includes opulence under the head of abundance. "Institute of Political Economy," 307.
87. Thompson, *Inquiry*, 187–91.
88. Ibid., 180–83.
89. Ibid., 191–95.
90. Ibid., 8. One might point out that there are many forms of physical exertion that are both pleasurable and do not involve the creation of wealth or accumulation, including many forms of recreation, such as walking, hiking, cycling, and so on. Of course, none of these would be considered *labor*, and this does not detract from Thompson's point.
91. "Labor Rewarded," 105.
92. For Bentham, see *The Theory of Legislation*, 101–102.
93. Thompson, *Inquiry*, 515.
94. Ibid., 520–23.
95. Ibid., 448.
96. Ibid., 449.
97. Ibid.
98. It bears at least a passing resemblance to Smith's argument against bounties. *Wealth of Nations*, bk. IV ch V.
99. Thompson, *Inquiry*, 451.
100. Ibid., 291.
101. Ibid., 451.
102. Ibid., 448.
103. Or, as the Epicureans might have it, katastematic pleasure—relief from the pain of anxiety.
104. Thompson, *Inquiry*, 422.
105. As Dooley says rather dryly in a footnote annotation in Thompson's *Appeal*, "Women as represented in nineteenth-century law were treated as being of no significance or worth in their own right." *Appeal of One Half of the Human Race, Women, against the Pretensions of the Other Half, Men, to Retain them in Political, and Thence in Civil and Domestic, Slavery; in reply to a paragraph of Mr. Mill's celebrated "Article on Government"* (Cork, Ireland: Cork University Press, 1997 [1825]), 118.
106. Ibid., 176–81.
107. Ibid., 118.
108. Ibid., 176.

109. Jeremy Bentham, "Radicalism Not Dangerous," in *Works of Jeremy Bentham,* ed. John Bowring (Edinburgh: W. Tait; London: Simpkin, Marshall, 1843), vol. III, 610.
110. Thompson, *Inquiry,* 21; italics removed.
111. Ibid., 22.
112. Ibid., 23.
113. Ibid.
114. Ibid., ch. 1, Sec. 1–9. Bentham would largely agree on this point—as was noted above, Bentham associates wealth with well-being.
115. Ibid., ch. 1, Sec. 14.
116. Ibid., 53.
117. Smith, *Wealth of Nations,* vol. I, 18.
118. Thompson, *Inquiry,* 52.
119. Ibid., 54.
120. See, e.g., Max Horkheimer and Theodor W. Adorno, *Dialectic of Enlightenment: Philosophical Fragments,* trans. Edmund Jephcott (Stanford: Stanford University Press, 2002). For a more recent critique, see Robert J. C. Young, *White Mythologies: Writing History and the West,* 2nd ed. (London and New York: Routledge, 2004).
121. Thompson, *Inquiry,* 49.
122. Ibid., 47. There is little difference, really, between Thompson's discussion of the advantages of the division of labor and labor cooperation (see, especially, ibid., ch. 1, sec. 7) and Smith's. The difference has to do with the appropriation of the surplus (which will be discussed below).
123. Ibid., 48–49.
124. Ibid., 50.
125. Marx, *Capital,* vol. I: 132.
126. Ibid., 135.
127. Thompson, "Labor Rewarded," 11.
128. Ibid., 11–12. See also *Inquiry,* 98–99.
129. *Inquiry,* 51.
130. Ibid., 63–64.
131. Ibid., 64.
132. Ibid., 101.
133. Ibid., 36. Thompson's theory of surplus value, and its relation to Marx, will receive more attention in the discussion of his political economics in the next chapter.
134. Ibid., 51.
135. Ibid., 67.
136. Ibid., 50.
137. Ibid., 55.
138. Ibid., 67.
139. Ibid.
140. Ibid., 370.

141. Ibid., 504. Thompson distinguished between selfishness and self-interest, and, as I will discuss in the next chapter, condemned the former but not the latter.
142. Ibid., 514–15.
143. This is not to say that they *haven't,* but there is no evidence that they *have.*
144. That said, Bentham also predates this division, but he can easily be characterized as an advocate of SWB.
145. Gasper, "Human Well-being," 35.
146. See, e.g., Doyal and Gough, *A Theory of Human Need*; Noonan, *Democratic Society*; Soper, "Review"; Patricia Springborg, *The Problem of Human Needs and the Critique of Civilisation* (London: G. Allen and Unwin, 1981).
147. See, e.g., Alexander Kaufman, ed., *Capabilities and Equality: Basic Issues and Problems* (New York and London: Routledge, 2006); Martha Nussbaum and Amartya Sen, eds., *The Quality of Life* (Oxford: Oxford University Press, 1993); Avner Offer, ed., *In Pursuit of the Quality of Life* (Oxford: Oxford University Press, 1996); Amartya Sen, *Choice, Welfare, and Measurement* (Cambridge: MIT Press, 1982); *Commodities and Capabilities* (New York: Elsevier Science Publishers, 1985).
148. Gasper, "Human Well-being," 55–57. One author identifies no fewer than thirty-nine different lists. Sabina Alkire, *Valuing Freedoms: Sen's Capability Approach and Poverty Reduction* (Oxford: Oxford University Press, 2002).
149. Len Doyal, "Review of *On Human Needs* by Kate Soper and *The Problem of Human Needs and the Critique of Civilization* by Patricia Springborg," *Critical Social Policy* 3 (1983): 138.
150. Springborg, *Problem of Human Needs.*
151. Ibid., 252–74.
152. This may be in no small part because its originator, the economist Amartya Sen, makes great use of abstract analytical methodologies, especially in some of his earlier essays, for example, Sen, *Choice, Welfare*; *Commodities.*
153. "Capability and Well-Being," in *The Quality of Life,* ed. Martha Nussbaum and Amartya Sen (Oxford: Oxford University Press, 1993), 31.
154. *Choice, Welfare,* 353–69.
155. "Capability," 40.
156. Martha Nussbaum, "Capabilities as Fundamental Entitlements: Sen and Social Justice," in *Capabilities Equality: Basic Issues and Problems,* ed. Alexander Kaufman (New York: Routledge, 2006), 52–53.
157. Doyal and Gough, *A Theory of Human Need.*
158. McGillivray, "Human Well-being," 3.
159. See, e.g., Doyal, "Comment," 59–69; Noonan, *Democratic Society,* 54–56; Sen, *Commodities.*
160. McGillivray, "Human Well-being," 3–4. Greater affinity for the Epicurean notion of katastematic pleasure is evident in this list.

161. For example, a methodology referred to as "time-sampling" involves having participants note down their state of mind at the time and what they were doing at various times of the day. Veenhoven, "Advances," 17.
162. Or, in the case of the objective measurement of subjective happiness, whether the subject appears to be happy.
163. This is not the place to engage in a critique, but in many of his articles Veenhoven acknowledges the existence of strong objections to the subjective approach, including the instability of the measurements, for example, Ruut Veenhoven, "Happiness as an Aim in Public Policy: The Greatest Happiness Principle," in *Positive Psychology in Practice*, ed. Alex Linley and Stephen Joseph (Hoboken: John Wiley and Sons, 2004).
164. Ibid., 3–4.
165. "Advances," 16–17.
166. At the same time, postmodernism's refusal to accept the possibility of universal human characteristics comes under harsh criticism, especially from writers on human needs, as in, for example, Doyal, "Comment," 12–21, 27–34; Noonan, *Democratic Society*, ch. 13.
167. Sen, *Commodities*, ch. 3.
168. For a good discussion of the nature and diversity of the list approach to well-being, see Sabina Alkire, "Dimensions of Human Development," *World Development* 30, no. 2 (2002).
169. Thompson, *Appeal*, 90.

Chapter 4. Happiness and Utility

1. United effort and common property are presented as a single principle because they are, for Thompson, inseparable, as will be evident from the discussion below.
2. Bentham, *The Theory of Legislation*, 98.
3. *IPML*, 11.
4. Ibid., 11 fn a.
5. Appropriations of Bentham, especially within the economics literature, often confuse utility and happiness. For example, Daniel Kahneman (a psychologist awarded the Nobel Prize in economics) claims he is borrowing the term *utility* from Bentham when he says, "Being pleased or distressed is an attribute of experience at a particular moment," an attribute he calls "instant utility ... best understood as the strength of the disposition to continue or to interrupt the current experience." But for Bentham, utility is a property of the object, not an attribute of the experience. Kahneman's "instant utility" really is much closer to Bentham's idea of pleasure. For Bentham, whether or not something contributes to happiness is what constitutes its utility. But for Kahneman, utility (both as instant utility and as what he refers to as "remembered utility") is a kind of building block for happiness. So Kahneman inverts Bentham's

system, making utility a determinant of happiness rather than the other way around. Daniel Kahneman, "Objective Happiness," in *Well-Being: The Foundations of Hedonic Psychology,* ed. Daniel Kahneman, Ed Diener, and Norbert Schwartz (New York: Russell Sage Foundation, 1999), 4.
6. Bentham, *IPML,* 12.
7. Ibid., 11.
8. Kelly claims that "[t]he principle of utility as a practical principle is not concerned with the balance of pleasure over pain. Instead, it requires individuals to act in accordance with rights and legal norms which direct action toward the end of the maximum of social well-being." Kelly, *Bentham and the Civil Law,* 68. But, within a Benthamite framework, what is "social well-being" without a consideration of the balance of pleasure over pain?
9. Bentham, *IPML,* 11–12. Bentham blurs the distinction when he makes reference to the "principle of utility, or, for shortness sake, to utility." Ibid., 12.
10. Ibid., 11–12 n. b.
11. Ibid., 12 n. b.
12. *A Fragment on Government,* 3.
13. Of course, the state is not the only social force that has this function. Bentham identifies four "sanctions" or "sources from which pleasure and pain ... flow." These are "the *physical,* the *political,* the *moral,* and the *religious.*" These are the means by which "any law or rule of conduct" may be given "a binding force." *IPML,* 34.
14. Bentham notes that there are different varieties of "equality," such as "political equality" and "civil equality." He says, "When used by itself, the word is commonly understood to refer to the distribution of property. It is so used in this treatise [*Theory of Legislation*]" (and, we may assume, his other works). *The Theory of Legislation,* 97.
15. In his own writing, Bentham ordered them in different ways at different times. For example, in the *Theory of Legislation,* they are ordered subsistence, abundance, equality, security. Ibid., 96. In the *Institute of Political Economy,* they are listed as I have them here: subsistence, security, abundance, and equality, explicitly identifying subsistence as primary but not indicating any further order. *Institute of Political Economy,* 307. In a late manuscript, Bentham placed subsistence, abundance, and equality *under* (or within) security, as "Maximizing universal security" involves "securing ... subsistence ... , maximizing ... abundance [and] securing ... equality." Kelly, *Bentham and the Civil Law,* 106.
16. From one perspective, security is subordinate to subsistence because security's object is subsistence. Looked at another way, however, subsistence follows from security, making security the most important. It is important to remember, however, that neither is the final end, as all are subordinate to the principle of utility.

17. Bentham, *The Theory of Legislation*, 101.
18. Ibid., 99. This will be discussed in greater detail below.
19. In *Bentham and the Civil Law* Kelly provides a vigorous defense of Bentham on the question of distributive justice, and he is often cited as an authority on the question. However, in my reading I found numerous methodological and interpretive problems that limit the work's value. The most serious problem is that Kelly equates distributive justice with equality, but the two are, in fact, quite different, as distributive justice can produce outcomes that are manifestly unequal (see, e.g., Aristotle, *Politics*, 103). All that said, there are elements of Kelly's work that are useful, so although his conclusions may be called into question elements of his exposition and analysis are still valuable.
20. Stark, "Liberty and Equality," 69.
21. Frederick Rosen, "Introduction," in *An Introduction to the Principles of Morals and Legislation* (Oxford: Clarendon Press, 1996), xxxvii.
22. Bentham, "Radicalism Not Dangerous," 610. With this Bentham seems to come closest to the phrase often attributed to him: "Each to count for one, and none to count for more than one."
23. *The Theory of Legislation*, 103–104. Emphasis in the original. See also Stark, "Liberty and Equality," 73–74.
24. Bentham, *The Theory of Legislation*, 120.
25. Ibid.
26. Gerald J. Postema, "Bentham's Equality-Sensitive Utilitarianism," *Utilitas* 10, no. 2 (1998).
27. Bentham, *The Theory of Legislation*, 123.
28. Locke, *An Essay*, 549. Hume makes an almost identical statement. David Hume, "Enquiries concerning Human Understanding and concerning the Principles of Morals," ed. L. A. Selby-Bigge and P. H. Niddich (Oxford and New York: Oxford University Press, 1975), 192–204; see also Kelly, *Bentham and the Civil Law*, 80–81.
29. Bentham, *The Theory of Legislation*, 206–207.
30. "Supply Without Burthen," 290–92.
31. *Official Aptitude*, 342. This should not be interpreted as Bentham arguing that property is the *only* subject pertaining to justice. In fact, he criticized Locke for making such a claim. "Article on Utilitarianism," 315.
32. Kelly, *Bentham and the Civil Law*, 155.
33. In arguing that utilitarianism is not particularly interested in the concept of ownership as such, Ryan notes that Bentham has no extended discussion of the concept outside of the *Theory of Legislation* (and the *Principles of the Civil Code*, which are derived from it), and that "Bentham is curiously reluctant to go far into the definition of property." Alan Ryan, *Property and Political Theory* (Oxford: Basil Blackwell, 1984), 95–96. This is not to say that Bentham ignores the subject, as it comes up not infrequently, but the general absence of a sustained discussion is

somewhat odd considering what, from my perspective, seems to be a rather important subject.
34. Bentham, "Nonsense upon Stilts," 322–35.
35. *The Theory of Legislation,* 114. The quotation given here is from Bentham's text (written in English, translated into French, and then translated back into English again), which, according to Aaron Thomas, editor and translator of the most recent English edition of Beccaria's work, may have come from an English translation based on a bastardized French edition (2010, personal correspondence). Beccaria raises his concern in a section entitled *Theft,* in which he discusses punishments for theft committed "without the use of violence," noting that (in Thomas's translation) it is "a crime of that unhappy segment of men for whom the right of property (a terrible and perhaps unnecessary right) has left them nothing but a bare existence." Cesare Beccaria, *On Crimes and Punishments and Other Writings,* ed. Aaron Thomas, trans. Aaron Thomas and Jeremy Parzen (Toronto: University of Toronto Press, 2008), 43.
36. Bentham, *The Theory of Legislation,* 114; italics removed.
37. Smith, *Wealth of Nations,* vol. II, 232.
38. Bentham, *The Theory of Legislation,* 119.
39. Kelly, *Bentham and the Civil Law,* 185–99. See also Bentham, "Supply Without Burthen."
40. *The Theory of Legislation,* 118.
41. Kelly, *Bentham and the Civil Law,* 166.
42. Bentham, *The Theory of Legislation,* 202–206.
43. Ibid., 207. Richard Hildreth, an active abolitionist who translated Dumont's French text into English in 1864, was moved to insert a note at this point that "[r]ecent experience in the West Indies seems to contradict this theory."
44. "Principles of the Civil Code," in *The Works of Jeremy Bentham,* ed. John Bowring (Edinburgh: William Tate, 1838), vol. I, 312–13. *The Principles of the Civil Code* published in Bowring's *Works of Jeremy Bentham* is based on, but differs in numerous ways, from the version published by Dumont. As a result, this one of those places where it is difficult to tell what is Bentham's thought, what is Dumont's, and what is Bowring's, so this particular statement could have come from any one of them.
45. *The Theory of Legislation,* 207–209.
46. *First Principles Preparatory to Constitutional Code,* ed. Philip Schofield, *The Collected Works of Jeremy Bentham* (Oxford: Clarendon Press, 1989), 233.
47. "Institute of Political Economy," 311.
48. "Leading Principles of a Constitutional Code, for Any State," in *Works of Jeremy Bentham,* ed. John Bowring (Edinburgh: William Tait, 1843), vol. II, 235–36. As will be discussed in the next chapter, his concern with sinister interest is what led him to become a champion of democracy.

49. *First Principles,* 235.
50. Baujard, "Collective Interest," 630.
51. Ibid., 611.
52. Bentham, *IPML,* 12.
53. Baujard, "Collective Interest," 620–24.
54. Ibid., 626.
55. Englemann offers an excellent discussion of this in his essay on Bentham's "Indirect Legislation." Engelmann, "'Indirect Legislation.'"
56. Thompson, *Inquiry,* 1.
57. I do not mean to suggest that racial domination and the oppression of women by men are not features of our own times, but at least they are no longer directly enforced by statute.
58. Hobbes's view of competition seems strikingly similar to Thompson's when he asserts that in consequence of competition "amongst men there ariseth on that ground, Envy and Hatred, and finally Warre," although it should be noted that in this passage he is referring to competition for "Honour and Dignity," not wealth. Thomas Hobbes, *Leviathan,* ed. C. B. Macpherson (New York: Penguin Books, 1968), 225–26.
59. Harrison comments that "there is little evidence that . . . Thompson was indebted to Ricardo." Harrison, *Quest,* 67. Reisman calls the label "unfortunate. . . . Apart from the labour theory of value, the subsistence standard, the rivalry between wages and profits, there is little in Ricardo that . . . Thompson may be said to have borrowed." David Reisman, "Introduction to Volume 1," in *Thomas Hodgskin and William Thompson: Ricardian Socialism,* ed. David Reisman, *Democratic Socialism in Britain: Classic Texts in Economic and Political Thought: 1825–1952* (London: Pickering and Chatto, 1996), lxi. Indeed, Claeys argues that the labels "Lockean socialist" or "Smithian socialist" may work as well or better as descriptors of the so-called Ricardian socialists in general. Claeys, *Machinery,* xxiii–xxv. Ricardo and Thompson may have known each other, but direct evidence is lacking. Thompson comes up in a very curious way in an October 1819 letter from Bentham to Ricardo in which he says he "had to thank you" for a recent letter "from my—I will venture to say from our—Hibernian friend," whom the Editor, according to a note, takes to be Thompson, although the letter he is referring to is missing. Bentham, *Correspondence,* 9: 362–65.
60. By "competitive" he means supporters of the system of individual competition, or capitalism. Thompson, "Labor Rewarded," 39–94.
61. Malthus is quoted, but not cited, in a passage in which Thompson refers to the "*false position, that "increased comfort will necessarily lead to increase of improvident breeding."* Thompson argues that the problem of "improvident" population increase is the effect, not the cause, of "the misery of the majority of the community." *Inquiry,* 425–26.
62. Ibid., iii–vii.
63. Ibid., 103–44.

64. Political economists may find Thompson's theory incomplete. Harrison notes that, in general, Owenite political economy is marked by its "refusal to be limited by its [classical political economy's] declared boundaries," as their concerns "were not those which were primary or central in classical political economy." Thus, their economic theory was "both more and less than a theory of economics: more in that it was an attempt to reassert the values of an older, pre-capitalist concept of 'moral economy' ... less in that it was not a coherent and complete theory of the functioning of an economy." Harrison, *Quest*, 74.
65. Roncaglia, *The Wealth of Ideas*, 189–90.
66. Thompson, *Inquiry*, 19–20.
67. Ibid., 44.
68. Smith, *Wealth of Nations*, vol. I, 72–73.
69. Ibid., 74.
70. David Ricardo, *On the Principles of Political Economy, and Taxation*, 3rd ed. (Harmondsworth: Penguin Books, 1971), 57.
71. Ibid., 83–86.
72. Ibid., 115.
73. Ibid., 119. There is no difference between Smith and Ricardo on this point; see Smith, *Wealth of Nations*, vol. I, 95.
74. Roncaglia, *The Wealth of Ideas*, 196.
75. Frederick Engels, *Anti-Dühring* (London: Electric Book Company, 1878), 259.
76. Thompson, *Inquiry*, 166. The reference to "wages" in the second sentence is mysterious; perhaps he means the capital set aside for wages (not a reference to the labor power contributed).
77. Ibid., 166, 171.
78. Ibid., 167.
79. Karl Marx, *Selected Writings*, ed. Lawrence H. Simon (Indianapolis: Hackett, 1994), 58.
80. Thompson, *Inquiry*, 166–67.
81. More recently, David Ellerman argues that instead of capitalists renting labor (his take on the labor contract of employment), labor should rent capital. David Ellerman, "Property and Contract in Economics: The Case for Economic Democracy," Basil Blackwell, http://www.ellerman.org/Davids-Stuff/Books/p&c.htm, ch 1.
82. Thompson, *Inquiry*, 61.
83. "Capitalism," according to the *Oxford English Dictionary*, did not enter the English language until the 1850s. "Capital," meaning the use of stored value in such a way as to produce more value, and "capitalist," an adjective that denoted someone who makes productive use of capital, were already in fairly wide use in Thompson's time.
84. Thompson, *Inquiry*, 423.
85. Ibid., 133. As Marx and Engels express it, "The history of all hitherto

existing societies is the history of class struggle." Karl Marx and Frederich Engels, *The Communist Manifesto* (London: Penguin Classics, 2002), 219.
86. See, e.g., Thompson, *Inquiry*, 36.
87. Marx and Engels, *Communist Manifesto*, 221.
88. He also refers to the "inequality of wealth" as "the radical defect in the constitution of society, that which must necessarily engender every other evil." Thompson, *Inquiry*, 221. He is not, however, consistent on this point. In the context of his feminist argument in the *Appeal* he argues that there are natural causes of inequality (the superior strength of men, for example), social causes (such as the denial of education), and political causes (the denial of political rights), without identifying any of these as primary.
89. Although it is a silent attack: Bentham is not mentioned. But the position he attacks is clearly Bentham's.
90. Thompson, *Inquiry*, 147–49.
91. Ibid., 175.
92. Claeys, *Machinery*, 91. Claeys is correct to point out that Thompson recognizes some advantages from competition, but Thompson clearly argues that these are outweighed by its evils. It may be that I am reading Thompson's works as more polemical than does Claeys. In my reading, Thompson presents the strongest argument for competition that he can, only to then demonstrate its failure and the superiority of the position he advocates. We might note that in arguing that capitalism is a stage in the historical development toward communism, Marx also praises certain aspects of the competitive system, in particular improvements in the standard of living and technological advancement. See Marx and Engels, *Communist Manifesto*, 222–26; see also Stedman Jones's discussion in Gareth Stedman Jones, "Introduction," in *Karl Marx and Friedrich Engels: The Communist Manifesto*, ed. Gareth Stedman Jones (London: Penguin Classics, 2002), ch. 12. Indeed, Thompson also saw the "removal of feudal restraints" to be a positive step, Thompson, *Inquiry*, 134.
93. "Labor Rewarded," 65.
94. *Inquiry*, 370.
95. Ibid.
96. Ibid., 392.
97. Ibid., 180.
98. Ibid., 274.
99. Ibid., 337.
100. To put this in some context, in early nineteenth-century debates on workers' education, supporters (who were generally in the minority) emphasized its importance in developing "habits of submission and respect for their superiors" and to "lay the foundation of obedience,"

which would "make them contented in the station which Providence has appointed to them." On the other hand, a "controlled education" was seen by reformers as "a safeguard against social disorder" in the face of widespread destitution even as late as 1834. Gregg, *History of Britain*, 246–47.
101. Thompson, *Appeal*, 113.
102. Ibid., 113–14.
103. *Inquiry*, 313.
104. Ibid., 319.
105. Ibid., 176.
106. Ibid., 446.
107. Ibid., 466.
108. Ibid., 595.
109. *Appeal*, 127.
110. Ferguson, "Radical Ideas." Thompson's arguments are broader and more forceful than Wollstonecraft's, but it is incorrect to suggest, as Ferguson does, that Wollstonecraft did not also refer to women's status in marriage as a form of slavery. Mary Wollstonecraft, "A Vindication of the Rights of Woman," in *A Vindication of the Rights of Men and A Vindication of the Rights of Woman*, ed. Sylvana Tomaselli (Cambridge: Cambridge University Press, 1995), 69.
111. Thompson, "Labor Rewarded," 15.
112. *Appeal*, 142; emphasis added. When Thompson says that everyone should be "made" happy, he means that they should be able to make themselves happy, as he argues elsewhere that happiness is something that generally comes out of active engagement rather than passive acceptance.
113. James Mill, *The Article on Government, Reprinted from the Supplement to the Encyclopaedia Britannica* (London: Encyclopaedia Britannica, 1821), 16.
114. Ibid., 20–21.
115. Thompson, *Appeal*, 62.
116. Mill, *Article on Government*, 9.
117. Ibid., 7.
118. Thompson, *Appeal*, 62.
119. Thompson never married (given his argument in the *Appeal* one can see why), and his view of the conditions of wives in Britain may have been strongly influenced by that of his close friend Anna Doyle Wheeler, whom he names as co-author of the ideas presented in the book (referring to it as their "joint property." Ibid., 47). Wheeler's own marriage, at fifteen, to Francis Massy-Wheeler, ended after twelve stormy years with her "fleeing" to the home of her uncle. Dolores Dooley, "Introduction," in *Appeal*, ed. Dolores Dooley (Cork, Ireland: Cork University Press, 1997), 6, 22. Some authors identify them as "lovers," see, e.g., Peter

Collins, "Thompson, William," in *The Oxford Companion to Irish History,* ed. S. J. Connolly (Oxford: Oxford University Press, 2002). However, evidence of this is lacking—contemporary sources (such as John Minter Morgan's eulogy, given in part in the voice of Anna Wheeler's *nom de plume,* Vlasta) do not mention it, and there is no record of them having produced any children. Morgan, *Hampden,* vol. II, 294 ff.
120. Thompson, *Appeal,* 68.
121. Ibid., 66.
122. Ibid., 96–97.
123. Ibid., 92.
124. Ibid., 127.
125. Ibid., 64.
126. Ibid.
127. Ibid., 65.
128. Ibid., 64–65.
129. Ibid., 101.
130. Ibid., 106.
131. Ibid., 128.
132. Ibid., 209.
133. Ibid., 76.
134. Ibid., 89–90.
135. *Inquiry,* 423.
136. *Appeal,* 91.
137. Ibid.
138. Ibid., 127.
139. *Inquiry,* 504.
140. Ibid., 178.
141. Ibid., 2–3.
142. James Mill, *Elements of Political Economy* (London: Baldwin, Cradock, and Joy, 1821), 52.
143. Thompson, *Inquiry,* x–xiv. For his sake, Smith says that the First Book of the *Wealth of Nations* is concerned with discovering the "order, according to which [the produce of the productive powers of labor] is *naturally* distributed among the different ranks and conditions of men in the society." Smith, *Wealth of Nations,* vol. I, 2 (emphasis added). Smith uses the word *natural* quite frequently throughout the *Wealth of Nations,* never saying what he means by it. For example, he refers to the "natural rates of wages, profit, and rent" and the "natural price" of a commodity at one point (ibid., 62), and later that, "The produce of labour constitutes the natural recompense or wages of labour" (ibid., 72), but it is not clear that the term means the same thing in both places.
144. Thompson, *Inquiry,* 535. We should not read this reference to "rights" as a reference to the concept of natural rights; we may assume that Thompson rejects the idea on the same grounds as his mentor. Bentham,

"Nonsense upon Stilts," 330. But as this shows, Thompson did not reject the concept of rights; we may assume that he, like Bentham, saw rights as established and guaranteed by law. Bentham, *The Theory of Legislation*, 82–87.
145. Thompson, *Inquiry*, 178. The "natural laws" developed in the first chapter of the *Inquiry* are summarized in its last section, 173–78.
146. Ibid., xiv.
147. Ibid., xiii.
148. *Practical Directions*; *Inquiry*, ch. 6; "Labor Rewarded."
149. The same could be said of state ownership, but the difference here is one of scale: The members of the cooperative community remain much closer, physically and epistemically, to their joint property, than in a system of state ownership. For a brief but enlightening discussion of this point, see Buber, "Comments on the Idea of Community."
150. Thompson, *Inquiry*, 386–91.
151. Ibid., 240–41.
152. Ibid., 245.
153. Ibid., 590.
154. *Practical Directions*, esp. the chapter on "Agriculture."
155. He explicitly argues that only "fully-formed" communities should attempt to engage in exchange for their necessities; nascent communities should focus on self-sufficiency and only consider producing a surplus for exchange of items of "secondary utility." Ibid., 135–36.
156. *Inquiry*, 523–26.
157. Ibid., 529.
158. This may reflect either a lack of familiarity or a lack of consideration of major debates in classical political economy of his time, particularly Ricardo's theory of comparative advantage. Thompson never discusses why Ricardo's theory would not apply to the cooperative communities.

Chapter 5. The Politics of Happiness

1. David Trend, "Democracy's Crisis of Meaning," in *Radical Democracy: Identity, Citizenship and the State*, ed. David Trend (London and New York: Routledge, 1996), 7.
2. Sheldon Wolin, *Politics and Vision: Continuity and Innovation in Western Political Thought*, expanded ed. (Princeton: Princeton University Press, 2004), 591.
3. "Norm and Form: The Constitutionalizing of Democracy," in *Athenian Political Thought and the Reconstruction of American Democracy*, ed. J. Peter Euben, John R. Wallach, and Josiah Ober (Ithaca: Cornell University Press, 1994).
4. Indeed, for some mainstream theorists, the perceived lack, or insufficiency, of democracy at the level of the state leads them to consider

democracy at the social level—for example, Robert Dahl, *A Preface to Economic Democracy* (Berkeley: University of California Press, 1985).
5. Bentham, author of the "Radical Reform Bill" and "Radicalism Not Dangerous," was certainly considered a radical in his time. To refer to him as "mainstream" is anachronistic in that sense. However, his theory can be understood to be solidly in the mainstream of democratic theory today.
6. Schofield dates to 1822, and the drafting of his constitutional code, the point at which Bentham became convinced that the only form of government that could be expected to effectively promote the interests of the people was one based on representative democracy. Schofield, *Utility and Democracy*, 250. This should be seen as the end point of a process, rather than a sudden shift. See note 15, below.
7. With a rather important qualification, as will be discussed below.
8. It should be noted that in this early period—prior to 1793—his views changed over time: initially he argued for a property qualification, although he thought it should be quite low, and the exclusion of women, but by the end of his efforts to contribute to the development of the French system he was arguing that security of property was not, in fact, threatened by political equality, and that the exclusion of women from the franchise was "ridiculous." Schofield, *Utility and Democracy*, 85–91.
9. From a letter of 1792, quoted in ibid., 81.
10. J. R. Dinwiddy, "Bentham's Transition to Political Radicalism, 1809–10," *Journal of the History of Ideas* 36, no. 4 (1975): 683.
11. A loose translation of "*tout a peu pres est déjà fait et bien fait de ce qui sembleroit demander une représentation égale pour le bien faire*," quoted in J. H. Burns, "Bentham and the French Revolution," *Transactions of the Royal Historical Society* 16, Fifth Series(1966): 98.
12. Ibid.
13. Quoted in Schofield, *Utility and Democracy*, 101.
14. Ibid., 102.
15. There is some debate about the timing of his "conversion" or "transition" and the role of James Mill in bringing this about that need not concern us here; see, e.g., Mary Peter Mack, *Jeremy Bentham: An Odyssey of Ideas 1748–92* (London: Heinemann, 1962); Dinwiddy, "Bentham's Transition"; Schofield, *Utility and Democracy*, 78–83, 137–40. A common theory is that this turnabout was a result of his meeting James Mill in 1808. Schofield refers to it as the "standard account" but casts doubt on the idea, noting that Bentham had started writing on the need for parliamentary reform slightly before their meeting. Schofield also argues that Bentham's thinking went through more of a "transition" than "conversion." Ibid., 137–40.
16. See, e.g., Plato, *The Republic*, 112–13 (421b–c).
17. Bentham, *IPML*, 223.
18. According to Schofield, the phrase first arose in 1797 in writing on the

poor laws, but in 1804 he began to use it regularly in writing on judicial evidence and procedure. Schofield, *Utility and Democracy*, 109.
19. Ibid., 125.
20. Jeremy Bentham, "The Elements of the Art of Packing, as Applied to Special Juries, Particularly in Cases of Libel Law," in *Works of Jeremy Bentham*, ed. John Bowring (Edinburgh: W. Tait; London: Simpkin, Marshall, 1843), vol. V, 91; see also Schofield, *Utility and Democracy*, 135, ch. 10.
21. Quoted in *Utility and Democracy*, 272.
22. Ibid., 274. Note that it is Schofield, not Bentham, who refers to official aptitude and popular sovereignty (discussed below in the text) as among the "securities against misrule." Ibid., 348.
23. Ibid., 224–25.
24. Bentham, "Constitutional Code, Vol. 1," 25–26.
25. "Radical Reform Bill, with Extracts from the Reasons" in *Works of Jeremy Bentham*, ed. John Bowring (Edinburgh: W. Tait; London: Simpkin, Marshall, 1843), vol. III, 558.
26. "Constitutional Code, Vol. 1," 25–26.
27. *Securities Against Misrule and Other Constitutional Writings for Tripoli and Greece*, ed. Philip Schofield, *The Collected Works of Jeremy Bentham* (Oxford: Clarendon Press, 1990), 68.
28. Frederick Rosen, *Jeremy Bentham and Representative Democracy: A Study of the Constitutional Code* (Oxford: Clarendon Press, 1983), 12.
29. Bentham, "Radical Reform Bill," 559–60.
30. "Projet of a Constitutional Code," in *Rights, Representation, and Reform*, ed. Philip Schofield, Catherine Pease-Watkin, and Cyprian Blamires, *The Collected Works of Jeremy Bentham* (Oxford: Clarendon Press, 2002), 231, 46–49.
31. *The Theory of Legislation*, 81. This could be an example of what we might call the "Dumont effect," as was noted earlier.
32. Schofield, *Utility and Democracy*, 144.
33. Bentham, "Radicalism Not Dangerous," 599. This essay was written in response to critics of the reform bill. Ironically, in the Reform Bill itself he rejects the qualifier, "virtual," saying that by "universality ... no man appears to mean that females should vote." "Radical Reform Bill," 559.
34. Lea Campos Boralevi, *Bentham and the Oppressed* (Berlin and New York: Walter de Gruyter, 1984), 25.
35. Jeremy Bentham, "Constitutional Code," in *Works of Jeremy Bentham*, ed. John Bowring (Edinburgh: William Tait, 1843), vol. IX, 108–109. Ball argues that, in making this argument, Bentham might be accused of having committed two fallacies he condemned: the Procrastinator's Argument and the Snail's Pace Argument. Ball, *Reappraising Political Theory*, 190–91; see also Boralevi, *Bentham and the Oppressed*, 17. Ball and Boralevi agree on this point, but disagree sharply over whether

Bentham can properly be considered a feminist. Much of their argument is concerned with issues outside of the question of the suffrage and need not detain us here. In my view both arguments have merit; this is clearly not a topic on which Bentham maintained a great deal of consistency.
36. Schofield, *Utility and Democracy,* 348.
37. Ibid., 259.
38. Bentham, "Political Tactics," 310.
39. "Constitutional Code, Vol. 1," 35–36.
40. *Securities Against Misrule,* 54–55; *First Principles,* 56–59. See also Schofield, *Utility and Democracy,* 261.
41. Bentham, *Securities Against Misrule,* 63–64.
42. Ibid., 67–68.
43. Although in retrospect it seems obvious, I must thank Philip Schofield for pointing this out to me.
44. Thompson, *Inquiry,* 387.
45. Ibid., 210.
46. In fact, Thompson will later say that he thinks a true identity of interests in this sense is "impossible." *Appeal,* 91.
47. Ira Katznelson, Mark Kesselman, and Alan Draper, *The Politics of Power: a Critical Introduction to American Government,* 4th ed. (Belmont, CA: Wadsworth/Thomson Learning, 2002). 13.
48. Thompson, *Practical Directions,* iv.
49. *Inquiry,* 212–13 note.
50. Smith, *Wealth of Nations,* vol. II, 303.
51. Thompson, *Inquiry,* 291.
52. Ibid., 290.
53. Ibid., 291–92.
54. *Appeal,* 143–44.
55. Wollstonecraft, "A Vindication," 90. Thompson certainly knew Wollstonecraft's work. In fact, he criticizes her for her "narrow views which too often marred [her] pages and narrowed their usefulness"—possibly a reference to her statement that she was mainly concerned with middle-class women. Thompson, *Appeal,* 47; Wollstonecraft, "A Vindication," 76. However, Thompson may owe Wollstonecraft more of a debt than he realizes, as his arguments against subordination bear a fairly strong resemblance to hers.
56. Thompson, *Inquiry,* 292.
57. Ibid., 292–93.
58. Readers familiar with J. S. Mill's writing in this area may find rather strong parallels between Thompson's argument and Mill's claim that, as Pateman puts it, "It is at the local level where the real educative effect of participation occurs, where... the issues dealt with directly affect the individual and his everyday life." Carole Pateman, *Participation and Democratic Theory* (Cambridge: Cambridge University Press, 1970), 31.

59. Thompson, *Inquiry*, 293.
60. Thompson refers to local districts of two or three hundred thousand (ibid.), so it seems that such assemblies would be quite impractical, unless there were a large number of them in each district. In the "Addenda" to *Labor Rewarded,* Thompson provides a brief outline of a national constitution that he says could be applied "to the extent of hundreds of millions of persons" through a system that would start with open assemblies at the local level, which would elect delegates to the next higher level, which would itself elect delegates to a national assembly (inserting as many intermediate levels as required). As a sample national constitution it is quite thin, especially compared to Bentham's *Constitutional Code*. Interestingly, it shares many characteristics with the decision-making structures adopted by some social movement organizations in the late 1970s and early 1980s, such as the Abalone Alliance, which formed in the mid-1970s to oppose the Diablo Canyon nuclear power plant near San Luis Obispo, California. Steven E. Barkan, "Strategic, Tactical, and Organizational Dilemmas of the Protest Movement against Nuclear Power," *Social Problems* 27, no. 1 (1979): 29.
61. Thompson, *Inquiry*, 358.
62. Ibid., 358–59.
63. Ibid., 101.
64. "Labor Rewarded," 41.
65. Ibid., 43–44. We can but speculate about the reasons for this change of heart. It may be significant that this comes after the failure of Owen's New Harmony community, and he may have gotten an earful from Owen about conditions in America. He also may have been concerned about the establishment of a dynastic system in the United States with the election of John Quincy Adams, the son of a former president, as president.
66. Ibid., 44.
67. It is important to remember that Thompson is writing in the context of the United Kingdom of the early nineteenth century, so much of his critique is focused on the exclusion of the vast majority of the population from the vote. Still, there are points at which his arguments apply even to systems with universal suffrage, and it is on these that I will concentrate.
68. Thompson, *Inquiry*, 218.
69. Ibid., 220.
70. Ibid., 221.
71. Ibid.
72. As it turns out, the implementation of universal suffrage seems to be only a minor inconvenience when it comes to their maintaining their dominance. I refer here to the increasing—in fact, stunning—disparity in wealth in early-twenty-first-century America and the consequent

disparity in political power. G. William Domhoff, "Power in America: Wealth, Income, and Power," http://sociology.ucsc.edu/whorulesamerica/power/wealth.html.
73. Thompson, *Appeal*, 58.
74. Ibid., 64–65.
75. See, e.g., Robert Dahl, *Democracy and its Critics* (New Haven: Yale University Press, 1989), 30–33, 84–87.
76. See, e.g., *On Democracy* (New Haven: Yale University Press, 1998), ch 14; Katznelson, Kesselman, and Draper, *Politics of Power*, ch 1; C. B. Macpherson, *Democratic Theory: Essays in Retrieval* (Oxford: Oxford University Press, 1973), ch 1.
77. This is true whether or not the inverse is true—that democratic practice presumes equality.
78. Chantal Mouffe, "Radical Democracy or Liberal Democracy?," in *Radical Democracy: Identity, Citizenship, and the State,* ed. David Trend (New York and London: Routledge, 1996), 20.
79. Trend, "Democracy's Crisis," 14; Laclau and Mouffe, *Hegemony*, 181.
80. *Hegemony*, 163.
81. J. Peter Euben, "Taking it to the Streets: Radical Democracy and Radicalizing Theory," in *Radical Democracy: Identity, Citizenship, and the State,* ed. David Trend (New York and London: Routledge, 1996), 69, 73.
82. Michel Foucault, *The History of Sexuality: An Introduction,* trans. Robert Hurley, 3 vols, vol. 1 (New York: Vintage Books, 1978), 92–96.
83. See, e.g., Dahl, *Democracy and its Critics*, ch. 9.
84. These terms were fairly commonly used by first-wave feminists, as early as the 1690s by Mary Astell, in the 1790s by Wollstonecraft, and by Thompson himself in the *Appeal*. Mary Astell, *Political Writings,* ed. Patricia Springborg (Cambridge: Cambridge University Press, 1996); Wollstonecraft, "A Vindication."
85. There are a number of points on which Thompson could be criticized for essentializing women, assuming that they will be at a disadvantage under competitive conditions, but this would not affect the overall thrust of his argument.
86. Thompson, *Appeal,* 53, 163. There is an interesting parallel between Thompson's argument on this point and Marx's argument in *On the Jewish Question,* where he argues that political and civil rights for Jews should not be confused with emancipation in a capitalist society based on exploitation. I do not mean to suggest that Marx lifted Thompson's argument, as there is no reason to believe that Marx would have read the *Appeal,* at least not by 1842 when he wrote his response to Bauer.
87. Sheldon Wolin, "'Fugitive Democracy,'" *Constellations* 1, no. 1 (1994).
88. Thompson, *Inquiry,* 390.
89. Ibid., 421.

90. Ibid., 461–62.
91. Ibid., 466.
92. Ibid., 467. In general he downplays the cost of exit, suggesting that "[i]f these establishments were numerous and in different places, changes of abode and occupation... would be mere excursions or experiments of pleasure.... Nothing could be more useful for every community than these voluntary individual exchanges: by means of them, all the uncongenial members of every community would be gradually withdrawing to societies more attractive to them... operating as safety valves for the retiring of every irritating and irritated member." Ibid., 494–95. Might there be a community made up of curmudgeons and irritable misfits?
93. Ibid., 508.
94. Thompson also discusses public opinion in the same way as Bentham, for example where he says that "[n]o wishes... can conjure away exclusions, can alter laws. The laws must be repealed. If this public opinion be sincere, they will, as a matter of course, be repealed." *Appeal,* 174. By the same token, it could be said that Bentham recognizes the function of public opinion to regulate the behavior of individuals through his discussion of the moral sanction and the pleasure of reputation, but this certainly is not something he would consider as a political function, whereas Thompson sees it as a central component of the politics of the community.
95. *Inquiry,* 509.
96. John Stuart Mill, "On Liberty," in *On Liberty and Other Essays,* ed. John Gray (Oxford: Oxford University Press, 2008), 8.
97. Ibid.
98. Thompson, *Inquiry,* 390.
99. Radical democrats might challenge Thompson's arguments regarding the possibility of an identity of interests because it effaces the existence of significant differences. Thompson certainly can be criticized for a kind of Enlightenment universalism, but in his defense the notion of an "identity of interests" can be interpreted as limited to particular, significant areas, for example the distribution of wealth within the community, or individuals' health and well-being, rather than complete and total identity.
100. Thompson, *Inquiry,* 497.
101. Ibid., 496.
102. Ibid., 383.
103. Ibid., 315.
104. Although Thompson himself has a different perspective, suggesting that it would be easy for members to leave with no real harm done to the community: "[F]or the stock and all the operations are on so large a scale, that the withdrawing of any individual member with his share thereof, could produce no effect on the prosperity of the whole: there

would be therefore no need to insist on the consent of the community... to the withdrawing of any individual members." Ibid., 494. He does not consider the possibility of a factional split that results with a substantial portion of a community deciding to depart—as in fact happened under Owen at New Harmony. Harrison, *Quest,* 165.
105. Thompson, *Inquiry,* 434.
106. Ibid.
107. Ibid., 434–36.
108. Ibid., 579. For Thompson's explicit arguments against revolution and against the use of force generally, see ibid., 599.
109. Hunt, "Utilitarianism," 560.
110. See, for example, the articles that appeared in the 2000 edition of the Communities Directory published by the Fellowship for Intentional Communities (http://www.ic.org/pnp/cdir/2000/index.php).
111. He discusses issues of natural inequality extensively in the *Appeal* in support of his argument for political rights for women. However, because here I am discussing these issues specifically in the context of the cooperative communities, my attention will be exclusively on his arguments in the *Inquiry*.
112. Thompson, *Inquiry,* 470–71.
113. Joyce Rothschild and J. Allen Whitt, *The Cooperative Workplace: Potentials and Dilemmas of Organizational Democracy and Participation* (Cambridge: Cambridge University Press, 1986), 70.
114. Jane J. Mansbridge, "Fears of Conflict in Face-to-Face Democracies," in *Workplace Democracy and Social Change,* ed. Frank Lindenfeld and Joyce Rothschild-Whitt (Boston: Porter Sargent, 1982), 126–27.
115. Carmen Sirianni, "Learning Pluralism: Democracy and Diversity in Feminist Organizations," in *Critical Studies in Organization and Bureaucracy,* ed. Frank Fischer and Carmen Sirianni (Philadelphia: Temple University Press, 1994).
116. Thompson, *Inquiry,* 498.
117. Ibid., 497.

Chapter 6. From Theory to Practice

1. Thompson, "Lease of an Estate."
2. Even to the extent that a statue of him stands in Manchester at the entrance to the rather impressive set of buildings that once housed the offices of the Cooperative Wholesale Society (CWS) and associated offices of the British cooperative movement.
3. For example, Fairbairn's otherwise excellent examination of the development of the Rochdale Principles does not mention Thompson at all, and he gets only a passing mention in Thornes's similarly valuable

essay. Fairbairn, "The Meaning of Rochdale"; Thornes, "Change and Continuity," 33.
4. As Claeys puts it, "Unable to control the new movement... he withdrew his support and attempted to frustrate measures he disagreed with." Gregory Claeys, "Introduction," in *Robert Owen: A New View of Society and Other Writings,* ed. Gregory Claeys (London: Penguin Classics, 1991), xvii.
5. Brett Fairbairn, "Social Movements and Co-operatives: Implications for History and Development," *Review of International Co-operation* 94, no. 1 (2001): 26.
6. Ibid., 25–26.
7. Birchall's work is an excellent example of this. While it provides a very valuable overview of the historical development of cooperatives internationally from the last half of the nineteenth century through the twentieth century, it includes only a very brief discussion of the period before Rochdale, and while it includes very interesting discussions about the political associations of cooperatives, it has almost nothing at all to say about ideology. Johnston Birchall, *The International Co-operative Movement* (New York: St. Martin's Press, 1997).
8. Or "socialism." In this period the terms seem to have been used more or less interchangeably.
9. The origins of the romanticized version may be traced to the first history written of the Rochdale pioneers by George Jacob Holyoake, the first edition of which was published in 1857. Holyoake may have good reason to claim, as he does in his Preface of 1893, that this work, which was published in serial form in Britain and by Horace Greeley in the *New York Tribune,* translated into French, Spanish, Italian, German, and Hungarian, and quoted by J. S. Mill in his *Principles of Political Economy,* played a major role in spreading the Rochdale model worldwide. G. J. Holyoake, *Self-Help by the People: The History of the Rochdale Pioneers,* 3rd/10th ed. (London: Swan Sonnenschein, 1900). He provides a much fuller history, including a lengthy discussion of the earlier work by Owen, Thompson, and others, as well as various other experiments similar to Rochdale, in his two-volume work, *The History of Co-operation in England.*
10. Fairbairn, "The Meaning of Rochdale," 4.
11. "Social Movements," 28.
12. Peter Gurney, "Labor's Great Arch: Cooperation and Cultural Revolution in Britain, 1795–1926," in *Consumers against Capitalism? Consumer Cooperation in Europe, North America, and Japan, 1840-1990,* ed. Ellen Furlough and Carl Strikwerda (New York: Rowman and Littlefield, 1999), 137.
13. G. D. H. Cole, *A Century of Co-operation* (London: George Allen and Unwin, 1944), 25. Dr. William King, in his journal *The Co-operator,* offered an estimate of "about one hundred and thirty societies established"

at the end of 1829, a number that had grown to three hundred when he published his last number on August 1 of 1830. William King, "The Co-operator," in *Dr. William King and the Co-operator, 1828–1830,* ed. T. W. Mercer (Manchester: The Co-operative Union, 1922), 82, 114. The rate of growth, for a movement of low-income or impoverished workers, seems excessive; this may reflect expressions of interest or perhaps plans as much as real entities established.
14. Mercer, *Co-operative Commonwealth,* 29.
15. The Pioneers appear never to have taken steps to establish a community, but it should be noted that by an 1852 act of Parliament they were forbidden to engage in "banking, mining, or wholesaling or to hold land." The landholding provision was removed in 1855, but a ban was placed on expenditures for the purpose of education. Gurney, "Labor's Great Arch," 139.
16. Fairbairn, "The Meaning of Rochdale," 3.
17. Besides Owen's and Thompson's work, a well-known essay, published in 1825, was John Gray's *A Lecture on Human Happiness,* which is primarily an attack on the unequal distribution of wealth and power and the capitalist mode of production. John Gray, *A Lecture on Human Happiness, Being the First of a Series of Lectures on That Subject in Which Will Be Comprehended a General Review of the Causes of the Existing Evils of Society* (New York: Augustus M. Kelley, 1971). Given the date, we do not know the extent to which his views may have been influenced by Thompson's *Inquiry*. It is not clear if this was ever delivered as a lecture before a live audience. It was originally published in England in 1825; an American edition came out in 1826, published along with the Preamble and Constitution of the Friendly Association for Mutual Interests established at Valley Forge, Pennsylvania.
18. First Armagh Co-operative Society, "The Laws of the First Armagh Co-operative Society," in *Owenism and the Working Class: Six Pamphlets and Four Broadsides, British Labour Struggles: Contemporary Pamplets 1727–1850* (New York: Arno Press, 1972), 13.
19. First Salford Co-operative Society, "Principles, Object, and Laws, of the First Salford Co-operative Society" (Manchester, 1831).
20. First London Co-operative Society, "The First London Co-operative Association: Objects and Laws," in *Owenism and the Working Class: Six Pamphlets and Four Broadsides, 1821–1834* (New York: Arno Press, 1972). We don't know who the members of this society were, but Thompson refers to "our London Society" in a letter of 1826. Thompson, "Correspondence," 185. But since Thompson's letter is from 1826 and the Laws of the First London Co-operative Society referenced above are from 1829, they may not be the same.
21. A Member, "An Address Delivered at the Opening of the Birmingham Co-operative Society" (Birmingham: W. Plastans, 1828).
22. Dooley, *Equality in Community,* 29–30. This is the same William Pare,

discussed in the introduction, who acted as executor of Thompson's will and produced the abridged edition of the *Inquiry*. According to Birchall, Pare, always an active missionary for Owenism, was responsible for its spread to Scandinavia. He remained a leader of the British cooperative movement as late as 1869, when he made the first (unsuccessful) attempt to establish an international association of cooperatives. Birchall, *The International Co-operative Movement*, 37.

23. Robert Owen, "Resolutions, &c. Passed at the First Meeting of the Co-operative Congress" (Manchester, May 26 and 27, 1831).
24. John and James Powell, "Proceedings of the Second Co-operative Congress" (Birmingham, Oct 4–6, 1831).
25. William Carpenter, "Proceedings of the Third Cooperative Congress," in *Owenism and the Working Class: Six Pamphlets and Four Broadsides, 1821–1834, British Labour Struggles: Contemporary Pamphlets 1727–1850* (New York: Arno Press, 1832), 108–17. We may note that a delegate from the Rochdale society, William Harrison, was in attendance at the 3rd Congress, which required travel to London. Two different cooperative societies from Rochdale had delegates at the first Congress, held nearby in Manchester. They did not, however, attend the 2nd Congress, nor did they send a letter of support.
26. The "Law the First" and the most important of the operating rules are excerpted in Appendix 1.
27. Paul Lambert, *Studies in the Social Philosophy of Co-operation*, trans. Joseph Létargez (Manchester: Co-operative Union, 1963), 294–97.
28. Fairbairn points out that none of their original rules stipulated democratic procedures, suggesting, "Most likely democracy was left out because it was taken for granted.... [O]ne may take the omission of the principle of democracy as an indication of its centrality to Rochdale co-operation." Fairbairn, "The Meaning of Rochdale," 7. A "one member, one vote" rule was explicitly adopted in August 1845. Ibid., 7–9.
29. Marx, *Capital*, vol. I: 874.
30. Marx discusses these conditions at length, mostly quoting from parliamentary commissions of the time into the working conditions of what were then referred to as the "laboring classes." Ibid., ch. 15.
31. Andrew Sharp, ed. *The English Levellers,*in *Cambridge Texts in the History of Political Thought* (Cambridge: Cambridge University Press, 1998), 116.
32. Ibid., 129.
33. Gareth Stedman Jones, *Languages of Class: Studies in English Working Class History 1832–1982* (Cambridge: Cambridge University Press, 1983), 102.
34. Gregg, *History of Britain*, 152–57.
35. Stedman Jones, *Languages of Class*, 104–105.

36. James Bronterre O'Brien, quoted in ibid., 109.
37. Claeys, "Introduction," xvii–xxii.
38. Harrison, *Quest*, 75.
39. Ibid., 67.
40. Ibid., 64.
41. Harrison says that it would be "an easy matter, though tedious, to document the use by Owenites of the key concepts of Enlightenment rationalism." Ibid., 83.
42. Ibid., 79.
43. Ibid., 80.
44. Perhaps this is unremarkable. After all, late-twentieth-century and early-twenty-first-century Marxism owes much more to subsequent theoretical developments than it does to Marx's own work.
45. Harrison, *Quest*, 216–24. Indeed, it is at meetings held at the branch in Manchester that a young Friedrich Engels was first exposed to the ideas of socialism. Claeys, "Introduction," xxii.
46. Harrison, *Quest*, 225.
47. Cole, *A Century of Co-operation*, 48.
48. Thompson, *Weavers of Dreams*, 141.
49. Holyoake, *Self-Help by the People*, 80.
50. Thompson, *Weavers of Dreams*, 22.
51. Holyoake, *Self-Help by the People*, 80–81.
52. Holyoake's account is corroborated by one of the Chartists-cum-Pioneers, who was quoted in a 1901 interview as saying that the Pioneers' meetings started in the Chartist meeting room, but, "After a while there was a quarrel, the Co-operators in the Society seceded and some of them were amongst the members of the Pioneers' Cooperative Society." Thompson, *Weavers of Dreams*, 23.
53. Stedman Jones, *Languages of Class*, 124.
54. Carpenter, "Proceedings," 60–61.
55. Stedman Jones, *Languages of Class*, 127.
56. Harrison, *Quest*, 200.
57. Thompson, *Weavers of Dreams*, 19. Stedman Jones refers to Lovett as an "ex-Owenite." Stedman Jones, *Languages of Class*, 126.
58. Harrison, *Quest*, 215.
59. Stedman Jones, *Languages of Class*, 130.
60. Thompson, *Weavers of Dreams*, 21.
61. Cole, *A Century of Co-operation*, 57.
62. Indeed, in the wake of the second failure of the People's Charter in Parliament in 1848, membership in the Rochdale cooperative surged from 140 to 600 in just two years. Fairbairn, "The Meaning of Rochdale," 10.
63. Stedman Jones, *Languages of Class*, ch 3.
64. The Chartists were somewhat more universal, as they included male

servants whom the Levellers would have excluded. But the Chartists, like the Levellers, were accused of threatening private property, a charge which they, like the Levellers, denied. Ibid., 91. Of course, both excluded women.
65. Fairbairn, "The Meaning of Rochdale," 17, 22.
66. I have not been able to find an affirmative decision to abandon the idea of community, so it is not possible to determine when or how it occurred. It may have merely faded away.
67. Thompson, *Practical Directions,* i. Some of the text in this passage is in quotes, but we do not know if Thompson is referencing a particular political economist, political economists in general, or simply setting the text apart.
68. Fairbairn, "The Meaning of Rochdale," 11.
69. Holyoake, *Self-Help by the People,* 108–11.
70. Fairbairn, "The Meaning of Rochdale," 13.
71. Ibid., 11. It has been suggested that this expansion marks the invention of what we now call the chain store. Birchall, *The International Co-operative Movement,* 9.
72. Fairbairn, "The Meaning of Rochdale," 11–12.
73. Birchall claims the CWS "virtually invented modern retail distribution." Birchall, *The International Co-operative Movement,* 10.
74. Fairbairn, "The Meaning of Rochdale," 13.
75. Beatrice Potter Webb and Sidney Webb, *The Consumers' Co-operative Movement* (London and New York: Longman's, Green, 1921), 182–87. Another point in the debate was whether or not consumer cooperatives should serve nonmembers. The concern was that if they did, then the members would benefit at the expense of the nonmembers, which was precisely the kind of exploitive relationship they wanted to get away from. Lambert, *Studies,* 66.
76. Webb and Webb, *Consumers' Co-operative Movement,* 185–86.
77. Paul H. Casselman, *The Cooperative Movement and Some of Its Problems* (New York: Philosophical Library, 1952), 10–11.
78. James Peter Warbasse, *Cooperative Democracy,* 4th ed. (New York and London,: Harper and Brothers, 1942), 137.
79. Ibid., ch. X. Warbasse does not reference Marx, but he must have been aware that he was advocating for the same ends through different means.
80. Fairbairn, "The Meaning of Rochdale," 13–14.
81. ICA, "Introduction to ICA," International Co-operative Alliance, http://www.ica.coop/ica/index.html.
82. "Statistical Information on the Co-operative Movement," International Co-operative Alliance, http://www.ica.coop/coop/statistics.html.
83. Deller et al., "Economic Impact of Cooperatives."
84. NCBA, "About Cooperatives," National Cooperative Business Association, http://www.ncba.org/abcoop.cfm. Estimating the number of

Americans who are members of cooperatives is difficult for two reasons: First, because many memberships are really household memberships that cover several persons. Also, many people may be members of more than one cooperative—for example, a credit union as well as a retail co-op. We do know approximately how member total memberships there are, and based on the fact that there are eighty million memberships in credit unions, because people are less likely to belong to multiple credit unions, the estimate of 120 million is probably fairly accurate, and even conservative.

85. ICA, "Statistical Information." See the caveat above regarding counting the number of members. In some countries, such as England, where most people belong to a national association or federation of cooperatives rather than individual enterprises, it is much easier to get an accurate (or more-accurate) count of memberships.
86. Secretary-General, "Cooperatives in social development" (New York: United Nations General Assembly, 2009).
87. ICA, "What Is a Co-operative?" International Co-operative Alliance, http://ica.coop/en/whats-co-op/co-operative-facts-figures.
88. Birchall identifies six basic forms: Consumer, credit, agriculture, worker, housing, and health. But credit cooperatives (also known as credit unions) and housing and health cooperatives can all be understood as varieties of consumer cooperatives, having to do with banking, housing, and health care provision respectively. Deller, et al., identify a fourth form, purchasing cooperatives, in which otherwise independent businesses form a cooperative for the purpose of purchasing supplies. Deller et al., "Economic Impact of Cooperatives," 10. This includes some fairly large companies, such as Ace Hardware, True Value Hardware, and Best Western Hotels. However, this form is not included among any of the ICA's categories and, because it is the most distant from both the Rochdale model and Thompson's theory, I have excluded it from my discussion here.
89. Financial cooperatives, including credit unions (with more than eighty million members) are in fact the largest in terms of both number of members and assets in the United States, although because they rarely publicize themselves as cooperatives, they are not so visible as cooperatives when compared to, for example, a local retail cooperative that puts "co-op" or "cooperative" in its name, as do most of the grocery stores found in the Cooperative Grocer Network's directory (http://www.cooperativegrocer.coop/coops).
90. With annual revenue of more than $7 billion in 2006, Land o' Lakes is the largest agricultural cooperative in the United States and thirty-eighth largest overall in the world Hassan Kashef, "International Co-operative Alliance Global 300 list" (Geneva: International Co-operative Alliance, 2008).

91. Other forms of worker ownership exist, such as Employee Stock Ownership Plans (ESOPs), but worker cooperatives are distinct in their commitment to egalitarian principles and the subordination of capital to labor.
92. Although worker cooperatives tend to be small, there is one significant exception: Mondragón, a conglomeration of some 256 companies, of which half are cooperatives. Due to rapid expansion over the past 20 years, the portion of worker-members fell to only about a third of its workforce of 85,000 (Mondragón, "Frequently Asked Questions: Corporation," Mondragón Cooperative Corporation, http://www.mondragon-corporation.com/language/en-US/ENG/Frequently-asked-questions/Corporation.aspx), although, partly in response to an international outcry of concern that the flagship of the workers cooperative movement was failing to live up to its principles, by the end of 2010 this had been increased to 85 percent. "Annual Report," (Mondragón, Spain: Mondragón Corporacion Cooperativa, 2011), 10. This is not the place for any extended discussion of Mondragón's history or their adherence to cooperative principles, but there is a fairly extensive literature on the subject. See, e.g., Saioa Arando et al., "Assessing Mondragon: Stability and Managed Change in the Face of Globalization," in *Employee Ownership and Shared Capitalism: New Directions in Research,* ed. Edward J. Carberry (Champaign, IL: Labor and Employment Relations Association, 2011); George Cheney, *Values at Work: Employee Participation Meets Market Pressure at Mondragón,* updated ed. (Ithaca: Cornell University Press, 1999); Sandra Harding, "The Decline of the Mondragón Cooperatives," *Australian Journal of Social Issues* 33, no. 1 (1998). Mondragón has engaged in what appears to be genuine self-criticism on some of the challenges it faces. Mondragón, "Mondragón Corporacion Cooperativa: The History of an Experience" (Mondragón, Spain: Mondragón Corporacion Cooperativa, 2006).
93. These were drafted by a small international committee chaired by Ian MacPherson, supported by a Consultative Committee that included forty-eight participants from twenty-nine countries on almost every continent (except Australia), and released along with a Background Paper that discusses the process by which the Principles were adopted and provides historical context and an in-depth explanation of their content. Ian MacPherson, *Co-operative Principles for the 21st Century,* Studies and Reports (Geneva: International Co-operative Alliance, 1995).
94. The complete Statement of the Cooperative Identity is reproduced in Appendix 2.
95. MacPherson, *Co-operative Principles,* 5.
96. Ibid., 6–7.
97. Zeuli et al., take it as a matter of fact that "[n]ot all cooperatives adopt all of the ICA principles. The basic three 'defining principles'

(user-ownership, user-control, and proportional distribution of benefits) are more commonly accepted as the only principles necessary to guide cooperatives. Many cooperative leaders and scholars believe that the additional principles should serve only as recommendations. They may not be appropriate... for all co-ops in all environments." Kimberly A. Zeuli, Robert Cropp, and Marvin A. Schaars, *Cooperatives: Principles and practices in the 21st century* 4th ed. (Madison: University of Wisconsin Center on Cooperatives, 1980), 45.
98. W. P. Watkins, *Co-operative Principles: Today and Tomorrow* (Manchester: Holyoake Books, 1986), 4.
99. Fairbairn, "The Meaning of Rochdale," 24.
100. This is perhaps best exemplified by the fact that it was not until 2009 that the ICA elected a woman as president. There have, however, been some notable cases of women holding leadership positions. For example, Emmy Freundlich, an Austrian who was a member of the ICA executive and a socialist member of Parliament, was imprisoned by fascists during World War II. Birchall, *The International Co-operative Movement*, 50.
101. The £1 fee to join The Co-operative Group in the UK, which at one time represented about two weeks' wages for the average working-class household, now is virtually meaningless.
102. Birchall, *The International Co-operative Movement*, 222–34.
103. See, e.g., Rita Rhodes, "The Internationalism of the Co-operative Movement," in *Towards the Co-operative Commonwealth: Essays in the History of Co-operation,* ed. Bill Lancaster and Paddy Maguire (Loughborough, Leicestershire: The Co-operative College, 1996). This has not kept the ICA from taking strong, principled stands on issues that are of international importance—for example, against fascism in the 1930s or, more recently, against the Israeli bombardment and invasion of the Gaza Strip in 2009. Ivano Barberini and Iain Macdonald, "Statement on the Israeli-Palestine Conflict" (2009), http://www.ica.coop/publications/pressreleases/2009-palestine.pdf. This stand was taken at the urging of "co-operators from Israel, Palestine and Iran... calling on the international co-operative movement to demand an immediate end to the violence in their region." Ibid.
104. Fairbairn, "The Meaning of Rochdale," 29.
105. For example, REI, on its Web page promoting membership (http://www.rei.com/help/membership_join.html? mem_ind_REI_sidebar), features "the dividend" prominently as the reason people should join. Only after a list of several items having to do with special discounts members receive are "voting privileges" for the board of directors mentioned. The Cooperative Principles are nowhere to be found on their Web site.
106. Lambert, *Studies*, 75.
107. Ibid., 74.
108. Gurney, "Labor's Great Arch," 138–39.
109. Lambert, *Studies*, 79.

110. Ibid.
111. The committee that developed the set of principles adopted in 1994 specifically cites Watkins's work as one of two primary sources that set "the theoretical context" for the revision. MacPherson, *Co-operative Principles*, 13.
112. Watkins, *Co-operative Principles*, 5–13.
113. The set of principles adopted by the ICA in 1994 does not include one called "Association," but as will be evident from the discussion below, the principle is embodied in the first and sixth ICA Principles of Voluntary and Open Membership and Cooperation among Cooperatives.
114. Watkins, *Co-operative Principles*, 18.
115. This is the direction taken in the British system through the establishment and development of the Cooperative Wholesale Society, which ultimately opened up its own bank, production facilities, and farmland.
116. Watkins, *Co-operative Principles*, ch 2.
117. Ibid., 32.
118. Ibid., 58.
119. This problem is often referred to as "managerialism," and there exists a fairly extensive literature, specifically with respect to public management. An excellent treatment of the problem of managerialism in cooperatives may be found in Peter Davis, *Managing the Cooperative Difference: A Survey of the Application of Modern Management Practices in the Cooperative Context* (Geneva: International Labour Office, 1999).
120. Watkins, *Co-operative Principles*, 109–11.
121. Ibid., 54.
122. Lambert, *Studies*, 67.
123. Ibid.
124. Some consumer cooperatives, for example the Black Star Brewery in Austin, Texas (www.blackstar.coop), include employees on their board of directors.
125. Lambert, *Studies*, 66.
126. Watkins, *Co-operative Principles*, 68.
127. Lambert, *Studies*, 66. In light of Lambert's claim, Hoyt's report that nonmembers often account for more than fifty percent of sales in retail food cooperatives is cause for concern. Ann Hoyt, "Consumer Ownership in Capitalist Economies: Applications of Theory to Consumer Cooperation" in *Cooperatives and Local Development: Theory and Applications for the 21st Century*, ed. Christopher D. Merrett and Norman Walzer (Armonk, NY: M.E. Sharpe, 2004), 274.
128. Lambert is clearly referring to an assembly of members. Large-scale cooperatives may conduct elections by mail, but response rates may still be relatively low. For example, only a little more than 1 percent of REI's 4.7 million members participated in a recent election for members of the board of directors. Catherine Walker, "Annual Membership Meeting" (Seattle: Recreational Equipment, Inc. [REI], 2011).

129. Lambert, *Studies,* 73. There is more that might be said about this from the perspective of democratic theory—indeed, a whole chapter could be dedicated to the question of translating democratic theory into practice specifically in the context of cooperatives. However, there is no space for that discussion here.
130. It is certainly no coincidence that, from their beginnings, women have always had equal rights in cooperative governance, even when they were denied the suffrage in state institutions—although their ability to participate fully has not been effectively realized in practice. See note 139, below.
131. Thompson, *Inquiry,* ch 4.
132. MacPherson, *Co-operative Principles,* 6.
133. For an especially passionate argument, see Tim Huet's *Cooperative Manifesto.* Tim Huet, "A Cooperative Manifesto," *Grassroots Economic Organizing,* no. 61 (2004).
134. Birchall, *The International Co-operative Movement,* ch 4–6.
135. MacPherson, *Co-operative Principles,* 12.
136. Pateman, *Participation,* 105.
137. Sidney Verba, Kay Lehman Schlozman, and Henry E. Brady, *Voice and Equality: Civic Voluntarism in American Politics* (Cambridge: Harvard University Press, 1995).
138. MacPherson, *Co-operative Principles,* 13–14.
139. C. J. Kroeker, "Individual, Organizational, and Societal Empowerment: A Study of the Processes in a Nicaraguan Agricultural Cooperative," *American Journal of Community Psychology* 23, no. 5 (1995); Corinne L. Shefner-Rogers et al., "The Empowerment of Women Dairy Farmers in India," *Journal of Applied Communication Research* 26, no. 3 (1998); Linda Mayoux, "Alternative Vision or Utopian Fantasy?: Cooperation, Empowerment, and Women's Cooperative Development in India," *Journal of International Development* 7, no. 2 (1995). Surely, if it were the case that women had equal status within the cooperative movement, MacPherson would not consider it necessary to remind his readers that cooperatives must "ensure that doors are open to women as members, elected leaders, staff and managers," both as a matter of social justice and "in keeping with the basic commitments obvious in co-operative circles from their beginnings." MacPherson, *Co-operative Principles,* 67–68. More broadly, this points to the difficulty of establishing institutional structures based on equality in a society in which social relationships are often hierarchical.
140. Some of these tensions, between the benefits and dangers of consolidation, are on full display in Gonzales's study of Italian social cooperatives. Vanna Gonzales, "Italian Social Cooperatives and the Development of Civic Capacity: A Case of Cooperative Renewal?" *Affinities: A Journal of Radical Theory, Culture, and Action* 4, no. 1 (2010): 230.

141. To my knowledge, no empirical research exists that confirms this, so at this point this is an assertion, not an observation.
142. But this may be changing. In 2011 The Co-operative Group came out with an advertising campaign in the UK that makes strong references to principles and presents itself as a model for progressive social change. It is significant, on political terms, that this is part of an aggressive campaign to double its membership to twenty million by 2020—fully one-third of the national population.
143. Mark Kaswan, "U.S. Cooperatives as a Social Movement" (paper presented at Reclaiming the Economy: the Role of Cooperative Enterprise, Ownership and Control; An International Conference on Cooperative Forms of Organization, Cardiff, Wales, September 6–8, 2006). As Curl notes, however, from the early nineteenth to the early twentieth century it played a very important role as a movement for social change. John Curl, "The Cooperative Movement in Century 21," *Affinities: A Journal of Radical Theory, Culture, and Action* 4, no. 1 (2010).
144. Huet, "A Cooperative Manifesto." In fact, it was with a great sense of irony that I regarded the 2009 debate over the establishment of large-scale health care cooperatives in the United States, especially since the supporters of the plan were conservatives who railed against the move to "socialism" that would occur if a government-controlled single-payer system were implemented. Little did they know that their cooperatives were every bit as "socialistic"—perhaps even more so—as what they were decrying.
145. MacPherson, *Co-operative Principles,* 58–69.
146. It is worth noting that cooperatives are prominently featured in a number of works that consider what a postsocialist, postcapitalist society might look like. Alperovitz, *America Beyond Capitalism*; Hahnel, *Economic Justice and Democracy*; Schweickart, *After Capitalism*; Alperovitz, *What Then Must We Do*; Wright, *Envisioning*.
147. Thompson, *Inquiry,* 579.

Conclusion

1. W. B. Gallie, "Essentially Contested Concepts," *Proceedings of the Aristotelian Society* 56, New Series (1955–56).
2. Ibid., 184.
3. Bentham, *A Fragment on Government,* 28.
4. Bruni and Porta, "Introduction," 20.
5. Thompson, "Labor Rewarded," 65.
6. Although these sorts of communities do exist: The Federation of Intentional Communities lists some 1,602 communities in the United States alone, although many of these are "forming," and many have a

religious basis that would have troubled Thompson. Also, most if not all are much smaller than his target size of five hundred to two thousand persons. FIC, "Intentional Communities: Geographic Community List," Federation of Intentional Community, http://directory.ic.org/iclist/geo.php. Still, some come quite close to his ideas, especially the members of the Federation of Egalitarian Communities, which range from a community of three to one with more than one hundred (including children) (www.thefec.org).
7. Security seems to have dropped out as a concern, or at least it is not expressed directly. This may, in effect, be a concession to the liberal regimes in which they operate, considering the fact that the original idea of the cooperative community has been replaced by the enterprise model and the fact that the consumer cooperative model, where securing the full produce of labor to the laborer is not recognized as a value, is the most common type.
8. Stiglitz, Sen, and Fitoussi, "Economic Performance and Social Progress."
9. For example, the six million member Co-operative Group in the UK (the descendant of the Rochdale Society and the CWS) is organized into seven regions, each of which has a number of subregions, giving it forty-eight Area Committees, each with an elected board that participates in the governance of the cooperative. Cooperative Group, "Area Committees," The Cooperative Group, http://www.co-operative.coop/membership/have-your-say/our-committees/area-committees/.
10. That said, in the United States at least, the level of inequality of wealth between the vast majority and those at the top now rivals that of early nineteenth-century Britain. Domhoff, "Power in America."
11. See, for example, Smith's comment that "the accommodation of an European prince does not always so much exceed that of an industrious and frugal peasant, as the accommodation of the latter exceeds that of many an African king, the absolute master of the lives and liberties of ten thousand naked savages." Smith, *Wealth of Nations,* vol. 1, 16.
12. Regina Gagnier, *The Insatiability of Human Wants: Economics and Aesthetics in Market Society* (Chicago: University of Chicago Press, 2000).

Appendices

1. Lambert, *Studies,* 292 ff.
2. ICA, "Statement on the Co-operative Identity," International Co-operative Alliance, http://www.ica.coop/coop/principles.html.

Bibliography

A Member. "An Address Delivered at the Opening of the Birmingham Co-operative Society." Birmingham: W. Plastans, 1828.
Alkire, Sabina. "Dimensions of Human Development." *World Development* 30, no. 2 (2002): 181–205.
———. *Valuing Freedoms: Sen's Capability Approach and Poverty Reduction.* Oxford: Oxford University Press, 2002.
Alperovitz, Gar. *America Beyond Capitalism: Reclaiming Our Wealth, Our Liberty, and Our Democracy.* 2nd ed. Takoma Park, MD, and Boston: Democracy Collaborative Press and Dollars and Sense, 2011.
———. *What Then Must We Do?: Straight Talk About the Next American Revolution.* White River Junction, VT: Chelsea Green Publishing, 2013.
Annas, Julia. *The Morality of Happiness.* New York: Oxford University Press, 1993.
Anon. "Lecture on Cooperation." *Manchester Times & Gazette*, 4 June 1831, 600.
Aquinas, Thomas. "The *Summa Theologica* of St. Thomas Aquinas." http://www.newadvent.org/summa/. Accessed March 19, 2012.
Arando, Saioa, Fred Freundlich, Mónica Gago, Derek C. Jones, and Takao Kato. "Assessing Mondragon: Stability and Managed Change in the Face of Globalization." In *Employee Ownership and Shared Capitalism: New Directions in Research*, edited by Edward J. Carberry, 241–72. Champaign, IL: Labor and Employment Relations Association, 2011.
Aristotle. *Nichomachean Ethics.* Translated by Roger Crisp. Edited by Roger Crisp. Cambridge: Cambridge University Press, 2000.
———. *Politics.* Translated by Sir Ernest Barker. Oxford: Oxford University Press, 1995.

Astell, Mary. *Political Writings*. Edited by Patricia Springborg. Cambridge: Cambridge University Press, 1996.
Ball, Terence. "The Formation of Character: Mill's 'Ethology' Reconsidered." *Polity* 33, no. 1 (Autumn 2000): 25–48.
———. *Reappraising Political Theory: Revisionist Studies in the History of Political Thought*. Oxford: Clarendon Press, 1995.
Barberini, Ivano, and Iain Macdonald. "Statement on the Israeli-Palestine Conflict." 2009. http://www.ica.coop/publications/pressreleases/2009-palestine.pdf. Accessed Dec. 13, 2009.
Barkan, Steven E. "Strategic, Tactical, and Organizational Dilemmas of the Protest Movement against Nuclear Power." *Social Problems* 27, no. 1 (1979): 19–37.
Baujard, Antoinette. "Collective Interest Versus Individual Interest in Bentham's Felicific Calculus. Questioning Welfarism and Fairness." *European Journal of the History of Economic Thought* 17, no. 4 (2010): 607–34.
Beccaria, Cesare. *On Crimes and Punishments and Other Writings*. Translated by Aaron Thomas and Jeremy Parzen. Edited by Aaron Thomas. Toronto: University of Toronto Press, 2008 [1766].
Beer, Max. *A History of British Socialism*. One Volume ed. New York: The Humanities Press, 1940.
Bentham, Jeremy. *Chrestomathia*. Edited by M. J. Smith and W. H. Burston. *The Collected Works of Jeremy Bentham*, edited by J. H. Burns (1961–79), J. R. Dinwiddy (1977–83), F. Rosen (1983–94), F. Rosen and P. Schofield (1995–2003), P. Schofield (2003-). Oxford: Clarendon Press, 1983.
———. *A Comment on the Commentaries and a Fragment on Government*. Edited by J. H. Burns and H. L. A. Hart. *The Collected Works of Jeremy Bentham*, edited by J. H. Burns (1961–79), J. R. Dinwiddy (1977–83), F. Rosen (1983–94), F. Rosen and P. Schofield (1995–2003), P. Schofield (2003-). Oxford: Clarendon Press, 2008.
———. *Constitutional Code, Vol. 1*. Edited by F. Rosen and J. H. Burns. *The Collected Works of Jeremy Bentham,* edited by J. H. Burns (1961–79), J. R. Dinwiddy (1977–83), F. Rosen (1983–94), F. Rosen and P. Schofield (1995–2003), P. Schofield (2003-). Oxford: Clarendon Press, 1983.
———. *The Correspondence of Jeremy Bentham: January 1817 to June 1820*. Edited by Stephen Conway. *The Collected Works of Jeremy Bentham*, edited by J. H. Burns (1961–79), J. R. Dinwiddy (1977–83), F. Rosen (1983–94), F. Rosen and P. Schofield (1995–2003), P. Schofield (2003-). Oxford: Clarendon Press, 1989.
———. *The Correspondence of Jeremy Bentham: July 1824 to June 1828*. Edited by Luke O'Sullivan and Catherine Fuller. Vol. 12. *The Collected Works of Jeremy Bentham*, edited by J. H. Burns (1961–79), J. R.

Dinwiddy (1977–83), F. Rosen (1983–94), F. Rosen and P. Schofield (1995–2003), P. Schofield (2003-). Oxford: Clarendon Press, 2006.

———. *Deontology; Together with a Table of the Springs of Action; and the Article on Utilitarianism.* Edited by Amnon Goldworth. *The Collected Works of Jeremy Bentham*, edited by J. H. Burns (1961–79), J. R. Dinwiddy (1977–83), F. Rosen (1983–94), F. Rosen and P. Schofield (1995–2003), P. Schofield (2003-). Oxford: Clarendon Press, 1983.

———. *First Principles Preparatory to Constitutional Code.* Edited by Philip Schofield. *The Collected Works of Jeremy Bentham*, edited by J. H. Burns (1961–79), J. R. Dinwiddy (1977–83), F. Rosen (1983–94), F. Rosen and P. Schofield (1995–2003), P. Schofield (2003-). Oxford: Clarendon Press, 1989.

———. *A Fragment on Government.* Edited by J. H. Burns and H. L. A. Hart. New authoritative ed. Cambridge and New York: Cambridge University Press, 1988 [1776].

———. *An Introduction to the Principles of Morals and Legislation.* Edited by J. H. Burns and H. L. A. Hart, with an introduction by F. Rosen. *The Collected Works of Jeremy Bentham*, edited by J. H. Burns (1961–79), J. R. Dinwiddy (1977–83), F. Rosen (1983–94), F. Rosen and P. Schofield (1995–2003), P. Schofield (2003-). Oxford: Clarendon Press, 1996.

———. *Jeremy Bentham's Economic Writings: Critical Edition based on his printed works and unpublished manuscripts.* Edited and with an introduction by W. Stark. 3 vols. New York: Burt Franklin and London: Allen and Unwin, 1952–54.

———. *Official Aptitude Maximized; Expense Minimized.* Edited by Philip Schofield. *The Collected Works of Jeremy Bentham*, edited by J. H. Burns (1961–79), J. R. Dinwiddy (1977–83), F. Rosen (1983–94), F. Rosen and P. Schofield (1995–2003), P. Schofield (2003-). Oxford: Clarendon Press, 1993.

———. "Pannomial Fragments." In *Selected Writings/Jeremy Bentham,* edited by Stephen G. Engelmann, 240–80. New Haven: Yale University Press, 2011.

———. *Rights, Representation, and Reform: Nonsense Upon Stilts and Other Writings on the French Revolution,* edited by Philip Schofield, Catherine Pease-Watkin, and Cyprian Blamires, 317–401. *The Collected Works of Jeremy Bentham*, edited by J. H. Burns (1961–79), J. R. Dinwiddy (1977–83), F. Rosen (1983–94), F. Rosen and P. Schofield (1995–2003), P. Schofield (2003-). Oxford and New York: Clarendon Press, 2002.

———. *Securities against Misrule and Other Constitutional Writings for Tripoli and Greece.* Edited by Philip Schofield. *The Collected Works of Jeremy Bentham*, edited by J. H. Burns (1961–79), J. R. Dinwiddy

(1977–83), F. Rosen (1983–94), F. Rosen and P. Schofield (1995–2003), P. Schofield (2003-). Oxford: Clarendon Press, 1990.

———. *The Theory of Legislation*. Translated (into French) and edited by Etienne Dumont. Translated (into English) by R. Hildreth. London: Routledge and Kegan Paul, 1931.

———. *The Works of Jeremy Bentham, published under the superintendence of his executor, John Bowring*. 11 vols. Edinburgh: William Tait, 1838–43.

Bernard, Paul R. "Irreconcilable Opinions: The Social and Educational Theories of Robert Owen and William Maclure." *Journal of the Early Republic* 8, no. 1 (Spring 1988): 21–44.

Birchall, Johnston. *The International Co-operative Movement*. New York: St. Martin's Press, 1997.

Bonner, John. *Economic Efficiency and Social Justice: Development of Utilitarian Ideas in Economics from Bentham to Edgeworth*. London: Edward Elgar, 1995.

Boralevi, Lea Campos. *Bentham and the Oppressed*. Berlin and New York: Walter de Gruyter, 1984.

Brogan, A. P. "John Locke and Utilitarianism." *Ethics* 69, no. 2 (1959): 79–93.

Brown, Wendy. "At the Edge." *Political Theory* 30, no. 4 (Aug. 2002): 556–76.

Bruni, Luigino, and Pier Luigi Porta. "Introduction." In *Economics and Happiness*, edited by Luigino Bruni and Pier Luigi Porta, 1–28. Oxford and New York: Oxford University Press, 2005.

Buber, Martin. "Comments on the Idea of Community." In *Martin Buber: On Intersubjectivity and Cultural Creativity*, edited by S. N. Eisenstadt. Chicago: University of Chicago Press, 1992.

Burns, J. H. "Bentham and the French Revolution." *Transactions of the Royal Historical Society* 16, Fifth Series (1966): 95–114.

———. "Happiness and Utility: Jeremy Bentham's Equation." *Utilitas* 17, no. 1 (March 2005): 46–61.

Caillé, Alain, Christian Lazzeri, and Michel Senellart. *Histoire Raisonnée de la Philosophie Morale et Politique: Le Bonheur et L'utile*. Paris: La Découverte, 2001.

Carpenter, William. "Proceedings of the Third Cooperative Congress." In *Owenism and the Working Class: Six Pamphlets and Four Broadsides, 1821–1834. British Labour Struggles: Contemporary Pamphlets 1727–1850*. New York: Arno Press, 1832.

Casselman, Paul H. *The Cooperative Movement and Some of Its Problems*. New York: Philosophical Library, 1952.

Cheney, George. *Values at Work: Employee Participation Meets Market Pressure at Mondragón*. Updated ed. Ithaca: Cornell University Press, 1999.

Cicero. *De Finibus Bonorum Et Malorum*. Translated by H. Rackham. 2nd ed. Cambridge: Harvard University Press, 1931 [45 BCE].
———. *On Duties*. Edited by M. T. Griffin and E. M. Atkins. Cambridge: Cambridge University Press, 1991.
Claeys, Gregory. *Citizens and Saints: Politics and Anti-Politics in Early British Socialism*. Cambridge: Cambridge University Press, 1989.
———. "'Individualism,' 'Socialism,' and 'Social Science': Further Notes on a Process of Conceptual Formation, 1800–1850." *Journal of the History of Ideas* 47, no. 1 (Jan.-Mar. 1986).
———. "Introduction." In *Robert Owen: A New View of Society and Other Writings*, edited by Gregory Claeys. London: Penguin Classics, 1991.
———. *Machinery, Money, and the Millennium: From Moral Economy to Socialism, 1815–60*. Cambridge: Polity Press, 1987.
Cole, G. D. H. *A Century of Co-operation*. London: George Allen and Unwin, 1944.
———. *A History of Socialist Thought: The Forerunners 1789–1850*. 2 vols. Vol. 1, London: Macmillan, 1953.
———. "Introduction." In *Robert Owen: A New View of Society and Other Writings*, edited by G. D. H. Cole. London and New York: Everyman's Library, 1927.
Collard, David. "Research on Well-Being: Some Advice from Jeremy Bentham." *Philosophy of the Social Sciences* 36, no. 3 (September 2006): 330–54.
Collins, Peter. "Thompson, William." In *The Oxford Companion to Irish History*, edited by S. J. Connolly. Oxford: Oxford University Press, 2002.
Commons, John. *Institutional Economics: Its Place in Political Economy*. 2 vols. Madison: University of Wisconsin Press, 1934.
Cooperative Group. "Area Committees." The Cooperative Group, http://www.co-operative.coop/membership/have-your-say/our-committees/area-committees/. Accessed March 14, 2010.
Curl, John. "The Cooperative Movement in Century 21." *Affinities: A Journal of Radical Theory, Culture, and Action* 4, no. 1 (Summer 2010): 12–29.
Dahl, Robert. *Democracy and Its Critics*. New Haven: Yale University Press, 1989.
———. *On Democracy*. New Haven: Yale University Press, 1998.
———. *A Preface to Economic Democracy*. Berkeley: University of California Press, 1985.
Davis, Peter. *Managing the Cooperative Difference: A Survey of the Application of Modern Management Practices in the Cooperative Context*. Geneva: International Labour Office, 1999.
Deller, Steven, Ann Hoyt, Brent Hueth, and Reka Sundaram-Stukel.

"Research on the Economic Impact of Cooperatives." Madison: University of Wisconsin Center for Cooperatives, 2009.

Dinwiddy, J. R. *Bentham*. Oxford and New York: Oxford University Press, 1989.

———. "Bentham's Transition to Political Radicalism, 1809–10." *Journal of the History of Ideas* 36, no. 4 (1975): 683–700.

Domhoff, G. William. "Power in America: Wealth, Income, and Power." http://sociology.ucsc.edu/whorulesamerica/power/wealth.html. Accessed March 13, 2010.

Dooley, Dolores. *Equality in Community: Sexual Equality in the Writings of William Thompson and Anna Doyle Wheeler*. Cork, Ireland: Cork University Press, 1996.

———. "Introduction." In *William Thompson: Appeal,* edited by Dolores Dooley. Cork, Ireland: Cork University Press, 1997.

Doyal, Len. "Comment: Thinking About Human Need." *New Left Review*, no. 201 (July/Aug. 1993): 113–28.

———. "Review of On Human Needs by Kate Soper and the Problem of Human Needs and the Critique of Civilization by Patricia Springborg." *Critical Social Policy* 3 (1983): 138–40.

———, and Ian Gough. *A Theory of Human Need*. New York: The Guilford Press, 1991.

Drakopoulos, Stravos, and Anastasios Karayiannis. "Human Needs Hierarchy and Happiness: Evidence from the Late Pre-Classical and Classical Economics." In *Handbook on the Economics of Happiness*, edited by Luigino Bruni and Pier Luigi Porta. Cheltenham, UK, and Northampton, MA: Edward Elgar, 2007.

Duncan, Grant. "After Happiness." *Journal of Political Ideologies* 12, no. 1 (February 2007): 85–108.

Easterlin, Richard. "Does Economic Growth Improve Human Lot? Some Empirical Evidence." In *Nation and Households in Economic Growth: Essays in Honor of Moses Abromowitz,* edited by P. A. Davis and M. W. Reder. New York and London: Academic Press, 1974.

Ellerman, David. "Property and Contract in Economics: The Case for Economic Democracy." Cambridge, MA: Basil Blackwell, 1992 (edition cited is available from http://www.ellerman.org/Davids-Stuff/Books/p&c.htm).

Ellis, Peter Berresford. *A History of the Irish Working Class*. London: Pluto Press, 1985.

Engelmann, Stephen G. *Imagining Interest in Political Thought: Origins of Economic Rationality.* Durham: Duke University Press, 2003.

———. "'Indirect Legislation': Bentham's Liberal Government." *Polity* XXXV, no. 3 (April 2003): 369–88.

Engels, Frederick. *Anti-Dühring*. London: Electric Book Company, 1878.

———. *Socialism, Utopian and Scientific*. Translated by Edward Aveling. Chicago: Charles H. Kerr, 1910.

Epicurus. "Letter to Menoeceus." Epicurus.info, http://www.epicurus.info/etexts/Lives.html#I40. Accessed April 26, 2012.
———. "Principal Doctrines." Epicurus.info, http://www.epicurus.info/etexts/PD.html. Accessed March 5, 2010.
———. "Vatican Sayings." Epicurus.info, http://www.epicurus.info/etexts/VS.html. Accessed April 26, 2012.
Euben, J. Peter. "Taking It to the Streets: Radical Democracy and Radicalizing Theory." In *Radical Democracy: Identity, Citizenship, and the State*, edited by David Trend, 62–78. New York and London: Routledge, 1996.
Everett, Charles W. *The Education of Jeremy Bentham*. New York: Columbia University Press, 1931.
Fairbairn, Brett. "The Meaning of Rochdale: The Rochdale Pioneers and the Co-operative Principles." In, *University of Saskatchewan Centre for the Study of Cooperatives Occasional Paper Series* (1994). http://www.usaskstudies.coop/pdf-files/Rochdale.pdf. Accessed Nov. 1, 2009.
———. "Social Movements and Co-operatives: Implications for History and Development." *Review of International Co-operation* 94, no. 1 (2001): 24–34.
Ferguson, Susan. "The Radical Ideas of Mary Wollstonecraft." *Canadian Journal of Political Science / Revue canadienne de science politique* 32, no. 3 (Sept. 1999): 427–50.
FIC. "Intentional Communities: Geographic Community List." Federation of Intentional Community, http://directory.ic.org/iclist/geo.php. Accessed Jan. 5, 2010.
First Armagh Co-operative Society. "The Laws of the First Armagh Co-operative Society." In *Owenism and the Working Class: Six Pamphlets and Four Broadsides. British Labour Struggles: Contemporary Pamplets 1727–1850.* New York: Arno Press, 1972.
First London Co-operative Society. "The First London Co-operative Association: Objects and Laws." In *Owenism and the Working Class: Six Pamphlets and Four Broadsides, 1821–1834.* New York: Arno Press, 1972.
First Salford Co-operative Society. "Principles, Object and Laws, of the First Salford Co-operative Society." Manchester, 1831.
Foucault, Michel. *The History of Sexuality: An Introduction*. Translated by Robert Hurley. 3 vols. New York: Vintage Books, 1978.
Fowler, James H., and Nicholas A. Christakis. "Dynamic Spread of Happiness in a Large Social Network: Longitudinal Analysis over 20 Years in the Framingham Heart Study." *BMJ* 2008; 337: a2338 (2008).
Foxwell, H. S. "Introduction." In *Anton Menger: The Right to the Whole Produce of Labour,* edited by H. S. Foxwell. New York: Augustus M. Kelley, 1962.

Gagnier, Regina. *The Insatiability of Human Wants: Economics and Aesthetics in Market Society.* Chicago: University of Chicago Press, 2000.

Gallie, W. B. "Essentially Contested Concepts." *Proceedings of the Aristotelian Society* 56, no. New Series (1955–56): 167–98.

Gasper, Des. "Human Well-Being: Concepts and Conceptualizations." In *Human Well-Being: Concept and Measurement,* edited by Mark McGillivray, 23–64. New York: Plagrave Macmillan, 2007.

Gonzales, Vanna. "Italian Social Cooperatives and the Development of Civic Capacity: A Case of Cooperative Renewal?" *Affinities: A Journal of Radical Theory, Culture, and Action* 4, no. 1 (Summer 2010): 225–51.

Gordon, Pamela. *The Invention and Gendering of Epicurus.* Ann Arbor: University of Michigan Press, 2012.

Gray, John. *A Lecture on Human Happiness, Being the First of a Series of Lectures on That Subject in Which Will Be Comprehended a General Review of the Causes of the Existing Evils of Society.* New York: Augustus M. Kelley, 1971 [1826].

Gregg, Pauline. *A Social and Economic History of Britain: 1760–1980.* 8th ed. London: Harrap, 1982.

Gurney, Peter. "Labor's Great Arch: Cooperation and Cultural Revolution in Britain, 1795–1926." In *Consumers against Capitalism? Consumer Cooperation in Europe, North America, and Japan, 1840–1990,* edited by Ellen Furlough and Carl Strikwerda, 135–72. New York: Rowman and Littlefield, 1999.

Hahnel, Robin. *Economic Justice and Democracy: From Competition to Cooperation.* New York: Routledge, 2005.

Harcourt, Bernard E. *Illusion of Free Markets: Punishment and the Myth of Natural Order.* Cambridge: Harvard University Press, 2011.

Harding, Sandra. "The Decline of the Mondragón Cooperatives." *Australian Journal of Social Issues* 33, no. 1 (1998): 59–76.

Harrison, J. F. C. *Quest for the New Moral World: Robert Owen and the Owenities in Britain and America.* New York: Scribner, 1969.

Harrison, Ross. *Bentham.* London and Boston: Routledge and Kegan Paul, 1983.

Helliwell, John F., and Robert D. Putnam. "The Social Context of Well-Being." *Philosophical Transactions: Biological Sciences* 359, no. 1449 (Sept. 29, 2004): 1435–46.

Hobbes, Thomas. *Leviathan.* Edited by C. B. Macpherson. New York: Penguin Books, 1968.

Hodgskin, Thomas. "Labour Defended against the Claims of Capital; or, the Unproductiveness of Capital Proved with Reference to the Present Combinations Amongst Journeymen." In *Ricardian Socialism,* edited by David Reisman. London: Pickering and Chatto, 1996.

Holub, Renate. *Antonio Gramsci: Beyond Marxism and Postmodernism.*

Critics of the Twentieth Century, edited by Christopher Norris. London: Routledge, 1992.

Holyoake, G. J. *The History of Co-operation in England: Its Literature and Its Advocates.* New York: AMS Press, 1971 [1906].

———. *Self-Help by the People: The History of the Rochdale Pioneers.* 3rd/10th ed. London: Swan Sonnenschein, 1900.

Horkheimer, Max, and Theodor W. Adorno. *Dialectic of Enlightenment: Philosophical Fragments.* Translated by Edmund Jephcott. Stanford: Stanford University Press, 2002.

Hoyt, Ann. "Consumer Ownership in Capitalist Economies: Applications of Theory to Consumer Cooperation." In *Cooperatives and Local Development: Theory and Applications for the 21st Century,* edited by Christopher D. Merrett and Norman Walzer, 265–289. Armonk, NY: M. E. Sharpe, 2004.

Huet, Tim. "A Cooperative Manifesto." *Grassroots Economic Organizing,* no. 61 (2004).

Hume, David. *Enquiries Concerning Human Understanding and Concerning the Principles of Morals.* Edited by L. A. Selby-Bigge and P. H. Niddich. Oxford and New York: Oxford University Press, 1975.

Hunt, E. K. *History of Economic Thought: A Critical Perspective.* 2nd ed. Armonk, NY, and London: M. E. Sharpe, 2002.

———. "Utilitarianism and the Labor Theory of Value: A Critique of the Ideas of William Thompson." *History of Political Economy* 11, no. 4 (Winter 1979): 545–71.

ICA. "Introduction to ICA." International Co-operative Alliance, http://www.ica.coop/ica/index.html. Accessed Dec. 1, 2009.

———. "Statement on the Co-operative Identity." International Co-operative Alliance, http://ica.coop/en/what-co-op/co-operative-identity-values-principles. Accessed July 7, 2006.

———. "Statistical Information on the Co-operative Movement." International Co-operative Alliance, http://ica.coop/en/whats-co-op/co-operative-facts-figures. Accessed Dec. 1, 2009.

———. "What Is a Co-operative?" International Co-operative Alliance, http://www.ica.coop/coop/index.html. Accessed Feb. 10, 2006.

Jevons, H. Stanley. *Economic Equality in the Co-operative Commonwealth.* London: Methuen, 1933.

Jevons, W. Stanley. *The Theory of Political Economy.* Reprints of Economic Classics. Fifth ed. New York: Augustus M. Kelley, 1965.

Johnson, James, and Dana R. Villa. "Public Sphere, Postmodernism and Polemic." *The American Political Science Review* 88, no. 2 (1994): 427–33.

Jose, Jim. "Contesting Patrilineal Descent in Political Theory: James Mill and Nineteenth-Century Feminism." *Hypatia* 15, no. 1 (Winter 2000): 151–74.

Kahneman, Daniel. "Objective Happiness." In *Well-Being: The Foundations of Hedonic Psychology,* edited by Daniel Kahneman, Ed Diener, and Norbert Schwartz, 3–25. New York: Russell Sage Foundation, 1999.
Kashef, Hassan. "International Co-operative Alliance Global 300 List." Geneva: International Co-operative Alliance, 2008.
Kaswan, Mark. "U.S. Cooperatives as a Social Movement." Paper presented at Reclaiming the Economy: the Role of Cooperative Enterprise, Ownership and Control; An International Conference on Cooperative Forms of Organization. Cardiff, Wales, 6–8 September 2006.
Katznelson, Ira, Mark Kesselman, and Alan Draper. *The Politics of Power: A Critical Introduction to American Government.* 4th ed. Belmont, CA: Wadsworth/Thomson Learning, 2002.
Kaufman, Alexander, ed. *Capabilities and Equality: Basic Issues and Problems.* New York, London: Routledge, 2006.
Kelly, P. J. *Utilitarianism and Distributive Justice: Jeremy Bentham and the Civil Law.* Oxford and New York: Clarendon Press; Oxford University Press, 1990.
King, William. In *Dr. William King and* The Co-operator, *1828–1830,* edited by T. W. Mercer. Manchester: The Co-operative Union, 1922.
Kroeker, C. J. "Individual, Organizational, and Societal Empowerment: A Study of the Processes in a Nicaraguan Agricultural Cooperative." *American Journal of Community Psychology* 23, no. 5 (1995): 749–64.
Laclau, Ernesto, and Chantal Mouffe. *Hegemony and Socialist Strategy.* London: Verso, 1985.
Lambert, Paul. *Studies in the Social Philosophy of Co-operation.* Translated by Joseph Létargez. Manchester: Co-operative Union, 1963.
Lane, Fintan. "Review." *Irish Economic and Social History* XXX (2003): 158–59.
Layard, Richard. *Happiness: Lessons from a New Science.* New York: Penguin, 2005.
———. "This Is the Greatest Good." *The Guardian,* 14 September 2009, 32.
Leonhardt, David. "Money Doesn't Buy Happiness. Well, on Second Thought..." *New York Times,* April 16, 2008, C1.
Locke, John. *An Essay Concerning Human Understanding.* Oxford: Clarendon Press, 1975.
———. "Second Treatise of Government: An Essay Concerning the True Original, Extent, and End of Civil Government." In *Two Treatises of Government,* edited by Peter Laslett. Cambridge: Cambridge University Press, 1988.
Lowenthal, Esther. *The Ricardian Socialists.* Studies in History, Economics and Public Law. Edited by Columbia University Faculty of Political Science. Vol. 114, New York: Columbia University, 1911.
Lyons, David. *In the Interest of the Governed: A Study in Bentham's Philosophy of Utility and Law.* 2nd ed. New York: Oxford University Press, 1991.

Mack, Mary Peter. *Jeremy Bentham: An Odyssey of Ideas 1748–92*. London: Heinemann, 1962.

Macpherson, C. B. *Democratic Theory: Essays in Retrieval*. Oxford: Oxford University Press, 1973.

———. *The Life and Times of Liberal Democracy*. Oxford and New York: Oxford University Press, 1977.

MacPherson, Ian. *Co-operative Principles for the 21st Century*. Studies and Reports. Geneva: International Co-operative Alliance, 1995.

Maloy, J. S. "Real Utopias in a Gilded Age: The Case of American Populism." *New Political Science* 34, no. 3 (2012): 372–79.

Mansbridge, Jane J. "Fears of Conflict in Face-to-Face Democracies." In *Workplace Democracy and Social Change,* edited by Frank Lindenfeld and Joyce Rothschild-Whitt, 125–37. Boston: Porter Sargent, 1982.

Marx, Karl. *Capital: A Critique of Political Economy*. Translated by Ben Fowkes and David Fernbach. 3 vols. London: Penguin Classics, 1990–92.

———. *The Poverty of Philosophy*. Translated by H. Quelch. Amherst, NY: Prometheus Books, 1995.

———. *Selected Writings*. Edited by Lawrence H. Simon. Indianapolis: Hackett, 1994.

———, and Frederich Engels. *The Communist Manifesto*. Edited by Gareth Stedman Jones. London: Penguin Classics, 2002.

Mayoux, Linda. "Alternative Vision or Utopian Fantasy?: Cooperation, Empowerment, and Women's Cooperative Development in India." *Journal of International Development* 7, no. 2 (1995): 211–28.

McCready, Stuart, ed. *The Discovery of Happiness*. Naperville, IL: Sourcebooks, 2001.

McGillivray, Mark. "Human Well-Being: Issues, Concepts, and Measures." In *Human Well-Being: Concept and Measurement,* edited by Mark McGillivray. *Studies in Development Economics and Policy,* 1–22. New York: Palgrave Macmillan, 2007.

McMahon, Darrin M. *Happiness: A History*. New York: Grove Press, 2006.

Menger, Anton. *The Right to the Whole Produce of Labour*. Translated by M. E. Tanner. With an introduction and bibliography by H. S. Foxwell. New York: Augustus M. Kelley, 1962 [1899].

Mercer, T. W. *Towards the Co-operative Commonwealth: Why Poverty in the Midst of Plenty?* Manchester: The Co-operative Press, 1936.

Mill, James. *The Article on Government, Reprinted from the Supplement to the Encyclopaedia Britannica*. London: Encyclopaedia Britannica, 1821.

———. *Elements of Political Economy*. London: Baldwin, Cradock, and Joy, 1821.

Mill, John Stuart. *Autobiography*. London and New York: Penguin Books, 1989.

———. "On Liberty." In *On Liberty and Other Essays,* edited by John Gray. Oxford: Oxford University Press, 2008.
Mondragón. "Annual Report." Mondragón, Spain: Mondragón Corporacion Cooperativa, 2011.
———. "Frequently Asked Questions: Corporation." Mondragón Cooperative Corporation, http://www.mondragon-corporation.com/language/en-US/ENG/Frequently-asked-questions/Corporation.aspx. Accessed Dec. 5, 2009.
———. "Mondragón Corporacion Cooperativa: The History of an Experience." Mondragón, Spain: Mondragón Corporacion Cooperativa, 2006.
Morgan, John Minter. *Hampden in the Nineteenth Century, or, Colloquies on the Errors and Improvement of Society.* 2 vols London: E. Moxon, 1834.
Mouffe, Chantal. "Radical Democracy or Liberal Democracy?" In *Radical Democracy: Identity, Citizenship, and the State,* edited by David Trend, 19–26. New York and London: Routledge, 1996.
NCBA. "About Cooperatives." National Cooperative Business Association, http://www.ncba.org/abcoop.cfm. Accessed Aug. 4, 2006.
Noonan, Jeff. *Democratic Society and Human Needs.* Montreal: McGill-Queen's University Press, 2007.
Nussbaum, Martha. "Capabilities as Fundamental Entitlements: Sen and Social Justice." In *Capabilities Equality: Basic Issues and Problems,* edited by Alexander Kaufman, 44–70. New York: Routledge, 2006.
Nussbaum, Martha, and Amartya Sen, eds. *The Quality of Life.* Oxford: Oxford University Press, 1993.
Offer, Avner, ed. *In Pursuit of the Quality of Life.* Oxford: Oxford University Press, 1996.
Ogden, C. K. "Introduction." In *Jeremy Bentham: The Theory of Legislation,* edited by C. K. Ogden. London: Routledge and Kegan Paul, 1931.
Owen, Robert. *A New View of Society and Other Writings.* Edited and with an introduction by Gregory Claeys. London: Penguin, 1991.
———. "Resolutions, &C. Passed at the First Meeting of the Co-operative Congress." Manchester, May 26 and 27, 1831.
Pankhurst, R. K. P. *William Thompson (1775–1833): Britain's Pioneer Socialist, Feminist, and Co-operator.* London: Pluto Press, 1991.
Pateman, Carole. *Participation and Democratic Theory.* Cambridge: Cambridge University Press, 1970.
———. *The Sexual Contract.* Stanford: Stanford University Press, 1988.
Pitkin, Hannah F. "Slippery Bentham: Some Neglected Cracks in the Foundation of Utilitiariansim." *Political Theory* 18, no. 1 (Feb. 1990): 104–31.
Plato. *The Republic.* Translated by Tom Griffith. Cambridge: Cambridge University Press, 2000.

Postema, Gerald J. "Bentham's Equality-Sensitive Utilitarianism." *Utilitas* 10, no. 2 (July 1998): 144–58.
Powell, John and James. "Proceedings of the Second Co-operative Congress." Birmingham, England, Oct. 4–6, 1831.
Quinn, Michael. "Post-Modern Moments in the Application of Empirical Principles: Power, Knowledge, and Discourse in the Thought of Jeremy Bentham vs. Michel Foucault." In *Revue d'études benthamiennes [En ligne]* (2011). Published electronically March 1, 2011. http://etudes-benthamiennes.revues.org/245#article-245.
———. "Subsistence, Security, Abundance, and Population in the Political Economy of Jeremy Bentham." In *ISUS-X, Tenth Conference of the International Society for Utilitarian Studies*. Berkeley, CA, 2008.
Reisman, David. "Introduction to Volume 1." In *Thomas Hodgskin and William Thompson: Ricardian Socialism*, edited by David Reisman. *Democratic Socialism in Britain: Classic Texts in Economic and Political Thought: 1825–1952*. London: Pickering and Chatto, 1996.
Rhodes, Rita. "The Internationalism of the Co-operative Movement." In *Towards the Co-operative Commonwealth: Essays in the History of Co-operation,* edited by Bill Lancaster and Paddy Maguire, 105–108. Loughborough, Leicestershire: The Co-operative College, 1996.
Ricardo, David. *On the Principles of Political Economy, and Taxation*. 3rd ed. Harmondsworth: Penguin Books, 1971 [1821].
Roncaglia, Alessandro. *The Wealth of Ideas: A History of Economic Thought*. Cambridge: Cambridge University Press, 2005.
Rosen, Frederick. "Epicureanism and Utilitarianism: A Reply to Professor Lyons." *Utilitas* 18, no. 2 (2006): 182–87.
———. "Introduction." In *Jeremy Bentham: An Introduction to the Principles of Morals and Legislation*. Oxford: Clarendon Press, 1996.
———. *Jeremy Bentham and Representative Democracy: A Study of the Constitutional Code*. Oxford: Clarendon Press, 1983.
Rosenbaum, Stephen E. "Epicurean Moral Theory." *History of Philosophy Quarterly* 13, no. 4 (1996): 389–410.
Rothschild, Joyce, and J. Allen Whitt. *The Cooperative Workplace: Potentials and Dilemmas of Organizational Democracy and Participation*. Cambridge: Cambridge University Press, 1986.
Ryan, Alan. *Property and Political Theory*. Oxford: Basil Blackwell, 1984.
Saint-Just, Louis. "Sur le Mode d'Exécution du Décret Contre les Ennemis de la Révolution." http://www.royet.org/nea1789–1794/archives/discours /stjust_decret_ennemis_ revolution_03_03_94.htm. Accessed Sept. 15, 2008.
Scarre, Geoffrey. "Epicurus as a Forerunner of Utilitarianism." *Utilitas* 6, no. 2 (1994): 219–31.
Schofield, Philip. *Bentham: A Guide for the Perplexed*. London: Bloomsbury Academic, 2009.

---. *Utility and Democracy: The Political Thought of Jeremy Bentham.* Oxford: Oxford University Press, 2006.
Schweickart, David. *After Capitalism.* Lanham, MD: Rowman and Littlefield, 2002.
Secretary-General. "Cooperatives in Social Development." New York: United Nations General Assembly, 2009.
Sen, Amartya. "Capability and Well-Being." In *The Quality of Life,* edited by Martha Nussbaum and Amartya Sen, 30–53. Oxford: Oxford University Press, 1993.
---. *Choice, Welfare, and Measurement.* Cambridge: MIT Press, 1982.
---. *Commodities and Capabilities.* New York: Elsevier Science Publishers, 1985.
Shackleton, R. "The Greatest Happiness of the Greatest Number: The History of Bentham's Phrase." *Studies on Voltaire and the Eighteenth Century* 90 (1972): 1461–82.
Sharp, Andrew, ed. *The English Levellers. Cambridge Texts in the History of Political Thought,* edited by Raymond Guess and Quentin Skinner. Cambridge: Cambridge University Press, 1998.
Shefner-Rogers, Corinne L., Nagesh Rao, Everett M. Rogers, and Arun Wayangankar. "The Empowerment of Women Dairy Farmers in India." *Journal of Applied Communication Research* 26, no. 3 (1998): 319–37.
Sirianni, Carmen. "Learning Pluralism: Democracy and Diversity in Feminist Organizations." In *Critical Studies in Organization and Bureaucracy,* edited by Frank Fischer and Carmen Sirianni, 554–76. Philadelphia: Temple University Press, 1994.
Sismondi. "On the History of the Middle Ages—No. 1." *The New Monthly Magazine and Literary Journal* II (1821): 508–14.
Smith, Adam. *An Inquiry into the Nature and Causes of the Wealth of Nations.* Chicago: University of Chicago Press, 1976.
Soper, Kate. "Review: A Theory of Human Need." *New Left Review,* no. 197 (1993): 113–28.
Springborg, Patricia. *The Problem of Human Needs and the Critique of Civilisation.* London: G. Allen and Unwin, 1981.
Stark, W. *The Ideal Foundations of Economic Thought: Three Essays on the Philosophy of Economics.* Fairfield, NJ: Augustus M. Kelley, 1976 [1943].
---. "Introduction." In *Jeremy Bentham's Economic Writings: Critical Edition Based on His Printed Works and Unprinted Manuscripts,* edited by W. Stark, 11–78. New York: Burt Franklin, 1952.
---. "Liberty and Equality Or: Jeremy Bentham as an Economist." *The Economic Journal* 51, no. 201 (April 1941): 56–79.
Stedman Jones, Gareth. "Introduction." In *Karl Marx and Friedrich Engels: The Communist Manifesto,* edited by Gareth Stedman Jones. London: Penguin Classics, 2002.

———. *Languages of Class: Studies in English Working Class History 1832–1982*. Cambridge: Cambridge University Press, 1983.

Stiglitz, Joseph E., Amartya Sen, and Jean-Paul Fitoussi. "Report by the Commission on the Measurement of Economic Performance and Social Progress." Commission on the Measurement of Economic Performance and Social Progress, 2009.

Taylor, Eve. *Eve and the New Jerusalem*. New York: Pantheon Books, 1983.

Thompson, David. *Weavers of Dreams: Founders of the Modern Co-operative Movement*. Davis, CA: Center for Cooperatives, University of California, 1994.

Thompson, E. P. *The Making of the English Working Class*. New York: Pantheon Books, 1964.

Thompson, William. *Appeal [of One Half of the Human Race, Women, against the Pretensions of the Other Half, Men, to Retain Them in Political, and Thence in Civil and Domestic, Slavery; in Reply to a Paragraph of Mr. Mill's Celebrated "Article on Government."]* Edited by Dolores Dooley. Cork, Ireland: Cork University Press, 1997 [1825].

———. "Correspondence." *The Register for the First Society of Adherents to Divine Revelation at Orbiston*, Dec. 13, 1826, 183–85.

———. *An Inquiry into the Principles of the Distribution of Wealth Most Conducive to Human Happiness, Applied to the Newly Proposed System of Voluntary Equality of Wealth*. New York: B. Franklin, 1968 [1824].

———. "Labor Rewarded: The Claims of Labor and Capital Conciliated: Or, How to Secure to Labor the Whole Products of Its Exertions." In *Ricardian Socialism*, edited by David Reisman. *Democratic Socialism in Britain: Classic Texts in Economic and Political Thought, 1825–1952*. London: Pickering and Chatto, 1996 [1827].

———. "Lease of an Estate for Ever, with Liberty to Purchase the Fee at Convenience." *The Weekly Free Press and Co-operative Journal* V, no. 239 (Feb. 6, 1830).

———. *Practical Directions for the Speedy and Economical Establishment of Communities on the Principles of Mutual Co-operation, United Possessions, and Equality of Exertions and of the Means of Enjoyments*. London: Strange, and E. Wilson, 1830.

———. *Practical Education for the South of Ireland, in Letters Addressed to the Proprietors of the Cork Institution, Etc*. Cork: West and Coldwells, 1818.

———. "To the Industrious Classes of Britain and Ireland; Particularly to Our Neighbors, the Distressed Spitalfields Weavers." *The Co-operative Magazine and Monthly Herald* 1, no. 11 (1826): 337.

———. "To the Members and Managers of the Mechanics Institutions in Britain and Ireland." *The Co-operative Magazine and Monthly Herald* 1, no. 1 (1826): 23.

Thornes, Robin. "Change and Continuity in the Development of Co-operation, 1827–1844." In *New Views of Co-operation,* edited by Stephen Yeo, 27–51. London: Routledge, 1988.
Trend, David. "Democracy's Crisis of Meaning." In *Radical Democracy: Identity, Citizenship, and the State,* edited by David Trend, 7–18. London and New York: Routledge, 1996.
Veblen, Thorstein. "Why Is Economics Not an Evolutionary Science?" *The Quarterly Journal of Economics* 12, no. 4 (July 1898): 373–97.
Veenhoven, Ruut. "Advances in Understanding Happiness." *Revue Quebecoise de Psychologie* 18, no. 2 (1997): 29–74.
———. "Happiness as an Aim in Public Policy: The Greatest Happiness Principle." In *Positive Psychology in Practice,* edited by Alex Linley and Stephen Joseph, 658–78. Hoboken: John Wiley and Sons, 2004.
———. "Subjective Measures of Well-Being." In *Human Well-Being: Concept and Measurement,* edited by Mark McGillivray. 214–39. New York: Palgrave Macmillan, 2007.
Verba, Sidney, Kay Lehman Schlozman, and Henry E. Brady. *Voice and Equality: Civic Voluntarism in American Politics.* Cambridge: Harvard University Press, 1995.
Villa, Dana R. "Postmodernism and the Public Sphere." *The American Political Science Review* 86, no. 3 (1992): 712–21.
Walker, Catherine. "Annual Membership Meeting." Seattle: Recreational Equipment, Inc. (REI), 2011.
Warbasse, James Peter. *Cooperative Democracy.* 4th ed. New York, London,: Harper and Brothers, 1942.
Warke, Tom. "Multi-Dimensional Utility and the Index Number Problem: Jeremy Bentham, J. S. Mill, and Qualitative Hedonism." *Utilitas* 12, no. 2 (July 2000): 176–203.
Watkins, W. P. *Co-operative Principles: Today and Tomorrow.* Manchester: Holyoake Books, 1986.
Webb, Beatrice Potter, and Sidney Webb. *The Consumers' Co-operative Movement.* London and New York: Longman's, Green, 1921.
Wolin, Sheldon. "'Fugitive Democracy.'" *Constellations* 1, no. 1 (1994): 11–25.
———. "Norm and Form: The Constitutionalizing of Democracy." In *Athenian Political Thought and the Reconstruction of American Democracy,* edited by J. Peter Euben, John R. Wallach, and Josiah Ober, 29–58. Ithaca: Cornell University Press, 1994.
———. *Politics and Vision: Continuity and Innovation in Western Political Thought.* Expanded ed. Princeton: Princeton University Press, 2004.
Wollstonecraft, Mary. "A Vindication of the Rights of Woman." In *A Vindication of the Rights of Men and A Vindication of the Rights of Woman,* edited by Sylvana Tomaselli, 65–294. Cambridge: Cambridge University Press, 1995.

Wood, Neal. "Tabula Rasa, Social Environmentalism, and the 'English Paradigm.'" *Journal of the History of Ideas* 53, no. 4 (1992): 647–68.
Wright, Erik Olin. *Envisioning Real Utopias*. London and New York: Verso, 2010.
Young, Robert J. C. *White Mythologies: Writing History and the West.* 2nd ed. London and New York: Routledge, 2004.
Zeuli, Kimberly A., Robert Cropp, and Marvin A. Schaars. *Cooperatives: Principles and Practices in the 21st Century.* 4th ed. Madison: University of Wisconsin Center on Cooperatives, 1980.

Index

Abundance, 42, 72–73
Agricultural cooperatives, 180, 183, 188, 263n90
Alperovitz, Gar, 215n4
Annas, Julia, 21, 223n12
Aquinas, Thomas, 24–25
Aristotle, 26, 86, 198, 222n5
Armagh Co-operative Society, First, 167–68
Association. *See* cooperative communities; intentional communities; voluntary association
Ataraxia (tranquility), 21, 23
Atomism, 22
Autarkic cooperative community model, 13–14, 69–70, 129–130, 178, 179, 200, 202

Basic human needs. *See* human needs
Baujard, Antoinette, 105–106
Beccaria, Cesare, 55, 103, 244n35
Bentham, Jeremy, 5, 8–9, 10–12
  analysis of economic power, lacking an, 48–49
  on community as a kind of fiction, 47–48, 124–25, 220n52
  on democracy: instrumental theory of, 138–40; as a means of obtaining good government, 133–34, 137–38, 140; support for universal male suffrage, 171, 252–53n35
  on expectation vs. experience, 34, 35–36, 40
  on government: role in providing security and happiness, 43–44, 54, 137, 199–200; on sovereign power, 136–38
  on happiness (theory of), 19, 29, 31–32; based in individual interests, 10, 48–49, 95; on "eudaemonics," 38; expectation vs. experience of, 34, 35–36, 40; the "felicific calculus," 32–33; on the maximization of pleasure, 31, 33; on monetary value as a measure of happiness, 41–43, 48–49, 52, 53; on pleasure (and exemption from pain) as the prime motive, 34–39, 49–50, 56, 98, 198
  Hobbesian ideas in, 39, 66
  on the importance of property rights, 40, 46–47, 102–103
  individualism in, 10, 47–51, 56, 95–96

Bentham, Jeremy *(continued)*,
   on interests and self-interest: "extra-regarding interest," 34; self-interest as the basis of human activity, 5, 50–51, 105, 199; on singular interest vs. plural interests, 34–35, 36, 226n18; "sinister interest," 105–106, 136–38, 234n40, 244n48
   legal reform a primary focus, 9–10, 31, 48, 99
   Lockean ideas in, 40, 75, 102
   on Panopticon prisons or poorhouses, 46, 50, 95, 231n98
   on security, 5, 38–41, 75, 77–78, 101, 102, 137; as avoiding harm or pain, 36, 44, 45, 50; conflict of security and equality, 43–47, 99–101, 103, 200; distributive justice and, 43–47, 103–104, 243n19; government role of providing, 43–44, 50, 54; "securities against misrule," 137. *See also* security: Bentham on
   theory of utilitarianism (*see* utilitarianism: in Bentham)
Benthamism, 64, 199, 225n1
Bernard, Paul R., 61
Birchall, Johnston, 182–83, 258n7
Birmingham Co-operative Society, 168
Brown, Wendy, 2, 3, 221n55
Bruni, Luigino, and Pier Luigi Porta, 198
Burns, J. H., 225–26n2

Capabilities approach, 86–87, 88
Capitalism, 193, 246n83
   "capital without capitalists," 129
   conflict over wages under, 109–10
   conflicts of interest and, 125
   the cooperative movement and, 14, 182–83, 184, 192–93
   the creation of desire and, 53, 207
   critiques of, 13, 29, 82–83, 112, 113–18
   involuntary exchange of labor under, 82–84
   Marxist analysis of, 3, 112, 113, 119, 129, 170, 219n40, 247n92, 260n30
   paradox of, 207–208
   people's interests served under, 50–51, 65–66, 199–200
   See also exchange (of goods); competition; private property; Thompson, William: on the "system of individual competition"
Character formation, effect of circumstances. *See* philosophy of necessity
Chartism/Charter movement, 164, 166, 170–71, 173–76, 184, 261n52 and 62, 262n64
Chartist Cooperative Land Society, 174
Cicero, 50, 223n16, 231n97
Civil unrest, 103–104. *See also* revolution
Claeys, Gregory, 8, 115, 215–16n5, 217n16, 245n59, 247n92
Class conflict, 113. *See also* capitalism
Classical liberalism, 50, 101
Coercion, 65, 82–83, 84, 106, 109, 113, 126–27, 155, 201. *See also* involuntary exchange
Collective ownership. *See* property, collective
Collectivization of property, 126, 128–29, 202
Common property. *See* property, collective
Communities
   not composed of isolated individuals, 124–25, 127
   as "corporate" entities, 130–31
   as a fictitious body, 47–48, 124–25, 220n52

intentional, 159, 177, 257n110, 268–69n66
self-sufficient (autarkic), 13–14, 69–70, 129–130, 178, 179, 200, 202
Competition, 75, 117, 153, 208, 245n58
  absence in cooperative communities, 156, 168
  for power, 66, 149–51, 174
  for property (wealth), 5, 8, 62–63, 85, 114–17, 118–19, 130–31, 193, 201–202, 237n75, 247n92
  See also inequality; Thompson, William: on the "system of individual competition"
Condorcet, Nicolas, Marquis de, 11
"Constitutive Authority," 138, 139–40
Consumer cooperatives, 178–79, 180, 184–85, 188–89, 193, 204, 262n75, 263n88, 266n124, 266n127, 266n128, 269n7
Consumerism
  hedonic happiness and, 42–43, 52–54
  as purchasing pleasure, 51–52
  See also money
Cooperative communities, 6, 63, 68, 71, 82, 128–31, 157–61, 163–64, 167, 235n56, 250n149
  alignment of self- and social interest within, 155
  compared with capitalist society, 153–54
  absence of conflict within, 156–57, 159
  democracy within, 154–57
  equality within, 151, 153–54
  failures and decline of, 174–75, 176–79, 204
  goal abandoned by Rochdale pioneers, 174
  relationships between, 129–30
  role of public opinion within, 155–56, 160, 256n94
"Cooperative commonwealth," 178–79
Cooperative Congresses, 6, 168
Co-operative Group (UK), 193, 267–68n142, 269n99
Cooperative models
  enterprise model, 2, 161, 179–80, 192–93, 203–205, 211, 269n77; contrasted with the community model, 176–78; current extent of, 179–80; principles of, 180–89, 211–13; effects of professionalization in management (managerialism), 182–83, 186–87, 204, 266n119; types of cooperatives in, 180. See also cooperative movement: contemporary
  Owenite (community) model, 13–14, 62, 164, 167, 168; Thompson's version compared with Owen's, 4, 108
  Rochdale model, 164–65, 166, 169–70, 176, 177–78, 184, 203, 258n99, 259n15
Cooperative movement, 2, 3, 163, 194–95
  basis in Thompson's ideas, 1–2, 161, 163, 165, 190–94
  from the community model to the enterprise model, 176–79, 203–204
  contemporary, 179–81, 262–63n84, 263n85, 263n 88, 263n 89, 263n90; challenges to, 204–205. See also cooperative principles and theory; International Co-operative Alliance
  ideological foundations of, 183–94, 205

Cooperative movement *(continued)*,
  social change and, 2, 4, 158, 192,
    194–95, 205, 267–68n142,
    268n143
Cooperative principles and theory,
    181–89
  cooperative commonwealth,
    178–79
  democratic participation, 151–55,
    182–83, 187–89, 204
  ethical values, 183
  first principle, 183–90
  ICA Cooperative Principles, 2,
    181–83, 190–94, 211–13,
    264–65n97
  Rochdale Principles, 169–70, 176,
    209–10
  Thompson's principles and ideas of
    (*see* Thompson, William: cooperative theory and principles; as voluntary associations; voluntary association)
Cooperative societies, pre–1844
    (Birmingham, First Armagh,
    Hull Anti-Mill, London,
    Salford), 167–68
  size and extent, 258–59n13,
    259n18, 259n20
Co-operative Union, British national,
    176
Co-operative Wholesale Society
    (CWS), 178, 179, 266n115
Cooperatives. *See* agricultural cooperatives; consumer cooperatives; cooperative movement: contemporary; credit unions; worker cooperatives
Credit unions (financial cooperatives),
    180, 183, 204, 263n84, 263n88,
    263n89
CWS. *See* Co-operative Wholesale
    Society (CWS)

Dale, David, 62
Declaration of Independence, 1, 26

Declaration of the Rights of Man,
    26
Democracy, 45, 133, 160, 191
  Bentham and Thompson contrasted
    on, 10–12, 134–35, 144, 146,
    148, 155–56, 201
  Bentham on: instrumental theory
    of, 138–40; as a means of
    obtaining good government,
    133–34, 135, 137–38, 140, 199;
    public opinion and, 141–42;
    on representative democracy,
    135–36, 199; support for
    universal male suffrage, 134, 135,
    139–40, 252–53n35
  democratic participation in cooperatives, 169, 182–83, 187–89,
    204, 266n128, 266–67n129
  mainstream theories of, 133–34,
    151–52, 250–51n4, 251n5
  radical democratic theory, 2, 133,
    134, 152–53, 256n99
  representative democracy, 10, 151,
    170–71, 208
  Thompson on: as integral to
    cooperative communities, 14,
    154–56, 157–58; education and,
    144–46, 190, 191; participatory
    democracy, 146–47, 153, 160; as
    a principle of social interaction,
    11–12, 153–54, 155–56, 201;
    public opinion in cooperative
    communities and, 155–57, 159,
    160–61, 256n94; representative
    democracy, 12, 143, 144–51;
    self-government, 143, 154–57,
    159; as a subsidiary principle to
    utility, 9, 128–29, 132, 153–54,
    194
Desire, 22–25, 52–53, 197–98
  creation of (in capitalism), 53, 207
  pleasure not the satisfaction of,
    22–23
  as the root of action, 25, 64
  See also pleasure

"Disappointment-prevention principle," 40
Distribution of wealth, 40, 68, 72, 78, 80, 100–101, 103–104, 109, 124, 125, 153, 156, 190, 201–202, 203, 256n99, 259n17
"natural laws" for, 13, 126–28, 200
See also inequality
Distributive justice, 102, 103–104, 243n19
"Divi, the" (dividend, or patronage refund), 166, 183–85, 265n105
Division of labor, 12, 13, 71, 81–82, 145, 177, 239n122
Dooley, Dolores, 67, 216n15, 218n26, 238n105
Doyal, Len, 87, 241n166
and Ian Gough, 44, 88, 90–91

Easterlin, Richard, 53
Economic activity (GDP), as measure of happiness, 52–53
Economic power, 48–49, 64–65, 83, 91–92, 113, 127, 149, 150, 178, 186, 199–200, 206, 207. *See also* capitalism; elite rule; power
"Economy of labor," 69–70, 158
Education, 57–58, 59, 61, 62, 81, 108, 145, 147–48, 190, 234n31, 247n88, 247–48n100, 259n15
and cooperatives, 178, 181, 183, 184, 185, 209, 212
universal, 116–17, 247–48n100
See also knowledge
Elites
that government represents the interests of, 113, 145–46, 149–51
rule by, 138–40, 144–46
Employee Stock Ownership Plans (ESOPs), 264n91
Engelmann, Stephen G., 35–36, 227n24, 245n55
Engels, Frederick, 7, 111
and Karl Marx, 113, 219n40, 246–47n85

Enlightenment, 26–27, 57, 60, 174, 261n41
universalism, 81, 256n99
Epicureanism, 21, 26, 29, 197–98, 223n14, 224n32
on desire, 22–23
katastematic vs. kinetic pleasure, 21–24, 25, 27–28
on pleasure as the absence of pain, 21–22, 24
on virtue, 23, 198, 223n16
Epicurus. *See* Epicureanism
Equality, 12, 42, 46, 88, 119–20, 123, 190, 199, 203, 229n76, 243n19
Bentham and Thompson contrasted, 5, 11–12, 77–78, 96, 107–108, 128, 132, 200
within the cooperative community, 13–14, 151, 153–54, 155–56, 159–60
in the cooperative movement, 190, 194, 203, 211–12, 267n130, 267n139
democracy and, 11, 134, 138, 151–54, 255n77
forms of (legal, economic, social), 45–46, 152, 242n14
fundamental equality of all humans, 77–78, 126–27
security and, 5, 99–101, 103–104, 127, 131–32, 202, 229n71
as a subsidiary principle of utilitarianism, 38, 45, 99–101, 128, 132, 242n15
See also inequality; women: subordination of
Eudaemonism ("eudaemonics"), 1–2, 19–23, 28–29, 38, 47, 54, 66–67
vs. hedonic happiness (hedonism), 19, 207–208
social character of, 79–80, 91–92, 207–8, 215n3
See also Aristotle; Epicureanism; happiness

Exchange (of goods or labor), 71, 80–81, 178–79. *See also* labor; involuntary exchange; voluntary exchange
Expectation (as motivation), 34, 35–36, 39–40. *See also* security

Fabian socialists, 178
Fairbairn, Brett, 166, 177–78, 183–84, 257–58n3, 260n28
Feminism (anti-subordination), 2–3, 11, 77, 108, 119–24. *See also* women: political rights; women: subordination of
Ferguson, Susan, 119, 217n17
Feudal system, devolution of, 25
Financial cooperatives. *See* credit unions
Foucault, Michel, 9, 152–53
Free market, 28, 41, 49, 50–52, 53, 65–66, 80, 90, 199–200, 237n78. *See also* capitalism
French Revolution, 135, 148–49

Gallie, W. B., 197
Gasper, Des, 52, 87, 224n37
Global economy, 179–80, 191, 203
Godwin, William, 109
Government
  on a national constitution, 254n60. *See also* People's Charter
  representing interests of the capitalist elite, 113, 145–46, 149–50
  role in ensuring happiness, 36–37, 137
  role in ensuring subsistence, 43, 199
  role in providing security, 39, 43–44, 199
Gramsci, Antonio, 64–65
Grassroots Economic Organizing, 3
Gray, John, 259n17
Greatest happiness principle. *See* utilitarianism

Greek conceptions of happiness, 19–21, 26, 197, 222n5. *See also* Aristotle; eudaemonism; Epicureanism; Stoics

Habermas, Jürgen, 9
Happiness, 85, 200–201, 222n3
  assumption of equal capacity for, 77–78
  Bentham's theory of, 19, 28–29, 31–32; based in individual interests (individualism), 47–48, 49–50, 56, 58, 95; on "eudaemonics," 38; expectation vs. experience of, 34, 35–36, 40, 41–42; the "felicific calculus," 32–33; liberty and, 50–51; on maximizing happiness, 98–99, 104, 135; on maximizing pleasure, 31, 33, 67; on money as its measure, 41–42, 48–49, 52–53; on pleasure (and exemption from pain) as the prime motive, 34–39, 49, 50, 56, 98, 123, 198; relationship to (subjective) well-being, 31–32, 37–38, 51, 198
  equal right to, 26–27, 100, 127
  Greek conceptions of, 19–21, 26, 197, 222n5. *See also* Aristotle; eudaemonism; Epicureanism; Stoics
  as the maximization of pleasure (*see* pleasure)
  political character of, 1, 20, 26–27, 36–37, 96, 131, 198
  relationship to desire, 23–25, 53
  relationship to pleasure, 21–25, 27, 32–8, 54, 66–70, 73
  relationship to well-being, 28–29, 31–32, 37–38, 51
  religious conceptions of, 24–25, 26, 221–22n2
  social character of, 21, 79–80, 84
  temporal frame of, 27–28. *See also*

katastematic pleasure; kinetic pleasure

Thompson's theory of, 19, 57, 70, 91–92; as eudaemonistic, 1–2, 66–67, 79–80, 91, 207–8; on the general happiness, 124, 127; on happiness as (objective) well-being, 66–7, 90–92; on the hegemonic construction of happiness, 64–66, 78–79; on maximizing happiness, 80, 132; on maximizing pleasure, 67; on the means of happiness, 66–70, 90, 124; moral value and, 67, 71, 78; as a social theory, 56–57, 90–92 (*see also* social institutions; social science); wealth and, 70, 72–73

See also eudaemonism; hedonism; well-being

Harrison, J. F. C., 61, 171–72, 174, 216n5, 245n59, 246n64, 261n41

Harrison, Ross, 31, 226n3

Health/health care, 44, 68, 69, 70, 89, 256n99, 263n88, 268n144

Hedonism (hedonic happiness), 19, 21, 24–25, 42–43, 47, 48, 51–54, 66–67, 79–80, 95, 197–98, 207, 215n2, 224n37
ascetic, 24
consumerism and, 42–43, 52–53, 63
the "hedonic treadmill," 53, 207
modern, 24–25, 28–29, 48, 51–52
pleasure and desire in, 20–25, 42–3, 89, 198
political dimensions, 28, 203
religious dimensions, 24–25
self-interest and, 34–35, 36, 50, 51–52, 123, 131
subjectivity and, 28, 86
wealth or consumption and, 42–43, 52–53, 63, 67–68, 89, 100–101

Hegemony
Gramsci on, 64–65
hegemonic construction of happiness, 62–66, 78–79
See also power

Hetherington, Henry, 174

Hobbes, Thomas, 39, 66, 83, 108, 254n58

Hodgskin, Thomas, 6

Holyoake, G. J., 167, 173, 177–78, 219n34, 258n9, 261n52

Huet, Tim, 195, 267n133

Human needs, 44–45, 86–88

Hume, David, 44, 55, 102, 243n28

Hunt, E. K., 8

ICA. *See* International Cooperative Alliance

"Ill-being," 33

"Income paradox," 53–54

Individualism, 47–51, 54, 61, 185–86
modern hedonism and, 28, 48–49
political economy and, 51–54, 95, 185
"system of individual competition" as undermining social relations, 13, 84–85, 107–108, 113–18, 119, 127–28, 149–50, 168, 201–202
See also Bentham, Jeremy

Industrial Revolution, 25, 55, 170, 206

Inequality, 80, 103–104, 108, 117, 142, 159–60, 201–202, 257n111
of capacity assumption, 78–79
as undermining democracy, 149–51, 152, 206
in knowledge and education, 145, 149
of security, 114
as a social and political evil, 73, 100–101, 119–24, 150, 168–69, 247n88

Inequality *(continued)*,
See also equality; Thompson,
William: on the "system of
individual competition"
Insecurity, 39, 76, 158, 202, 206
capitalism as a system of, 114, 155
of the produce of labor for workers,
76, 108, 114, 151
See also security: Thompson on
Instrumental theory of democracy,
138–40, 142
Intentional communities, 159, 177,
257n110, 268–69n6. See also
voluntary association
Interests
Bentham on: "extra-regarding
interest," 34; self-interest as
the basis of human activity, 5,
50–51, 105, 199; on singular
interest vs. plural interests,
34–35, 36, 226n18. See also
"sinister interest"
Thompson on, 81; conditions for
an identity of interests, 124–26;
conflicts of interest and social
institutions, 115–16, 123, 124,
125, 156; on identity of interests
in married couples, 120–24,
125; on "natural" vs. "factitious"
motives, 73–75, 154–55; true vs.
false interest, 58, 80–81, 84
See also motivation/motives;
self-interest
International Co-operative Alliance
(ICA), 2, 176, 179–82, 265n100
ICA Cooperative Principles,
181–82, 185–87, 189, 191–92,
211–13, 264–65n97
International Year of the Cooperative
(IYC), 203, 205, 216n10
Involuntary exchange, 82–84, 237n75

Jevons, H. Stanley, 51–52, 54, 90. *See
also* neoclassical economics

Justice, 27, 86, 88, 102

Katastematic (static) pleasure, 21–24,
25, 27, 42, 222–23n9, 226n18,
235n45, 238n103
difficulty of measurement, 27–28
wealth and, 42–43
Kelly, P. J., 45, 102–3, 104, 242n8,
243n19
Kinetic pleasure, 21–24, 25, 27, 33,
35, 42, 222–23n99
King, William, 258–59n13
Knowledge, 60–61, 69, 70, 75,
80–81, 83, 84, 89, 108, 116–17,
123–24, 138, 139, 145, 147–48,
149, 154, 174, 235n56

Labor
division of, 71, 81, 145, 177,
239n122; unpaid (domestic), 53.
See also involuntary exchange;
voluntary exchange
subordination to capital, 13, 66,
76–77, 82–85, 119–24, 126,
152, 180, 201–202, 263–64n91.
See also subordination
Labor theory of value, 13, 70–72,
126–27. *See also* surplus value,
theory of
Laborers' right to the full produce of
labor, 126–27. *See also* produce of
labor
Laclau, Ernesto, and Chantal Mouffe,
2–3, 152
Lambert, Paul, 184–85, 187–89,
262n75, 266n127, 266n128
Law the First, 167, 169, 177, 209. *See
also* Rochdale Principles
Layard, Richard, 53, 208, 225n42
Levellers, 171, 175
Liberal capitalism, 1, 2, 29, 49, 86,
108, 152, 185–86, 192, 201,
206–207. *See also* capitalism
Liberalism, 50, 88, 101

Liberty, 51, 87, 122, 152, 171, 199, 231n94
  negative (as the pursuit of self-interest), 26, 50, 88, 118, 131
  positive (as fulfillment of basic needs), 88
Lieberman, David, 225n1
"Life-satisfaction," 28, 89. *See also* well-being
Locke, John, 40, 75, 102, 243n31, 245n59
  hedonic happiness in, 25, 215n2
  on private property, 72, 102, 228n47, 228n48, 237n82
  on the *tabula rasa*, 57–58, 233n8
London Co-operative Society (Association), 6, 7, 168, 174
Lovett, William, 174, 261n57
Lowenthal, Esther, 8, 217n16, 219n48, 221n59
Luther, Martin, 24

Maclure, William, 61
MacPherson, Ian, 195, 264n93, 267n139
Macpherson, C. B., 50–51
Male suffrage (universal), 120–21, 125, 141–42, 170–71, 262n64
Malthus, Thomas, 44, 109, 245n61
Managerialism (in cooperatives), 186–88, 204, 266n119
Mansbridge, Jane J., 160
Marriage
  identity of husband's and wife's interests in, 120–21, 122, 125
  subordination of women to men in, 121–22, 123–24, 125
  women as slaves in, 119–20, 122, 248n110
  See also women
Marx, Karl, 82, 119, 170, 207, 255n86, 260n30
  Frederick Engels and, 113, 219n40, 246–47n85
  preceded or influenced by Thompson, 2, 7, 85–86, 111, 112
Marxism, 3, 96, 129, 261n44
McGillivray, Mark, 88
McMahon, Darrin M., 26
Menger, Anton, 7, 221n59, 231n101
Menger, Carl, 51
"Methodological individualism," 47–48. *See also* individualism
Mill, James
  on identity of interests in marriage, 120–21, 124, 125
  influence on Bentham, 251n15
  on the "natural laws" of distribution, 126
  on self-interest and exploitation, 121, 122–23, 150
  on universal male suffrage, 120–21, 124, 125, 139, 171
Mill, John Stuart, 7, 61, 253n58, 258n9
Modern hedonism, 28–29, 51–52
  vs. ancient (ascetic) hedonism, 24–25
  individualistic character of, 48–49
  See also consumption, kinetic pleasure; subjective well-being (SWB)
Mondragón Cooperative Corporation, 264n92
Money, 110, 210
  as a measure of happiness, 41–42, 48–49, 52–53
  as purchasing pleasure, 51–52
  as the determination of value, 49
Moral aptitude, 137–38
Moral philosophy, 31, 55, 59, 98, 99, 142, 198, 215n2, 215n3, 234–35n40
"moral science," 56
Moral reasoning and judgment, 56, 117, 123, 135, 202, 236n70
Moral sanction, 142, 242n13, 256n94

Moral value
  of actions, 67
  of education, 116–17
  equal, of persons, 12, 78
  of (voluntary) exchange, 71, 81–82
  in social relations undermined by competition, 115–16, 207
Morgan, John Minter, vi, 9, 220n49, 233n88, 249n119
Motivation/motives, 43, 63–64, 68, 85, 15, 137–38, 145, 226n19, 230n77, 234n38
  and desire, 25
  "natural" vs. "factitious" motives, 73–75, 154–55
  pleasure (self-interest) as primary, 32, 34–36, 50, 56, 66–67, 73, 81, 100, 118, 137, 200
  security and, 38–39, 72, 75, 83, 146–47
Mouffe, Chantal, 152

"Natural laws for the distribution of wealth," 13, 116, 126–28, 200
Neoclassical economics, 28–29, 51–54, 90, 199, 203, 231n100
  GDP as the measure of happiness, 52–54
  relationship to Bentham, 51, 54
New Harmony cooperative community, 61, 163, 234n27, 234n28, 254n65, 257n104
New Lanark, 62, 234n31
Nussbaum, Martha, 88

Objective well-being (OWB), 28–29, 86–90
O'Brien, James Bronterre, 174
O'Connor, Feargus, 174
Occupy movement, 208
Official aptitude (moral, intellectual, active), 137–38, 140, 145–46
Orbiston cooperative community, 163
OWB. *See* objective well-being

Owen, Robert, 4, 6, 55, 64, 164
  Association of All Classes of All Nations, 174
  on formation of character by the social environment ("philosophy of necessity"), 57–59, 61, 201
  contrasted with Bentham, 59–62
  cooperative community model of, 13–14, 108
  that ideas of happiness/interest are shaped by the social environment, 62, 63, 80
  the Rational Society (Universal Community Society of Rational Religionists), 172, 173
Owenism (Owenite socialism), 4, 109, 164, 166, 170, 171–74, 175–76, 205, 216n55, 246n64, 260n22
Owenite socialists, 172, 216n5
Owenite communities, 4, 13, 62, 163, 167, 172. *See also* New Harmony cooperative community

Pain. *See* pleasure and pain
Paley, William, 55, 107
Panopticon prisons or poorhouses, 46, 50, 95, 231n98
Pare, William, 6, 168, 172, 219n34, 259–60n22
Pateman, Carole, 191, 253n58
People's Charter. *See* Chartism
Philosophy of necessity, 57–59, 61, 63–64, 73, 78, 80–81, 107, 172, 201
Pitkin, Hannah F., 34–35
Plato, 19–20
Pleasure and pain
  on different types of pleasure, 21, 67–69, 73, 123, 145, 155
  felicific calculus and, 32–33
  happiness as avoidance of pain, 38–40, 67
  on the maximization of pleasure, 24, 31, 33, 67

pleasure as the absence of pain, 21, 22–23
as the basic principle of psychology (motivation), 67, 98, 102, 123, 198
sexual pleasure, 68
See also desire; happiness; katastematic pleasure; kinetic pleasure; motivation/motives; well-being
Polis (city-state), 20
Political economy, 43, 52–54, 80, 108–109, 112, 113–14, 115, 117–18, 126, 171–72, 201–202, 216n15, 217–18n20, 220n53, 246n64, 250n158
in cooperative socialism, 129, 236n72
differences between Bentham and Thompson on, 12–13, 95–96, 131–32, 200
private property and, 13, 41, 49, 85, 91, 100, 101, 102–104, 110, 113–15, 117–19, 126, 128, 130, 157, 201–202, 228n47 and 48
productive vs. unproductive labor, 71–72
as socially structured practices of production and exchange, 57
subjective well-being and, 27–29
subordination and, 119–20
theory of surplus value and, 109–112
See also distribution of wealth; inequality; labor theory of value; neoclassical economics; wealth
Political rights, 77, 144–46, 170–171, 247n88, 255n86
in cooperative communities, 129, 153
of women, 5, 77, 119–22, 124, 125, 135, 139–40, 141–42, 143, 144, 153, 169, 251n8, 257n111, 262n64. *See also* suffrage
See also Chartism

Popular sovereignty, 136, 138. *See also* democracy
Power
economic, 48–49, 186, 199
of elites (elite rule), 138–40, 145–46, 149–50
functions of, 48, 61, 64
intellectual, 145–6, 155
in marriage, 123–26
political, 74, 76, 96, 113, 150–51, 156, 158, 175, 192, 202, 204, 221n55, 254–55n72, 259n17
relations of, 2, 11, 65, 78–79, 83, 96, 113, 122–123, 125, 127, 142, 150, 159, 221n55
"soft" power, 65
sovereign power, 136–38, 139
See also coercion; hegemony; subordination
Predestination, 24–25
Principle of utility. *See* utilitarianism
Principles subsidiary to utility. *See* subsidiary principles
Producer cooperatives. *See* agricultural cooperatives
Professionalization (in cooperative management), 186–88, 204, 266n119
Produce of labor
effects of securing (or not) to the laborer, 80, 82, 83, 108–10, 114, 116, 117–18, 126, 127, 146–47, 149, 201
security and, 39–40, 114–15, 117, 129
surplus value and, 111–12
Property
collective (common), 128–29, 184, 190, 192–93, 203–204, 212; as a subsidiary principle to utility, 9, 96, 107–108, 128–29, 132, 190, 194, 202–203, 241n1
private, 13–14, 113–15, 243–44n33; vs. cooperative ownership, 153–54;

300 Index

Property *(continued)*
　elimination of, 126, 128–29, 202; injustice and, 102; as the motive for selfishness, 84–85, 118–19; importance of security to, 40, 46–47, 102–3; as a social institution, 91–92. *See also* capitalism; political economy; social institutions; Thompson, William: on the "system of individual competition"
Public and private spheres, 9, 10–11, 96
Public opinion
　in cooperative communities, 155–57, 159, 160, 256n94
　Public Opinion Tribunal, 10, 12, 141–42, 147, 155

Radical democratic theory, 2, 133, 134, 152–53, 256n99
Ralahine cooperative community, 163
Rational Society (Universal Community Society of Rational Religionists), 172, 173. *See also* Owen, Robert
Rationalism, 58, 61, 84, 157, 160, 172, 174, 236n71, 261n41. *See also* Enlightenment
Recreational Equipment, Inc. (REI), 193, 265n105, 266n128
Reformation, modern hedonism and, 25
Religious conceptions of happiness, 24–25, 26
Representative democracy. *See* democracy
Revolution, 107, 158, 184, 257n108
Ricardian socialists, 109, 172, 217n16
Ricardo, David: the economy as a "web of exchanges," 110
　theory of comparative advantage, 250n158
　theory of surplus value, 108–12, 114, 245n59
Rights of women. *See* suffrage; women: political rights
Rochdale Co-operative Manufacturing Society, 177–78
Rochdale Principles, 169–70, 176, 181, 187, 190, 209–10, 257–58n3, 260n28
　Law the First, 167, 169, 209
Rochdale Society of Equitable Pioneers, 164–67, 169–70, 173, 178, 181–82, 184, 190, 258n9, 259n15, 261n52
　abandonment of community cooperative model, 176
Rochdale cooperative (enterprise) model, 176, 177–78, 180, 182, 203, 258n9
Rosen, Frederick, 100, 139
Rothschild, Joyce, and J. Allen Whitt, 160
Ryan, Alan, 243–44n33

Salford Community, First, 168
Schofield, Philip, 139, 140, 141, 251n6, 251n15, 251n18, 252n22, 253n43
Security
　Bentham on, 5, 38–41, 75, 77–78, 101, 102, 137; abundance (opulence) and, 72; civil unrest and, 103–104; conservative character, 104; distributive justice and, 43–47, 103–4, 243n19; as ensuring future pleasure or avoiding future pain (harm), 36, 38–39, 44, 45, 50; equality vs., 5, 96, 99–101, 199, 229n71; expectation and, 40, 75, 102; happiness and, 39–40; as the main object of law, 39; not a motive, 38; of property distribution and civil unrest, 103–104;

problem of quantification, 53; role of government in providing, 10, 36, 43–44, 50, 54, 95, 199; "securities against misrule," 137–38; slavery and, 104–105; as a social concept, 39, 227n40; relationship to subsistence, 38, 43–47, 100, 103, 200, 242n16; wealth and property and, 41–43, 46, 102–103, 104–105, 228n58, 251n8; well-being and, 32, 70. *See also* subsidiary principles

Thompson on, 5; for capitalists, 113–14; competition and, 116, 151; expectation and, 76; importance for production of wealth, 109; involuntary exchange and, 83; inequality for capitalists and workers, 113–14; in the produce of labor for laborers, 126–27, 128–29; reconciliation with equality, 96, 101–102, 107–108, 127, 200, 202; slavery and, 114; subsistence and, 75–77, 128, 151; voluntary exchange and, 127; absence of for women, 77; absence of for workers, 76, 80, 108, 114, 115–18, 151, 202. *See also* subsidiary principles

Self-help, 169, 183, 190–92, 211

Self-interest
alignment with social interests, 5, 12, 14, 81–82, 85, 105–106, 118–19, 193
as a basis for exploitation, 121, 122–23, 150
as the basis for human activity, 5, 50–51, 60, 105, 199
"enlightened," 59–60, 81
as a matter of individual pursuit, 47–48, 58
influence of social institutions on, 62, 63, 80
liberty as the pursuit of, 50, 118, 131
true and false, 80–81
vs. selfishness, 118–19
See also interests

Self-sufficient communities. *See* autarkic cooperative community model

Sen, Amartya, 52, 88, 208

Sense perception, 48

Sexual pleasure, 68

"Sinister interest," 105–106, 123, 136–38, 145, 150–51, 156, 234n40, 244n48

Slavery, 104–105, 113–14, 120, 148, 206
marriage as a form of, 119–20, 122, 248n110

Smith, Adam, 12–13, 44, 80, 103, 109, 112, 132, 145, 245n59, 249n143, 269n11
on the conflict over wages under capitalism, 109–10
influence on Bentham, 12, 51
influence on Thompson, 12–13
labor theory of value, 111
on surplus value, 110
theory of wages, 109–111

Social change, and the cooperative movement, 2–3, 4, 163, 192, 194–95, 205, 267–68n142, 268n143
as evolutionary, 158

Social character of happiness. *See* happiness: social character of; happiness: Thompson's theory of

Social environmentalism. *See* philosophy of necessity

Social institutions, 11–12, 14, 29, 45, 48–49, 96, 172, 194, 203, 206, 208, 224–25n41
hegemony and, 64–65
human needs and, 87
as shaping individual character or interests, 58–59, 63, 64, 74–75, 84–85, 118–119, 123, 201

political character of, 5, 134, 152, 192, 207–208
as structuring social conditions (relations), 56–57, 64, 90–92, 96, 99, 131–32, 134, 152, 192, 201
Social interest, alignment with self-interest, 5, 12, 14, 81–82, 85, 105–106, 118–19, 193
Social science, 11, 27, 56, 64, 172, 198, 221n56, 224n39, 232n4
Social theory of utility. *See* Thompson, William: and utilitarianism; utilitarianism: in Thompson, William
Socrates, 19
Springborg, Patricia, 87
Standard of living, 54, 117, 130, 191, 206, 247n92
Stark, W., 46, 100
Stedman Jones, Gareth, 171, 173, 174–75
Stiglitz, Joseph E., 203, 208, 225n42
Stoics, 26
Subjection. *See* subordination
Subjective well-being (SWB), 28–29, 54, 86, 88–90, 197, 198, 225n42, 241n162, 241n 163
Subordination, 3, 5, 11, 13, 66, 84–85, 107–108, 117, 119–24, 125, 145, 253n55, 264n91
as a feature of capitalism, 76–77, 119, 202
as reflected in social institutions, 84
social subordination, 152
as undermining the greatest happiness, 119
of women, 5, 11, 13, 119–24, 148–49, 192, 245n57, 253n55
See also labor: subordination to capital
Subsidiary principles
in Bentham, 8–9, 38, 42, 96, 99–100, 131, 199, 202 (*see also*
abundance; equality; security: Bentham on; subsistence)
in Thompson, 8–9, 96, 107, 128, 131–32, 151, 190, 194, 202 (*see also* democracy: Thompson on; equality; property: collective; security: Thompson on; united effort; voluntarism)
See also utilitarianism
Subsistence, 39, 50, 59, 72, 116, 128, 177, 202, 229n77
basic needs and, 44–45
as a principle subsidiary to utility, 9, 38, 99–100, 107, 199, 200, 202, 242n15, 242n16
on the right to, 47
security and, 38, 43, 45–47, 76
wages and, 110, 245n59
Suffrage, 136, 138, 139, 142, 150–51, 267n130
universal, 11, 135, 138, 143, 144–45, 205, 254–55n72
universal for men only, 120–21, 134, 141–42, 170–71, 199, 262n64
women's exclusion from, 121, 139–40, 142
See also women: political rights
Surplus production, 130
Surplus value, theory of, 108–12, 114
that surplus value should belong to labor, 126–27
SWB. *See* subjective well-being (SWB)

The Cooperative Group, UK, 193
Thompson, William
Anna Doyle Wheeler and, 5, 6, 7–8, 248–49n119
as blending Benthamism and Owenism, 63–64, 66
compared with Bentham: on democracy and democratic theory, 10–12, 134–35, 144–46, 148, 201; on equality, 77–79,

128, 132; on happiness, 4–5, 8–9, 19, 20, 29, 55, 67, 77–78, 79, 86, 91–92, 203, 235n45; on intellectual aptitude, 146; on interests and motives, 73, 75, 80–81, 106, 118–19, 123, 124–25, 145; on the object of moral and social inquiry, 56–57; on political economy, 12–14, 95–96; on political theory, 143–44, 201; on principles subsidiary to utility, 96, 200, 202; on public opinion, 155; on security, 75–76, 114; on slavery, 114; on social relations and institutions, 64–66, 201; theories of utility, 95–97, 106–107, 131, 200, 202; underlying philosophy, 9–14, 134–35; on wealth, 70, 72–73, 202

cooperative theory and principles, 2, 3, 63, 68, 71–72, 107, 128–30, 134, 143, 144, 153–58, 164, 177, 193–94; common ownership (collectivization) of property, 14, 108, 126, 128–29, 132, 190, 192, 202, 204; on the economy of labor, 69–70; providing ideological foundations of the cooperative movement, 163, 183, 189–92, 194, 202–203, 205; "principle of a virtuous disposition," 154–55; public opinion and, 155–57; on the voluntary exchange of labor, 64, 72, 81–82, 84, 85

on democracy and government: role of education, 145–48, 247n88, 247–48n100, 253n58; on public opinion, 156–57, 159, 160, 256n94; on self-government, 12, 143, 147, 154–57, 159. *See also* democracy: Thompson on; government

on education, 4–5, 63, 81, 108, 116–17, 145, 147–48, 190

efforts to found a cooperative community, 6, 161, 163–64

William Godwin and, 109, 219n48

on happiness (theory of), 19, 57, 70, 91–92; as eudaemonistic, 1–2, 66–67, 79–80, 91, 200–201, 207–8; on the general happiness, 124, 127; on the hegemonic construction of happiness, 64–66, 78–79; on maximizing happiness, 80, 132; on maximizing pleasure, 67; on the means of happiness, 66–70, 90, 124; moral value and, 67, 71, 78; as a social theory, 56–57, 90–92 (*see also* social institutions; social science); wealth and, 70, 72–73, 202; as (objective) well-being, 66–7, 90–92

on the individual, 69, 85

on interests and self-interest, 81; conditions for an identity of interests, 124–26; conflicts of interest and social institutions, 115–16, 123, 124, 125, 156; identity of interests in married couples, 120–24, 125; on "natural" vs. "factitious" motives, 73–75, 154–55; self-interest vs. selfishness, 85, 118–19, 123, 155, 240n141; social interest and self-interest aligned, 5, 12, 14, 81–82, 85, 105–106, 118–19, 193; on true and false interest, 58, 80–81, 84. *See also* interests; self-interest

Jeremy Bentham and, 57, 63–64, 218n26, 220n49, 219n48, 225n1

life and works, 4–9, 218n28

Karl Marx compared to, 7, 85–86, 112

Thompson, William (continued)
  Thomas Malthus and, 109, 245n61
  objective well-being (OWB) and, 29, 90–92
  on the philosophy of necessity, 63–64
  as a political economist, 8–9, 13, 108–109, 112, 132, 246n64
  as a Ricardian socialist, 217n16, 219n48
  Robert Owen and, 4, 6, 57, 62–63, 64, 108, 164, 168, 171–72, 174, 254n65, 256–57n104
  that security includes subsistence, 75–77, 128, 132, 151
  social and political philosophy of, 11–14
  on social relations and institutions, 11–12, 90–92, 131, 148, 172, 232n2, 267n139; community (social) context of individuals, 14, 56–57, 81–82, 85, 90–91, 96, 117, 119, 124–25, 128–29, 132, 146–47, 154–55, 160, 207–208, 256n92, 256n94; on equality in, 96, 128, 132, 151, 153–54; as establishing the conditions of people's lives, 56–57, 64–5, 79, 96, 131–32, 134, 201; happiness and, 90–92; individual character (interests and motives) shaped by, 74–75, 84–85, 118–19, 123; political character of, 5, 11–2, 64–65, 84, 134, 207–208; subordination as a social and political evil, 119–24, 247n88. See also social institutions
  on social science, 11, 56–57, 64, 172, 221n56, 232n44
  on the "system of individual competition" (capitalism), 6, 13, 29, 63, 71–72, 80, 107–108, 125, 132, 149; that competition undermines social relations, 84–85, 113, 114–17, 125, 149, 177, 201–2, 247n92; that government serves the interests of the capitalist elite, 76, 117–18, 149–51; and the "natural laws for the distribution of wealth," 128; the opposition of security and equality under, 108; power relations under, 76–77, 82–84, 113, 115, 117–18, 159, 201; private property as the motive for selfishness, 84–85; private property as a social institution, 91–92; on private property and wage labor, 113–15; as a system of insecurity for workers, 76–77, 108, 113–114; as undermining happiness, 16, 113–18, 201–202. See also coercion; inequality; insecurity; involuntary exchange; subordination; surplus value, theory of
  on (systems of) subordination: as a social and political evil, 119–24, 247n88. See also labor: subordination to capital; marriage; subordination; Thompson, William: on the "system of individual competition"; women: subordination of
  and utilitarianism (social theory of utility), 96, 131–32, 202; the alignment of social interest and self-interest, 5, 12, 14, 81–82, 85, 105–106, 118–19, 193; subsidiary principles, 8–9, 96, 107, 128, 131–32, 190, 194, 202. See also utilitarianism: in Thompson
  utopianism in, 159, 163, 221n59
  Mary Wollstonecraft and, 119, 146, 248n110, 253n55

on women's civil and political rights, 120–21, 124, 125, 143–44, 148–49, 153
Tranquility (*ataraxia*), 21, 23

United (common) effort, as a subsidiary principle to utility, 9, 96, 107, 108, 128–29, 132, 202, 241n1
United Nations, 180, 203, 205, 216n10
United States political system, 136, 148–49, 254–55n72. *See also* slavery
Universal suffrage. *See* suffrage
Utilitarianism (greatest happiness, principle of utility), 1, 5, 19, 21, 25, 27, 51–52, 56, 142–43, 227n32, 243n33
  in Bentham, 31, 95–98; the distribution of wealth and,100–101; equality and, 100–101; vs. happiness, 97; individualism and, 48–51, 95–96; interest paradox, 105–106; liberal character, 49–51, 95–96; micro and macro aspects of, 98–99, 102, 131, 135, 139; orientation toward pleasure vs. well-being, 32, 37–38, 198–99; as a political principle, 37, 75, 98–99, 105, 135, 137, 199; private property and, 102–105; role of democracy, 135, 138–40, 201; as a "sentiment of approbation," 98; subsidiary principles, 8–9, 38, 42, 96, 99–101, 131, 199, 202; theory of marginal utility, 100–101; use value, 42; vs. utility, 97–98
  in Thompson, 190–91; capitalism and, 107–108, 113–18, 200–202; connection to Bentham's, 106–107; the distribution of wealth and, 68; education and, 146–47; (in)equality and, 13, 68, 74, 123–24; the "natural laws for the distribution of wealth" and, 126–28; political economics and, 131–32; as a political principle, 75, 96, 142–43, 148, 150–51; role of democracy, 142–43, 148, 150–51, 201; social character, 96; subordination and, 119–24; subsidiary principles, 8–9, 96, 107, 128, 131–32, 151, 190, 194, 202

See also subsidiary principles
Utility, as a property of objects, 97–98. *See also* utilitarianism
Utopianism, 115
  cooperative communities and, 159, 163, 221n59

Veblen, Thorstein, 52, 63
Veenhoven, Ruut, 89, 241n163
Virtue(s), 20, 222n5
  as civic duty, 50, 81, 83, 119, 146, 153, 154–55, 157, 231n97
  Epicurean focus on, 22–24, 197–98, 223n16
  self-interest and, 81
Voluntarism, 64, 80–84, 127, 151, 156, 157, 190, 194, 200
  as a principle subsidiary to utility, 9, 96, 107, 128, 132, 190, 194
Voluntary association, 82, 84, 96, 155, 189–90, 194
  in cooperatives and cooperative communities, 13, 68, 128, 156, 159, 177, 181, 185–87, 190, 191–92, 195, 200, 203, 211, 266n113, 268–69n6
  marriage and, 122
Voluntary exchange (of goods or labor), 13, 64, 71, 72, 80–83, 84–85, 112, 114, 115, 127, 153, 200, 256n92

Voting rights. *See* political rights; suffrage

Wage labor, 44, 83, 121–22, 127, 184, 229–30n77, 237n78, 245n59, 249n143
　conflict over, in capitalist society, 109–10
　private property and, 113–15
Walras, Leon, 51
Warbasse, James P., 178, 262n79
Warke, Tom, 51
Watkins, William P., 185–87, 255–56n111
Wealth, 70–73, 228n54
　abundance (opulence), 5, 42, 72–73, 104, 116
　accumulation of (as private property), 5, 49, 65–66, 73, 85, 102–104, 107–108, 113–15, 207
　alienation of, 128
　comforts vs. superfluities, 70–71
　distribution of, 68, 78, 80, 103–104, 109, 113, 124–25, 191, 202, 203, 217–18n20, 247n88, 249n143, 256n99, 259n17, 269n10
　happiness or well-being and, 29, 32, 42–43, 54, 56–57, 67–68, 69, 72–73, 100–101, 116, 202, 236n65, 238n90, 239n114
　materialism and, 53, 68, 69–70, 73
　national aggregation of, 109, 132
　"natural laws for the distribution" of, 13, 126–28, 200
　production of, 71–73, 80, 108, 109, 113, 127–28, 201–202
　security and, 10, 43–47, 75, 102–103, 108
　social and political power of, 113, 149–51, 152, 206, 208, 254–55n72
　theory of marginal utility and, 100–101
　See also inequality; private property
Webb, Beatrice Potter and Sidney, 178–79, 262n75
Well-being, 19, 62, 99, 201, 215n3
　in Bentham, 31–33, 37–47, 50–51, 58, 99, 104, 227n31
　as the conditions of life, 19, 28–29, 66–67, 87, 89, 96, 198, 200, 203
　contemporary cooperatives and, 190–91, 205
　the "felicific calculus" and, 32–33
　the "higher" pleasures and, 202
　interest and, 35–36, 118
　as "life-satisfaction," 28, 89, 229n64, 241n168
　the means of happiness and, 66–70, 124
　reduction to pleasure, 51–54, 89, 199
　relationship to happiness, 31–32, 37–38, 51, 66–7, 88–92, 198, 200, 224n37
　security and, 43–47, 104
　social character, 59, 79–80, 91–92, 242n8
　in Thompson, 66–73, 79–80, 85–86, 131–32, 200, 207, 256n99
　wealth and, 41–43, 239n114
　See also ataraxia; happiness; katastematic pleasure; objective well-being (OWB); subjective well-being (SWB)
Wheeler, Anna Doyle, 5, 6, 7–8, 248–49n119
Wolin, Sheldon, 154
Wollstonecraft, Mary, 119, 146, 248n110, 253n55
Women, 26, 53, 78, 104, 125, 154, 224n32, 235n41, 235–36n58, 238n105, 255n84, 255n85

cooperative movement and, 182, 192, 212, 262n64, 265n100, 267n130, 267n139
political rights, 5, 77, 119–22, 124, 125, 135, 139–40, 141–42, 143, 144, 153, 169, 251n8, 257n111, 262n64
subordination of, 5, 11, 13, 119–24, 148–49, 192, 245n57, 253n55

See also marriage; political rights; subordination

Wood, Neal, 57–58, 233n8
Worker cooperatives, 178, 180–81, 188, 204, 263n91, 263–64n91, 264n92

Zeno, 26
Zeuli, Kimberly A., Robert Cropp, and Marvin A. Schaars, 264–65n97

www.ingramcontent.com/pod-product-compliance
Lightning Source LLC
Chambersburg PA
CBHW022047230426
43672CB00008B/1092